Misinterpreting Modern Russia

Misinterpreting Modern Russia

Bruno S. Sergi

continuum

NEW YORK • LONDON

2009

The Continuum International Publishing Group Inc
80 Maiden Lane, New York, NY 10038

The Continuum International Publishing Group Ltd
The Tower Building, 11 York Road, London SE1 7NX

www.continuumbooks.com

Library of Congress Cataloging-in-Publication Data

Sergi, Bruno S.
Misinterpreting Modern Russia: western views of Putin and his presidency / Bruno S. Sergi.
p. cm.
Includes bibliographical references and index.
ISBN-13: 978-0-8264-2772-4 (hardcover: alk. paper)
ISBN-10: 0-8264-2772-3 (hardcover: alk. paper) 1. Russia (Federation)—Politics and government—1991-2. Russia (Federation)—Social conditions—1991-3. Russia (Federation)—Economic conditions—1991-4. Putin, Vladimir Vladimirovich, 1952-I. Title.

DK510.763.S443 2009
947.086—dc22

2007039141

Printed in Great Britain by the MPG Books Group, Bodmin and King's Lynn

To the memory of journalists

Paul Klebnikov, *Forbes*

Anna Politkovskaya, *Novaya Gazeta*

Table of Contents

Acknowledgments

I drafted this book's content page when I was an adjunct professor of Political and Economic Development in Comparative Perspectives at New York University in the summer of 2005. I continued through the final typescript in the summer of 2007, yet again at New York University, while I was teaching a class on the same subject.

Because these two periods of teaching affected this book, I owe particular appreciation to New York University's students who attended my courses. Equally, I express thankfulness to my students in Italy and across East-Central European universities where I gave a variety of academic courses, guest lectures, and seminars on transition economics and international business through the past several years. Truthfully, I have been more than fortunate to lecture very gifted students. Intense class interaction coupled with abiding public debate have been essential sources of research inspiration and enriched my intellectual curiosity about multifaceted new market economies enough to concentrate more on certain themes than on others and not to overlook ethical questions. The latter became noticeable during the finale of a moribund communist system, transformed in several ways ever since former President Mikhail Gorbachev brought perestroika and glasnost to Russia by the mid 1980s, and skyrocketed after Gorbachev abandoned the political scene at the end of 1991. Thus all through the research phase of this book, I took students' suggestions seriously for their rousing contributions to my research work; they have been so important that they need warmhearted acknowledgment here.

Likewise, throughout my journey into Russian affairs, I profited from an immense channel of communication with those who really want to better comprehend the nature of Russia's evolution. Similarly, a truly supportive environment came through a continuous dialogue and exchange of ideas with colleagues. Although I am not mentioning these colleagues explicitly, my intellectual debt goes to those who—by means of pedagogic and unfailingly constructive criticism—fed my conception of the realities that have come into sight in Russia, coaching and contributing to the shaping of my research philosophies. They encouraged me in many ways to follow a realistic approach, and to be sufficiently attentive to ethical matters without seeking to be a scholarly know-it-all. They added dimensions to this book's chapters in countless ways. Friends and colleagues Vadim Anufrijenko, Bill Bagatelas, Youssef Cohen, Marshall Goldman, Pavel Machitski, Peter Oppenheimer, and Vladimir Tikhomirov all read and commented on several portions of the manuscript. They made suggestions that contributed to closing several gaps in earlier versions of the manuscript, helped eliminate critical flaws from my earlier drafts, and offered precious advice—quite extensively at times—about reformulating certain thoughts. Although these people might still disagree with some conceptual frameworks of this book, they put me right on analyzing absorbing aspects of Russia's complex circumstances. I deeply appreciate them.

What is more, I would like to pay a special tribute to Dr. David Barker, Continuum Publishing's editorial director in New York. Every author would like to work with this kind of editor. David offered me trustworthy support and willingness to publish the book, especially his ability to appreciate the value of this challenging work, from the preliminary stages of my book proposal to accepting the title for the worldwide prestigious reading list at Continuum Publishing. I also wish to thank the staff of Continuum Publishing for their cooperation and their excellent job on the original manuscript, pointing me to several sections that needed clarification and to the logic and arguments made in several chapters.

Summing up, I am obliged to my colleagues and students for unflinching help, to the many people who carefully read portions of the text to increase its readability, and to my managing editor at Continuum for strong promotion of this worthwhile project.

Bruno S. Sergi
New York
August 4, 2007

Prologue

Misinterpreting Modern Russia begins in New York in the summer of 2005 and ends in the summer of 2007. These two dates separated a seemingly interminable time, even as I kept my writing in a holding pattern over a span of two years flanked by my teaching in the summer term of 2005 and of 2007 at New York University. Given the substantial complexity of the subject, an enigmatic wakefulness has accompanied my writing experience regarding the grounds that make possible in the West an absolute misreading of the modern Kremlin's triumphs and failures. What is more, additional complexity emerges from the very nature of this work, which calls attention to numerous economic and political aspects to examine, obstacles to highlight, probable criticisms to counter. After having updated, expanded, perfected, and finished up the revisions of old drafts of the manuscript, I took the completed work to the publishing table.

Nevertheless, walking through and breathing in the absorbing atmosphere in the heart of New York University's Greenwich Village in Manhattan has been important. It has fueled my intellectual curiosity to reach more persuasive and knowledgeable conclusions about the multifaceted subject of Russia. Discussing the subjects of transition economics and politics with students in the United States and from all across Europe, who have solicited me—more often than not—to explain the weight of business ethics and political and economic developments in new market economies has affected this book a great deal. I simply took off the typical blindfold of western intellectuals!

Russia's President, Vladimir Putin, was (and is still at the time of writing) absolutely a brawny leader on both domestic and world stages while I wrote groundwork chapters. As the Russian Constitution binds any president to the limit of two consecutive four-year terms, and as Putin ascended to the Kremlin—wherein is based the Russian government—in March 2000 and was reelected for a second time in March 2004, he is set to step down in March 2008. Because both the end of the term of Putin's Kremlin and my book publication date will almost coincide, this timing could not have been more opportune. Due to this fortuitousness, my thoughts might be perceived as more bipartisan and coming from a different perspective than they would be if Putin were still in power at the Kremlin today.

Above and beyond Putin's forceful approach to politics, he has faced a great deal of criticism worldwide, much like the majority of western political leaders who undergo the benefit of international visibility. Unlike certain western influential political leaders who fell into widespread disparagement and lost consensus some time after having been elected, Putin's personality came under heavy attack from the day when he ascended to the Kremlin. Shortly thereafter, top intellectual circles—the so-called Kremlinologists—viewed him negatively due to his former association with the KGB and its successor agency Federal Security Service—known by its Russian initials FSB, and censure has been growing rapidly and continues as I write. Yet, far less criticism surrounded him in Russia where he has received a noteworthy popular support that began long before the beginning of his tenure and has increased since then.

Likewise, Russia's realities have followed a similar trajectory in the West as its reputation has been open to constant attack by Kremlinologists; that is, in the same way as the West has been cynically criticizing Putin's Kremlin, Kremlinologists have censured and condemned Russians for having legitimized Putin's Kremlin. Regardless of the logic behind the high level of popular support for the Kremlin among Russians, the West seemingly mistrusts voting masses beyond western boundaries and this criticism adheres to a western strategy to misunderstand Russia. Thus, the West has fully understood neither Russia nor the country's developmental logic during the 1990s. In a nutshell, the logic of cynicism and double standards will come up frequently in the storyline of my book.

The truth of the matter is that to describe a political leader's interaction with domestic citizens and groups of power and the overall governance in a country that is even now on its own way toward becoming a normal one is an energizing intellectual task. At the same time, no single interpretation can fully capture Russia's socioeconomic development during the past two decades, much less the entire logic of Russia's communist saga. In light of this, experienced and talented people could have concentrated on the entire logic of history rather than just narrow perceptions of Putin's era. Without a courageous reassessment and a new approach, I could end up with the same type of failed interpretation that has occurred until now.

Finally, I feel the intellectual need to size up the country. To achieve the goals of objectivity and impartiality, I probe into the policies, tactics, and approaches of the Russians' and President Putin's Kremlin in a unifying methodology—common Russian people set at the center of a greater coherent interpretative theme. I then bring these together while also dissolving certain stereotypes and linking economics, business, and politics notions in order to bring the worldwide reading public up to date on Russia's problems, challenges, and international opportunities.

The West's Rhetoric and Proper Causal Relationships

The irony is that the West has continued to express, resolutely and definitively, already disputed, inattentive views about Russia. The conventional western approach failed in several respects, and these are flaws that I would like to avoid here. That said, there is one point of agreement between Russia's supporters, the Kremlin haters, and those who, like me, point toward a balanced analysis: the country's story is astonishing. This basic understanding is a good and realistic step from which to start our long journey to sort out how to interpret contemporary Russia.

We are almost at the end of President Putin's Kremlin course now—what I term *the third vision for a modern Russia*, after those introduced by ex-presidents Mikhail Gorbachev and Boris Yeltsin. In light of the *three visions* for reforms, my endeavor proves even more challenging because I undertake my writing experience and analysis while residing in the West and for western readers. The West in its entirety bears a large degree of culpability for having subjected Russia's whole story to insubstantial scrutiny if not hypocrisy. One of the possible errors Kremlinologists have made is in considering Russia to have already become a *normal country* by the mid-1990s, when in fact Russia was in complete chaos at the time.

Another point the West regularly neglects is the country's vastness. Geographically, Russia is simply the largest country in the world. With its eleven time zones, the country benefits from boundaries that stretch from the heart of Western Europe to the Pacific Far East, from the Arctic to China. Being so huge, Russia carries the geographical advantage of being a gate among cultures and markets, but it also requires a geopolitical strategy and an international specific policy. That is, the country's sheer scale and its geographical and cultural position render Russia important and unique. Yet rather than recognizing the contingencies resulting from Russia's size, the West has done quite the reverse and closed its eyes to this factor. Russia's strategic position, alongside its past as a nuclear power, may easily prompt stark criticism of whatever Russian authorities do.

In connection with this, I argue that Kremlinologists might perceive any kind of decision taken by the Kremlin as suspicious given the complicated international issues and problems on the current regional and world stage. There has been in the West a tendency to systematically criminalize non-western leaders whenever they become somewhat powerful. Even worst, in recent years, the international community has committed serious faults in Rwanda, in the vast Sudanese desert region of Darfur, and in Iraq, to mention just three cases involving rapes and slaughters of civilians. The world could have worked to build up a broad antiterrorism alliance when the terrorist attacks of September 11, 2001, revealed that all modern nations are unstable and weak. And given the portentous return of Russia on the world political stage, having Russia as a full-fledged member in an international and peaceable partnership would be both possible and helpful. In one sense, it is better for Russia to be self-assured inside the fold than threatening outside, as it was during the communist era. In other words, due to the march of domestic and international events, it is time to demand a far better logic and balanced awareness of a country that is in serious need of transformation into a just and *normal country* and that would benefit from an equal, credible partnership in the international consensus.

Besides its inattentiveness to real world consensus, the West also has a tendency to use rhetoric. Given these defects in its approach, the West has overlooked many details about the transition from communism to noncommunism in Russia. It is not surprising, therefore, that we have assessed and debated political strategies in the 1990s incorrectly and Putin's naturally ensuing pro-stability response inaccurately. As an alternative to previous inaccuracies, I map the way that geopolitical realities and circumstances developed after 1985. Misinterpreting realities, omitting facts, and overlooking proper causal relationships as other Kremlinologists have done would result in one more job wide of the mark.

Russians gave President Vladimir Putin the electoral go-ahead in 2000 and 2004 in order to pursue a strategy that, it was hoped, would lead to stability and calm—both of which were missing under Gorbachev and Yeltsin. Russians shared the same ideals of stability and fairness, ideals akin to people's beliefs in every corner in the world. I am perfectly conscious that interpreting the authentic meaning of these ideals is quite a difficult job. Notions like these are interconnected and intellectually loaded. They sometimes become cliché, and are vulnerable to double standards that become visible when the West confronts its own image. The West is cynical and wary about questioning the genuineness of democracy, and it still attacks the search for stability in Russia. Answering this question requires that we become more aware of the way that money, lobbies, and entrenched groups' interests are able to jeopardize that supposedly authentic democratic vote that it is purported to exist in the West. The harshest western critics have painted present-day Russia—under Putin, not his predecessors.—as a *managed democracy*, that is, as a state of affairs characterized by elections that take place with the results known in advance. Without a doubt, we are not and have not been able to see beyond our noses!

After all, I find very inspiring the address of Vaclav Havel—the celebrated writer and dramatist, last president of Czechoslovakia (1989–1992), and the first president of the Czech Republic (1993–2003)—to the U.S. Congress on February 21, 1990. Havel argued that the process of establishing democracy is a continuing one, but that we "may approach it as one would the horizon in ways that may be better or worse, but it can never be fully attained." Money and business interests, which were not clean at that time, were significantly and extensively involved in Russia's "democratic experiment" in the 1990s. Although the "democratic experiment" was considered fully democratic in the West, it actually was not. Therefore, the Russian experiment in the 1990s was far from Havel's concept of "horizon." Notwithstanding, those zealots sent from the West to Moscow have assured us that the 1990s were a truly democratic period developing in Russia. The most advanced, tested, practical, recognizable form of democracy is the electoral one that we all have come to know; I take this type of functioning for granted in Russia today.

The West's Superior Values?

Now I address another major problem of the West's rhetoric: a disputable attitude to impose superior values. The West has performed poorly at several levels of analysis, and *naïveté* may be an even better word to describe West's general lack of awareness. One only sees at present an overall biased and faulty explanation concerning the many problems the Russian leadership had to confront and the poor after-effects of Russian affairs on both the domestic and international level during the 1990s. Yet I want to allow readers to identify the logical progression of such things rather than relying on anecdotal episodes of contemporary Russian affairs that have been reported to the reading public everywhere, either in quite a distorted fashion or without the comprehensive approach with respect to specific, well-defined facts, that is, without understanding the realities of the economic reforms, the social contradictions, and the painful transformation and its impact on the daily lives of common Russians. Without mastering the rationale and respective measurable achievements of the *three visions* for a modern Russia, from Gorbachev's perestroika and glasnost in 1985 through the rise of Putin at the end of the 1990s, the West would neglect the comprehensiveness of such Russian common sense, yet again. As I do not evade important questions or deny evidence or facts that colleagues have shown, but rather hope to provide insight regarding Russia's political actuality, I address these issues in a different spirit, without resorting to rhetoric.

In dodging both rhetoric and flaws, I am obliged to ascertain a few rational pillars of analysis. Most of the events that occurred in Russia in recent years can be associated with a newfangled "managerial culture" born under Gorbachev's early rule. While Gorbachev create favorable expectations of a political and societal U-turn in both the short and long term, he conceived measures that logically resulted in the depressing business results of the 1990s. Russians did not expect this disappointing end product. The transition from Gorbachev's style of government to the wild and uncontrollable context of Yeltsin's political economy, when business groups were fighting each other much of the time, has been quite straightforward. However, Yeltsin's policies have been more detrimental to the country overall than have Gorbachev's. At that time, the growth of the oligarchs—in terms of both power and influence—included the obvious recognition of their gaining control of the oil and gas industry and other lucrative national resources at the time of Yeltsin. Rampant corruption created a bleak picture of the country. Common Russians became impoverished while watching the country backslide; a few became wealthier.

Conventional Kremlinologists' views refer to this as a minuscule side effect of the transformation; yet I refer to it as to chaos.

It is blatantly obvious that when Vladimir Putin ascended to the Kremlin he stepped into an office still struggling with people's discontent and general dissatisfaction, which became major issues to address. The West has failed to consider him as a leader who could cope—admirably or not—with the repercussions from hastily improvised western-inspired transformation policies, which Russia's business insiders and certain clans of interests have managed for their own benefit and not for the benefit of most Russians.

It is true that Putin has had to face a growing tide of unethical behavior, business corruption, wild business practices, extortion, and common rituals of paying briberies that Russians had to confront routinely in order to get anything done. The Putin Kremlin pursued specific forms of restraint on the country's uncertain business sector. More than anything else, Putin was able to introduce a minimum of institutional stability back to the country. Naturally, Russians and Kremlinologists engulfed us with debates about the qualitative role and the exact range of top authorities in the country's affairs and influence. It is possible that Putin and his critics started and continued to confuse each other through seemingly understandable criticism that they directed at each other. We look at the Kremlin through a long series of disarticulated events or snapshots, but the Kremlin followed a logical strategy—shrewd or not.

These varying perspectives explain much of the confusion. The public kept watching whether Russia was developing in a way that emulated the West, and evaluated the country accordingly. It seemed that the West reproached the Russian president's behavior for refusing to act on western strategic lines for Putin's alleged acknowledgment that his policies were systematically pushing Russia further away from the initiatives of the 1990s. Such a critical assumption was offered primarily by the West in an attempt to blame on the new Russian course that was not that much in its own selective image. Although western intellectuals continue to censure Russia, the country is properly adhering to the kind of electoral democracy we have in the West and this way of blaming Russia in the West is characteristic of the flawed double interpretative standards we carry out in the West. The absence of this premise meant that western censure directed against Putin and the advancement of Russian economic, financial, and political events, continued to lack an ethical foundation. In the end, we failed to establish a logical central premise.

The sudden spike in criticism over Russia was a signal that, unbeknownst to us, Russia may have not entered a truly democratic setting in the 1990s. Conversely, the West has understood quite the opposite: its economic and political commentators were reporting enthusiastically on the new Yeltsinian course, the recourse to formal, free elections, the coming out of a *normal country*, and the extent of privately produced national income—much the same as western-fashion democratic systems. Without good starting assumptions and central premises, the West focused most heavily on Putin's and others'

KGB network—as if the KGB had never previously existed or broken in the country's affairs—which was judged to remain the most serious threat to democratic principles.

Western interpretations of Russian affairs have been negligent and selectively distorted. If Putin undertook a firm reaction against political instability and big business distortions on the whole, and most Russian citizens felt their livelihoods under the Putin presidency had improved economically, accusing Putin of being altogether crooked in the pure economic realm would be partially grim. Alleging that Putin's Kremlin is utterly lacking in democratic principles or that the Russian people have historically been attracted to dictatorship should be readdressed more logically, as the 1990s developed quite in a different manner than the West is inclined to think.

A Paradox?

All this leaves us with a paradox. Savvy businesspersons purchased natural resources from the state in exchange for almost nothing while they were influential counselors to top politicians or financially influential in the country, and neglected to pay taxes. The Kremlin has done well to unveil a new anticorruption campaign against illegalities and other means used by certain business sectors to be able to avoid pay of taxation.

For the moment, the Kremlin's policies have only partially been triumphant. Fraudulent activities keep flourishing as Russia continues its transition on the road to being a *normal country*. The West was pleased with the Shleifer and Treisman (2005) proposition that Russia had become such a normal middle-income country over time—that is, a country with a per capita income of some $8,000 a year, with a growing prosperity, degrees of political and economic freedom, and levels of corruption and inequality comparable to those of Mexico or Turkey. I am in agreement with Shleifer and Treisman. However, on this ground perhaps and in the eyes of western critics, it sounds as if western intellectuals themselves would be happier if Putin had not taken any action instead of proposing even more cogent and resolute actions against the country's corruption and dishonesty that were escalating to new highs. The West ignored Russia's right to make the most of selling on the international markets. One could ask a larger question: would it have been better not to curb any illegal activities for fear that such a policy reaction would automatically incite observers to label Russia's leaders as despots without any systematic analysis of the facts? I would say no!

Experts and readers may hold different opinions about Russians and the significance of the Putin presidency. Nevertheless, illuminating the rationale behind the politics in which Putin has been engaged for nearly eight years is without a shred of doubt a job full of twists and turns. I set sights on depicting the Russians and Putin correctly, even arguing partially against a huge stack of books that insensitively and utterly criticize Putin's politics, Russians' thoughts, and Russia's use of its naturally endowed richness. Equally, recent work in the West paints a bleak picture of a post-Yeltsin Kremlin hijacked by a dictatorial frame of mind and mad citizens who get confused when they go to the polls. I find especially aggravating Kremlinologists who interpret democracy in Russia as being at risk of the Kremlin's dictate or simply nonexistent or who say that these votes come from common Russians. Critics create this sort of picture of Russia. I do not buy it at all.

Still, I am not too dismissive of the uncertain effects of Russian's Kremlin. Nor do I doubt the harshness of the Kremlin today. Russia and its current president are worldwide examples of both triumphs and failures. I do not want to foment intellectual warfare with this statement; however, the spectacle of a nasty, terrible Russia being disseminated by the world media is no doubt offensive to ordinary Russians. Consequently, I must investigate Putin's Russian evolution unconventionally yet still thoughtfully, giving way to hypocritical scrutiny based on double standards and allowing insights into specific areas of interest. In this context, readers must be informed about the main dilemma between the state of modernization and social justice in Russia.

It is beneficial, if not essential, to review the country's choices as they have been carried out in the past as well as likely economics and political perspectives. Modern Russia is no longer the Russia that initiated a de-Stalinization course fifty years ago, nor is it the Russia at the time of the Cold War. Russia is now a country of immense resources and expertise, interdependent with the West, with fantastic business opportunities—a country that exhibits sizeable oil and natural gas reserves and exports that are serving an increasing demand from Western and Eastern Europe, China, and other countries in Central Asia. Russia stands at the center of a fantastic strategic scenario.

Along with this good news, the social strata of very moneyed, the somewhat rich, and the poor represent another face of modern Russia. The social problems of a new society, combined with rapid development of retailing activities and business prospects, offer readers a completely different perspective on post – Cold War Russia, its newest, post-Yeltsin leadership, and its prospects.

A New Perspective on Modern Russia

In partial contrast to the scholars who stay at the two poles and analyze the present Russian situation by referring to the past authoritarian Russia, or who simplistically use western tools of analysis to interpret Russia, I do not sidestep the reality of the laborious and extremely complex end of communism all the way through the present-day Russia. I focus on the real changes that the rationale of Russian leaders of the 1980s and 1990s brought us to today. Explained simply, I look backward from the present and from the past to the present, as if I was on a pendulum, looking back at where I have been, and explain the events evolving from the past to the present using a unified rationale. I provide broad perspectives as a way of letting all readers interpret events, gain possible answers, and awaken to a new understanding of Russia as a whole. Because this implies a strategic and systematic familiarity with Russian reality, the material I have put together throughout this book endeavors to reflect upon and interweave both political economy and moral principles into a single overarching and unifying concept. One must be principled when considering Russian society and how the developments have been turned out as compared to how Russia has been perceived by the rest of the world. The most important element lacking in earlier interpretations was an understanding of the basic ethics behind the evolution of the 1990s and an assessment of how groups of power shaped the country overall and how this affected both Russian people's views and Putin's decision making.

The need to have this cohesive look at Russia is important, as it enables us to explain the logic of single events linked one to another and to see the point of developmental evolution. During the era of communism in Russia, the paternalistic state was a warden of people's goods, rooted in the citizens' belief in the country's authority. This did not work well, and once Russian citizens began to understand it better thanks to Gorbachev's inspired reforms, Russia initiated a phase of modernization but indecisive deregulation. During this passage from communism to noncommunism, and a hasty move from a state-controlled economy to market-based economic setting and resource distribution, certain groups in power paid absolutely nothing to get control of the state's firms and natural resources. Deceptive privatization schemes were being sett up purposely. My reading of Russian affairs centers on a unifying approach that serves to bring together politics, economics, and a dose of pragmatism. This approach has the critically important benefit of not leaving readers in a quandary about the implication that unfairly distributed wealth and vast natural resources have had on the country.

No serious observer can suppose that socioeconomic realities are not important in the shaping people's sentiments and any leader's decisions. This is especially so when unfairness goes beyond critical bounds of legality and social disruption. On the one hand, western politics has recurrently misconstrued that business and political collusion went well beyond any imaginable critical limits of legality and social acceptance. They were not single cases of abuses and corruption, though: they were pieces of a wittingly corrupted puzzle. On the other hand, attempting to understand this complexity requires deep thought about the realistic options Russian leaders had in the late 1990s to drive the country out of crisis.

Therefore, a fresh interpretative approach provides proper views of this recent past and its prospective future. Still it must also be realized that my appraisal of political and civil society actors in the name of Russian social justice and modernization is a critique of the erroneous understanding of the realities of Putin's Kremlin. In analyzing Russian realities, I strive to be realistic, pragmatic, but I am also a firm critic of the 1990s and Putin's Kremlin when such criticism is logically warranted (realistic alternatives to Putin's efforts to stabilize the country were not available then) and based on facts. The truth of the matter is, as long as unprejudiced interpretations of Russia and coherent communication to readers are absent from our agenda, western society will remain at risk of getting the wrong idea about Putin's Kremlin and the Russians. Thus, a few more observations will help.

First, let's be clear that a great majority of Russians have expressed discontent about how the privatization method has been contrived and put into practice—not about the privatization process per se. Russia suffered from unfortunate living conditions as the move to a market economy and the incredibly corrupt privatization process cropped up. Buyers of public resources did not always have good enough money handy to pay for them. In point of fact, if enterprises to privatize had been valued at a fair market price, it would have been almost impossible to procure as much money as necessary. That same common Russian majority openly expressed a sentiment that the above process and logic had to be upturned, either partially or fully.

The fortunate buyers, however, could leverage the managerial skills they learned in the school of communism, take advantage of accumulated past experiences, and exploit political connections into the clout that was needed to control resources. Unfortunately, this course of action occurred at the expense of the least connected and most vulnerable people. This unfair situation created the basis for the events that characterized the unstable 1990s in Russia. Perhaps this provides a true understanding of Russians' sentiments. Undoubtedly, one thing that sets the West and its economic missionaries apart is their insistence that Moscow authorities had to keep the privatization process going and privatize whatever they could.

If this unfortunate sequence of events had occurred in the West, it would have brought into being a gigantic scandal prompting government agencies to react. When Russian government agencies—rightly or not—reacted to the threatening business environment, western pundits described Putin's Kremlin as on par with tyranny and not democratic whatsoever. It is just another case of western double standards when interpreting Russian transitions.

These conditions and the West's culpability on this subject explain Russians' anger about the 1990s. Common Russians themselves completely understand what went wrong in the 1990s, and they acknowledge having supported Gorbachev and Yeltsin with enthusiasm. They came to have an aversion—quite naturally—to the deceitfull way that privatization had been engineered, which Russians had also ingenuously supported by depositing their savings into bank accounts, unaware that they were beefing up such deceptive schemes. All this negatively affected their living conditions overall. They abhorred the method and disappointing outcomes of privatization. Given that they initially trusted the reforms and used their savings to acquire vouchers and shares, and that a foolishly planned system hurt their interests, their anger was understandable. The winners of this game were members of the victorious party leadership—from the Yeltsin political circle—and some other former young communists. They became extremely wealthy by paying nothing to the state—or only nominal sums—benefiting from opportunities they found in unfairly organized competitive bidding programs.

Second, I take issue with a widespread view in the West stemming from our desire to find criminals in every corner: that the majority of Russians want their country to climb back to a nuclear superpower status. They desire a reinforced central power, or a soft superpower, true, as part of an effort to preserve the country's unity. Today, except for the risk of small atomic bombs falling into the hands of terrorist groups, the issue of nuclear superpower status as a means to destroy the world is history. Readers should not construe that yearning for stability and unity as a wish to return to dictatorship but rather as a desire to have stable political institutions to protect the country against the anarchy and false-hearted reforms experienced in the 1990s. The West has this well-known sense of stability, and I find simply ridiculous and objectionable that the West does not get it. We simply share the very same set of values here in the West. More to the point, Russians are against real socialism and the growing number of millionaires and well-off people are evidence. If the West does not understand these facts, it continues to misinterpret Russia.

A third observation is about young Russian billionaires. As this has become a "commercial affair," *Forbes* magazine, the Manhattan bible of the richest men and women the world over, began listing a couple of them in the 1990s. The magazine now officially identifies several dozen Russian billionaires, most of them young. There is nothing wrong with this; however, the aberration of the 1990s was that many young communists became very rich in a matter of a couple of years. This should not have happened without arousing suspicion. It was a legal result in most of the cases, but it is fascinating that there are close to 100,000 millionaires in Russia—a number as large as in Manhattan. It has created another astonishing perspective of analysis that touches on the social sphere of development. Thousands of millionaires represent the very social newness of Russia's recent history, but nobody wants to look at these facts.

Fourth, a huge surprise in the new Russia was that Yeltsin preferred Putin—a former KGB official, one of Yeltsin's closest collaborators at that time, and virtually unknown to the country—as acting prime minister in August 1999. Then, the state Duma—Russia's lower house of Parliament that was historically renamed in the 1993 Russian constitution—approved his appointment on August 16. Afterward, Russians voted him in, in March of the following year and in March 2004, to modernize the country. Russians were willing to back him, and no one candidate has emerged as a clear frontrunner among opposition parties, even among the communists.

My last and fifth observation: what I suggest and continue to believe about Russia is that a cultural response to a modern managerial need was born during communism, but that managerial skills learned during the 1980s have turned out against the country's interest in the 1990s. A class polarization occurred during the era of communism, when the majority was on one side and a tiny group of leaders existed on the absolute other side of the social ladder. A bunch of chronic muddles is the culprit of a communist school of thought, which created some of the basis for the wild 1990s: Russians knew it and said no to its return. The impact on poverty of Russia's economic collapse in the 1990s—greatly accentuated by widening increase in wealth disparity—adds to the obstacles to understanding why things developed as they have in Russia. Observers should and must be aware of the huge gap between the rich and increasing numbers of poor in Russia, a fact that may encourage people to express social distrust and discontent.

* * * *

These are truthful observations and not ideological notions. Many in the West see Russia's moving struggles through the eyes of most of its citizens, who are considered democratically inexperienced by western Kremlinologists. Yet, I refrain from using rough, old-style western interpretative methodology and instead try to explain a variety of facts in such a way as to keep pace with Russia's realities and Russians' perceptions. I do not simply document the move from a centrally planned economy to a market economy, but rather I scrutinize the rationale that allowed only a few Russians to win huge fortunes while the extreme majority of the Russian population became poor. To be able to establish the evolution of politics and economics in Russia, I follow a particular line of judgment ranging from the three *visions for a modern Russia* through the fraudulent 1990s and the recent growing visibility of Russia due to the country's valuable natural resources, which are key to success in the world and a seemingly mighty aspect of a country's foreign policy.

In light of an intriguing geographic proximity to a great many other countries, modern Russia has a renewed, fundamentally important role to play in global issues. Interacting with Asian regions and Western Europe, possessing incalculable amounts of oil and natural gas, and considering that current events are of momentous importance for Russia to win back its role on the international stage, are all issues that call for further examination. My suggestion here is that relying on the country's history and the historical attitudes of ordinary Russians may be inadequate for figuring out modern Russia—a fact that should, in my opinion, cause us to be wary of the pronouncements of some who relied on such conventional analyses. Yet a disinterested analysis that reads between the lines provides a truthful interpretation of the status of Russia's progress.

To conclude, connecting politics and society in the name of Russian social and legal modernization shapes the primary contours of this book. I would like to believe that the West will start having clear sympathies with and will not ostracize modern Russia, but there has been no evidence of such a tendency in the recent past. I hope prospective readers will appreciate this work, which may truly affect the continually evolving debate about what has turned out right throughout the transition period in Russia, as well as contemporary worries among the least fortunate Russians. I firmly believe that it is high time somebody brings this new perspective to light.

A Final Note to Readers

I would like to explain a problem of terminology readers will encounter throughout this book. Two specific terms have been strewn around for the past several decades: *Russia* and the *KGB*. I use *Russia* (Russian Federation) and *Russians* throughout the text, although Russia is only one of the resulting republics—the biggest one—of the federation; Russians make up only one ethnic group, although it is the prevalent group in the total population.

The second term is *KGB*, which indicates the secret police originally created by Lenin in December 1917. The secret police became an extreme tool to control the masses and a weapon against "countless conspiracies and countless attempts against Soviet power" by political opponents. *Cheka* was its original name, but it was later renamed in various ways as, for example, GPU, OGPU, NKVD, MGB, and MVD. These were precursors of the KGB prior to 1954, when the newly renamed KGB became responsible for guaranteeing internal security and conducting foreign intelligence and was subordinated to the Council of Ministers. The Federal Security Service, known by its Russian initials FSB, replaced the KGB in November 1991 to perform state security functions. It should be noted that the new shield badge has the imperial eagle on top—as preferred by the Kremlin—instead of the original sickle and hammer. Abandoning previous symbols of Soviet communism has been a main theme in my writings on Russia, and even though the name of the agency has changed, the KGB remains the most recognizable name connected with secret police in Russia and in other countries of the former Soviet Union, except Belarus, which has kept the old name. I therefore use *KGB* quite frequently in this book.

Because my work is written to be readable and appeal to younger generations who did not live through the transitions I have studied, I use terms such as *Russia* and *KGB* which are historically predominant in the language and minds of people. Additionally, they roll off the tongue much more easily. I can blame custom for my use of such terms in place of their actual current names.

Chapter One

From the Reign of Lies to Modern Russia—An Astonishing Story

In seeking authentic insight into Russian history, this book examines the past three decades, from former president Mikhail Gorbachev's high hopes, through the former president Boris Yeltsin's years, and finally to the rise to power of Vladimir Putin. I disentangle problems and interpret the gross social injustice that set the stage for Putin's policy response on behalf of the Russians. This requires dissolving stereotypes that are quite widespread in the West and creating liaisons among economics, business, and politics at the center of a greater coherent and unified interpretative theme, thereby bringing some fresh perspectives to the eight years of Putin's presidency. Above all, it is important to note that until the gap between Russian reality and the western interpretation of Russian issues narrows, and the West deals with Russia in a far more pragmatic manner, the western assessment of Putin will continue to be off the mark. Unlike previous studies, this examination offers a better approach and down-to-earth media coverage.

As per my unifying methodology positioning Russians at the center of a greater coherent interpretative scheme, I steer away from focusing on specific events and prefer to reflect on the overall picture of Russia. Why? Because I am concerned with the nature and trajectory of Russian politics, Russia's economic development, and how the country played a role in both opening and closing the past century politically, in line with what has been written by the historian Kapuscinski (Kapuscinski, 1994). Although history never totally repeats itself, Russia now seems well situated to play an important role at the opening of this new century.

The very celebrated *Potemkin* uprising in 1905 initiated the twentieth century. This event politically forced Czar Nicholas II to establish the first Russian Duma—the general assembly that functioned until the Russian revolution in 1917 and enjoyed limited legislative and oversight power. The uprising came about on June 27—June 14 according to the Julian calendar then in use in Russia—and began on the famous Russian battleship moored in the Ukrainian port of Odessa, which became a naval base, an important logistical one during the Soviet era. After being served rancid meat, more than 600 sailors spontaneously rebelled on that famous battleship, perhaps foreshadowing the growing discontent of the intensely separated social classes in Russia after 1991—a Russian society split between rich and poor, with no middle class, that provided economic fortunes in developed, wealthier countries, and that helped keep government power in check. Similarly, a uniquely distressing system of wealthy landowners and poor peasants (*barin* and muzhik, respectively) gave birth to the dawn of the twentieth century's political arena and may provide an analogical explanation of Russia in the 1990s.

Afterward communism committed itself to dominating and transforming a society. Following a Leninist utopian ideology that had been imposed on the country in 1917, Russia subsequently passed through a period of Stalinist communism. Communism did not address the interests of Russia as a whole, and has not ever assured greater fairness in politics and economics nor safeguarded fundamental rights. The communist ideology transformed the poor czarist country into one that Boris Pasternak, in his 1958 novel *Doctor Zhivago,* termed the "inhuman reign of the lie." That novel on the Bolshevik Revolution and the Bolshevik's impact on the country, for which Pasternak—born into a prominent Jewish family in Moscow—won the Nobel Prize for Literature in 1958, an award kept secret from Russians through the Gorbachev era until the novel was published by *Noviy mir*, the same journal that had refused to publish it in 1956. (Pasternak had to decline the honor because of the protests in his home country and he was expelled from the Union of Soviet Writers.) Note that after the novel was banned by *Noviy mir* due to what was considered its spirit of refusal of the socialist revolution, the novel was published first in Russian and in Italian by the Italian publisher Feltrinelli in 1957; the English translation appeared in 1958 and soon after it was published in several other languages. As in Pasternak's novel, the lie has become a pillar of the communist state, as Aleksandr Solzhenitsyn wrote in 1990.

Russian citizens have suffered so much from lies over the past several centuries that they are still determined to achieve the better times that they deserve. The issues of the divided society reemerged in 1991 and again during Putin's tenure. Mirroring the events of 1905, Putin's Kremlin started the new century by echoing the widespread discontent of the people.

The Passage from the Past to the Current Century

Let me put this in a broader context. The passage from one century to the next and the *visions* that have steered Russians and Russia for the last two decades have generated much optimism. Mikhail Gorbachev's perestroika and glasnost, concepts introduced in 1985, have been quite straightforward in principle: freedoms of speech, writing, and entrepreneurship—simply the opposite of oppression and lies. These ideals have a longstanding history in the West but not in Russia. A few questions bring together the difficulties behind the genuine meaning of these words and how they were actually implemented in Russia, if at all, to end communism. Judicious and clear-cut interpretations call on experts to reconsider Russia, especially from those who do not see below the surface. Glasnost and perestroika inspired high hopes in the Russians, creating a sort of modern *Potemkin*-like nonviolent uprising guided from the top, the Kremlin, this time. Unfortunately these high hopes were left largely unfulfilled, and they were reshaped in 1991 when both the Soviet Union and the twentieth century came to a close. Under Yeltsin's economic and business growth agenda, unethical conduct played a big part in the shady distribution and misuse of natural resources and business opportunities.

However, Kremlinologists—whether academic or not—still deny that these problems represented ethical lapses. This position seems shocking and irresponsible to maintain. At most, only technical failures of tactical timing flaws faced by Russia at that time have been acknowledged. Crucial western financial support to Russia under Yeltsin allowed economists—who in reality had little sense of economic cause and effect—to pursue self-serving economic theories instead of attempting to address the ethics involved in the Russian reality.

The century ended with Russians trying to make of communism an episode of the country's history, to put the experience of lies out of their minds. Common Russians had supported the variously envisaged new reforms since the mid-1980s; however, although the aim of the proposed reforms could be regarded from first sight as fair, their actual application had been accompanied by many grievances. Russians were bled economically over the course of the decade, they saw their country moving into political instability quickly, they suffered unfair income redistribution, and they reckoned that some groups were stealing from the state. They felt really unhappy and insulted as well. Given the current situation in Russia, the need to understand the Russian people and Vladimir Putin has never been greater, especially given the growing importance of Russia's relationship with the western world.

In the afternoon on the last day in 1999—Putin was designated acting prime minister in August and acting president at the end of the year—it became clear that Boris Yeltsin had designated Putin as his rightful political heir. This new Russia left behind the end of the century but it was about to open a new century. Putin was soon linked to KGB and to the post-KGB system, an observation that made sense from a formal or institutional viewpoint.

The West viewed Putin altogether negatively and saw that Russia's democracy was running on fumes, which created the impression that the West was eager to critique him. Likewise, the West did not consider Putin as a political leader who could cope with the destabilizing aftereffects of hastily improvised western-inspired policies emanating throughout the 1990s. A class of new politicians and businesspersons engineered distorted and deceitful reforms that resulted in economic and ethical failure. Regardless, Putin was seen as a sinner because of his personal history at the KGB.

Currently, much attention is being paid to Russia's wealth in hydrocarbons. Russia is the world's second-leading oil-producing and-exporting country and is quickly moving to the top, and tops the world's list for proven natural gas reserves and likely export development. Russia's natural resource exports now provide a sizeable percentage of total European-nation imports, and increasingly of one-time economic competitors like China and Japan, among others. Despite a commitment to modernizing production techniques, diversifying sources of energy production, and becoming more efficient overall, all advanced and developing economies are becoming dependent upon oil. As these countries' options are limited for meeting growing demand from industry and people for year-round electricity and heating, they will be in desperate need of Russia's oil and gas supply in the near future. And Russia is currently in good economic shape under these circumstances because Putin, unlike Yeltsin, is able to direct most of the proceeds of escalating export and high global oil prices directly into general Russian economic growth. This is a critical issue to bear in mind when considering Russia's recent role in the world and what the post-2008 Kremlin administration stance will be. It is important to keep this in mind because much of Russia's economic revitalization depends upon its ability to bring vast oil and natural gas resources into play for the country's modernization.

Two Foundations of the Astonishing Russian Story

These few facts elucidate why interpreting Russia is problematic and why the aftereffects of the 1980s and 1990s should be regarded as clues to the emergence of wealth disparity, social chaos, and discontent that occurred under Yeltsin. These conditions were all but utterly unacceptable to the vast majority of Russians. Let me also accept as fact, as do the majority of Russians, that these new Russian billionaires became wealthy during communism itself, purchased large amounts of natural resources from the Russian state for almost nothing or for a price much below the fair one, and then sometimes sold them for outrageous profits. The Russian people will never forget that this disparity was achieved through the state capture and the spiteful, corrupted governments of the 1990s. It is incredibly irresponsible to continue denying this. We, in the West, have no choice but to accept the honest views of the Russian people.

There are two likely foundations of this story. The first one is a long-standing dispute that flourished long before the 1990s among international scholars studying Soviet communism and its later and recent passage to noncommunist society. Of particular interest to everyone involved, the quarrel raged over what fueled the survival of the Soviet regime from 1917 to 1991. The survival of communism for more than sevety years was a central theme of scholarly activities concerning Soviet communism. The followers of the totalitarian approach argued that oppressive Soviet power forced the populace to work as components within a larger system, thus insuring the regime's survival.

On the other hand, revisionists held that the populace itself provided enough support to keep any regime afloat. The opposing sides contested each other, providing recourse to critiques of these differing views, which occasionally led to harsh disagreements. Few scholars voiced an intermediate stance. Nevertheless, I notice some truth in both these two differing views.

Given the implosion of communism in the country, an ethical discussion about Russia is of paramount importance. In addition, how Russians perceive the changes that have occurred is equally essential. But the majority of experts will continue to miss this most important issue concerning these ongoing debates—how and why ethics and ethical judgment fit then and now into this current discourse. Obviously, primary analyses performed by Kremlinologists have failed to see these aspects. The ethical interpretation of modern Russia matters very much when comprehending present realities, which is why they were not important to Russian leaders while they were trying to survive the transition. Instead, they forged the passage to a noncommunist state of affairs in such a way that benefits themselves at the expense of the majority of Russians.

The second foundation of this story is the notion of political power, ethics, and economics combining at one time to produce social changes. These negative social changes emerged during the 1990s in Russia as well as in other countries, and continue to have a complicated impact today, playing themselves out in contemporary Russian realities, which are very intricate in nature.

Let me explain. Russia moved from a situation with relatively equal communist distribution of income, although at a low level by any international standards, to become the most unequal industrialized society in the world. While oligarchic reforms and the looting mentality of some were becoming entrenched by the end of the 1990s, the European Union and the United States were granting Russia the status of a market economy country—clearly a paradoxical situation.

Yet, such considerations were for naught with respect to realities ensuing during the implosion of the former Soviet system. While opposing these developments, the West continued and continues to discuss these issues, and questions were raised, but their causes and intimate developmental logic remained sketchy and poorly explained. This shortcoming continues to persist because of the minimal or nonexistent focus on the ethical considerations of Russia's changes and subsequent policy.

Kremlinologists were able to write with authority but were in a seemingly difficult position for exerting matter-of-fact influence over the pragmatic debate on Russian development or even to interpret it persuasively. That is why the West's great attempts to help have proven extremely unfortunate and unsuccessful. Russia's so-called reformers had set their sights on western economic symbols and strategies for help in rebuilding the Russian economy and even society. However, a more objective view of Russia would allow the West itself a historical opportunity to greatly improve its overall relationship with Russia both politically and economically, no matter who the leader of Russia was.

Portraying Russia without Downplaying the Kremlin's Faults

A potential snag in the attempt to explain why the Russians behaved as they did is that standardized talks, lectures, and professional journal articles had already misled the international community. In light of this, any attempt to make sense of what really happened in Russia will be quite tricky indeed, but at the same time such an investigation will be thought-provoking and will challenge mainstream interpretations of this subject. Russia and its citizens must be portrayed judiciously and realistically to better understand what they have experienced, the troubles they face, and the better days they are expecting.

Without these elements, a true critical analysis of political tides in post–Cold War Russia and of Russia's economic and social prospects cannot be rendered. An honest, reality-based assessment of Putin's two-term tenure as president cannot be accomplished without first understanding the socioeconomic shortcomings facing Russian citizens before, during, and after the formal transition to the rule of law and to a democratically elected government. Unfortunately, a positive outcome in any analysis of Russians' expectations and Putin's work will prompt much criticism from the scholars who have misinterpreted the lasting unethical consequences of the transition period. Many of these scholars have spent recent years reading only superficially events taking place in Russia, and have not been happy with Putin's techniques and strategies. It is true that some of the Kremlin's most recent choices seem dubious and of questionable international consequences. However, the widespread portrayal of the current Russia's administration shows it as completely mad and undemocratic, and operating with no concern for the people's interests with the cynicism has been a hallmark of Putin's presidency—as opposed to a dispassionate search for truth, fairness, and accountability—as Steven Lee Myers posits in the *New York Times* (2007). Is this cynicism exclusively a prerogative of the Kremlin today? Do no other important, relevant countries in our current world resort to cynicism as a normal way of creating domestic and international policies?

Critics have made it very difficult for a new interpretation to take root and flourish. However, it is time to take a factual look at what Russia and its citizens have faced and how they have dealt with the very different leadership styles of the three post-communist leaders' visions for a noncommunist era in Russia. It is time to look at the ethical aspects of what happened and what continues to happen, with an eye on what is real for Russians and not necessarily focusing on only that which is vital to lobbies in the West and Russia.

In doing so, some may think that the analysis is one-sided and largely silent about certain aspects of current Russian affairs. They may blame that one-sidedness on what I consider the heavy and unavoidable response from the state after Putin took office. Yet the analysis that I provide throughout this book does not downplay the culpability of some groups of bureaucrats, the phenomenon of state capture—or powerful actors who gained control over the state's fortunes to their personal advantage and buying off politicians to shape the legal and regulatory environments in their own interests, and the Kremlin's harshness as a whole. What this analysis does, instead, is look at the transition period with a clear eye toward the Russian realities of the era, rather than with the clouded perspective of pundits who do not glimpse the intricate social and economic pressures of internal Russian politics.

A Quick Look at a Disheartening Reality

The idea of prospective censures of this book is sufficient motivation to steer readers to challenge the old mind-sets and perspectives about Russian citizens and the current Russian political leadership. Of primary concern is that a new look at this timeframe must confront the paradox of the balance between the ethics and the legality of events or strategies, and the majority of scholars have confused these two aspects of leadership.

On the other hand, Russia in the 1990s could also be interpreted through a narrow, misleading, or distorted lens, and this is equally wide of the mark. A simple rule of thumb in the West has been to see Yeltsin's work as plain enough to paint him as a novel democratic reformer during the 1990s. Although Gorbachev did come from the top, one of the western paradoxes is to have seen him—as well as his successors—as a novel, immaculate democratic reformer, even as a pioneer. Did Russia not welcome a wave of true reforms conceived overnight? That is, the West believed Yeltsin to be an unparalleled and positive reformer able to fix societal problems, despite all of the negative events and programs that came out of that era. Persisting in this kind of illogical rationale forced many to misunderstand Russia's passage from one political dimension to a completely different one, and even worse, to get the wrong impression about why the majority of Russians got angry during the 1990s and why they are still bothered by that fallacious rationale today. Nobody has been able to make sense of the Russians' greatest of all political delusions, of delusions they have gotten from early political personnel who came into power promising dreamland but then who turned out to be as bad as the previous communist leadership.

Given the disheartening absence of a coherent central premise among Kremlinologists painting an altered portrait of present-day Russia, approaching Russia logically might be a good start for derailing distorting news propagated all across the world. Avoiding irrationality can make all the difference. Official criticism by these so-called experts on Putin and the ways in which Russian economic and social reforms are progressing lacks the necessary basis to be grounded in reality.

Westerners increasingly contradict themselves when blaming Putin's Kremlin for his actions and programs, while the common perception in Russia about the same subject is different. Western experts continue to do so when they censure those Russians—the majority, if we look at elections and opinion polls—who contend that the Kremlin coherently and resolutely had to get involved in the "game" to be able to curtail most of the activities that began in the 1990s. A new government, powerful enough to make decisions, sometimes strict and firm decisions, was much welcomed by the populace, in order to reverse the events that occurred in the late 1980s and 1990s.

Once in power, Putin's Kremlin undertook reforms and firm restrictions against distortions and inefficiencies as the first step in reinforcing political stability—which was endangered by oligarchic reasoning—and supporting the country socioeconomically. The Kremlin successfully restored the country's stability in 2000. More to the point, if most Russian citizens feel their livelihoods under the Putin presidency have improved economically, then it is difficult to understand why the West systematically blames the *Kremlin* for being unscrupulous toward Russians' hopes. The weight of injudicious oligarchy was overwhelming in the 1990s, and the risks of major social and ethical drawbacks on the road to improving the welfare of Russian citizens were quite a reality at that time. True, not all reforms were designed well or worked out well, and that is a failure of the Kremlin.

Likewise, mounting economic weaknesses were felt by common Russians. Despite the new social contract called for by Putin during his first important presidential speech in July 2000, salaries and pensions remained unpaid at times in many parts of the country. But wage arrears were an economic chaos inherited from Yeltsin's years. Putin had to deal quickly with the repercussions of a financial crisis that was severely weakening the country, and a society that was very displeased with the fact that a majority of citizens lived near or below the poverty line as a result of the reforms of the 1990s.

Before Putin's rule, the Kremlin seemed unable or unprepared to undertake any concrete measures to overcome Russia's economic depression, to help ordinary Russians, and to be in favor of state interests. Russia had to ask international creditors for further debt rescheduling because it was incapable of repaying its debts. The state budget had to be beefed up with taxes, especially tax revenues from the oil and gas industry. Russians would have rallied around a better tax control, such as that which in fact showed up several years after Putin's election (though it was still far from being an extremely efficient tax system). Afterward, in the new century, Russia acquired strength enough to repay its external debt, enhancing its financial stability with consistent credit rating upgrades to the investment level by all major international rating agencies and its ability to take steps in the social sector.

From Failure over Failure

The Kremlin's job was not that straightforward and painless, nor without failures. Putin found himself between a rock and a hard place when he was elected at the Kremlin, and he and the Russian government found themselves caught between standard western plans to help Russia move beyond the crisis and the reality of Russia's social and economic nightmares. Under an institutional angle of analysis, it is worth reviewing few points recent Russian history provides.

First, after the de facto implosion of the genuine communist credo at the hands of Gorbachev's government, Russia experienced three distinct waves of reforms, which I call the *three visions for a modern Russia*. These visions actually overlapped each other, compounded by failure after failure, each one carrying over all its failures into next vision, and finally into Putin's Kremlin. Putin had to cope with the Kremlin's own failures, which had accumulated and were escalating dangerously, beefed up by earlier failures. Gorbachev attempted to revise communism through glasnost and perestroika, Yeltsin's system fostered oligarchy and corruption, as well as associated instability, and then finally Putin's Kremlin implemented reforms aimed at reestablishing a minimal rule of law.

Second, political institutions created in the 1990s were based upon a sort of electoral democracy—not a vibrant democracy whose government is accountable to citizens, as we believe that we have in the West—but rather real involvement of Russians in the country's government. Russians had to choose Yeltsin because he imposed himself on the Russian public, which finally gave him its trust. There was no realistic alternative to Gorbachev other than Yeltsin, who was the only visible leader to Gorbachev's vision in 1991. Although Yeltsin was the first "democratically" elected president of Russia in 1991, clans of businesspeople robbed the country after his election. The West praised those reforms because we were looking at both technicalities rather than social justice and systematically overlooking growing social discontent and that Russians wanted the government to confront these unethical realities.

Third, Russia's living conditions, like living conditions in any country at any given time, are a direct reflection of the governing policies of the time. In Russia, the standard of living for most citizens was significantly impacted by the visions of each administration during the 1990s, and no less so under Putin.

Fourth, although Putin was advanced and chosen by Yeltsin's Kremlin, he was perceived as capable of bailing out Russia from the collapse, corruption, and weaknesses that were seen as Yeltsin's legacy. Russia's panorama and the debate about country's political future have become more interesting since then. A specific criticism of Putin early on in the process was his former association with the KGB. This was perceived as his Achilles' heel—his original sin. As a result, his political steps against business clans were criticized indiscriminately. Members of these business clans clearly had a great deal of money and spent part of this money to fund critical propaganda against Putin's Kremlin both from inside the country and internationally. It is easy to believe that westerners jumped right on board with it. The second inconsistency of Western criticism is that Russians themselves have been calling on the government for even more resolute strategies to prevent further bribery payments and inefficiency. The fact that Russians called on the government for resolute strategies can be appreciated if we look at the history of Russia and attitudes of Russians themselves after years of chaos.

As I have said, the West continues to take an increasingly negative view of Putin's Kremlin and the Russian people's dissatisfaction with his presidency. Nevertheless, such unsympathetic assessments do not accurately reflect the reality in today's Russia.

It is a mistake to refuse to recognize that dishonesty, bankruptcy, and fraud occur all over the world and that national governments and judiciary systems try to rein in these tendencies. That is, western hypocrisy reaches its peak when one compares, in basic terms, the ongoing situation in Russia to international practices and values regarding corruption and corporate extortion. Once western governments recognize and address their own national cases of dishonesty and fraud at all levels, their criticism of Russian political problems appears naïve and idealistic, scrutinizing Russia solely on principle and not based on the practices the West applies at home.

What Are the Relevant Questions?

To wrap up this comprehensive analysis, we should be able to address the questions that no one has asked up till now. This exciting process gets us thinking about new questions that standard interpretations proffered in the past did not allow. A short list of such questions in this case might include:

- Were business activities in the 1990s a product of the deceitful implementation of western capitalistic practices or merely the product of conflicting tribes of bandits or thieves during the institutional chaos of the 1990s?
- What would the 2000s in Russia have looked like if Putin had not become leader of the Kremlin?
- Would Putin's policy have taken a different course without anti-corruption reforms?
- How far and deep would western countries' legislation go in dealing with domestic instability and social chaos?
- What is the state of social justice and modernization in Russia today after Mikhail Gorbachev's and Boris Yeltsin's visions for reform?
- Should the legal action taken be attributed to Putin himself and/or to the Russians' wishes that the Kremlin take action against escalating unpleasantness within the business and bureaucratic sectors?
- What should an oil- and natural gas – rich country realistically do with these commodities?
- What meaningful and realistic alternative do western zealots suggest Russia follow in selling oil and natural gas? Here, I refer to western fanatics of the 1990s and now harsh critics of the Kremlin and its policy in the oil-gas sector.

- What is wrong with Russia seeking to maximize profits from the country's export of oil and gas? Is it not true that other exporting countries act exactly the same way when they maximize export revenues?
- How should other countries approach their foreign policy when the West's foreign policy is seemingly driven by double standards?
- Will the West get wise and team up with Russia?

These thoughts represent the central questions within an in-depth analysis of Putin and his presidency as it draws to a close. I have endeavored to articulate answers to these questions about the state of noncommunist Russia. Any serious scholar needs to come up with concrete answers grounded in basic Russian realities; therefore, the proper procedure is to follow a logical classification of details and single out facts. The logical pillars supporting this analysis are the ethical chaos occurring in Russia and the necessity to confront it. The complete absence of any ethics in the business and political realms ended the hopes of ordinary Russians that their country would be normal and brought about more inequalities and the economic troubles of the 1990s. These inequalities clearly caused social injustice and unequal opportunities, and were entirely economically detrimental.

Proper Interpretations

Interpreting these Russian pillars by rigorous western standards and presuming that Russia's leaders could curb the phenomena previously analyzed through recourse to a trouble-free policy is misleading. The highly corrupt system of the 1990s and the general social discontent that became manifest necessarily entailed a vigorous response from the state. Commentators are still afraid to address these issues, as the central aspect of the West is not to understand Russia and to strongly critique the Kremlin.

Any country's leadership must deal with challenging realities from a policy perspective. In the case of modern Russia, however, one must address several additional aspects of the situation, such as natural resource issues in one of the world's most abundant countries and the sudden dramatic appearance of numerous millionaires and billionaires. It was blatantly evident that only a few people were enjoying most of the country's wealth, and some of them seemed to become rich overnight. In addition, widespread corruption and poverty figures among certain groups of people throughout the country were and are staggering, especially when viewed alongside others that indicated that other tiny groups were getting rich. How is this situation different from that of other developing countries? How are the political leaders supposed to handle this? In two words, not easily, although most leaders have spent more time talking about short-term virtual outcomes instead of long-term ethical aspects of the situation. But history is recurrent, and there is one point no one mentions: it is not surprising that the beginning of this new century, like the previous one, has been punctuated again by Russia's growing influence in Europe and beyond. Russia's mammoth natural resources give the current and future Kremlin administrations an influential role, but prior uneven distribution of these natural resources also created unending socioeconomic imbalances among the Russian citizenry that demand resolute action and response.

The distortions produced in the 1990s created the same issues that have pressured Putin to reform the country. The pulse of reality is measured by people's aspirations, yet the West gives birth to a one-sided debate on democracy in Russia and ends up with misplaced conclusions at times. Yet I cannot interpret Russian circumstances if I do not look at the logical progression of facts. I provide a broad perspective and means for readers to interpret these events and explanations as to why Russians want their government to act tough in these areas. This may incite criticism; however, my perspective brings with it the important advantage of acknowledging the limited options any leadership would have had in the late 1990s to move the country forward in a positive direction and pull Russian society safely through economic and social outcomes.

During the 1990s, only a few western intellectuals understood that that decade had produced more bad things than good. But the majority in the West has been calling on intellectuals to pressure Russia not to make thoroughgoing improvements in the stability sphere. No analysis of Russia should ignore the impact that unfairly distributed wealth is still having on Russia. Nor can one theorize that the uncertain development of socioeconomic realities in Russia was unimportant in this context. A steady crusade against corruption and economic thievery was an important aspect of Russia, although the current Kremlin has fallen quite short; still, the crusade should continue as both economic and moral policy, making further government reforms a priority.

A well-developed analysis of Russians and Putin must, by its nature and scope, be structured logically around the central idea that the 1990s were a failure in Russia, particularly because ordinary Russians' expectations were not and have not been met. Once this point has been established, the decision by Yeltsin's Kremlin to opt for the most moderate politician at that time and the Russians' electoral support of Putin represent a logical step in the development of the country.

For the West, identifying with Russia and Russians from the proper coherent perspective is a necessity. It is unclear why the denigration only works as long as introducing an ethical discourse is not legitimate in Russia. It is also necessary to ascertain why the West does not, or does not want to, fully understand the realities of Russian social and economic challenges. Therefore, I take steps toward a clearer understanding by offering a rather controversial analysis of President Putin and his activities. With an integrated and consistent, logical breakdown of existing evidence in the areas already highlighted, readers will have the opportunity to see Russian affairs and Putin from a different perspective, which will make it easier to understand Russian events and why they developed the way they did. Putin's Kremlin was forced to act in a way that would best move Russia and Russians through a chaotic period in history toward better times.

It benefits the reader in two ways to know that Russia grew amid unethical and unlawful practices during the 1990s; we would expect any government around the world to engage in a war against these harmful conditions. But the West's persistent mental block in dealing with any Russian leadership team not sharing specific leadership goals and concepts shared by the West has led to the undervaluation of Russia's transition onto the modern world stage and the country's social and economic issues. Failure to rectify this glaring weakness has resulted in policy flaws in the West. It is essential to comprehend the very strong support Putin has enjoyed throughout Russia; his economic programs and policies have certainly benefited many more Russians than any Yeltsin post-communist policies. Perhaps most troubling is the very real possibility the West has deliberately chosen not to assess Russia through any lens other than the shallow, distorting prism it currently uses.

Therefore, readers who are anxious to understand the Russian political and economic transition, readers who want a snapshot of the roots of modern Russia and the barriers to long-term reasonable economic growth there, and readers who deserve a reasoned view of why the market did not behave as it was expected to in Russia need a comprehensive analysis of events over the period that commenced with Gorbachev's perestroika and glasnost in the mid 1980s. Seeing Putin's Kremlin from a perspective different from that of the Kremlinologists is the last step of this process. Serious, well-supported, and responsible explanations concerning these subjects will allow readers to be *au fait* with the evolving Russian story, despite the fact that critics will strenuously and nervously take issue with my approach.

Chapter Two

Modern Russia—Three Reforming Visions

As mentioned in the previous chapter, the past century began and ended with Russia, and there is no doubt that Russia played a big role then, just as it is doing in this century. This fact is of some significance in the overall assessment of Russian affairs and the country's alleged inclination toward autocracy.

Not least important is the perception that current Russian realities draw a historical parallel with the Russia of a century ago, when wealthy landowners and impoverished peasants were in continuous conflict with one another. Some have compared those conflicts with the class disputes that emerged during the 1990s, a potentially explosive situation in the absence of serious resolutions to this economic divide in Russia; the growing instability of the gap between the rich and the poor was adding critical complexity to the development of the transformation strategy and threat to the changing social structure of modern Russia's society. Dealing with this has required a serious, constructive, ethical effort to interpret reality as it is rather than hiding behind the political spin of the few people who benefit from the situation.

There are two key lessons to bear in mind when appraising the formation of modern Russia. First, we have the divided class structure in Russia, with oligarchs and billionaires on one side and huge numbers of poor citizens on the other. These two classes are the primary actors in the unfolding story of Russia's noncommunist development as overseen by the current Kremlin's actions, which are widely perceived among most of Russia's citizens as coherently tied to the country's new realities, but recognized far less in the West.

Second, there were serious flaws in past leaders' policies as they attempted to muddle through the widespread unlawfulness. These policies did not prove advantageous to the majority of Russians, and illegal actions were numerous; this milieu became a powerful validation of the inevitability that Putin had to take matters in hand immediately upon taking office. As a result, this situation contributed to Mikhail Gorbachev's and Boris Yeltsin's drop in popular approval and to Putin's credibility throughout Russia today. Because Gorbachev and Yeltsin did not take action toward offering the country any sort of stability, they eventually lost credibility and support. In a certain sense, Putin's ability to provide the country and ordinary Russians with a sort of stability is emphasized by his predecessors' failure.

The endeavor to transform a communist country into a pro-market, fair society saw Russia through three different visions for reform, all of whose mistakes now overlap: the Gorbachev era with its experimentation and high hopes, then the disgraced Yeltsin era of rampantly unethical business practice and oligarchy, and finally the current leadership of Putin, which is moving closer and closer to its final stages and continuing its attempt to reestablish political stability while spurring economic growth.

Mikhail Gorbachev

The appointment of Mikhail Gorbachev, as the very last secretary-general of the Soviet Communist Party, was proposed by Andrei Gromyko, the long-standing Soviet minister of foreign affairs from 1957 until 1985, who labeled him the *man with a nice smile but with iron teeth*. This phrase, quite common among Kremlinologists, comes from the notoriously dour Andrei Gromyko—who was kicked out of government after twenty eight years as foreign minister. The Kremlin knew it needed someone youthful and vigorous and Gorbachev, at age fifty four the youngest member of the Politburo, moved quickly to consolidate his personal power.

The Politburo approved the appointment on March 11, 1985. Gorbachev played a key role in bringing the Soviet era to a close. He was much lauded in the West for initiating democratic reforms but become widely loathed in Russia for paving the way to the economic ethical debacle, which brought enormous wealth in to the hands of few well-connected people but plunged many ordinary Russians into humiliating poverty. Building something so novel in Russia proved tremendously difficult for Gorbachev, who had no experience whatsoever in political democratization, economic reform, or societal changes. Western governments appreciated Gorbachev's efforts, which maximized the likelihood of a complete implosion of the system, but overlooked the societal impact.

By the mid-1980s, Gorbachev shared a pioneering vision that would reform the way his immense communist country worked, embracing a multiparty system and adopting the new goal of humane, democratic socialism that he proposed to the Central Committee plenum—the de facto governing body of the Soviet Union. That goal was officially adopted on February 7, 1990, but quite plainly had unintended results, because of course Gorbachev did not intend to break up the Soviet Union. In producing his plans for reform, his primary goal was that all people, including consumers and entrepreneurs, would enjoy political and economic freedom. Global response to his ideas was acclamation for Gorbachev, vis-à-vis positive reaction to the reform efforts he initiated almost immediately. Gorbachev had almost seven years to make decisions, but rather than results, he seems to have produced committees and working groups that proposed unrealistic reforms.

One unexpected focus of Gorbachev's reform was the anti-alcohol campaign discussed at the Politburo—the governing body of the Communist

Party—on April 4, 1985. Gorbachev was wise to focus on this issue of tremendous importance to Russian society: almost 90 percent of ill patients started drinking before the age of fifteen and one-third of them started before the age of ten, according to Kaiser (1992). Gorbachev also supported the economic reforms envisaged by Yuri Andropov—Gorbachev's most important patron. During a speech to a Communist Party official on April 8 that year, Gorbachev supported the principle of giving more independence to enterprises and changing the way the economy was managed. Soon after, on April 23, the approximately 300 members of the plenum of the Central Committee endorsed a vague reform program outlined by Gorbachev himself.

But while some doubts were rising within the party's bureaucracy, two meetings with U.S. President Ronald Reagan brought notoriety to Gorbachev in November 1985 and October 1986. The two leaders met for the first time in Geneva, Switzerland, where they discussed issues such as the Strategic Defense Initiative. On October 11, 1986, Gorbachev and Reagan held a major summit in Reykjavik, Iceland, concerning the reduction of nuclear weapons, but due to fighting in Afghanistan and Central America, the meeting ended with no concrete outcomes. Nevertheless, that meeting was always considered the first major meeting between the two leaders. The meeting was both very important and very controversial, because President Reagan unexpectedly proposed to Gorbachev that both Russia and United States eliminate their long-range, strategic offensive missiles, which represented a reduction in ballistic nuclear missiles by 50 percent and an end to the placement of intermediate-range missiles in Europe—a so-called "zero option" agreement. Reagan's chief ally in international affairs, Margaret Thatcher of Britain, said she was shocked that her close friend and ally, Reagan, would unilaterally attempt to do such a thing without consulting her, NATO, and others. Gorbachev responded to the proposal by telling Reagan that the Soviets would agree to it only if Reagan and the United States completely dropped plans to build the new SDI or "Star Wars," as many observers called the controversial program supported by Reagan. Reagan refused Gorbachev's official response and the Reykjavik summit broke up at that point. Reagan was blamed for the collapse of the summit because he was not flexible regarding SDI. Therefore Gorbachev, the darling of the world at that time, was generally not blamed for being unable to embrace Reagan's original offers or for the collapse of the Reykjavik summit. While no agreement was signed during the summit, both leaders still felt that the meeting was a success and opened the way for further progress.

After Reykjavik, Gorbachev landed on *Time* magazine's front cover in 1987 as Man of the Year and 1989 as Person of the Decade—former president Richard Nixon even suggested that Gorbachev be named Man of the Century. He met with the Pope in Vatican City on December 1, 1989. On December 2–4, he met with then – U.S. president George H. W. Bush at the Malta summit. Gorbachev was awarded the Nobel Prize for Peace on October 15, 1990, for his role in ending the Cold War. The West continued to watch him closely.

Margaret Thatcher stated, "I like Mr. Gorbachev: we can do business together," even before Gorbachev won top seat at the Kremlin. George H. W. Bush offered him economic assistance. The West was easily impressed and enthusiastic about Gorbachev's rehabilitation of truth, ethics, and human values. The Soviet Union was in the midst of a crisis and needed to be reshaped.

There were two parts to Gorbachev's vision, his new ideas of glasnost and perestroika. Glasnost (meaning "openness"), was the counter-censorship program that Gorbachev first talked about at the end of 1984, even before he become party leader, when he expressed the idea that political power should talk to citizens truthfully, rather than superficially and insincerely. In fact, the word comes from the era of Czar Alexander II, whose Emancipation Manifesto emancipated the serfs in 1861 and also introduced other reforms. In any case, Gorbachev's glasnost, inaugurated by 1985, allowed freedom of speech and print, and transparency in government's activities in the Soviet Union. A new magazine called Glasnost began to appear by June 1986.

Perestroika was the name of major economic reforms that Gorbachev introduced on February 25, 1986, during the Twenty-seventh Party Congress. These reforms applied to the economic mechanisms of industry, agriculture, and foreign trade. In truth, perestroika was not a term coined entirely by Gorbachev alone. He may have had the courage to start reforming the country, but the term actually originated (in a political sense) in a speech given by Soviet leader Lazar Kaganovich—a top member of the Politburo during Stalin's tenure. Kaganovich used this term fifty seven times during the Seventeenth Communist Party Congress in 1934 (Ellman and Kontorovich, 1992; Sergi, 2004).

In 1987, Gorbachev published *Perestroika: New Thinking for Our Country and the World* (1987a). A key component of his economic restructuring program was resorting to the autonomy of government enterprises, an ideological attempt toward a radical decentralization of decision making from top ministerial circles in Moscow down to individual plants and units. Under the Law on State Enterprises that went into effect in 1988, this was to be accomplished in stages and through an evolutionary process. Enterprises producing 60 percent of the country's industrial output were to implement the new system in 1988, and enterprises producing the remaining part were required to implement the new "independent, self-accounting, self-financing, and self-managing" system by 1991. In late 1990, this principle was further extended as enterprise managers were to operate in the interests of their employees and "stockholder-owners" in determining all aspects across firm management conforming to market demand and supply evolutions. At a Central Committee plenum on March 15, 1989, Gorbachev suggested that a "green revolution" was necessary in agriculture.

In 1988, the *man with a nice smile but with iron teeth* removed Andrei Gromyko and appointed Eduard Shevardnadze as the new minister of foreign affairs, convened with President Ronald Reagan, and rehabilitated one of Lenin's closest comrades Nikolai Bukharin—who had been thrown out of the Politburo, arrested, and killed by Stalin's purges. Taking all of these steps made

Gorbachev's policy so estemed in the West that Archie Brown (1996) referred to "the Gorbachev factore" and Robert Kaiser (1992) lauded Gorbachev's courage to turn his country in a new direction. Meanwhile, many Russians spoke of "two Gorbachevs," the apparatchik and the reformer; that is, one man who was trying to square a circle of efforts toward reforming the system while hurting the enormous Soviet apparatus as little as possible. Clearly, these two tendencies were at odds. Enemies of this new process warned that glasnost might turn out to be a double-edged sword that could come back and hurt the person using it, but Gorbachev began speaking openly about the existence of perestroika's opponents beginning in the second half of 1986. At that time, when Gorbachev started to recognize the existence of internal opponents to perestroika, he was quite clear in expressing his ideas and clear about the fact that opposition was mounting in the party.

It soon became clear that rapidly escalating political and economic developments were driving the Soviet Union toward implosion. In the space of six months, from June 1991 to end of 1991, the Soviet Union peacefully imploded. A kind of dual Gorbachev-Yeltsin vision for Russia operated for about six months after the elections, until the end of 1991, when Gorbachev's political leadership ended on Christmas Day. The dispute between Gorbachev, Soviet president and Yeltsin, Russian president, became irreversible. Yeltsin tried to incite the protest against Gorbachev's Soviet Union in order to let the Union implode. There was dual power in Moscow and in Russia until Gorbachev resigned and the USSR officially ceased to exist at the end of 1991.

On September 6, 1991, the Soviet government recognized the independence of the three Baltic States. Then, on December 8, 1991, Boris Yeltsin, president of Russia, along with the presidents of Ukraine and Belarus, erased the Soviet Union from the world map. The meeting at a hunting lodge near Minsk resulted in a declaration that the Soviet Union was dissolved and replaced by the Commonwealth of Independent States. Gorbachev described this as a constitutional coup. On December 1, 1991, Ukraine declared its independence from the Soviet Union after a popular referendum in which 90 percent of voters opted for independence. Meanwhile, the Soviet economy continued to deteriorate and collapse from internal economic contradictions.

Gorbachev was still opposed to any rapid market reforms, but Yeltsin decided to disband the Soviet Union in accordance with the Treaty of the Union of 1922 and thereby to remove Gorbachev and the government of the Soviet Union from power. This was seen as a forced measure to save the country from a complete economic collapse and was, at the time, widely supported by Russia's population, as by December 1991 food shortages in central Russia resulted in the introduction of food rationing in the Moscow area for the first time since World War II. Three weeks later, on December 25, 1991, Gorbachev resigned as Soviet Union's president, and all official Soviet institutions ceased operations by December 31, 1991, as individual republics assumed the central government's role.

Ineffectiveness and uncertain political strategy ended Gorbachev's era before reform efforts could take hold. The new course that he championed was popular with Russians in the beginning, but became less popular toward the end when several problems produced by these half reforms could be readily seen. Signs of increasing problems and dashed hopes were just around the corner. In some ways, Gorbachev still represented the former Soviet Union, and he lacked the legitimacy of a democratically elected leader.

It is interesting to note that after resigning, Gorbachev started a career as a professional speaker, receiving up to $90,000 for each public appearance. This is a mark of the positive reputation and respect Gorbachev gained among western political leaders and intellectuals, who were extremely impressed by Gorbachev's innovative reforms, although these reforms scarcely had an impact in the country. When Gorbachev ran for reelection in Russia in 1996, he received only about 1 percent of the vote from his constituents.

Happiness with Gorbachev Turns to Discontent

Perestroika and glasnost were parts of an overall program of economic, political, and social restructuring. The growing role of dissidents since the 1960s, and the systemic weakening of the system, had had profound repercussions on Gorbachev and his reform efforts (Horvath, 2005).

Notwithstanding this, the reforms were intended to revive a moribund system, and no one can contradict the fact that these reforms played a positive role in inspiring domestic intellectuals to become more dynamic and vivid, and shaping debates and cultural discussions among thinkers. The way in which they were conceived and implemented, however, became a clear invitation to rob state resources and push them en route for the tangled track of Yeltsin's era.

Rodric Braithwaite (2002), the former British ambassador to Moscow from September 1988 to May 1992, explains in his *Across the Moscow River: The World Turned Upside Down* that economics and politics often go hand in hand, and despite an apparent enthusiasm, signs of disappointment over Gorbachev's programs began to appear by November 1990. The first to feel the effects of this disappointment were insider politicians in Russia. Gorbachev's popularity was high when the last Soviet troops left Afghanistan on February 15, 1989, and when the Congress of People's Deputies elections were held as the first ever nationwide multi-candidate election on March 26 of 1989. But many of the Communist Party candidates running for election were voted down, and Yeltsin appeared to win the match because he received 90 percent of the votes in Moscow. Only the composite electoral system and resolution of numerous election problems ensured the majority for Gorbachev to be elected First Executive President on May 25, during the opening session of the Congress of People's Deputies.

Internal troubles were on the increase. Gorbachev's closest allies left him the following year. Shevardnadze resigned as foreign minister on December 20, blaming an orchestrating specter of an "approaching dictatorship" (Gorbachev 1995: 490). Prime Minister Nikolai Ryzhkov—formerly Gosplan's chairman before the Gorbachev years—quit. Grigory Yavlinsky also resigned from his post as deputy prime minister for economic reform. On January 19, 1991, the year of the attempted coup d'etat in the summer, Nikolai Petrakov, one of Gorbachev's economic advisers, resigned, citing as a reason that economic reforms were hard to implement under the (then) current circumstances.

This was, in fact, the beginning of further chaps, banditism, or the state capture society, which goes back to the end of the 1980s. Even during perestroika, bright young men were leaving the party and jumping into the market ideology and business, as reported by Braithwaite on the occasion of a joint venture agreement between a British company and a cooperative to manufacture hot-air balloons in Russia. It was April 1989, and in his own words, it was his "first encounter with the Perestroika phenomenon of the ex-Party businessman: bright young men who were getting very rich by moving into business and taking Party funds with them" (Braithwaite 2002: 288). A large number of former Party *nomenklatura* "reinvented themselves as *businessmen*" (Braithwaite 2002: 318) and new radical reformers. Soviet leaders preferred to plunder their country of its wealth rather than risk losing everything in clashes with the population as had happened in other countries in Eastern Europe in 1989. The immense Soviet elite, armed to the teeth with loyal internal forces and weapons, failed to defend the system, but for some authors it can resemble a mystery story (Kotkin, 2001) Gorbachev could not prevent the final implosion of the system. Despite loyal internal forces and a corpulent *nomenklatura*, elites could not defend the system and the absence of an all-consuming conflagration can be simply explained because the economic and political symbols of communism had already disappeared by the early 1980s. In the end, the Soviet economic history increased in numbers without establishing firm bases for the populace's well-being.

Finally, yet importantly, workers started criticizing Gorbachev for promises that went awry—especially the health-care sector, which really underprovided services to Russians. However, two different viewpoints collided here. On one side, Gorbachev was under attack for having gone too far with reform efforts, but on the other side, people complained that many reforms were not thought through well enough. Gorbachev was tied to the old system to such an extent that "in the face of imperialism's aggressive policy and threats we must not permit military superiority over ourselves. Such is the will of the Soviet people" (Gorbachev 1987b: 102). What Gorbachev was trying to introduce did not harm *nomenklatura* utterly, but Gorbachev was obliged to introduce ways to tackle industrialization and build support services in the trade and financial sectors.

The previous twenty five years had seen capital accumulation expand by 6 to 9 percent, but the accumulation could not continue at this pace, and by the end of the 1970s, capital accumulation was decreasing and returns were diminishing. Participation in the workforce was still extremely high—higher than in the United States—and the population was growing at less than 1 percent per year after 1970. Gorbachev had to take action. The new economic accounting idea or self-financing mechanism (*khozraschet*) that had been introduced as part of former Soviet premier Alexei Kosygin's various economic reforms in the mid-1960s (Kosygin shared overall power with Leonid Brezhnev, General Secretary of the Communist Party) was designed to reform and modernize Soviet agriculture, industry, and trade. Kosygin, in fact, gave incentives to industrial managers, tried to provide more flexibility in the production system, and sought to reform the agriculture and construction sectors. Unfortunately, central planners disbanded Kosygin's reforms and fought off proposals for more flexible economic planning. Gorbachev, however, was more pragmatic and became resolved to modernize the economy and make it work without political interference. He reactivated an accounting system from January 1988—made possible through a state enterprise law that was voted into effect in 1987—that attempted to toughen budget constraints, thus forcing decentralization and using profits and sales rather than the absolute volume of output to steer economic principles and make self-financing work. Besides the fact that this reintroduced Kosygin's mid-1960s reforms, it was an attempt to modernize the country while keeping the political structure intact. This attempt, however, led to price increases, output reductions, and other microeconomic distortions (Ellman and Kontorovich, 1992). The new system would have created the basis of economic accounting and self-financing principles and several factory managers looked at it favorably. Nevertheless, mechanisms for guaranteeing equal starting conditions for all enterprises were not in place yet.

Other Gorbachev reforms involved the reorganization of the state's methods of regulating and limiting social capital investment, and increasing the efficiency of noncentralized capital investments. In the end, the man with a nice smile but iron teeth could invigorate the image of the Soviet Union abroad as he traveled quite widely, consolidated his personal power, and made preliminary steps toward streamlining a huge bureaucracy. Nevertheless, he did not move decentralization too much and did not introduce definitive, final free-market mechanisms, so as not to endanger the party's power. Even internationally, Gorbachev expressed the image of an ambitious country and was determined to compete deliberately with the United States and the West.

Boris Yeltsin

After supporting Gorbachev, the world community shifted support to Boris Yeltsin. Yeltsin's father had been convicted of anti-Soviet agitation in 1934 and sent to a gulag for three years; Boris was practically from the class of muzhik, the class of poor peasants which set against the wealthy landowners *(barin)*. Yeltsin was extremely popular with the Russian people; when he ran for president on June 12, 1991, he received 90 percent of the votes in Moscow. Symbols of the communist regime imploded: Yeltsin had, in fact, resigned from the Communist Party on July 12, 1990, and the system started moving toward a form of electoral democracy based on presidentship. Yeltsin then introduced a second official vision for Russian economic and political strategy. The two political visions were quite different, as were the political contexts in which Gorbachev and Yeltsin were operating (see Breslauer, 2002; Sakwa 2002). The main difference between the two periods, however, was that under Yeltsin the country suffered considerable political instability—far more than under Gorbachev—and widespread corruption.

Yeltsin triumphed over Gorbachev politically in 1991 by winning the Russian presidential elections in June of that year. However, the April 1993 referendum on his reform proposals led to a conflict with the Russian Parliament, and prompted Yeltsin to order the army to surround the Parliament palace in September of that year. A referendum on the new Russian Constitution was held in December 1993, and Yeltsin definitively won the presidential election in July 1996. On this latter occasion, I recall that Yeltsin was supported by Anatoly Chubais, who was head of the State Privatization Committee, then first deputy prime minister in charge of economics and finance from 1994 to 1996, and then chief of the presidential administration after Yeltsin's reelection in 1996 until March 1997. Chubais lent a hand to recruit a group of oligarchs to bankroll the Yeltsin campaign and guarantee crucial financial support and favorable media coverage for Yeltsin's reelection. Loans from the International Monetary Fund helped a great deal as well. However, his overall support and sympathy declined to depressing levels, and in the run-off on July 3 he won slightly less than 54 percent while the Communist leader Gennady Zyuganov had 40 percent or so. Still, the voters in Moscow offered him almost 83 percent of the vote. Yeltsin won electoral backing to stay in power thanks to Russia's oligarchs, who became immensely wealthy and used their treasures and media to simply return the favor to him. After realizing the inconclusiveness of the first wave of privatization, Yeltsin engineered a second wave of privatization, the so-called "loans-for-shares" privatization. The oligarchy quickly took possession of state property and resources for its own benefit. Former President Gorbachev ran for president again, receiving meager support. In contrast to the mainstream western understanding of Russia, I assert that genuine democracy in the mid-1990s Russia was a labile notion, and election results were often subject to bribery.

Western Kremlinologists and international organizations seemingly took the new Yeltsin state structures for granted. They appeared to believe that new programs would transform the country into some form of immediate example of stability, and even prosperity, including effective representation of regular citizens' aspirations. While international observers were demonstrating overly optimistic assessments of Yeltsin's effectiveness, however, tremendously unethical and incredibly corrupt conduct was occurring behind the scenes throughout the Yeltsin era of the 1990s. By 1999, Yeltsin was so disgraced within Russia that he felt compelled to appoint Vladimir Putin as prime minister and to resign on December 31 of that year, surprising most commentators around the world. The tremendous failure both of Yeltsin's political and of his economic performance was caused by an unparalleled failure in ethics by Yeltsin and his administration. Amazingly, adulation by outside observers continued regarding Yeltsin's shocking therapies and palpably corrupted privatizations, despite the reality of what was going on in the Russian business arena. The sanctioned thievery practiced by the *nomenklatura's* members was not popular among Russians and was certainly not what they had expected to happen in the transition to a noncommunist society. Praise for Yeltsin and his leadership by other world leaders, however, continued to follow him without interruption for most of his presidency. He died on April 23, 2007, at the age of seventy six.

Vladimir Putin

Putin represents the third vision of political and economic reality for modern Russia in the last fifteen years. Russians were afraid of how things were developing in the country. In fact, they desperately wanted someone to combat the instability created during Yeltsin's tenure. They supported Putin for a first four-year term on March 26, 2000. Prior to becoming president, Putin was a KGB functionary in the East German city of Dresden from 1985 to 1990, and may have trained agents to steal technological secrets from western countries. Much of today's hostility and a priori criticism of Putin are based on this affiliation with the original KGB and its successor agency, the renamed FSB, as I will explain below.

After he served in the KGB foreign intelligence service, Putin's political career was kicked off in Leningrad (renamed St. Petersburg after the breakup of the Soviet Union), which is, in fact, his hometown. The building of St. Petersburg, which begun in 1703, marked the first milestone in a new western type of action in Russia. Founded by Czar Peter the Great, it was the Russian capital until March 1918, when the capital was moved to Moscow, the capital ever since. The town was renamed Petrograd after the revolution in 1905 and renamed Leningrad three days after Lenin died in January 1924.

Putin came back to Leningrad from Dresden to become an aide to Leningrad State University's vice president in charge of international relations. After other appointments to the Leningrad—then St. Petersburg—City Council, Putin became deputy mayor of St. Petersburg from March 1994 through 1996. This occurred thanks to Mayor Anatoly Sobchak, Putin's former law professor in the mid-1970s. Putin also obtained a PhD in economics from the St. Petersburg Mining Institute in 1997.

In 1996, voters in St. Petersburg replaced Mayor Anatoly Sobchak with Vladimir Yakovlev after the town fell into an economic crisis and became pervaded by corruption and crime. The problem was so extensive that the town was considered the capital of crime in Russia, and voters wanted a crime fighter in office to replace Sobchak. After the election, Putin became a member of the presidential administration upon Anatoly Chubais's recommendation. He was then elevated to the Russian presidency's Central Control Bureau in the Kremlin, and named first deputy for the head of the presidential administration in May 1998. In July of the same year, he became head of the Federal Security Service, known by its initials FSB, which replaced the KGB. He served in this role and as Security Council secretary until March 1999. Finally, in early August, Vladimir Putin became first vice prime minister, and then acting prime minister, due to Yeltsin's firing of Prime Minister Sergei Stepashin. Putin was not a maximalist—not too radical—and this set him apart from other possible candidates, according to Yeltsin himself. Then, on New Year's Eve, Yeltsin handed over his office to Putin—who served as acting president of Russia—and new presidential elections were set for late March 2000, as mentioned above. Slightly less than 53 percent of Russians backed Putin at the time, but media sources were largely under the control of commercial interests, as Andrew Jack—a former Moscow Bureau Chief for the *Financial Times*—reminds us in *Inside Putin's Russia* (2004). Grigory Yavlinsky, the economist and Yabloko's party leader, and coauthor of the never implemented 400-day reform plan, ran for president but finished a distant third, with 4.8 percent. (Note that he also ran for president on June 1996, and came in a disappointing fourth with 7.3 percent, despite substantial financial backing from banks.) The Russian stock market rose with the news of Putin's election. These facts demonstrate that his background indeed looked favorable to a majority of Russians, despite his KGB affiliation, and Putin seemed to rise out of obscurity to the status of a portentous national leader. Solzhenitsyn remarked that considering Russia's vast array of problems, it is "by no means inappropriate to have a strong presidency" (1991: 96). Russians demanded an elected president with strong powers to become the champion of a total U-turn in social and economic policy. Putin hoped to make up further ground in politics and economics by wooing the voters with purpose, strengthening the unity of the country, and curbing the power of the oligarchy. Putin, who was not tainted in any way by association with unfairly acquired wealth, planned to develop a Russian route to liberalism and capitalism, reinforcing state, order, and law, and create a transformation in the social and human aspects of Russia's society and an associated improvement in the quality of human life.

However, Putin has been the undisputed national champion of stability, especially when it comes to visibility of institutions, and Russians favored him in March 2004. Russians paved the way for Putin's second four-year term on March 14, 2004, allowing him to continue his policies from the Kremlin until 2008 when his term expires. Russians were euphoric, and a large majority

71.2—percent—elected Putin; his closest opponent had less than 14 percent of the vote. It is not surprising that Russian voters got excited about Putin, making him stand apart from the previous two modern Russian leaders who lost popular consensus during their electoral mandates. Russians simply perceived him as a practical leader for such a project. The fact that Putin was elected by a minuscule majority in 2000 and enjoyed much broader and high ratings in the 2004 poll cannot be ignored at all or downplayed, as the West has done, nor can it be suggested—as Kremlinologists do—that he engineered a larger consensus because he was staying at the Kremlin. Elections were not characterized by blatant fraud, and a vast majority of votes for Putin in 2004 in a field of six candidates was a sign that Russians preferred stable leadership. Elections were democratic and the overwhelming support for Putin—although some wondered if the media virtually excluded coverage of other candidates. This support, coupled with the dominance in the Duma of pro-Putin parties, gave Putin a mandate to champion any agenda that he chose.

In both 2000 and 2004, Putin came into office promising to clean up corruption and stabilize the country. On the latter point he has partially succeeded, but he has made far less progress toward the former goal. He started with the benefit of the doubt, and after eight years, he does not deserve the political furor that is being expressed against him. Putin's work should not be triggering such dogmatic criticism, nor prompting critics to go back in Russian history and disparage Russians whose only crime was yearning for a convincing and reliable president in the Kremlin.

The rationale used by Putin's accusers is that he was with the KGB and carried out few resolute acts against corruption and instability; in addition to not having cut all appearance of corrupt practices, Putin's accusers lay blame on him because he would have offered widespread support to his entourage instead.

It is anachronistic to blame Putin for his accomplishments prior to his becoming president, yet such criticism continues. However, whether Putin has undertaken effective and resolute acts against corruption or whether he has molded clan interests to his satisfaction are two other real questions to reflect on.

Kremnologists saw opportunities for censuring Putin from the very beginning, condemning almost everything that he did in Russia. Yet, one indicator of the country's perception of Putin's leadership was the financial markets, which were an absolute novelty in modern Russia. Despite all the criticism and naysayers, the Russian stock market rose significantly with news of Putin's election. This was not surprising, because Russians were searching for strong leadership and saw Putin as capable of creating new development strategies for the Kremlin.

Oddly enough, much of the criticism of Putin's policy purports to be based on his personal experiences at the KGB. It is not necessary, in the context of Russian politics, to push this criticism any further. Perhaps more telling is the fact that Russians were extremely worried about the risk of seeing the country slide into chronic instability. Most Russians welcomed Putin's approach to government, and the main rationale for curbing the excesses of past governments lies in the fact that the country was in complete institutional chaos in the 1990s; otherwise they would never have elected him by such wide margins. Russians were very concerned that the elections needed to be accepted as legitimate, and seemed to favor a strong role for the government and their president. In a country plagued by corruption, Putin initiated policy administrative reforms at the central and subnational levels that addressed rife corruption—with varying effective outcomes—and the significantly unequal distribution of income. While Russians were inclined to support the costs of the transition from communism to a capitalistic market economy, and this occurred both under Gorbachev and Yeltsin, the benefits were enjoyed almost exclusively within the new bureaucratic-capitalist class. The rest of the country was unhappy with the outcome.

Endless Reform Proposals

After Gorbachev began introducing reform efforts, an endless number of plan proposals were suggested—although the majority of the proposed system changes really did merit the label of *reform*. Several economic reform proposals and dozens of alternative schemes were either quickly abandoned or dismissed completely by Gorbachev. Some of them may have been just simple ideas rather than coherent or strategic plans. The so-called "intensification and acceleration" and "compromise" plans, both proposed by Abel Aganbegyan—one of the early architects of perestroika—and the Grigori Yavlinski and Graham Allison plan (March 1985 and June 1991, respectively) topped and concluded the list of proposals. Economist Leonid Abalkin, deputy prime minister, chair person in 1989 of the 1989- State Commission on Economic Reform, and one of Gorbachev's major advisors, put together a far-reaching background report written for a conference on radical economic reform, held October 30 to November 1, 1989, in Moscow. This economic package included drafts of taxation, land use, trade unions, the property law, the banking system, and was very radical by Soviet standards. Abalkin's plan aimed to adapt a mixed economy with some state enterprises transferred to other forms of social ownership, although not entirely in private hands. Abel Aganbegyan instead suggested a total revaluation of private entrepreneurship. Operating within the notion of radical reform, Abalkin was influenced by a socialist market economy and the regulation of national economic processes. But in December 1989, the Congress of People's Deputies approved the Ryzhkov economic plan.

In addition, the economic situation was perceived as deteriorating by top apparatus members. In January 1990, Abalkin and Gosplan's chairman Yuri Maslyukov elaborated two variants: one suggested that the country had to be revived by more traditional Soviet methods, and the other suggested more market reforms. The Council of Ministers accepted the second, more radical variant and decreed in favor of accelerating the transition to a planned-market economy.

A radical reform plan was put forward by Nikolai Slyunkov and Yegor Yakovlev aimed at modifying the economy rapidly, and this plan was more reckless than Ryzhkov's. Gorbachev had envisioned the two plans quite differently, but in addition Nikolai Slyunkov and Yegor Yakovlev were too radical and the other, Ryzhkov, was much too cautious. Gorbachev, in his continuing indecisiveness over economic issues, did not opt for one or the other, but instead asked Ryzhkov to amend his plan by including elements drawn from Slyunkov and Yakovlev's.

In April 1990, Abalkin and Gosplan's chairman, Yuri Maslyukov, presented to the Presidential Council a program for a rapid transition to the market, thereby drawing attention to the costs involved in economic reform—e.g., open inflation, decline in production, inefficient enterprises, fall in living standards, and inequality. The program was rejected, and the one adopted in May was substantially more conservative.

From May to August of 1990, two teams were working on economic reform programs, one headed by Abalkin and one headed by academician Stanislav Shatalin. The latter produced the 500-Day Plan—unveiled on July 20—to steer the country to a free market system; it resembled the creation of a federation of republics with full market economy and full private ownership. This plan called for tax collections handled only at the federal level and proposed that foreign companies must be able to have up to 100 percent ownership of any investments made in Russia—not just joint ventures with Russian companies, as had been suggested by Gorbachev. The Abalkin-Ryzhkov plan was uncertain about how to create a new economic confidence, at least the way Gorbachev envisioned: the plan was quite different from Shatalin's program. Unfortunately, the long series of economic proposals and programs were not well conceived in terms of feasibility, and some of them were far too ideological to be implemented. By September 11, after having temporized quite a bit, Gorbachev declared a personal preference for the radical Shatalin's plan as more economically grounded, although he was aware that such a plan could have endangered the existence of the Soviet Union because of the need of federal taxes and the superiority not to undermine the role of the central government. On October 9, the Russian parliament approved that Shatalin's 500-Day plan. Then Gorbachev asked academician Aganbegyan to merge Shatalin's and Ryzhkov's programs, combining elements from both plans, and the Supreme Soviet approved an approach toward a "regulated market economy" on October 19. Abalkin resigned effective February 1991.

In these circumstances, Gorbachev's popularity steadily fell. The Russian economy worsened to such an extent that the Moscow city council implemented the rationing of meat, grain, and vodka by the end of January 1991, to take effect on March 1 of that year. But Russians elected Yeltsin president on June 12, and two weeks later Yavlinski and Allison submitted another economic plan that would include western aid. Aid was offered in July, but not on as large a scale as the Group of Seven meeting in London offered to Gorbachev in July. It was the beginning of the end of the Soviet Union.

George Soros's Secret Mission

A special note of merit is warranted for George Soros's activism, which he describes so candidly in his book, *Underwriting Democracy* (1991). He describes his self-financed secret mission to Moscow and the international task force of experts he sponsored himself. The first task force sponsored by Soros went to Moscow in early November 1988, after he met the Soviet ambassador, Anatoly Dubinin, in Washington, D.C. Soros's main idea was the concept of a market-oriented open-sector economy to be implanted within the body of the central planned economy, which could be understood as a way to avoid the faults of the previous long list of economic proposals and plans. While Ambassador Dubinin liked this idea and forwarded it to Moscow, Soros received the invitation by the chairman of the Council of Foreign Economic Relations. Soros's task force included experts on Soviet affairs, and a series of meetings culminated with a four-hour session with Nikolai Ryzhkov. They agreed to reinstate the task force, and in late January 1989, subgroups start working with at least twenty western economists, and more from Russia.

Unfortunately, Soviet interest overall was not high enough, and the mission received a cold reception. The outcomes of these subgroups and a formal, open-sector plan would have been officially presented in May that year, but Ivan Ivanov—deputy chairman of the Council on Foreign Economic Relations—sought a postponement, and eventually the whole effort ended in typical Soviet fashion. In fact, the Soviet counterpart neither refused nor accepted the scheme, and Soros said that the meetings were deteriorating into tourism. Soros was absolutely right to find an alternative way to the aforementioned myriad of economic plans, but also not aware that it was too early to decentralize so much of the control over these areas, if not decentralizing power to local communist party leaders. Nevertheless, Ivanov announced the impending creation of three such zones (Vyborg, Novgorod, and Nakhoda) in June 1989. In November, Ivanov did make known that three such zones were being allowed to operate in principle. They would have been zones of joint entrepreneurship where foreign currency could circulate with the ruble. Still, the center was not strong enough to carry out such ideas, as regional administrations and local nationalisms mattered most in the complete implementation of the plans. Over time, this led to a number of special tax zones within Russia—e.g., Ingushetia and Kalmykiya—where regional or local authorities had the right to offer tax concessions and exemptions to attract investments, but this right was widely abused by corrupt officials and primarily oil traders enjoyed tax exemptions.

Komsomol—A School of Capitalism

Legislation supporting private initiatives was introduced by December 1990. Russia moved in the direction of a private sector economy by adopting new laws regarding entrepreneurship, small enterprises, and the authorization of free enterprise zones. Gorbachev issued a decree in 1991 that approved the creation of such special zones throughout the Soviet Union, as well as joint ventures. Twelve free enterprise zones were announced by the early 1990s, and the number of foreign ventures accelerated. By January 1990, Soviet authorities had approved 1,274 joint ventures.

Nevertheless, changes after 1985 brought improvement in terms of the long wait for freedom and the opportunity for individual performance and expression. Because the necessity for transitioning to a market-oriented economy was imposed by the state, however, the actual effect was the expanding power of some groups and restrictions on the chances of others. This brought about risks concerning the country's ability to achieve a proper path with its own unique definition of continuing to develop in an ethical context. However, observers of Russian affairs are offering to busy educated readers in the West a reading excursus in the following way. Young communists became transformers, and created banks and joint business ventures. Especially during the late 1970s and early 1980s, the young communist members of the Party grouped in the powerful Komsomol—*Komsorg* in the Communist Party's jargon. This was the organization of young communists from the age of fourteen to twenty eight—functionaries could be older—that was established in October 1918 to bring together various youth organizations that had previously been involved in the Russian Revolution and served as the youth wing of the Communist Party. Through the Komsomol, they gained visibility, and active participation in the organization was an important factor in advanced membership and eventual leadership positions in the Communist Party. Although Komsomol had no direct influence on the Communist Party, experience in the youth organization was viewed as an important way for future leaders to gain recognition and visibility for a subsequent party career. This aspect, together with the loans-for-shares auctions in the mid-1990s, created the phenomenon of oligarchies in the country.

Active members of the Komsomol received privileges and political preference in promotions, and the majority of the population had belonged at one time or another. During the 1970s, the Komsomol had tens of millions of members, having reached a maximum of about fourty million in the 1970s and early 1980s. The reforms introduced by Gorbachev recognized, however, that the Komsomol was a haven for conservatism, bureaucracy, and the politically ineffective, and was not serving the interests of the youth. At the radical Twentieth Congress of the Komsomol held in April 1987, the rules of the organization were altered to reflect a more market-oriented approach. The reforms of the Twentieth Congress, however, eventually tore the organization apart. With fragmentation, lack of clarity of purpose, and waning interest, membership, and caliber of membership, there was simply no longer a need for an old-fashioned organization. The organization had to be transformed in a business laboratory as a springboard from which top youth members or the more politicallyconnected among them could benefit from the reforms introduced by perestroika. Komsomol members were given privileges in opening businesses, motivated by a desire to give youth a better chance. At the same time, many Komsomol leaders entered and headed the Russian regional and state anti-monopoly committees.

As a result, many Komsomol activists were given an unbelievably comparative advantage in business, and a new adage, "Komsomol is a school of capitalism," replaced the Lenin saying, "Trade unions are a school of communism." As a result, youth-formed entrepreneurial activities were the basis of student building teams that were formed at the university level. Besides small jobs during summer breaks, Komsomol members could raise money through the Youth Science and Technology Development Centers and the Youth Housing Cooperative. Komsomol began its involvement with the housing sector in 1971. This sector had been showing great distress, and had a direct and patent impact on the populace. One of the pillars of Gorbachev's campaign in 1985 dealt with the shortage of apartment units. The youngest members of society were directly impacted by this shortage and the new perestroika offered them an opportunity to build their own housing. Through Gorbachev's new initiatives, the idea was supported and more than fifty Youth Housing Cooperatives were created in Moscow alone. Perestroika simply gave young entrepreneurs broader chances to engage in business and this proved important to building Russian capitalism (Sergi 2004).

The second important route was the Youth Science and Technology Development Centers. These were created by decrees from the Soviet Council of Ministers and the Central Komsomol Committee that were issued in March 1987. By the beginning of the 1990s, there were more than 600 such centers across the country. The new system granted them the power to collect the money and then form the cradle of Russia's new business elite. These establishments did pay taxes, but only 3 percent of revenues went to the main organization, and 27 percent went to local branches. In the 1990s, the youth centers created a very profitable intermediary status for themselves within the society. Soon after the breakup of the Soviet Union, the youth centers covered the country with a network of raw material and consumer goods exchanges. Entrepreneurship was popping up in several other areas, for example the campaign to computerize the country during Gorbachev's tenure when the young business community acquired used computers from the West to resell them in Russia at very high prices. The Komsomol disbanded in 1991 due to the collapse of the Soviet Union.

Owning Russia by Owning Banks

A logical step forward in Gorbachev's modernization efforts was finding a mechanism for providing cash support to these young businesspersons. They found that the best way was to create and own a bank. In reality, the country was searching for a modern banking system, and Komsomol's functionaries were the avant-garde of the capital. The mono-bank (during communism there was one bank, performing the function of central banking and commercial banks) system of the communist era dominated by the central bank (*Gosbank*) was replaced by a two-tier banking system thanks to a decree in 1987. The new Soviet Central Bank started doing traditional monetary policy functions and banking supervision, while commercial banks operated for the people. The Sberkassa, which in fact existed during the mono-bank system as a state workers' saving bank, was consolidated into the Sberbank to collect deposits from citizens and grant credit to the government. The Promstroibank granted credit for investment purposes in the heavy industry, transport, communication, and construction sectors. The Agroprombank operated in the agricultural sector. The Zhilsotsbank operated in light industry and the residential construction arena. The Vneshekonombank was set up to handle the state's foreign creditors. A number of other banks were still transformed into something more, despite the absence of clear market regulations.

A law regulating cooperatives permitted the establishment of commercial banks and cooperative banks under private control. With the creation of Youth Science and Technology Development Centers and Youth Housing Cooperatives, the young people of the Komsomol could raise money through Gorbachev's perestroika. This entrepreneurial activity received strong political support by Gorbachev, to the extent that the system allowed new businesspeople to create small banks—called *pocket* or *agent* banks. As a result, the number of financial institutions grew from six at the end of the 1980s to more than 1,300 by the end of 1991, and to more than 2,500 by 1994—all this while the country's economy was collapsing. Very liberal licensing policies, in addition to low charter capital requirements and poor enforcement of infractions, helped this evolution of financial institutions. Initially, the young communists were transformed from what the West would term ordinary entrepreneurs into bankers, but over time a powerful group emerged in the banking sector and it is regularly referred to as the "rule of the seven" court banks—or *semibankirshchina*. This term refers to the phenomenon of seven most powerful and, indeed, close-to-Kremlin, financial groups in the mid 1990s. Its connotation is the historical *semiboyarshchina*, seven most powerful men of nobility who ruled Russia under Michael I (1613–1645). Since the mid-1990s, the chaotic Russian system provided a conduit between banking finance and the ownership of natural resources. Young communists transformed themselves again, through this conduit, into powerful oligarchs by the mid-1990s (Sergi 2004).

The demise of the state was well known, and these young communists took advantage of the chaos in government to gain power and wealth. They followed a slightly different route than the robber barons did in the United States, who at least created wealth from nothing. This difference is a significant one. The United States tackled of the dangers of monopolies through the anti-trust legislation of the Sherman Anti-Trust Act in 1890, as well as the Federal Trade Commission Act of 1914, which created a regulatory agency to administer and enforce antitrust regulations. The Russian method was to introduce an anti-monopoly agency, which has been operating since the 1990s. Although an important difference to acknowledge, it was not enough to interest ordinary Russians.

Thus, commercial banks were created out of a mono-bank system, and the number rose from just a few to an unnecessary level by the mid-1990s. The new central bank was trying to introduce sensible central banking, but the system was far from well run, with liberal licensing, low charter capital requirements (on the order of $200,000), poor enforcement of regulations, and a Central Bank deemed to be "almost surely home to enormous corruption under Gerashchenko's leadership," as Boone and Horder explain (1998: 57).

By 1992, Russia had about 1,700 banks that were generally weak because they each had an average of two branches per bank. The number of branches/bank increased to an average of 2.5 by 1994 and remained consistent in subsequent years with a generally poorly run banking industry. Not until April 1995 was a law passed to regulate the central bank of Russia, which thereby declared the bank independent and accountable to the State Duma and determined the independence of the chairperson. The two-tier banking system included private banks and the state bank.

Overall, this poorly controlled market prompted the new pocket banks to use their assets in the loans for shares auctions, and most of Russia's largest enterprises were sold. One may compare this logic with the savings and loan debacle in the United States in the 1980s. William Black's 2005 book *The Best Way to Rob a Bank Is to Own One* offers a great opportunity to increase one's understanding of what and why this occurred in the United States, and the picture he paints resembles Russia's pocket banks and the use of bank loans in Russia in the 1990s.

Putin's Third Vision

Objectively analyzing Vladimir Putin could be a problem for several reasons. First, Russians have chosen Putin as their political leader—a new czar, some posit—and we must review an accurate accounting of events so readers will be conversant with the exact details of the real Russian socioeconomic landscape. My object is not to accept the Russians' inclination or promote Putin blindly.

Observations show that democracy and new czarist elements are converging upon each other in Russia's political culture, but these facts require in-depth analysis of Russian passage from one to another system and what they might portend for the future.

In actuality, this modern era has included risks, trials, and contradictions for Russia, and new analysis may be helpful in conveying significance and more honest perspectives. There is not one definitive model for imagining a critical level of nationalism and its verbal abuse often in a very negative denotation among Kremlinologists and western chancelleries. Even if the Kremlin's rebounding identity policy bears any resemblance to it at all, I cannot fail to recall that many other patterns of nationalism are flourishing in Western Europe. What do the new French president Nicolas Sarkozy's approach and George W. Bush's high patriotism look like? When citizens are in favor of strong government but not a dictatorship, patriots rather than nationalists, they feel fearful of what the future might bring. I think we all should be attentive of seemingly opposed current waves of nationalism, and therefore look at both sides of the coin before jumping to any negative conclusion or invoking hostile reaction concerning the Kremlin's recent policy.

Second, western Kremlinologists and cultural elites all over the world connect the third vision for modernizing the country with the peril of an authoritarian regime and the absence of free elections. While this has to be debated carefully, the same observers skip over another equally possible risk, that of a democracy that must be insulated from money on national politics and big businesses, as it was during the 1990s in Russia.

We could draw a parallel here with the most recent experience in America. Conason (2007) introduces this peril in the age of George W. Bush in the United States, and says that for the first time since the Nixon era, Americans should doubt the future concerning the presence of democracy. Conason foresees the possibility of Americans living in a society where government conspires with big business and big evangelism; where ideologues and religious zealots attack logic and the scientific method; and where the ruling party encourages xenophobic nationalism based on irrational, manufactured fear.

In another influential book, *Selling Out: How Big Corporate Money Buys Elections, Rams through Legislation, and Betrays Our Democracy,* Mark Green (2002) a one-time (2001) New York mayoral candidate, lashes out against the risk of money enough to influence national politics. Green portrays how exactly the millions of dollars sloshing around the corridors of power shades and corrupts the system, and the poisonous role money has come to play in the political culture, with little accountability and no apparent shame among those responsible. In the same tone, data collected by Rodney Smith in *Money, Power, and Elections: How Campaign Finance Reform Subverts American Democracy* (2006) show that money matters now more than ever, as "essentially, campaign money buys speech, in all its various forms" (p. 61). When candidates lack money to buy media time and space, they are effectively silenced, says Smith. However, he believes that the United States has the opportunity to be the democratic republic that its founders intended as long as there is a process that discloses relevant information about campaign donors and recipients of donations.

In Russia, on the other hand, cultural elites assume that all free thought in Russia is censored, private entrepreneurship is absolutely prohibited, and political opponents and rich people are incarcerated—and the more fortunate could always seek asylum abroad. Putin is portrayed as an undemocratic leader.

Third, the challenge facing an analysis of Putin is that he is expected to step down by 2008 because the constitution simply prevents him from seeking a third consecutive presidential term. Despite recent rumors concerning a change in the Russian constitution that could allow him to remain in power at the Kremlin for an additional term, there is no evidence that Putin will lead the country in any way after the 2008 elections. Should he decide to run as the head of the party's list "United Russia," he could become a member of Russia's 450-seat Duma, one step down the government's ladder.

Regardless of these problems, an unprejudiced interpretation of Putin is welcome for one very specific reason. Across Europe and the West in general, there are standardized interpretations of the transformations that modern Russia has undergone in the past fifteen years. These interpretations are far too simplistic and based on erroneous or biased information about the country, which has courageously undertaken efforts to move from communism to a noncommunist market economy, and about common Russians who continue to express confidence that they will someday reap the benefits of a fair capitalist society. Indeed, while some omit any mention concerning recent Russian political history and the logic of the major events that unfolded during communist times, others insist on mentioning these facts, but without any deep enlightenment about what has actually been going on inside Russia.

A debate in the West regarding President Putin and his Kremlin began shortly after the beginning of Putin's first term in office (2000–2004). Disputes did not diminish during his second term (2004–2008), but instead intensified and become negatively focused against him. The primary issue in this debate among western analysts is what kind of a leader Putin is or has become. Most, if not all, of these analyses refer to increasing concern that Russia has veered off course and is headed toward an undemocratic future under President Putin. According to this version of the debate, Vladimir Putin and his *siloviki* allies—the hard-line Putin inner circle at the Kremlin whose members are referred to as partially and formally affiliated with the KGB—would establish rigid control over the economy and simultaneously weaken the genuine democratic features that mainstream analysts incorrectly assume have been a Russian reality since the 1990s. The basic underpinnings of this criticism imply that Russia experienced the birth of a western-style democratic system sometime between 1985 and June 1991, when Boris Yeltsin became the first democratically elected postcommunist Russian president. From a western perspective, Yeltsin's regime was by no means a failure and an honest democratic system endured during Yeltsin's regime, which clearly was not the case.

To provide another interpretation that is more harmonious with true post-communist Russian history, we will paint the current Russian landscape in a more complex, and accurate, setting. The reality of the current Russian situation must be assessed from the perspective of the Russian people themselves. In other words, we need to review how recent policy enacted by President Putin fits into the more ethical commitment by his government to improve the overall standard of living for all Russians, not just elites. The complexity surrounding this actual state of affairs, however, makes such an analysis much more challenging. The history of Russia over the past decades, as well as today, is truly an amazing, unfolding story. In reality, researching Russia's social and political fabric as well as its relationships with the rest of the world requires seeing Russia through much more objective eyes than the general scope of western interpretations have done thus far. To learn to understand the larger economic, socioeconomic, political, and cultural issues affecting Russia today and what actually happened as it transitioned from a communist country to a fledgling capitalist market economy, we must develop a more subjective outlook and interpretation than most western observers currently do.

Putin's Political Consensus and Asymmetric Game

Seeing modern Russia's struggles through the eyes of most of western citizens is hardly naïve. Simply launching into detailed western-style explanations or devices would be even worse. The pragmatic approach analyzes Russia with reference to who won and who lost the shuffle from a centrally planned economy to a market-driven one. What comes as somewhat of a surprise is that the winners of this socioeconomic redeployment were *nomenklatura* comrades and former young communists. This factor was the building block of a continuing split society. In this context, if Putin is alleged to have run the country by wielding the autocratic hand of a nineteenth-century czar, it is also true that Russian leaders were on the brink of opting between either shrewd modernization or a hazardous return to the absolute regimes of the past. According to western accusers, Putin did not put any limits on top businessmen because this would have brought the country back to communist times. In contrast to this mainstream view, I believe instead that the country would have returned to the past if a definitive oligarchization of the society had taken place. Russians have reacted quite favorably to Putin's efforts to stabilize the country and Putin has been pleased with this popular support. Russians displayed a strong reaction against fortunes being bizarrely acquired for trifling sums—but not many western commentators have reacted in the same negative way to this phenomenon. Russians reacted not against the creation of a new class of managers per se, but against the deformation of business acts which were in fact unlawful, a fraud for the country, and a massive theft from the state.

Nevertheless, Russians paved the way for Putin's second four-year term in March 2004, allowing him to continue his policies from the Kremlin until 2008 when his term expires. They were euphoric to vote him. During a news conference after the polls closed, Putin promised Russians that he would push ahead with economic reforms, and dismissed criticism from former U.S. secretary of state Colin Powell, who insinuated that Putin's rivals had been unable to get access to the media. Powell's criticism and criticism from the West in general is entirely illogical, even naïve, if we become aware that every single Russian knew who all candidates were and their degrees of political credibility. What is more, when former president Mikhail Gorbachev ran for president in 1996, he could exert a pull on an insignificant 1 percent or so of voters: his electoral support from Russian constituents remained low despite his high media visibility and incontrovertible talent in mobilizing public opinion. Thus the vote percentage accrued to Putin, and the electoral gap separating him from the others was not a problem of unequal access to the media, as some say, but instead is a direct corroboration of a specious western viewpoint. Although we could discuss almost endlessly about how staying in power can affect electoral outcomes, Putin continues to be the de facto most popular national leader in power today, as he has enjoyed the unbroken support of over 70 percent of the Russians, a record that has no parallels in other advanced democracies.

Many western observers are not pleased with Putin's performance, or with the many positive signs regarding the performance of the economy under Putin's Kremlin. After eight years of rule, Putin has achieved popular confidence and the Russian president, who is popular among Russia's citizens, has benefited from it, although disorders beneath both Russia's economic revival and achieved institutional stability are underscored by corruption and sometimes public-official incompetence. Analyzing divergent sentiments about Putin, whose policies will continue as long as he takes action against the oligarchy, requires a change in focus. While Russians may not have overtly demanded strong reaction against the new super-rich oligarchs, their life circumstances alone demanded attention, and Putin was within his obligation as a leader to intervene severely and resolutely in an effort to greatly reduce Russian poverty and reinstate stability.

Putin moved into this asymmetric game by putting his most powerful cards on the table, and he needed to play them well. He tried to appear soft-footed at the beginning, which was normally not possible in Moscow, and as he began to work against the oligarchy, the gap between the majority of Russians and the West grew larger. The incredible and portentous fortune that oil bestows on a country will eventually move the world to a more realistic account and interpretation of Russian events—something much closer to reality than hypocritical current western views.

The country's leadership needs to walk a bit more on eggshells in the future, because the interplay of Russia with other countries and interests will continue to increase. The distress of the population was and is visible, even though modern Russia still involves many risks and trials. While seventy years of communism has created feebleness and poverty for the majority of the population, the country was on the verge of either shrewd modernization or a hazardous return to absolute rules. When Putin was sworn in on May 7, 2004, to continue trying to strengthen his country and make it more secure, richer, safer, and more prosperous, as he said, a czar-style ceremony marked his willingness to do so. In the end, Putin received a standing ovation, which demonstrated that the entire country wanted a strong leader who was able to prevent the disintegration of the country and remedy the country's unanswered problems. Russians praised Putin because they perceived him as capable of offering something they had been chasing for a long time. Russian citizens had suffered so many wrongs, and recent leaders have not lived up to their expectations; therefore, the Russians wanted a strong person who promised them a decent living. Weighing up and despite all the negative criticism, Putin did not forget the common Russians, who were living in a country with a mix of deficient corporate governance and unevenly distributed income growth.

Chapter Three

The Distorted Logic of the 1990s in Russia

The rationale of Russia's transformation in the 1990s rested on the bureaucratic-capitalist class that emerged during that puzzling decade. This class would eventually come to dominate the political stage. Regarding the historical roots of criminality that observers trace back to the entire czarist and Soviet eras, although realistically so, they are not very relevant to comprehending the intimate causes of Russian development in the 1990s.

During the 1990s, oligarchs influenced elections to such an extent that the concept of *kleptocracy*, developed in sociology as a reference to corrupt regimes and bureaucracies in underdeveloped countries, could be meaningfully applied to the Russian situation. In fact, Russia was an emerging country in the early 1990s, although it was granted the status of a market economy by both the United States and Europe. This scenario created a powerful sentiment against the idea that predatory elites would support Yeltsin's legacy. The definitive goal of having a functioning bureaucratic apparatus for the country was not achieved, nor did it appear that business groups worked for the betterment of the country during the 1990s. Yet these two conditions, having an efficient bureaucracy and forward-looking businessmen, were initial requisites and had to be implemented at the very beginning of the 1990s, while the occurrences of the 1990s brought into being an overall system that has been perceived as lacking fairness and efficiency.

Dirty money, poverty, and inequality were liaising in a criminal framework. Raymond W. Baker's 2005 book *Capitalism's Achilles Heel*, which does not touch directly on the logic of 1990s in Russia but refers more to big U.S. corporations, effectively illustrates one side of dirty money in the world—that is, how certain businesspeople and *kleptocrats* perfected techniques to harm Russia's population. Financial scandals, tax dodging, and a mounting corrupted business system were not isolated cases in Russia, and negative externalities generated a spirit of lawlessness that undermined the Russian experiment and threatened the integrity of the market system experiment in Russia as a whole. These phenomena of corruption and tax dodging were not attributable to the Russian habit of avoiding the tax collector, but simply followed an unethical logic. The country fell into a profound ethical and political crisis—but this negative outcome was the logical consequence of the perverse 1900s rather than the outcome of Russian criminal history.

From this negative perspective of Russia, Putin was seen as a kind of undemocratic leader, laying himself open to criticism for placing aides in key bureaucratic posts. Alternatively, he was seen as being rather indecisive at the very beginning of his first term in that he could provide accurate diagnoses but could not implement the proper remedies. By exacting political influence on the oligarchy and limiting their authority on the economy, however, Russia could begin to force big businesses to operate in peaceful symbiosis and coexistence with the state and rules of law.

Following the anomalies and deformations that western-inspired reforms produced in Russia, it was clear that a break with events stemming from the 1990s was necessary. In such a context, Russian political institutions had to become effective, while business groups had to be ethically and legally oriented.

In reality, additional efforts toward achieving this broad goal were required. Observers initially placed harsh blame on Putin's short- and long-term achievements in his attempt to transform the country, fix the chaos of the 1990s, and prevent the powerful elite from taking over again. Still, the period of Russian history to blame for these situations is the one prior to Putin, which pioneered theft and enabled a lawless emerging market that gravely weakened Russia during the 1990s. As I said, I do not see any reason to blame Russia's history.

The Well-off and the Less Fortunate

Mikhail Gorbachev established basic conditions that were theoretically fundamental to moving the country toward more modern realities; reforms were not adequate to achieve significant accomplishments. Gorbachev's reforming strategies were resisted by political elites and reversed by bureaucracy even before 1991. When Boris Yeltsin's agenda, inspired by the *kamikaze crew*, privatization, the rule of bankers, and newly created oligarchs—sometimes clashing and conflicting with one another—controlled and single-handedly ran the economy, this pushed the state and the society into misfortune. A bloodless, permanent revolution of sorts drew the country away from communism into a silent managerial revolution. Instead, new forms of corrupt practices, business *nomenklatura*, criminal business practices, and theft from the pockets of small entrepreneurs and the like (what Russians call *bakshish*) emerged. Alena Ledeneva (2006) recalls the recognition of the worst practices in the 1990s: she refers to capturing the essence of post-Soviet systems through ample recourse to the use of personal networks (*blat*) for obtaining goods and services in short supply and for circumventing the inefficiencies of communism. This continues to operate today under a new generation of informal practices.

Mikhail Gorbachev's policy has been criticized widely by Russians, and partially by experts—but not by the West. In western eyes, Gorbachev has been a kind of hero. With global perception offering acclaim for Gorbachev because of the reforms he initiated almost unexpectedly in the mid-1980s, western political leaders declared he was someone with whom to do business. Margaret Thatcher was one of those leaders; in fact, she was the first to officially make such a statement in 1984. Glasnost and perestroika were widely praised at the time because the new course of action opened up private traders to operate legally, to set up private enterprises, and to initiate a policy of curbing communist economic distortions and benefiting from state-planned misallocations of economic resources. Russians, however, thought Gorbachev's legacy was primarily negative and blamed him for the collapse of a strong Russian system. They would have preferred that this had never happened, not because they were in favor of the communist system, but because they were unhappy with the complete chaos that befell the society and economy following 1991. It was the loss of superpower status that made some citizens long for the stability of the past. Likewise, it was the social and economic pandemonium that occurred after 1991 (when Gorbachev resigned), while Yeltsin reformists promised economic stability and economic well-being for all with market-based ethics, which caused Russians to turn against Gorbachev's legacy. Russians embraced the pledges that were extended to them after his term ended by international economic organizations, international experts, and amateur domestic experts—none of which materialized.

Similarly, it must also be said that, in addition to punctuating the end of the century, perestroika's long-term effects on the country cannot be disregarded. More importantly, what emerged during Gorbachev's years presaged a different type of revolution inspired by the Party's *nomenklatura*, which resulted in reforming the country's administrative structure without jeopardizing the architecture of the system. Perestroika attempted to steer the nation toward a new economic philosophy within a communist framework. While some liked it, famous dissidents such as Aleksandr Zinoviev—who returned to Moscow thanks to Gorbachev—have been very critical of perestroika itself. Perhaps arrogantly, or at least contrary to the Russian people's feelings, the West has continued to sympathize with the prospect of perestroika, as well as with the long-term effect of Gorbachev's reforms. All these realities must be considered within the larger context of Russia's own perceptions of successful reform.

Boris Yeltsin, meanwhile, pushed the country into an entirely new noncommunist fervor, which became the primary reason for the terrible economic injustices of the 1990s in Russia. Following these misguided ventures, Russians came to disparage the true outcomes of transitioning away from communist structures after Yeltsin surged to power in 1991 and introduced reforms and positive expectations in observers around the world who were interested in Russian affairs. Yeltsin's agenda produced a privatized economy and "free," western-style parliamentary elections—or such was the picture portrayed to the West, although oligarchs could control both the outcome of elections and top appointments. Although Kremlinologists welcomed these novelties introduced into Russian society, they did not welcome the terrible wealth disparity of Yeltsin's reforms; but these reforms were passed on as a by-product of the attempt to transform policy.

Yeltsin's business environment was not based on the respect of rules of law and orderly rules of business. A small number of entrepreneurs emerged and acquired control of former state assets for a price constantly below market levels, if anything at all. They simply collected money from the common Russians, planned deceptive privatization schemes, and paid the states nominal sums of money for companies that would become very powerful. Some of the oligarchs also won auctions through unjust means without having to pay market prices or use Russian investors' money. In addition, they most certainly did not pay enough in income tax obligations. Two of the more famous Russian billionaires—Mikhail Khodorkovsky and Boris Berezovsky—purchased shares in Yukos and Sibneft (global giants in petroleum production) for some $300 million and $100 million, respectively (Goldman, 2004). These were low figures because the actual value of the two oil companies was, in reality, twenty to thirty times higher at the time of the privatization, and would be many times over by the end of the 1990s. Khodorkovsky and Berezovsky won the auctions through several companies that they set up solely for that purpose. These were not isolated cases but instances of a common tendency snaking all across the country.

Another issue that the new country faced was a new class of entrepreneurs who obtained lucrative state contracts and became extremely rich in a country that was increasingly poor. It was unmistakable that the new entrepreneurs were not working for the good of the nation and its inhabitants, while massive corruption was shaping Russia's economic and political life. The whole system began identifying with names and symbols such as *mafia*, *business moguls*, *oligarchy*, and *bandit capitalism*. During the post-Soviet years, unethical practices among some bureaucrats and the new business elites led to many controversial and unjustified fortunes for some, as well as to the state's immoral idleness in dealing with the distorted results of the out-of-control 1990s. The economic prospects were bleak.

Fiascos in the 1990s: "Taxes" and "Sales"

There were two scenarios affecting the social and political fabric of the 1990s while Yeltsin's government tried to reform Gorbachev's reforms. The first issue to impact governmental efforts was the way the tax system was structured and control over the collection of taxes. The second issue affecting the fabric of daily life under Yeltsin was the way privatization was actually accomplished during this period. These two issues interconnected in a sociopolitical backdrop that contributed to the chaos of the 1990s and must be understood to fully interpret the events of that period.

The Tax System

Theoretically, any tax program can redistribute income among social classes in a way that benefits those who are less wealthy. As I see it, an accomplished tax policy is a main instrument in strengthening economic activities, increasing productivity, making labor markets work more efficiently, and, not least, increasing the influx of foreign investment. A tax system should provide state administrations with enough resources to offer an adequate economic infrastructure and effective levels of services that increase the country's competitiveness. All governments should develop these sorts of policies as long as they are fair to all and do not damage market efficiency. This should have happened in Russia as part of the transformation's long-term goals, but unfortunately, it did not occur in Russia during the 1990s. Even worse, as a component of the entire distorted logic of the 1990s, the tax crime was a deliberate scheme to evade tax obligations and file false tax returns. No one at the highest levels was found guilty of conspicuously evading taxes; no one state authority went far enough to pass wise laws to greatly improve the way the tax administration oversaw Russia's tax state of affairs. Oligarchs and various lobbies were powerful enough to keep their voices ringing out in the corridors of state Duma and other corridors of power in Moscow.

This issue was of immense importance in Russia in light of the transfer of state properties to private groups, which produced budget imbalances and precipitated the country into the financial crisis of 1998. Everyone can understand how much Russia needed serious tax reforms, and when the government failed to function, common Russians lost out. Again, private interests of big groups were so great and exerted so much power on the Duma that no serious tax reform was passed because nobody at the top level wanted to lose their benefits: therefore, ordinary or common Russians lost again! While other countries' privatization approaches attempted to enhance efficiency and bring money into the state's pockets, Russian privatization actually worked the other way, with the Russian government and ordinary Russians having, in fact, financed privatization. The Russian tax administration, state judiciary officials, and politicians were not working for the betterment of ordinary citizens. In the end, the only winners were the entrenched interests that supported the maintenance of the status quo.

The Russian tax system worked this way in the 1990s—failing to collect money from enterprises and other big business groups—and was incapable of offering adequate support to ordinary Russians because of this corrupt system. By 1997, Russia was able to collect about 40 percent of its legitimate national income at various institutional levels. Tax revenues were based on a system where regions and the federal government shared revenues. While the experience showed that changes were absolutely needed, opposite interests set in motion big businesses and regional governments to collaborate in concealing some of the revenue that was due to Moscow. Institutional chaos was an open invitation for tax evasion, no one feared lawsuits, and this reinforced the mutual interest of regional leaders and oligarchs in evading the central government and creating a tax avoidance phenomenon, while inevitably driving up costs for the state.

The Sale of the Century

Privatization policies in Russia could have encouraged efficiency and good corporate governance to the extent that Russia was thought to have started a well-developed and sincere market economy process. A state property fund in Russia, established to sell large heavy industrial companies and then select and monitor their paths to privatization, did not perform well either, from a purely ethical point of view.

The two basic privatization waves brought to light several problems. For one thing, the vouchers-for-shares strategy started in 1992, which implied the sale of major state-controlled corporations to private interests, allowed insiders to acquire a 51 percent ownership of share in certain stocks. The low-cost ownership cost up to 1.7 times the January 1992 assessed book value in an effort to keep the price extremely low in the face of high inflation rates, and by excluding important assets from the balance sheets (e.g., land and the right to explore mineral resources). Notably, up to 80 percent of the payment was covered by vouchers and came from enterprise funds, which were, in fact, created with workers' money. The unsold shares were left in the local property fund for auctioning off to the benefit of a bunch of insiders. The citizens supported Russia's first wave of mass privatization. At the outset, the public did not display antipathy toward how privatization was technically achieved, because they did not understand until later that it was a scheme designed to make the rich wealthier rather than to produce a fair economy. In addition to this, because of early lack of awareness among ordinary Russians about ubiquitous privatization schemes, Russians themselves supported privatization overall because restricting privatization ran the risk of allowing expansion of the state and ministries instead. However, the main paradoxical problem with the first wave of privatization was this: how could Russians realistically take part in the privatization of large industrial assets if they had not made enough money and capital to purchase state assets? Russia did not have an answer to this puzzle then, but there were some possible alternatives, such as avoiding a voucher strategy that would appeal to certain strong insiders but not to everyone, in the formation of western-type public companies. The fact that people who had not been born rich, or who grew up in relatively affluent families at most and had not inherited any fortune, became so rich has been quite puzzling. That is one problem.

The other problem is that a second wave of privatization was supposed to provide a way out of that impasse, and the influence of policy makers in corporate governance was one strategy to monitor the privatization process. The first stage in the state's program of privatization started in 1992, following Gorbachev's deregulation policies. It showed meager performance overall, as the paradoxical question I have asked above remained unanswered by the state. The government once again intervened by announcing legislative support to small businesses and set up a state committee designed to encourage small business development. At the same time, signs of the lack of protection for minority shareholders and powerless common Russians were quite widespread. The Law on Stock Companies and the Law on the Securities, both enacted in 1996, were aimed at protecting minority shareholder rights, but the public did not trust them. In principle, they were good attempts to correct a problem, but the infelicitous relationship between government officials and members of the business oligarchy led to abuse, with no transparency and absolutely no accountability.

Apart from the ensuing inflation and budget deficits, which are standard economic phenomena that affect the behavioral decisions of consumers and investors, the first wave of privatization, which consisted of a vouchers-for-shares privatization strategy in the period from 1992 to 1994, changed the attitudes and perceptions of ordinary Russians to privatization. Although 1992 was considered the starting point for organized small business formation, it was also a playground for more untold verities. It is true that by 1996, 77 percent of mid-sized and large enterprises were privatized, but it is also true that most of the newly privatized firms were performing poorly, with very low productivity and no means of raising working capital.

The process of small business formation stagnated from 1997 to 1999, although the process of creating a private business was, in fact, endless, and about 90 percent of small enterprises belonged to private owners by 1999. Nevertheless, the number of companies grew slightly from 841,737 to 868,008 in 1998, which provided 12 percent of the total jobs in the country—14.3 percent, if you include contract workers and combinations. Note that the number of small businesses in present-day Russia is roughly one million, thanks to the impressive positive impact and perspective of a growing economy and high expectations after 2002.

A second privatization might have been a success, say Maxim Boyko, Andrei Shleifer, and RobertVishny in *Privatizing Russia* (1995), but a clearer assessment of the situation would show otherwise. Most experts, both in the West and in Russia, believed in a shock-based method of transition and in the conventional wisdom of privatization. Russia adopted this strategy of freeing prices and instituting some form of deregulation, as well as selling the most efficient firms first and concluding with the least efficient ones. Nevertheless, while this strategy has been adopted everywhere in East Europe since the fall of the Berlin Wall in 1989 (although with different time frames), the Russian case was very special because of the original sin of unequal opportunities given to wealthy Russians and the strange way the voucher scheme was conducted. To further the rising ambitions of powerful groups' strategic ambition to grab state-controlled resources, a new auction-style form of privatization was initiated when the Russian federal government pledged its stock of industrial and transportation enterprises to raise the necessary cash to deal with a mounting state deficit and tax collection problems. Purposefully dishonest loans-for-shares agreements were made with banks that promised money in return for loans (McCarthy et al., 2004).

In the context of companies that were auctioned during the loans-for-shares process, the agreement operated in the following way: banks offered loans to the government, and the government provided them with shares in state-controlled companies that would be returned to the government when the debt was repaid. In the case of no repayment (which bankers thought would be the likely outcome), bankers would be allowed to auction the shares of stock in exchange for loan forgiveness. In fact, when the government was unable to repay the loans, bank oligarchs auctioned the shares in such a way that buyers acquired control of enterprises for only a bit more than the amount of the original loans, and sometimes buying it themselves. These pledge auctions characterized the new policies of privatization, the loans-for-shares approach, and the search for strategic investors, but the scheme was designed to create new economic elites in addition to those already created by the avant-garde capitalism of young, opportunistic communist members during the 1980s. Nevertheless, the scandalous loans-for-shares auctions drove the country toward an unbridled expropriation policy. A class of new businessmen ended up controlling a vast portion of national riches and the country's raw materials, media and much of the Duma, as we are remindinded by Chrystia Freeland—the *Financial Times* former Moscow bureau chief and Eastern Europe correspondent during the 1990s—in her book *Sale of the Century* (2000).

Yet, surprisingly, Andrei Shleifer and Daniel Treisman report, "the greatest asset-stripping scandals have concerned companies that remained under state control" and the companies "privatized to the oligarchs performed far better than those left under state control" (2005, p. 161). While economist Shleifer—who was one academic behind the working out of the foundations of Yeltsin's privatizations to promote market economic reforms in Russia—bears witness to the aforementioned logic and statement, I do not agree. The reading public has been made aware (in the literature, e.g., Shleifer and Treisman, and also in journalistic reports) that those companies that remained under state control at the beginning of transition were the less efficient ones. The basic strategy was to grab—without regard to whether a fair price was paid to the state or whether the auctions had been accessible to everyone—the most efficient and powerful business activities. For this exact reason, firms privatized to oligarchs seemed to show visible evidence of higher efficiency. Apart from how one can measure a firm's efficiency in a phase of transition economics, the overriding issue is that statements of those who said that the efficiency of privatized firms were visibly higher than that of non-privatized firms completely overlook the scandalous and bizarre takeovers of some of the best state companies, and the immoral business practices surrounding the privatization waves in Russia of those years.

In summary, the first phase of privatization from December 1992 to mid-1994 was a preferential method that helped insiders in banks and the former *nomenklatura*, even though vouchers were initially distributed fairly evenly throughout the population. However, information about the real worth of companies was incomplete, and an electronic voucher transaction system that could have offered a fair means of monitoring transactions was absent, leading to uncertainty and unequal outcomes for Russians, while "domestic and foreign middlemen bought up the vouchers from cash-hungry citizens"

(Desai, 2005). The second phase of privatization involved the creation of stocks for state-run enterprises and the sale of shares of those stocks with the goal of moving the economy successfully into a free-market system, increasing the production of domestic goods, reducing shortages, and improving the quality of consumer goods. However, the cultural and bureaucratic knowledge typical of *nomenklatura*, business, and political elites, as well as the abundance of natural resources, created a fortune-hunting phenomenon. Powerful groups of men who thirsted for control over their country manipulated the government to secure additional private interests over their public responsibilities.

After these two privatization waves, both oligarchs and the adopted method of privatization lost popular support in Russia. The pie was divided unevenly, with all of the country's natural resources and riches accruing to the upper new *nomenklatura*. It has been asked whether the state prevented the worst possible outcome, which explains why most Russians believe the role of the state is fundamental; hence Russians' endorsement of policies that increase state control (Jack, 2004).

And So Goes the Economy

Once Ex-president Yeltsin began heavily favoring the Russian oligarchs, both economically and politically, he gave away any hope for the postcommunist Russian economic transition to prevent a dramatic increase in the Russian wealth disparity. With Yeltsin's 1996 election victory guaranteed and controlled by the oligarchs, it was only a matter of time before wealth disparity in Russia reached the breaking point. Washington Consensus policies—an agenda of economic reforms based on simple rules of free trade and rigid monetary and financial stability promoted by several Washington-based financial institutions as essential to any economic recovery strategy program—dictated the immediate liberalization of prices in 1992. The International Monetary Fund (IMF) and the Washington Consensus historically exerted significant influence over domestic economies in Latin American countries, so it was natural to offer those strategies to other economies in difficulty around the world. Not surprisingly, the IMF and the ideology of the Washington Consensus also exerted significant influence over domestic economic strategies in Russia. Especially in the sphere of fiscal policy, they acted as distinctive advisors, and advocated bringing the government budget into equilibrium through the very injudiciously accomplished privatization idea of the mid-1990s. No doubt, it was not easy to deal with the numerous influences shaping economic variables, but that policy was definitively ascribed to the IMF and its growing involvement in Russian affairs

To understand this, one must be aware that the deregulation or liberalization of price controls in 1992 created an immediate inflation in Russia and wiped out the personal savings of many Russians. This led to increases in interest rates, which greatly compounded the ability of many, many Russians to buy (or increase their demand for) Russian products, or to borrow money and start a business. Yet sizeable ruble loans to the new class of business leaders were soon invested in U.S. dollars, to such a degree that the much expected ruble devaluation beefed up in value. All Russian employers—including the government, which had already borrowed money from Russian banks—now had a much more difficult time paying off their bank loans. The painful problems resulting from growing wealth disparity began to increase, culminating in the Russian financial collapse of 1998. Therefore, the official beginning of the western-inspired reform process in Russia set both the immediate and long-term stages for Russia's growing economic dilemma. Inflation cut demand, and subsequent higher interest rates designed to curb inflation created a nearly unpreventable explosion of wealth imbalance in Russia.

Once the oligarchs were created and supported by and for Yeltsin, massive asset stripping took place, creating a much-decreased government revenue stream. The Russian government's deficit and debt continued to grow because little to no revenue was received from privatization activities, and the repayment of loans owed to the IMF became increasingly difficult. Inflation decreased because no one had money to spend, but interest rates remained high and the combination of the two added to Russia's troubles. The IMF pressured the government to open up its capital accounts to allow a free flow of capital to take place, but instead the oligarchs and politicians who participated in privatization to capture state assets sold those assets for much more and immediately invested the ill-gotten wealth in foreign markets rather than in Russian enterprises.

The key point here is that Yeltsin's policies on one side and the IMF's on the other led to a situation that allowed interest rates to increase dramatically. The Asian economic crisis beginning in 1997 caused a great reduction in global demand for Russian oil. The price of oil itself dropped, but because it was a significant source of Russian government revenue, it lifted interest rates even higher, with the Yeltsin government unable to control massive increases in debt. Higher interest rates were also needed to defend the value of the ruble, because the IMF feared that devaluation would set off inflation again. Thus, falling oil prices and attempts to strengthen the ruble's value both put tremendous pressure on Russian interest rates. The ruble was clearly overvalued—domestic demand only existed for foreign imports, because Russian products were too expensive. This phenomenon brought inflation down from approximately 70 percent in 1995 to 3 percent in 1997 (before the financial collapse in August 1998), but it destroyed the competitiveness of Russian exports, and the premature opening of the Russian economy to an influx of capital led to the debt default and the collapse of the ruble. The IMF did not play fair, and did not advise Russia to adopt a more gradual strategy or more inflexible control of capital flight.

Consequently, the dramatic increase in Russian interest rates continued. This situation allowed the oligarchs to send money out of Russia and purchase

U.S. dollars, Swiss francs, and other strong currencies, thus increasing their private wealth at the expense of Russia's overall development. The overvalued stock market in the United States was a magnet for this kind of Russian wealth, and fueled an irrational curiosity in the United States stock market, making it even more difficult to keep money in Russia. Soon, Russia was paying interest rates of 60 percent on ruble loans, and these rates eventually rose to 150 percent. Russia had to and did default on its growing debt, again increasing the already growing global financial crisis.

Wealth disparity in Russia was the root cause of many of the problems—a key factor, in my opinion. Likewise, the pursuit of civil liberties and genuine freedom depends a great deal on the ability to reduce wealth disparity; such a reduction, if continued, could lead to improvements. By not forcing the oligarchs to pay higher taxes, Yeltsin created the beginnings of the overwhelmingly high pressure on Russian interest rates that crushed domestic productivity and demand, raised the ruble's value to the point where only foreign imports were affordable, and led to the Russian economic collapse in 1998 and threatened global financial turmoil.

Economic Deformations

The aspect of the Russian government in the economic process is very relevant here. What a pity it has been thus far that post – Cold War improvement in Russian living standards under Putin appears highly distorted outside Russia, as the West has consistently misinterpreted Putin's intentions and accomplishments. The realities of the 1990s must, therefore, be taken into account when analyzing the central question in the debate regarding the role of the state in fighting Russian instability and deficient entrepreneurship—all of which are very similar in the recent Russian past regarding Yeltsin's presidency.

The initial two processes of modernization created the conditions for a general submission to groups of power, economic elites, and elitism. The West was seemingly becoming an ingénue on Russian domestic affairs and the need to have Russia survive. How does such an ingénue to this political and economic global arena accommodate and contribute to Russia's survival? Furthermore, how does Russia define its priorities, nurture democratic institutions, or promote economic growth? Were the new waves of reform by Gorbachev and the democratic institutions of the Yeltsin era able to implement effective economic policy without forgoing basic democratic ideals? Was a weak democracy able first to implement economic reforms for growth and then foster stronger democratic values down the road? The cost of introducing and putting the final changes on a move away from communism to the general citizenship was already increasing before the Yeltsin era, when economic speculators and opportunist criminals were capitalizing on reformism and starting to have a huge amount of influence on Russian society.

It is important to understand one specific aspect of the 1990s, the economic performance of Russia between the end of the 1980s and the August 1998 crisis. Between 1989 and the August 1998 crisis, the gross domestic product plunged to roughly 60 percent of what it was in 1989—except in 1997, when it grew 1.4 percent, and when it started recovering again in 1999 and 2000, growing 6.4 percent and a robust 10 percent, respectively, according to Russian Federal State Statistics Service and all sensible statistical sources. Not all economists agree, though. In contrast to the numbers above, economist Anders Åslund (2002) suggests that output collapse was a myth; he calculates that Russia's gross domestic product could have dropped only by some 6 percent from 1991 to 1995, which is far less than people would have noticed and statistical offices recorded, because Russia was in far worse shape than generally perceived. Fortunately, not everyone followed Åslund's lead.

Nevertheless, debate is far less divisive when the subject is income distribution and economic reforms in Russia. Western experts are quick to say—as if they have something to hide—that the beginning of unfair income distribution started before the loans-for-shares privatization in the mid-1990s. However, they neglect to mention that there was another wave of privatization shortly after 1992, and that both privatization schemes surely exacerbated economic inequality in the country and jeopardized the ability of the majority of Russians to fairly compete in the new market—all this in the midst of inequalities that were bumping up and economic disequilibria that were deteriorating even-handed business opportunities. Undoubtedly, this represents an ethical gap, although some authors explain this state of affairs by alleging that income inequalities in Russia are in line with those in other middle-income countries (Shleifer and Treisman, 2005).

Matters look even worse as readers try to come up with a reasonable explanation about the roots of the problem. Whether income disparity created corruption or corruption created the income gap, the data shows that the 1990s was the era of increased income inequalities and unequal opportunities. The wealthiest people (20 percent of the population) accounted for about 31 percent of national income in 1991, and the least wealthy (20 percent of the citizens) accounted for about 12 percent. By the end of the 1990s, the wealthiest citizens reached 50 percent of national income, and the poorest dropped to about 6 percent. Does this information not require proper explanations? As unfair income distribution and a general impoverishment of the population took place on one side, on the other side a new class of entrepreneurs emerged. At the beginning of the 1990s—that is, before the official formation of oligarchy—Olga Kryshtanovskaya (1994) calculated that 12 percent of Moscow millionaires came from the *nomenklatura*, but that young parvenus were rising fast and criminal mafia connections were admitted by 40 percent of the business sector while 25 percent retained criminal connections of some kind.

If recent resistance to privatization or even renationalization of the oil and gas industry in Russia might also stem from nationalistic motives, I can look at similar situations in other developing nations where it is more evident. In Bolivia, for example, the indigenous population has strongly opposed the privatization of its natural gas industry. In Norway and in the Organization of the Petroleum Exporting Countries (OPEC)—the Vienna-based intergovernmental organization of eleven countries formed to help stabilize the oil market and insure that oil producers receive a reasonable rate of return on their investments—the oil industry is almost exclusively under state ownership. Russia's recent attempt to regain control of part of its oil and gas industry instead of leaving the entire industry in the hands of oligarchs or big foreign companies is partially explained by a nationalistic feeling of Russians; the primary explanation was the manifest injustice of the privatization process as it was managed in the 1990s.

This was Russia's economy in the 1990s. Something happened in the process of installing transparent and viable economic structures and has since devolved because of a lack of correct democratic values. What followed was an oligarchic interference with Russian politics aimed at reducing their own cost of doing business in Russia, but without lobbying "for other entrepreneurs to have access to an improved business environment" (Guriev and Rachinsky 2005: 145). Putin's decision to curb their political influence as an essential and initial part of his political campaign in 2000 was made to keep corruption under check while increasing the government's legitimacy as a direct consequence of the incorrect implementation of past privatization waves.

Yet much international opinion and scholarship rests primarily on the idea that this data is adequate to clarify Russia's events. This data is generalized; this is not the end of the story for Russia, though. Many conditions during the past two decades have combined to trap Russians in an ongoing, seemingly intractable and difficult scenario. One example is the *nomenklatura* members who took stock of the situation in the final communist years of the 1980s and used their superior managerial skills and power to become central actors themselves in the final years of Soviet collapse and beyond.

It is true that in a larger context Russia initiated new economic and social structures more than fifteen years ago, when Gorbachev initiated the perestroika that dissident Aleksandr Zinoviev quickly rebaptized *katastroika*. After that, the whole decade of the 1990s gave us an image of the power wielded by the previous *nomenklatura* well into the first decade of the twenty-first century. Competitors building new economic fortunes by squeezing control over state resources shaped the passage from communism to noncommunism. This was a generation of *megacapitalists* formed culturally during communism, as I have written elsewhere (2003, 2004), not a new class of managers and entrepreneurs, as much current literature asserts. These *megacapitalists* acquired their managerial skills during communism and not after it, as people wrongly perceive, and gained control over the Russian economy by acquiring state firms, state-indebted factories, and the rights to huge quantities of natural resources. Russia's massive transfer of state-owned property into private hands for nominal sums yielded enormous privilege, political influence, and economic power.

The statement by some experts that the wild business logic of the 1990s was not responsible for poor economic growth in Russia is fallacious. Although economists argue over whether or not the wickedness of that decade was responsible for the negative outcomes, links between the two aspects are clear. It is also not true that all oligarchs can be catalogued as irresponsible and unlawful.

Shleifer and Treisman's accurately note that this assertion would make little sense, as the decline in real GDP was linked to other factors, not in the least to the inexpert individuals that governed the country after 1991. If "the widespread image of Russia as a uniquely menacing disaster zone comes to seem like the reflection in a distorting mirror—the features are recognizable, but stretched and twisted out of all proportion," correctly state Shleifer and Treisman (2005, p. 52).

This economic disequilibrium benefited just a few overall, fueling an intense conflict over real assets, as Andrew Barnes (2006) describes in *Owning Russia*. When analyzing the collapse of the Soviet Union from the economic point of view of its gross domestic product performance, scholars generally debate the exact extent of this decline during the 1990s without showing much concern over distribution of this wealth. What it is possible to conclude is that we saw a partially failed transition to democracy and to a truly free market and also the prolonged struggle to control formerly owned state assets; this offers us diverse aspects to consider.

The Role of Self-Appointed Western Experts

During the late 1980s and the 1990s in Russia, new individuals without proper market experience or the least understanding of how markets function came to power and stayed in power for long time. In addition, Russia sought advice from very influential academic institutions in the West. Thus, a simplistic kamikaze definition of government and self-appointed experts on Russian economics had to guide an extremely difficult economic move toward capitalism, compounded by the growing reality of warring clans of Russian business elites. These experts started advising, broadcasting, writing, and drafting all manner of reports suggesting—very unrealistically, at best—economic reform principles for a system and society yearning for a noncommunist state of affairs. One major practical example was the first Russian *kamikaze crew*—as Yegor Gaidar (first deputy prime minister in 1991–1992 in charge for economics and now a moderate Putin opponent) and his ministers labeled the effort of his government to challenge the rules of the previous regime. That government was appointed in November 1991 and employed radical economic reforms and a free-market ideology. Conceivably, unquestioned (but not necessarily full-blown) western-style capitalism could suddenly be applied in a country that had previously held such concepts at arm's length. Supposedly, western experts sermonized at length about their new strategies to help Russia, pressuring the new Russian government to depend upon tribes of economists drawn from academia and international economic organizations. This western credo for how to make the transition in Russia became the guiding paradigm for the transparency of Russian finances and political economy. Overly simplified exhortations to carry out specific restructuring plans came from the same experts who were indispensable to planning and accomplishing such goals. Yet the resulting reforms did not work well for the country and for the general populace, although they did work for a very small number of the old *nomenklatura*, the new corrupt politicians, and anyone connected to them.

Similar poor analysis occurred concerning interpretations of Russia and Putin, this time offered by political and international relations commentators. Although economics is discussed much more than politics in Russian daily life, these commentators all pronounced the benefits of democracy, free markets, privatization, social well-being, international peace, and so forth. So did the aforementioned western experts who were supposedly helping with the economic transition process. Tragically for the Russians, however, the result of this sort of advice was a marked increase in social distress, thievery, corruption, and the near destruction of a normal Russian society. The same class of people who displayed ill-gotten wealth and unparalleled arrogance and deceitfulness toward their fellow Russian citizens brought about this state of affairs. Two differing and opposing groups appeared at that point. The unethical western response to all this was increased questioning and criticizing of even minor (but important) policy changes offered by the current Putin political leadership. Also, readers will come to recognize and understand that outsiders offered their advice and criticisms regarding overall Russian development as if it were part of an international tribunal against Putin, acting as if non-Russians were the only ones entitled to manage this crucial dialogue—obviously one of tremendous importance to the future of Russia itself.

What the Russian people really needed, instead, was for international experts to help alert the Russian government to a variety of ideas such as a complete awareness of the country's immense human resource potential and brainpower, but nothing else beyond such advice. This did not happen, of course—not even remotely. From a purely domestic Russian viewpoint, generations of new politicians and intellectuals have become notable in Russia today, as compared to earlier times of absolute, single-party rule. Now, both politicians of the old style, as well as new political recruits, are transforming into democratic participants (and, unfortunately, petty politicians as well, equally negative for Russia's current situation). That a former kind of political structure in Russia developed into a democracy is difficult to believe, even if open elections bear witness to such political conversion.

While the West officially tries to and wants to accept this partial democratic reality in Russia, it consciously emphasizes Putin's supposed Kremlin rigid control over the country, but underestimates excellent, economic progress for most Russians. While Russians are largely accepting of this recent economic tendency, Russians themselves wanted government protection from its downsides and this fact has became a dominating theme in the country. The economic conjuncture seemed to point to a comfortable combination of income growth and better economic expectations over time. It should also be apparent that that evidence showed support for the proposition that a positive correlation existed between economic performance and public support.

Western experts created, in effect, an eclectic kind of domestic and global censorship that governed advice to Russia's new governments, and used archetypal western standards of discernment and appraisal regarding Russia's democratic and economic needs. This was devastating for Russia, because unlike western nations that already have a strong middleclass (which creates democratic values unique to the West), such a middleclass is totally absent in Russia.

In effect, a new class of economists, at first youthful and inexperienced, with only basic and theoretical knowledge of free markets and their mechanisms, had begun to deregulate and regulate the entire country. This occurred by holding official conferences with western universities which only espoused very narrow ideological western economic and democratic views for noncommunist Russia. The cause of growing disagreement between Russia and its foreign advisors is that Russia needed economists who were strongly familiar with Russian economics and the national Russian economy, and understood the country's societal conditions. Instead, Russia received from its western advisors official economic assistance that was nothing more than primitive and basic economic, old-style western advice. In addition, there were scandals concerning economists who advised Russia's new governments and an utterly inefficient pedagogical attitude toward Russia and the entire bloc of transition countries in East-Central Europe. Some of these involved employees of the Harvard Project, including actual wrongdoing by other experts (Bombardieri, 2005). This raised additional ethical concerns about the general attitude of western rhetoric, and perhaps the lack of interest among Harvard circles, as the editors of the influential *Economic Newsletter* wrote: "A recent panel discussion with some of Yukos' American lawyers produced a very low turnout from the faculty and students. Memories are short and Mikhail Khodorkovsky has quite a task in front of him if he wants to keep his case a current concern" (*Economic Newsletter*, No. 3, 2005). This scant interest in the Yukos case among scholars and students at Harvard University where the newsletter was edited and published, draws on the fact that western scholars gave to the case a typical western interpretation (and morally wrong behavior!) while completely missing the ethical implications that tainted the entire course of events. Lacking a proper analysis, past events and other recent events simply created academic intrigues.

The resulting painful lessons for Russia were disasters, such as western advisors wrongly encouraging the liberalization of the Russian market, unfettered prices, and too many uncoordinated economic policies—all to attract foreign investors, which can often be excellent and positive. Such lessons are theoretically correct in their essence, although quite hard to implement all at once with a modicum of fairness. A brand-new class of rulers turned into a group of imprudent economists, managers, and economic development gurus who felt compelled to speak clearly about how to put all this advice together, but dramatically failed in the end.

In fact, these people were elitists. Elites fail to interpret the Russian path out of the crisis in more evenhanded ways. The point here is that Russian and western elites were making it more difficult to look objectively at Russian realities and were pushing acceptance of the idea that whatever works for the West should be accepted by Russia, and vice versa. The West's insistence, in this case, on supporting dogma and ideology regarding Russian development only served to strengthen those, both inside Russia and out, who wished to move Russia hastily and quickly toward a new development model. These forces also followed western tendencies, with the effects of trying to change Russia, thereby portraying Russia in the worst possible light.

As my methodological approach to educating the West about Russian realities is through analysis of multiple perspectives—by combining diverse factual interpretations from all sources, not just those of western persuasion, I want to make another revealing argument. A recent example by the West involving so-called official environmental concerns deals with a western oil company licensed in Sakhalin. During the autumn of 2006, the Russian Natural Resources Ministry, which oversees the environment, was accused of not complying with environmental regulations. If this allegation were true, this would clearly be another example of western hypocrisy in ostensibly caring about the environment while simultaneously destroying the environment in other countries if it feels the need to do so. Major oil companies have been accused of this wrongdoing ad infinitum. Such western hypocrisy makes it very easy for Russian elitists who do not fully understand Russian reality to apply dogma throughout the Russian debate on a variety of issues, and poison the strength of the Russian progressive movement. In this context, it is worth recalling the view expressed by Andrei Illarionov (an economic adviser to President Putin and Russia's representative to the Group of Eight, who was punished—some say—for his criticism over the Yukos bankruptcy procedure, and a censor of Russian bureaucracy). He strongly attacked the Kyoto protocol, which is intended to curb the air pollution blamed for global warming. The accord requires countries to cut emissions of carbon dioxide and other greenhouse gases. Some 141 countries, accounting for 55 percent of greenhouse gas emissions, have ratified the treaty, which pledges to cut these emissions by 5.2 percent by 2012. Russia ratified the treaty in November 2004, and its entry was vital because to become valid, the protocol had to be ratified by nations accounting for at least 55 percent of greenhouse gas emissions. This target was met after Russia joined the accord. The United States has not joined the treaty because it would be too costly to introduce and because its leaders feel the agreement is flawed; large developing countries, including India, China, and Brazil are not required to meet specific targets for now. Concerning this protocol, Illarionov (2004) wrote, "The Kyoto protocol is destructive for science and the environment, for public health and safety, for economic growth, and for the international fight against hunger and poverty.... Kyotoism is an attack on basic human freedoms behind a smokescreen of propaganda. Like those ideologies of human hatred, it will be exposed and defeated."

In a continuous effort to blame Russia's Kremlin, the West has not evaluated several seemingly negative aspects of the 1990s. While the country has not received adequate attention, I argue that we should reconsider what role the Russian government could have played in Russians' lives. By offering a sketch of the nature and moral significance of the 1990s in Russia, I argue that the country had not been hesitant to defend its political stability and social feasibility. Kremlinologists have argued without grounds that Putin's Kremlin, despite achievements and failures, has been immoral and detrimental to the country overall. However, western policy that weakens Russian progressive forces and the need to move the country toward a normal status, both inside Russian politics and throughout Russian society, represents a very powerful and negative influence on Russia's future development.

Chapter Four

Consciousnesses of Russia's Realities

I have already discussed the perverse logic that led the Russian economic environment to uncertain results starting in the late 1980s and allowed it to hit its worst economic and ethical situation in the 1990s. The years of Mikhail Gorbachev, the general support of Gorbachev's and Yeltsin's reforms, and the subsequent discontent with the results of those reforms should be key aspects of any analysis of the current Russian reality. Russians' initial support of economic reforms and the resulting widespread discontent over their ineffectiveness should have inspired intellectuals to formulate different point of views in response to such displeasure. This has not yet occurred, however, as intellectuals have failed to note the importance of the sequence of events and their negative ethical impact on Russians.

More disturbingly, the sequence and timing of the reforms have been fundamentally misinterpreted by those economists and international economic organizations involved in Russian affairs, and this has resulted in a case of intellectual arrogance. Serious observers would not fail to note the trust that Russians gave their new leaders in the 1980s and 1990s—elected democratically or not—repeatedly and unconditionally, as well as oaths those leaders made to Russians about changing their lives and improving their well-being.

The incredible emergence of new-fangled noncommunist *apparatchiki*, (officials who worked in the Communist Party bureaucracy, of whom there were several millions during communism and until Gorbachev came to power), of the modern companies' bosses, and of the new self-created class called the Manhattan Boys of Russia, is an underlying indicator of what was going on in Russia of the 1990s. Having once had a very equalized income distribution structure, Russia became the most unequal industrialized society in the world as a result of the 1990s. This change occurred, in a large part, because of looting by the oligarchy as the country transitioned from one form of economics to another, and because the West and certain western advisors have been mistaken in the economic sphere.

Western analysts must understand all this. Yet, some intellectuals have relied extensively on history to explain Russian attitudes and Russia's political system. They have provoked debates over the new experiment and its associated outcomes as a way of creating a blistering vision of the Putin

Kremlin. The intellectuals' foremost target has been Putin himself, but they have also tried to shift a sense of blame onto the Russians themselves. Besides criticizing Putin and his supposedly excessively conservative stance, however, intellectuals write and speak equally pessimistically about what they perceive as general Russian acquiescence to the current mainstream political system.

It has been said that the roots of the Russian attitude and acquiescence to authoritarianism can be found in the history of Russia itself. At the very least, it has been claimed that the Russian mind-set formed during the country's czarist past, and more recently during communism, and has influenced the way Russian voters express themselves during elections.

In reality, the Russian people's wishes and pleas during the 1990s were deep-rooted in much simpler concerns. They needed and wanted a government capable of building the economy, curbing distorted and dishonest practices, dealing decisively with the economic banditry that was strangling their country, and establishing fairness. Such is a correct, logically grounded interpretation of what motivated Russians at the end of the 1990s. Criticism of modern Russia, however, is quite sectarian and leans toward popular theory and demagogy rather than real research. An in-depth analysis would provide a reasonable explanation for a wider debate than is proposed here and discussed in other chapters of this book.

The enduring lack of economic prosperity for most Russians, along with current economic and political events—often interlinked—are so difficult to interpret that one needs only to glance at several different observations to feel overwhelmed regarding these Russian chronicles. Becoming familiar with Russia is not easy, beyond the unsophisticated concern over whether Russia has enjoyed free political elections since Putin took power. If Russian circumstances resemble a mix of imperfect corporate governance and grossly unevenly distributed income growth, an unequal, stratified society has been a constant in Russia's history, which lends partial support to the interpretation of Russian wishes from a historical perspective. Nevertheless, Russians' complex actuality has to be deciphered in a much simpler fashion.

The Path Dependence while Moving Toward Democracy

Certainly, anyone might assume that after seventy years of communism, or even centuries of czarism, specific forms of path dependence in the Russians' mentality are understandable. There have been so many undemocratic attitudes in Russian history that feasibility of a conduit from the past to the present can be realistically advanced by the experts who do so. Upon further analysis, however, the path dependence theory is not as critically important in explaining present-day Russia as these experts claim.

The well-known Harvard professor Richard Pipes (2005)—an adviser to President Ronald Reagan and a major advisor behind that administration's hair-line stance on Soviet affairs—interprets Russian events very much in this spirit in his very elegant book *Russian Conservatism and Its Critics: A Study in Political Culture*. Another wonderful book, *The Russians* by Hedrick Smith (1976)—who was the Moscow Bureau Chief for the *New York Times* from 1971 to 1974—also reports that even among Russian intellectuals, "Fearing what seems to them the chaotic turbulence of Western liberal democracies, most of them do not want democracy for Russia" (p. 507). Two books written at different points in time, from different perspectives, still enlighten these facets of Russian society.

Along this line of thought, as well as the ways in which other intellectuals describe Russians and modern realities, there are indubitably authenticities, but also interpretative transgressions. The concepts of the West and interpretative tools intersect at this point, straining some flawed interpretations concerning ordinary, and even the new rich Russians of our time. Although the communist regime was not stable and not very popular, says Pipes, Russians were searching for a democratic revolution of some sort. Pipes (2005) and Marc Garcelon (2005) believe that the educated middle class, the intellectuals, and the experts played a notable role during Gorbachev's era.

The idea of an organized middle class is a false impression of the past because it was absolutely absent in Russian society; or even if we accept the case of a most minuscule middle class, it was surely powerless. In truth, czarist and communist Russian society was highly polarized and stratified with a group of *nomenklatura* politicians, ballerinas, liberal intelligentsia, and intellectuals on top. The middle class, by western standards, was almost nonexistent. Perhaps it is a problem in terminology, but Russian society never had a stable western-style "middle class." Brezhnev communists' claim that Russian society had become classless was untrue because people were not all enjoying the same benefits; still, that society did not have a genuine middle class. However, that society was so highly stratified into two highly unbalanced extremities that the top pole enjoyed incomparable benefits in comparison to the very large opposite pole, and it was very difficult to move up the social ladder. The intelligentsia and top strata members had a much better chance of getting into university than the children of farmers and workers. Western scholars calculated the odds as almost 24:1, as Hedrick Smith asserts in his book.

When, in the 1960s, groups of sociologists and daring researchers began to think that economic reforms could be important and helpful rather than harmful to the country's interests, the Communist Party considered such ideas to be ideological sabotage spearheaded by the West. The West was complicit in the import of technology, computers, petrochemical plants, and so forth, which were made available to specific users in Russia while the state retained control over the economy and the country's ideology.

When Gorbachev shocked Russia and the West with an explanation and implementation of his reforms, the structure of the political system remained unaffected for the simple reason that it was untouchable. The much-acclaimed first democratically elected president of Russia, Boris Yeltsin, and his method of governing in the 1990s did not change the plight of ordinary Russians or disparage the activities of the new growing elite class. Yeltsin and his political cronies allowed business clans to steal from the state and even directly from Russians themselves. What the West had utterly and categorically miscalculated was that, after seventy years of communism and after ordinary Russians had entrusted that new democratic leadership which proved erroneous in the new *visions*, they went back to believing that a state could be the warden of the public's basic interest. This thrust does not reveal an activist reevaluation of communist years by ordinary Russians, as communist-style economics has been historically proven to not be the best option for any country. Yet, to understand Russians both during communism and after the transition to noncommunism requires that one comprehend how differently Russians regard their government.

A Dose of Ambiguity from Intellectuals

On occasion, some Russian experts offer criticism of recent events in Russia. In this respect, Elena Tregubova's (2004) *Tales of a Kremlin Digger* contains portraits of the Russian elite. She denies a transparent political process in Russia, and a sort of cult personality regarding Putin. For Tregubova—a journalist accredited by the presidential administration as a Kremlin reporter working for prestigious Russian newspapers such as *Kommersant, Russkii Telegraf*, and *Izvestia*—authoritarianism began with Putin. Although she tries to say that Mr. Putin reintroduced authoritarianism in Russian affairs, this claim remains ambiguous because any form of authoritarianism and oppression implies—among other things—that there are not truly open elections and that the leadership lacks social consensus. Such an extreme situation has not occurred yet in Russia, and no unfair election practices alleged to have happened in Russia are any worse than those that are rumored to be occurring in western elections on a regular basis.

More harshly critical of Putin's leadership was Anna Politkovskaya a famous journalist working for *Novaya Gazeta*. She wrote *Putin's Russia* (2005) to discuss multiple threats to Russian stability, and depicted a far-reaching state of decay with rampant corruption in business and certain sectors of the government, such as the judiciary and the army. She strongly condemned the ongoing war in Chechnya. Politkovskaya believed that Putin was moving the country back to a form of government similar to that of the old Soviet system. *Putin's Russia* fails to prove that Russia is currently reversing to something like its former Soviet days; and Politkovskaya's theory is also flawed by the observable fact that the modern Russian state no longer controls the means of production in any sector of commerce in Russia, with the exception of gas production and some parts of the oil industry. Moreover, as the increasingly long list of billionaires (*Forbes*, 2007) and millionaires demonstrates, the state is not in command of the economy completely.

Surely, these criticisms trigger several potential paradoxes. First, famous historians like Richard Pipes and Martin Malia (1994 and 1999), who have devoted a great deal of attention to the country, pointed to the suspected roots of Soviet tyranny in age-old autocratic traditions of the country's political culture to assert that it is unreasonable that it can take root in Russia soon. Their logic goes something like this: Russians are inclined to dictatorship or similar forms of governments and want to be presided over by a *strong man* capable of reinstating Russia's traditional model of government in which Russians would be relieved of their responsibilities for politics. Even if this were true—which it is not—we could not blame Putin himself and his Kremlin for having reintroduced forms of authoritarianism in a way unintelligible to Russians.

In fact, Padma Desai's book *Conversations on Russia: Reform from Yeltsin to Putin* (2006), in which eleven Russians and six U.S. citizens were interviewed about their views of their countries' direct or indirect involvement in past Russian reforms, Desai herself and the others state that Russians would be ready to accept a minimum dose of authoritarianism in exchange for stability and stricter control over social dysfunctions and to save the country from harm. However, although this would emerge as a sort of trade-off, the idea of a country that witnesses a dose of authoritarianism together with popular support seems illogical. Authoritarianism with popular support seems like a paradox. Either one interprets the notion of authoritarianism loosely or we simply talk of strong presidency as we have in place in several western democratic countries. Alternatively, perhaps people simply do not understand they are supporting a trade-off. That is, when citizens democratically elect a leader—twice in the case of Putin—and widely support his economic and political choices, we cannot have authoritarianism in principle, nor just a mild dose of it. When the Kremlin administration attempted to restrain the instability of the 1990s and sought to reinforce at minimum the country's unity following a general sentiment of ordinary Russians to have a more stable country, all this had nothing to do with a reversal of democratic reforms of Yeltsin, nor with an authoritarian state. We do not have enough evidence to express regrets at Putin's commitment to democracy and market reform. I am absolutely convinced that western citizens would have behaved in a quite similar fashion if they had to confront social instability and chaos. Still, critics fall into ambiguity when confusing the comprehensible search for a country's stability and unity with pro-tyrannical preferences of its citizenry. Certainly, Putin's Kremlin could have become diabolical between 2000 and 2004 and beyond, or a search for stability and unity could be misinterpreted for authoritarianism, but going so far as to blame Russian voters to have wittingly expressed tyrannical preferences is largely a blunder.

Moreover, if I assume that the country's history would make Russians disposed to authoritarianism, we should also assume those Russian politicians after 1985 have not been as democratic as the West has always thought. That is, if Russian history has been so pressing and capable of molding and fashioning Russians' attitudes, these "historical roots" should be equally important both for ordinary Russians and the political elite, and the West's notion of parallel groups of certain pro-democratic political leaders on one side and antidemocratic Russians on the other side would be a shortcoming. Instead, I suggest that modern Russia should be read as a country and a populace that have been moving toward democratic institutions, and there is no convincing evidence that Putin's Kremlin could revert Russia back to Soviet-type authoritarianism. Putin did not do so, and I do not believe post-Putin Kremlin leadership will do so.

Third, if some recognizable negative factors that are pervading Russian society are still so extensive and well-known to all—besides economic problems for a large part of society, the overall issue of the need to definitively move the country toward normal status— Russians and experts should invite the Kremlin to more resolute, stronger, yet still astute steps. However, calling on the Kremlin administration for stronger action in the face of the corrupt logic that was generated over the past decade sounds to western observers as too conservative and dictatorial. In other words, it is as if the West would be happier if Putin did not take any action. Would it have been better not to curb any illegal activities for fear that such a policy would instantly incite observers to label Russian leaders as despots without any systematic analysis of the facts? Such a question highlights the hypocrisy of western thought on the matter. There is no true external indication that Putin's recent choices have been too radical; still we could look at whether choices have been successful or not to weigh whether or not they are excessive. I do not see too much radical policy, if some failures in achieving proper results.

Fourth, perhaps westerners want to brand Putin as a harsh radical because of his work to seemingly reposition the country away from the western-style reforms of Boris Yeltsin, or because he is capitalizing on the reality that Russians traditionally accept authoritarian leadership. But those sorts of western-style reforms in the economic sphere have produced more cons than pros. And the theory of a conservative Putin would have us believe that he intends to push the country back to its previous communist philosophies, but this criticism is ill-conceived, inaccurate, and inconsistent. No one wants to theorize about what would have happened if no action had taken place after the Yeltsin fiasco. No one wants to piece together the way these aspects are linked to one another and the actual causality link between corruption and current policies, modern reforms and their consequences, or the disruption of the collective equilibrium that communism once provided to Russians. This, however, must be examined carefully. The equilibrium experienced during communism, for example, was not good for Russians, but we must be careful as we dissect it in relation to what Russians are experiencing today. The same communist leaders have been trying to reform the unique communist system of production by adopting western technology, incentives, flexibility, and productivity—that is, western-style notions. They have sought it all systematically, but have never succeeded—at least they tried.

One point made by Hedrick Smith (1976) in *The Russians*, however, assists us in the theory that a bridge can be drawn between Smith's perceptions of Russians in the past and those of Pipes and others recently. The years Smith spent in Moscow convinced him that Russians are seemingly less likely to undergo fundamental changes because he watched Russian authoritarianism adapt without surrendering its essence, and he concludes that Russians "find comfort in the stability and order that it provides" (507). He also believes that the past dual Russian elite that has been sandwiched between western ideals and the Slavophile ideological trend has shown a tendency toward the latter component—that is, the authoritarian government and restriction of human rights. The goal of his theory is to prove that Russians are intrinsically pro-authoritarian, nationalistic, and self-isolationist; but providentially, Smith's views refer to Soviet era and do not assist us very much today.

Russians Misled by Western Reforms

Liberal intelligentsia, academics, and others began pressing for real changes in the system starting back in the 1960s. In fact, when Gorbachev introduced reforms and high hopes for change, and when Yeltsin launched deep western-conceived economic reforms, Russians reacted quite enthusiastically to both of them—and perhaps much more enthusiastically to Yeltsin's more definite western-style reforms. Parts of the political bureaucracy and apparatus did not support such reforms, but the majority of Russians did. Lilia Shevtsova, one of the smartest analysts in Russian affairs, still does not detect a significant risk of Russia backsliding into communist-style politics, except within a hard-core 25 percent of the populace who are still nostalgic for the hammer and sickle (2005). However, this is not the morally correct way to interpret Russians today, or at least the majority of them.

The reality that we must be aware of in relation to Russian acceptance of transformation in the 1980s and 1990s is that they have been completely bamboozled by the West and by the ideas for reform that have been proffered by western academics and intellectuals. Public opinion data indicate that, except for a tiny nostalgic populace, what Russians continue to want is the final addition to liberal political and economic freedoms. The West has marketed these economic reforms to Russians as painless and positive, and painted them as beneficial to all. In the end, however, the majority of Russians did not benefit, and western thinkers—except for some courageous economists—still do not acknowledge this point the way they should. That is why some Russians express displeasure with the reforms, but they do not want to return to communism, as some experts claim, nor do they want to live with authoritarian leaders. They simply wanted a country shielded against chaos and instability in the same sense that we have taken pleasure in our societies in the West. Russians do not dislike the West, nor do Russians dislike western ideals and models. In fact, they have been quite enthusiastic about the implementation of many western ideas. Perhaps there was dislike or distrust in years past, but that no longer applies today. Consumption patterns, the import of luxury goods from Italy and the West in general, and new western car models are among the signs that show that there is not any prejudice against western culture. The anti-western rationale that governments of the communism era attempted to maintain, and the shield that was raised against any direct exposure to the culture of the West, are no longer realities.

Obviously, westerners misunderstand Russians in two ways. Russia, or part of it, has completely bought into western ideals, and now enjoys economic and cultural exchanges with western countries. For analysts to continue talking of a Russia that has not accepted the West or is against it some way is a bit specious. It would be foolish for Russia to detest the West, and luckily, this is not the case. Second, western ideals and models have been applied systematically and comprehensively in Russia for a long time, especially beginning in the 1990s—consider economic reforms, corporate governance, and so forth. What the Russian people find objectionable, however, is how such western models and ideals have benefited only a slight part of Russian society.

The West made one big mistake with its incorrect economic advice. Economic advice concerning the timing of reforms would have to become major, important and decisive steps if we were to reverse Russia's economic decline. Almost none of these attempts to reform the economy—which had become highly skewed and oligarchically controlled under Yeltsin—enjoyed much success. Unfortunately, attempts at political liberalization backfired and once opened, Pandora's box could not be shut again. Yeltsin lost control of the increasingly chaotic Russian system. When Gorbachev came to power in 1985 and Yeltsin came to power in 1991, they knew that there would have to be major reforms but we had to realize that economic reform could not succeed without a certain amount of political stability.

The West has also made another political misstep by labeling "good" and "bad" Russians according to their degree of sympathy for western values. The recent attempts by influential political leaders in the West—especially educated groups and even some intellectuals in the East—to conjecture about whether people are pro-West or pro-Russia in a clear attempt to divide those societies have been serious errors in judgment. For example, during the Ukrainian Orange Revolution in 2004, the West and western supporters engineered and inspired the country and its citizens to split into pro-West or pro-Russian factions. Most Ukrainians, however, were not conscious of such a demagogic division. The recent arrest in Georgia of four Russian military officers on espionage charges, although they were later released, sparked a diplomatic crisis between the two countries, in another clear example of the continuing oversights made by western observers with respect to Russian affairs.

The West has distorted the world's image of eastern societies by repeatedly stating the moral and economic superiority of the West and its institutional and governing models, and by psychologically dividing these societies into groups of people in favor of or against modern Russia. There is no doubt that the West has produced far better economic prosperity and political models based on democratic ideals in the several past decades of our western societies' development. The West, however, had to search for a more cooperative approach in dealing with Russian transformation, seeking ever more international cooperation instead of inspiring distrust and dislike of all that Russia does.

One part of the West's misaligned attempt to understand Russian culture today can be summed up by a remark by Hedrick Smith, who says that the West assumes that Russians want to be like westerners because "Russian life offers no obvious tourist exotica—women in saris or kimonos, figures of Buddha in temples, camels on the desert" (Smith 1976: 507). While Smith's point may drive home another equally incorrect conclusion—that Russians look like westerners except for this physical anomaly—the West has continuously misconstrued Russians, bypassing the basic issues of economic progress and social justice.

Young and old analysts alike present their own personal views and harsh feelings against Russia and some Russians, by intellectually shooting either Putin or the ideals that ordinary Russians actually believe to be in their best interest. Several public opinion surveys show that Russians are still alarmed by the real causes of corruption in the Russian system that originated in the 1990s. Vocal critics fail to recognize the complex reality of Russia and the very basic requests from Russians for things that we, in the West, consider basic everyday needs.

If a negative perception of the West exists at all with Russians, it is based on what went wrong during and especially after the period from 1985 to 1991. While the West and western institutions were professing the loveliness of the western model, Russians were reacting enthusiastically to and supporting the first vision of Gorbachev's reforms. When Yeltsin implemented a new vision of reform for Russians, people supported him equally and with much the same enthusiasm they had expressed and given to Gorbachev. People's discontent arose only after both visions yielded unconstructive results. Only when Russians were surveyed after Yeltsin's presidency did they begin to talk about missing a more paternal government—not in the original Soviet sense. Amid these years of economic shame and dishonor for ordinary Russians, influential western experts such as Richard Layard and John Parker (1996) were writing *The Coming Russian Boom: A Guide to New Markets and Politics*. Layard and Parker foresaw an encouraging Russian future based on events of the 1990s. However, the path of economic recovery was irrevocably altered by the profound changes Putin introduced (helped by the oil and gas industry to a large extent) several years after the book become available to readers. These authors based their work on facts that were true and observable to all at the time. But some observers in the West used those basic facts in the new landscape to interpret the new path of economic recovery as something to be blamed on Putin and the Russian people instead of recognizing the real changes introduced by the end of the 1990s and understanding their purpose.

Russian newspapers and magazines are filled with snide remarks about Europe and the United States. Russian media routinely show satisfaction with any unfavorable news emanating from these western blocs and any western mistakes in the conducting of foreign and economic policy corroborate the sense of frustration among many who feel that Russia is suffering from the results of poorly executed reform ideas by two presidents who were encouraged by western advice. Surprisingly, the Russian people do not disagree with westerners or metaphysical western notions; rather they did not appreciate Russian experts and leaders who applied those notions without respecting local realities. Western-inspired reforms were ill-used by Russian leaders, and Russians are well aware of this. Experts on transition economics still disagree on whether a gradual economic transition away from communist economics is superior or not to the shock of instant change. The latter simply suggests an abandoning of the current economy in a hurried fashion, but economists are still discussing the pros and cons of whether or not Yeltsin should have put wiser efforts into practice over time in Russia rather than rushing into it.

The West and Its Ambiguous Behavior

Reprimanding people is a job that requires patience and wisdom, and finding justifiable ways out of this ethical obligation is easy for the irresponsible. It is not easy, however, for Putin. There are those who have asked Putin to *square the circle*, in other words, to skip the mistakes made during the 1980s and 1990s when the country created oligarchs and gave power and money to them. Actually, the 1990s were not a clear example of genuine democracy, and the risks of a dictatorship were inherent during those days in Moscow.

The country needed full awareness of the reforms and opportunities initiated by Gorbachev and prolonged by Yeltsin, and this period has given Russians a taste of electoral democracy that would be difficult to eradicate at this point. It is true that those years helped free Russians from the shackles of Soviet communism, but oligarchs—by snatching political and economic power from the Russian people—began invasively interfering in Russian politics in a way that still affects the administration of governmental programs today. Even if the potential for Putin to become a dictator existed in Moscow then and exists hypothetically in present-day Moscow, it did not actually happen, and it will not happen. Prophets of the worst-case scenario worry that such sobering anti-Putin views might signal a return to communism, which is really unjustified criticism—unproved and a misinterpretation of current Russian society. Russians are afraid of prolonging what occurred during the Gorbachev and Yeltsin eras, yet Russians are not inclined to dictatorship any longer.

In addition, the country considered necessary transparency, the rule of law, fairness, and openness to shape a new business climate and forge structural reforms, but certain behaviors signaled a different message. The West witnessed several cases of economic debauchery, and no matter what negative image it created for Russia, it did represent truth. A special case of unethical behavior and a serious conflict of interest reported by U.S. newspapers was a project financed by the U.S. government through Harvard University, which enjoyed an exceptional position from which to exert academic and intellectual influence. The Harvard Institute for International Development had a project financed by the U.S. government and with the official high-profile mission of assisting in the rebuilding of the Russian economy, using the standard western philosophy of free markets and ethical, democratic principles. The project was financed by the U.S. government and led by Harvard economist Andrei Shleifer and lawyer Jonathan Hay, both top officials with the Harvard Institute for International Development, under contract with the United States Agency for International Development from 1992 to 1997, who were accused and condemned for defrauding the U.S. government by making personal investments in Russia. The Justice Department filed its initial complaint (*United States U.S. Harvard University*) on September 26, 2000. The case was initiated in 2004, when a judge in Federal district court in Boston found "Harvard, Teacher, and Lawyer to Pay US $30m," as Marcella Bombardieri's article in the *Boston Globe* was headlined (2005). Actually, top officials with the Harvard Institute for International Development under contract with the U.S. Agency for International Development from 1992 to 1997, would have conspired to defraud the U.S. government by failing to serve as impartial advisers about Russian economic reform. A year later, in August 2005, although neither the advisers nor Harvard admitted wrongdoing—Judge Douglas P. Woodlock dismissed the most serious charge against Harvard University, ruling that the university engaged in no institutional wrongdoing—some people agreed to pay the U.S. government, reports Bombardieri (2005). Harvard agreed to pay the U.S. government $26.5 million, with Shleifer paying a further $2 million, and Hay having to pay between $1 million and $2 million, depending upon his earnings over the next ten years. Note that the Department of Justice sued them for having not been impartial advisers on Russian economic reform, seeking $120 million in damages, although the government funded the previously mentioned Harvard project with some $34 million. If this case may be partly seen by viewing activities that were completely illegal and unethical, though perhaps they have received greater public awareness because of the official connection with Harvard, in the end the collapse of the Harvard project arrested work on a number of vital reform projects but it has helped to better focus on the outmost aspects of Russia. Also, this scandal led to the downfall of Larry Summers, who as President Bill Clinton's deputy secretary of the treasury, set up the Harvard project.

Janine Wedel's *Collision and Collusion* (1998) observed that some U.S. monetary aid was used to help former prime minister Chubais transition into the private sector and, indeed, economists working at Harvard assisted with that misuse of official funds that did not benefit the public. In addition, in light of the Bank of New York money-laundering scheme, Janine Wedel painted some western investors as "helping free market reformers to defeat their opponents" (Wedel 1998: 131), as the Chubais action was intended to develop a larger number of outsider owners and accelerate restructuring.

Overall, western experts were unethical and used very poor judgment when becoming directly involved in Russian privatization issues. Such poor judgment, however, may also have been exercised by economists during the 1990s, who were criticized for offering poor advice to Russia—they performed nothing illegal, but received huge amounts of money for their advice. This background may help shed light as to why there was an outcry against much of the West in general. Many western investor activities in Russia were unethical, although perhaps they received greater public awareness because of their official connection with important western institutions. In the end, the collapse of the Harvard project froze work on a number of vital reform projects, and only partially helped to better focus on the most critical aspects of Russian development.

Western Electoral Systems with No Disruption to Unity

Another factor was important in this complex picture. Attempts to introduce democratic elements into Russian society to satisfy the common objectives of Russians go back to the intellectual vivacity of the 1960s. Although intellectuals of this time period were becoming curious about it in an almost informal way—as communism did not allow any discussion of democratization—this feeling strengthened definitively after the 1970s and put pressure on the Soviet system through Gorbachev's first reform efforts. Waves of change and the political novelty that brought about the fall of communism also banished hopes for enduring reform. The country started to realign itself with global adaptations and western-inspired economic reforms. While domestic forces were characterizing a rigid Russian society, the exact transition away from communism was modeled and dictated by Yeltsin's corrupted and deceitful leadership, which explains why the realignment to western standards and models did not work well and actually created more issues. This unexpected outcome disappointed western experts and intellectuals, who had expected that Russia could align itself to western models easily and completely. The following issues that are poorly debated and that are about electoral democracy, the effort to maintain the country's unity, historical roots and religion, assume increasing relevance these days not only when we refer to Russia itself but also when we put Russia in confrontation with international realities.

On the one side, President George W. Bush posits that democracy in Russia may differ from democracy in the United States, although he is not specific as to how. If Bush is speaking in terms of the universality of democratic principles—that is, how elections are run (freely or not) and how political leaders become so—he is right. If he is trying to affirm that electoral systems and types of leaders cannot differ from one country to another, he is not. He is not right when he evades the rules of moral justice, which is an even more universal and accepted notion and one that absolutely merges with the universality of democratic principles. The Russia of the 1990s was a clear example of a separation between the organization of democratic elections and the morally and universally accepted laws of moral justice. Russia's development after 1985, especially during the Yeltsin years when Russia was complying technically with the concept of formal democracy, was marked by a systematic departure from the other and equally important task of molding a political system that is objectively right, fair, and morally righteous. As long as the West continues to confuse these two equally important angles of analysis, readers around the world will not gain a correct perception of Russia.

The beginning of a true functioning democracy, which did not occur in Russia prior to Vladimir Putin's presidency, implies that adjustments will be made and political institutions will be reinforced. What we watched, instead, was a slide toward anarchy and unfair justice prior to Putin's first term in office, as the inequality of natural resource distribution and a corrupt system led to a lack of moral justice, which is usually not associated with democracy. An electoral democracy is a prerequisite for moral justice, but there cannot be a universality of democratic principles without moral justice. Without a full understanding of Russian problems and dilemmas, a simplistic discussion of electoral democracy becomes ungenerously prejudiced against Putin's Russia, which is still based upon free electoral appointment.

The Country's Unity Perceived as a Value

On the other side, Russia's tighter control of regions and republics was not entirely an effort to instill a more authoritarian leadership, but rather a way of stopping the complete disintegration of the country—chaos was more than a risk by the end of the 1990s. In this context as well, much of Russia's situation was still only depicted in western books and manuals, which are equally faulty. Both of these direct and indirect western perspectives fall far wide of properly interpreting Russian events, and could mislead many readers. Putin, realistically, had no choice but to preserve and unify Russia and offer Russians real reasons to believe that progress could still be achieved. Aleksandr Solzhenitsyn supported the advantage of having a strong president in Moscow that could uphold the country's unity during a time of transition. Going a step beyond this philosophy, however, is the acknowledgment that social and economic issues have had much more impact on the need for a strong central authority than simply the need for a firm hand during an economic changeover. We must acknowledge Solzhenitsyn's view as a strong base upon which to build a more comprehensive reasoning that truly supports the legitimacy and effectiveness of a strong central Russian authority in most or all areas. Tendencies in other countries or regions put the importance of this issue right under our noses that the West thoroughly fails to notice. Movements toward decentralizing budgetary or political decisions all come about and are explained with the ultimate objective of making a country work better, efficiently, and cohesively. If Russian authorities looked at this issue, it was because there were obvious signs of governmental disintegration. No form of decentralization concept should produce any disintegration within the political system of the country. Instead, it has to be a by-product of a country's unity.

Another example is the European Union, where decentralization of policies could have helped in tightening institutional integration and control of regional and decentralized power and pressure groups. It is clear that a process of decentralization is compatible with unity as long as it is purposely conceived from the center and effectively applied to regional entities.

Historical Roots and Religion

An argument that the West makes is that Russia became continentally isolated—completely and purposefully unable to find a proper place in the international community. While there is no adequate justification to assume a direct link between the internationalization of the Russian economy and the delay in effecting reform policies, authors Richard Pipes and Martin Malia present an account of Russia's commitment to autocracy. They merely posit that Russians and Russian analysts believe the country can grow under autocracy. Stefan Hedlund (2005) states in his book *Russian Path Dependence* that Russia cannot be understood if one does not consider its history and the feelings of Russians themselves. If we do not consider the current mind-set of Russians and Russia itself, we cannot understand the winds of change. If one goes back a millennium in Russian history to the ninth century, it is clear that the issue of dependence and its impact on history mattered a great deal to the country's subsequent development. On the other hand, trying to tie recent developments in economic history to events in the past, however, is only looking at one tiny piece of the puzzle.

In fact, recent Russian development is the dominant intellectual legacy of Russia, as Pipes and others maintain. This is due to the vastness of its territory on one side, and the historical and social realities on the other. In contrast, the geographical vastness of Russia and the history of Russian politics and society are so well known that it is easy to accuse Russia of being inclined to authoritarian regimes. From a complementary angle of interpretation, another drawback is the tendency of western intellectuals to assume that recent attempts by the Kremlin to control the dynamics of certain situations are examples of a new wave of authoritarianism. Instead, these two observations actually reflect the national inclination to openness of the Russian people, and it is a much stronger reality than is often believed.

It follows that some could interpret maintaining the country's unity as isolationism. Richard Pipes and others accept this perspective as a trend of Russian isolation deep in its historical roots and religion. Western literature does not discuss why the current Russian leadership should not be attentive to maintaining country unity, nor does it report that the very same aspiration to preserve unity can be observed in every country in the world. Again, western commentators shift some culpability of this inclination to the country's history.

The preferred Russian religion of Eastern Orthodox Christianity—a derivative of Byzantium—caused Russians to feel a bit estranged from Catholic and Protestant Europe many years ago—not to mention the great philosophical distances between their form of Christianity and Islam and Buddhist Asia. Russian sovereigns from Ivan the Great to Peter the Great and Catherine the Great started borrowing ideas from the West on a limited basis in the area of elections, the so-called Legislative Commission in 1767, and in the discussion of a legal system to give rights to the representative of new estates. Italian architects eventually designed palaces in St. Petersburg and Moscow. Two of the Kremlin cathedrals, the Kremlin walls, and the Kremlin towers were conceived and built by Italian architects, but legend says that the same rulers prevented other socio-economic and political infections of western liberal ideas from being absorbed into Russia. Perhaps contact between members of the branches of Christianity in the East and West was much broader than originally thought, and the gap between Russia and the West was made to appear bigger than it was. Also, during the era of communism, technology from the West was being exchanged for Russia's raw materials—it was allowed in the Russian society, but only to reinforce it, not to radically transform it.

In contrast to what is alleged, religion plays a smaller role in the Russian society than it did in the past. If a sense of alienation and continental unfriendliness persists in secular form, it does not describe how Russians feel today. Analysts argue and pretend to use selected opinion polls to draw definitive arguments on Russian isolationism. If opinion polls show that a limited share of Russians regard the West as a foe and favor isolationism, it is truly only a small minority. This is not the sentiment of most Russians. A similar feeling is also measured if we look at opinion polls taken in the West concerning western feelings about Russia. This is not to say that some feelings of anti-Americanism have not been felt in the West. If some Russians are disaffected with the West, this is truly not related to the West, per se. In addition, if we find that a small number of Russians are hostile to the West, we can also find a similar small number who exhibit clear anti-Russian feelings, as well.

Does the West Have Only One Model to Offer?

The loss of a sense of empire was created by great progress in science and technology (such as the space program) achievements in the late 1950s and 1960s, and the system's subsequent collapse by the end of the 1960s and 1970s. This sense of loss contributed to the feeling of drifting apart from the rest of the world. The USSR was also the largest country in the world, and this spaciousness can contribute to a sense of alienation, as Russians take immense pride in the vastness of their land. This is not that different, though, from how other cultures interpret the size of their own countries. According to official communist dogma, alienation was an expected result of the capitalist ownership system, and experts reported that worker alienation, especially within the blue-collar working class, emerged after the 1960s and the failure of Aleksei Kosygin's reform attempts. Similar attitudes can be found in other populations and this is not the only reason to talk about alienation per se. Russians tend to think that they are not a country, like others, but rather a continent instead. Russians also believe that they are entitled to superpower status by virtue of their size, and as such, have a right to a decisive voice in world affairs.

The other factor that reinforces the idea of Russia's sense of isolation and hostility to the outside world for some scholars is Russia's antidemocratic, authoritarian tradition. That Russia had these characteristics is not in doubt. That Russia continues this tradition is an inaccuracy depicted by western critics. Although we widely perceived Russia as a radical country during the Soviet era, its radicalism was confined to Marxist-Leninist slogans meant exclusively for export (propaganda). In reality, it was a reactionary regime that had more in common with the autocracy of Nicholas I or Alexander III than with the socialist ideals of the radical intelligentsia. The Russian political tradition is solidly conservative—so much so that even its Marxism found a conservative coloring. Until 1991, Russia had abandoned autocracy only twice in its history—in the early seventeenth century and again in 1917. And in both cases, the collapse of autocracy led not to a liberal regime, but to anarchy—or, rather, to a dictatorship that resulted in the restoration of absolutism. The same process might have occurred in the 1990s when an electoral western-style parliamentary democracy and badly functioning institutional systems were hiding bandit capitalism with pervasive corruption, deceit, and other debauched business aberrations and abuses, wrote Stern and Stiglitz (1997).

Thus, since the beginning of Putin's Kremlin, the growing gap between rich and poor and political instability represented growing threats to long-term stability in Russia. The global media and policy experts virtually ignored these issues. They ignored the fact that when Putin ascended to the Kremlin, he had to struggle with Yeltsin's political-agenda effects of gloomy business fighting, outrageous corruption, endless social injustice, and entrenched interests, some actually existing from actual communist days of Mikhail Gorbachev. Once he stepped into such an astonishing office, Putin encountered the task of evening out the political scenery as well. It is likely that discontent built up among common Russians based on these consequences of the 1990s. That says it all! That alone would have justified a resolute reaction from any government. Common Russians supported Putin incessantly and increasingly. This book calls for taking a step back from an unbalanced-interpretative approach and opens a new approach vis-à-vis the realities that conditioned Putin's policy response. This glaring discrepancy is the primary cause of my concern, and I elevated this as the most important policy priority for the Kremlin in question at the end of Yeltsin's Kremlin. In this manner then, the Kremlin and primary institutions responsible for establishing policy priorities had to appreciate and realize the severity of a continuing and growing problem. Failure to elevate instability and chaos as the primary cause of all other economic, political, and social problems in Russia risked alienating entire segments of population. Such a growing disconnect between perceptions and reality regarding the actual cause of Russian social trauma made a comprehensive solution all but impossible to achieve. Instability was the fundamental reality and the primary force and form of causality, which leads to economic, business, political, and social responses by the Kremlin. Along with Russia's western advisors and western institutions in general, Russia clearly misunderstood from the outset of the post-communist development in 1980s and 1990s that preventing instability was the primary prerequisite for establishing successful, long-term development paradigms. By contrast, a small and well-connected group of powerful entrepreneurs made a killing from the privatization of Russia's public richness. This dimension was crucial to establishing the fact that the final years of Yeltsin's influence saw the largest, fastest-growing and most destabilizing of wealth concentration and institutional precarious realities, without precedent anywhere in central and Eastern Europe, post 1989.

Chapter Five

Experts Censured Modern Russia's Western – driven Economic Reforms

The failure of those economic reforms, which has been measured by western logic in terms of the volume of domestic output lost during the 1990s and other indicators that have likewise performed so disappointingly during the 1990s, has been an ignominy in Russia. The transition from communism to a free market economy has been a terrible and traumatic time for common Russians. Before the inception of new reformism, the western approach to Russian affairs was thought to be unproblematic, and only afterward did it become obvious that the opposite was true. This fact embodies another aspect of why President Putin and his critics continue to confuse each other. The western public and intellectuals took the soundness of the above strategy for granted and believed that it would have not been so painful at all in terms of output contraction and other variables. Through seemingly understandable criticism, the West has offered misleading appraisals of Russia and perhaps in search of good fortune in the quest to create the right environment for success. One specific harsh attack on the Putin Kremlin was that the economy could lose credibility and consensus among international investors, but those fears have not materialized.

The two bastions of 1990s reforms were macroeconomic variables set in such a way that all prices were allowed to move freely and there were waves of privatization concerning whatever the government could privatize. The latter continue to be very principled notions; however, given the Russian realities, these ideas were not feasible, and Russia was simply unprepared to jump suddenly into this new reality, especially while the new class of policy makers was deficient in ethical principles. The West's increasingly inattentive approach to Russia's affairs was the key factor behind worse-than-expected economic and social progress in molding a definitive consensus on Russian transformation. The market was still not competitive enough and it needed to be reinforced if the goal of a smooth transition was to be achieved, yet it brought the country to an unprecedented negative level of GDP reduction, a negative sign after 1989 which continued until 1996, an unprecedented fact in all central Europe The economic policy course adopted in Moscow illustrated the tendency to turn to pro-western advocates when deciding on the timing of reforms. All these ingenious ways of fixing national economic problems contributed in their own fashion to a negative process of modernization. Moreover, it appeared that the Yeltsin Kremlin had lost independence in the 1990s, becoming more receptive to external pressure, loosing the much-needed confidence of international investors, and failing to act more decisively on the country's most crucial issues.

Certain of the newfangled business sectors were similarly ethically unprepared for new challenges and the attempts by the oligarchy to deal with the communists' appalling legacy followed to that extent that people responded to this disillusionment in a way that appealed to a new, coherent, stable Kremlin. It should come as no surprise that the arbitrariness of western-inspired reforms received seemingly widespread support from the Russian political system during the 1990s.

Nevertheless, to establish the validity of the western criticism that Putin's economic governance is destructive, a mainstream examination should be able to assume that one point is true above all: that the western economic development paradigm is always an ethical one. But this is not always so. From any possible economic perspective on economic concepts, timing, and sequences of reforms, the arbitrariness and seemingly sincere western pedagogical activity seems doubtful. I would say that I level no criticism at the international economic organizations per se, as they had a difficult task, but rather I criticize the arguments and logic of reform that have been pursued in Russia. Moscow could not look to its neighbors to learn the rules of transformation, because Central European markets differed from Russian markets in terms of size and political stability. This missing political stability has been the biggest risk and it turned out to be complete chaos.

The West's subjective interpretation was not well focused. Putin's Kremlin has been greatly impeded against inheriting the groups of power who used political clouts to their own benefit through Yeltsin's reform programs. No one wants to give exact recognition and a proper weight to the occurrences above, but I want to put this issue back on everyone's interpretative perspective on Russian affairs. It would leave Putin's critics on this difficult path of confusing the concrete economic achievements and the schematic western concerns of rules of thumb, as both Putin's Kremlin critics and western ideological advisors and intellectuals inadvertently support an ideological basis for economic growth on the way to a materialistic society, rather than the spread of domestic social consensus. That is, while the social consensus on the new political course was intimately tied to an accurate anticommunist corollary, public consensus quickly collapsed.

These same western critics argued consistently that western development models offered solutions to development problems in East-Central Europe and other poor countries through international organizations' preferred economic approaches. Simply put, it is true that western economic aid did not work well in Russia during the 1990s because it was implemented so naïvely in an increasingly wild economic setting that was not conducive to economic fairness. Nothing that occurred during the 1990s enabled the market to respond quickly and efficiently to the changing business climate. None of these reforms enjoyed much success, and their nature and trajectory were atypical, which had negative ramifications for the development of both a normal capitalist economy and a liberal democracy. Russia's path during the 1990s was different from that of most advanced industrial countries, and even from many transitional states. As in the early twentieth century, a major problem was that leaders sought to introduce radical change in a situation in which many of the key components and actors and ethical bases were utterly missing. There was also the danger that Russian citizens' patience—even allowing for the fact that it appears to be greater than that of almost any other transition nation—would run out.

Thus, many of the problems of post-Yeltsin Russia could eventually have resulted in a virtual stalemate and stalled reforms; and the various ramifications of the near-absence of the bourgeoisie, including the rise of corruption, of the so-called oligarchs, and of the privatization of the *nomenklatura*, could be traced back to the distorting effects of the logic of communist economics. However, misguided western advisers must also share the blame for the problems the Russian economy has experienced in recent years.

While there is no reliable evidence against western criticisms of Russia, I cannot praise the outcomes of the western-driven reforms. However, western economic intellectuals deserve wide praise for having become aware of wrong and unethical outcomes that originated from the western-inspired reforms of the early 1990s.

Western Models Did Not Embrace Russia

Whatever results stemmed from western-style pedagogical meddling, the undemocratic economic tendencies identified by the same western critics do not exist in the post-Yeltsin Kremlin. Such inconsistent and unprincipled interpretation appears even more so when we realize that this is the primary western response to development issues, and this response may have contributed to the poor results in the countries in which it has been applied. Even when Washington-based international institutions sent their expert economists to Moscow without any real consideration, we simply overlooked the fact that the standard policy tools we worked with can work differently in different institutional environments. There is a gap between simple models and their applicability, and this discrepancy makes the usefulness of certain constructed models daunting (Sergi, 2006).

The western demagogic double standards caused by the ideological straitjacket that blinds western and eastern intellectuals and policy makers into assuming that any policy originating from a western economic judgment must be democratic and ethical is another reason for the general belief in the West that Putin is an unsuccessful economic leader—an erroneous view that is an unexplained critique and that is much too strong for the task at hand. The essential point here is that the Kremlin is a strong example of a new kind of approach, unique to Russia and Russian development over the past decades and even centuries, as identified in the extensive exploitation of crude oil and gas resources, an issue that will be discussed in chapter 7. But that western apprehension about Putin's leadership style weakens rather than strengthens the West's belief that Putin has been a poor leader from a purely economic perspective.

Therefore, I cannot take seriously western critiques of reforms proffered by Putin and the Kremlin administration, because the support structure for western criticism offered no practical reason, at the end of the 1990s, to continue following typical western models as examples of judicious development. Western missionaries have started interpreting Putin's conduct as an acknowledgment that his strategies have systematically pushed the Russian economic sphere away from the market model that the West offered to his predecessor in the 1990s, Boris Yeltsin.

When Putin came along, the West still believed in the development strategy that had been packaged and offered to Russia and other emerging countries, based on the definition of the essential points of western economic policy for raising common people's standard of living. But the standard of living was not raised when Russia stuck to western messages during the 1990s. Instead the worst development occurred, and it would have happened anyway in Russia, say western experts who are overly interested in the Russian and Central European transition. Despite that, our western meddling was responsible for the major technical errors of the time and the unethical foundations of those developments. Negative sentiments grew to such an extent within the population that many expressed sincere regret that the country had even attempted democratic reforms; the very poorest segments of the populace would rather forget the 1990s.

How can the development policies that Russia engaged in during the 2000s be called unethical when they have helped many more of Russia's citizenry than were helped in the period under Boris Yeltsin or during the rise of administrative skilled capital in the administrative command economy during Gorbachev's years in the 1980s? There is simply no ethical comparison between Russia's living standards under Yeltsin and those under Putin—not even considering the factors of instability and the pirating of state resources—and common Russians rejected the first modernization attempts altogether, effectively opting out for a *third vision*. The country, under the guidance of international experts, was not run efficiently and transparently, and the public was ripped off. Prompt action was needed to ensure fairness, and neither domestic nor international authorities were shouldering their responsibilities. There is no question that Russia was trying to recover from its worst period in the mid-1990s; only in the 2000s did entrepreneurial enterprises for diverse small industries begin to flourish and deliver robust economic growth. I can say unreservedly that without the oil and gas industry's immense resources, the country could not have benefited much in terms of economic growth. But in addition, living conditions under Putin improved much more quickly and for more Russians than under

Yeltsin, which leaves us again with the primary question of how we should judge Russian development priorities.

Certain Western Experts Now Censure What the West Did

I have pointed out (2004 and 2006), as have several experts, a number of faults and censures of what the West and international organizations did wrong (e.g., Peet, 2003), although the extent and the nature of these accusations differ from one author to another. Yegor Gaidar (1997)—the first deputy prime minister of the *kamikaze crew* in 1991–1992—argued that the West was simply forged by incapability. Jeffrey Sachs (2005), senior foreign economic advisor to the first Yeltsin economic teams that led the advisory team (1991–1993), recently offered candid assessments and observations of what went wrong and why development policies failed so completely and spectacularly in Russia. His assessment is unique and should be taken very seriously because he was an influential non-Russian economic advisor during the entire development process.

Other observers of the Russian reform process support Sachs's viewpoints and take his concerns further as well. The Economics Nobel Prize winner in 2001, Joseph Stiglitz—who from 1993 to 1997 was highly involved in Washington, DC, as a member of President Bill Clinton's Council of Economic Advisers (chairman in 1995) and senior vice president and chief economist at the World Bank in 1997—is another important figure in this debate. Stiglitz has been a ferocious critic of what the IMF has done in Russia in the 1990s, expressing opinions similar to Welfens's statement.

The notion that Russian failures in economic and political reform were not caused by ethical lapses under the first noncommunist Russian president, Yeltsin, and his senior economic advisory team led by Russian Yegor Gaidar, is not very credible. For that reason, it is highly plausible that Putin's Kremlin inherited a much narrower range of policy choices following the Yeltsin presidency.

The West has a credibility problem when it comes to its inconsistent criticism of Putin, and Yeltsin before him. As western critics asserted that reforms suffered mainly from Putin's undemocratic conduct, leaving most Russians impoverished and facing greater hardships than ever before, I must go through the evidence for what it really suggests. The West shares much of the responsibility because of its deliberate uncertainty over Russian reform all through the most important stages of the Russian transition. In other words, the West's sketchy approach to Russian economic affairs deliberately avoided policies that had been shown to be successful from prior development successes in other countries in Central Europe. A fairer economic policy would have served Russian reform efforts better, and I cannot blame Putin for criticizing the World Trade Organization and other international organizations and calling them archaic and nondemocratic and ineffective in tackling the world's problems, as he did during the economic forum celebrated in Saint Petersburg in June 2007.

These intentional policy choices by the West were made with full awareness of the implications for Russian development, and were clearly working poorly in light of what was known to be true in post-1991 Russia about the ruble and the West's responsibility to stabilize its short- and long-term value and related obligations compared with overall Russian development goals.

Once this fundamental truth was realized, it became very difficult to criticize Russia because western governments knowingly weakened any possibility for solid noncommunist economic and development reform. In other words, the unscrupulous policy decisions made by the West during the Yeltsin years and manipulated by underhanded business and political circles set in motion greatly increased radical and popular resistance within Russia that lasted for several years after the onset of noncommunist Russian reforms. This greatly altered the direction of economic and political reform in Russia, allowing anti-reform forces to gain power and dominate Russian politics and economics right up to and through the Putin years.

Toward a Financial Collapse — The 1998 Crisis

The year in which the financial crisis hit Russian society reminds me of important issues, in terms not only of the causes and effects of the crisis, but also of the bad advice that prompted the disintegration of the system. The West simply failed to recognize and crystalize main social losses that delivered a lost decade of economic stagnation. Therefore, a long decline and a new crisis represented the end of positive expectations. I could interpret this crisis as a market reaction to Moscow, or a signaling of negative perceptions of policies enacted or policies not enforced at all. It was unwise not to enforce stability or reduce the state deficit and having the ruble corridor (an exchange rate that cannot go beyond certain minimum and maximum limits) as the central themes of political economy. In addition, forcing the Russian government to liberalize capital inflows was a huge gaffe.

The fact that the country recorded only limited positive economic growth in 1997 was not enough to prevent a financial collapse, and the crisis of 1998 could be seen as the end of any expectation of lasting positive change. Russia was negotiating its foreign debt with the clubs of Paris and London. The Paris Club is an informal group of state creditors (having no legal basis) that dates back to 1956—when Argentina agreed to meet its public creditors in Paris—whose role is to find coordinated and sustainable solutions to the payment complexities experienced by governments with large claims on debtor nations. The London Club, on the other hand, is an informal group of commercial banks that team up to negotiate their claims against a sovereign debtor. Russia initiated talks with these clubs in April 1996 to try rescheduling repayment of massive inherited Soviet debts. The economy had experienced noticeable growth for the first time in 1997 (albeit below 1 percent), and the World Bank and the International Monetary Fund (IMF) were willing to provide Russia with more time. The prospect of international investors' restored confidence in Russia could possibly have come to fruition, considering the negotiations with the Paris and London clubs, had the Duma passed a more intelligent tax code. This did not happen.

Russia joined the Paris Club in September 1997, and at that time the country rescheduled a payment in excess of $60 billion in Soviet debt to other governments. In the meantime, in October 1997, Moscow achieved a $33 billion rescheduling agreement over a period of twenty-three years with the London Club. In reality, these agreements were due more to the political importance of Moscow and its long global history than to its realistic ability to show successful economic growth. Or to put it differently, the western circles who knew what was going on continued to back Russia, doing so fraudulently. The Paris Club decisions were based on an exchange rate of 0.6 rubles to the dollar (in contrast to the fluctuating band between 5 and 6 rubles), which was nonsense. Roughly 25 percent of the foreign assets due to Russia from Mongolia, Cuba, and Vietnam were, in practice, difficult to obtain and this undermined the financial strength of the Russian system. Nonetheless, there were some positive expectations on the horizon, so the Russian government lifted its restrictions on foreigners' ability to purchase government securities and nonresidents held by 30 percent of Russian short-term treasury bonds (i.e., GKOs). Russian banks began borrowing from foreign markets to a larger extent, so banks' foreign liabilities jumped from 7 to 17 percent in 1994.

Other events occurring in the country and abroad interacted with one another to negatively affect Russia. In July 1997, a financial crisis hit Asian countries, and this prompted international investors to become cautious about investing in financially weak countries—Russia was such a country then. As a result, the ruble first experienced a speculative attack in November 1997, and the Central Bank spent roughly $6 billion of its foreign exchange reserves in an attempt to support the ruble. Another billion or so was spent in May 1998, and much more all through the summer until the ruble was floated on September 2. Speculation about the Bank of New York's money-laundering scandal has been made in context with Russian financial troubles (Goldman, 2003).

Observers have theorized that the $4.2 to $10 billion reportedly sent from Russia to the Bank of New York was a case of capital flight in an effort to skip the tax collector. Some, however, have suggested that Russian banks and government officials used insider information to deal illegally with and make profits from Russian GKOs just prior to the collapse of the treasury bond market in August 1998. Other observers claim that the bulk of a $4.8-billion loan installment from the IMF in July 1998 went to the holders of GKOs, who converted the soon-to-be-worthless, ruble-denominated paper into the freshly received IMF dollars at highly favorable exchange rates, reaping huge profits. Nevertheless, nearly $4 billion of the IMF's $4.8-billion loan in the summer of 1998 never reached Russia, but was sold by Russia's Central Bank directly to eighteen of

Russia's commercial banks. Khodorkovsky's Bank Menatep was one of these, and it used its accounts in the Bank of New York from late July to the middle of August 1998 when the GKO market and the ruble both crashed. Only the tiny sum of $471 million went to support the ruble, which was the main purpose of the IMF loan.

Several hundred million dollars in other government funds were also embezzled, and at that time, no one was prosecuted for the crime, nor did it ever become clear what occurred despite several intensive investigations of Russian government officials for suspected insider GKO trading during the three and a half weeks prior to August 1998. Top politicians were involved, but nothing happened to them. Simply put, the ruble collapse had its origins in the Russian government's entrapment into large loans that were poorly managed by the IMF and other international economic organizations involved in Russian affairs, by a tight monetary policy imposed by these organizations' operating procedures, and by a careless fiscal policy to support the perverse logic of oligarchy. These policies were inconsistent and sent prices to skyrocketing levels, which inflicted suffering on the poorest, common Russians. It is unquestionably true that a dangerous inflationary process that usually harms vulnerable poor people did not have to take a back seat to other equally important concerns. The country could have reemerged by abandoning its episodic economic policy and in its place, giving preference to a more coherent policy mix. A foolish monetary and financial policy muddle was the main cause of the ruble's collapse in August 1998 and thus derailed Russian economic growth.

A Combination of Causes

In reality, Russia's financial situation was particularly weak due to a combination of causes. Foreigners understood the risk of a possible devaluation. Nonresident holders of short-term government bills secured contracts with the Central Bank to exchange rubles for foreign currency in an attempt to edge exchange rate risks for private companies and for the Central Bank to prevent runs on its foreign currency reserves. They introduced a ruble corridor at the time of the mid-1995 stabilization program and traded the ruble in the range of 5–6 rubles to the dollar. That exchange rate and the propensity of Russian authorities to defend the markets made it look impossible to sustain.

Contributing to this complex situation was the inefficient tax system, the weakness of state finances, and the unwillingness of the Duma to pass more effective tax legislation. The sharing of taxes between republics and Moscow was implemented in such a way that the republics could conceal portions of taxable profits, and the associated drop in fiscal revenues definitively collided with the interests of Moscow. Oligarchs were too influential to allow whatever endeavors the government and the Duma sought to collect that missing tax revenue.

The financial position of the government was not improving, and actually worsened significantly when the price of oil dropped from some $23 a barrel in 1997 to $11–$14 a barrel in 1998—although this negative trend started in December 1997, and this further impacted the government's shrinking cash reserves. The IMF certainly had in mind to back the reformers who were in fact running deceitful schemes for personal advantage, and this fact could not have been unknown to other top circles in the West. The IMF theoretically and institutionally tried to relieve pressures on prices and to help a financially struggling country, but domestic authorities could not do so. Furthermore, the reformers were too much involved in deceitful schemes to introduce a minimum of domestic financial discipline and sound policies. Russia's Central Bank wanted, illogically, to defend the ruble and sweep vital problems under the carpet, but this brought an increase of deficits and mounting foreign debts. If this chaotic situation reduced the interest of foreign investors in taking on Russian debt, someone could earn money, of course. It is widely proved in economics that chaos helps some individuals to benefit even though most people do not.

An additional issue was the endless expansion of money supplies to get to the bottom of fiscal imbalances. This creation of new money sped up the ruble devaluation, which rested on the incapacity of the Russian government to honor its debt.

By February 1998, a new tax law was submitted and approved by the Duma to cope with the danger of defaulting on Russia's foreign debt. However, capital flight rates were high, and the overall demand for Russian assets fell. Interest rates started to rise. Still, the Central Bank was overemphasizing shielding the ruble and squandering money on it.

On the political side, Yeltsin fired Prime Minister Viktor Chernomyrdin in March and appointed the thirty-five-year-old Sergei Kiriyenko to take his place. The new prime minister refused to meet with Lawrence Summers, who was monitoring Russia for President Bill Clinton, and markets suffered from the very visible strained relationship between the two countries. Another speculative attack on the ruble occurred soon after in April, but the West and the Russians were not communicating very well.

Oligarchs suggested a devaluation of the ruble to increase the value of their exports as a way of dealing with declining prices in the oil market. The situation was very confusing, and the country kept asking for financial assistance from the IMF. Stability was a precondition to obtaining further financial support, and the IMF was very worried about the political instability permeating the country. This prompted the IMF to postpone the release of a $670-million loan that was meant to help Russia's extended fund facility (a 1974-started IMF loan program to assist member countries' balance of payment problems caused by structural challenges; the program was intended to allow a longer period of adjustment than is possible under a traditional stand-by arrangement) and the extension of the loan to the end of 1999 with extra lending potential of at least $1 billion.

After the new government won endorsement from the Duma, the IMF emergency stabilization loan of $11.2 billion was part of a larger undertaking in July, while investors' expectations concerning crisis timing shifted from a period of one week to a longer one. Despite additional commitments and extra bailouts from the World Bank and Japan, the situation was about to worsen. The country had to repay a $2.5–$3 billion loan by the end of September, with an additional million ruble futures to mature in the fall, $4 billion capital flight occurring during the months of May through August, and the drop in oil revenue. Government bond yields swelled to 47 percent by mid-May and up to more than 50 percent by the end of the month. The Central Bank's key interest rate peaked to 150 percent by late May on increasing anxiety about the financial system and the anticipated default as well as the intention to defend the ruble against speculative attacks. The government stopped issuing short-term papers and offered investors the option of converting short-term treasuries that would mature before July 1999 into dollar-denominated seven- and twenty-year bonds with a guaranteed high annual yield.

Nevertheless, the Parliament postponed reforms considered necessary to qualify for IMF loans and Yeltsin reaffirmed that there would not be any devaluation of the ruble after an emergency parliamentary session on August 14. (Note that the stock and bond markets collapsed on the previous day.) Yet finally, on August 17, the government announced a devaluation of the ruble against the U.S. dollar until the end of the year, defaulted on the domestic debt, and stopped repaying the foreign debt, implementing a ninety-day moratorium. On August 26, the Central Bank declared that the fixed exchange rate could no longer be supported and the official floating which took effect on September 2 followed this announcement. Before that date, the IMF helped Russia because it was considered too important not to bail out. Before mid-August, the entire financial system was in a panic. Michel Camdessus, managing director of the IMF, announced a new line of credit to Russia on August 13. The government took definitive action on August 17, abandoning the ruble (with devaluation taking place four days later), declaring a default on $40 billion in domestic debt, and enacting a ninety-day moratorium on payments by commercial banks to foreign creditors.

Politically, the situation was worsening. Prime Minister Sergei Kiriyenko was thrown out, and Chernomyrdin's appointment to the post was not ratified by the Duma; Yevgeny Primakov, instead, was recommended by Yeltsin to be prime minister and approved by the Duma. The ruble crashed on August 25 and was left floating in early September 2, as I said, following the Central Bank's choice not to support the currency any longer and the government's default on its debt.

The Ruble and the IMF

The decision by the IMF and the West's insistence on keeping the ruble at an artificially high value were partly orchestrated by a dramatic increase in IMF lending to Russia. In this way, the high value of the ruble was maintained, but at the cost of a dramatic increase in foreign debt for Russia. The increase in foreign debt put western pressure on the Russian government. Major western banks, governments, and the IMF demanded that the ever-increasing Russian debt be repaid, which is much easier to collect—in this case from Russia—when currency is overvalued as opposed to undervalued. At the same time, Russian interest rates had to increase dramatically to keep a minimum of much needed foreign investment in the country Foreign investments were not materializing at all in Russia, while foreign investments were flowing into Central Europe and had indeed risen by a staggering rate. While helping to keep the national currency overvalued by increasing foreign demand for rubles that easily outstripped its supply, this also guaranteed that it would be much trickier for Russians to borrow money and generate domestic employment and higher wages when the ruble did come down. When this actually occurred, it greatly reduced the probability of and the conditions for Russian development. Rather than devaluing the ruble when Russia had much less foreign debt to repay, and keeping Russian interest rates low to generate an improvement in Russian living standards, the crash produced just the opposite situation.

All of this indicates that the West shares considerable responsibility for the problems facing Russia today and the significantly reduced democratic choices that Putin had when he became president (Stiglitz, 2002). Stiglitz's criticism—whose comments I share here—concerns the IMF's repeated refusal to support a lower-value ruble for Russia. The IMF said the measure would be inflationary, which was the primary concern of the IMF and the basic approach adopted by the IMF was to strengthen the ruble. Nevertheless, the policy adopted under the IMF's pressures failed to support the vulnerable ruble. Instead of the ruble being reinforced with several financial packages, Russia's currency crashed in the fall of 1992, in the winter of 1993, in the autumn of 1994, and again in the summer of 1998. In 1992, one U.S. dollar was worth around 415 rubles, but the rate had fallen to $1:28,000 rubles by the time Yeltsin left office. These events had the makings of a fiasco.

One specific censure involves the accumulation of external debt to $130 billion by 2001; another statistic can corroborate this depressing debt evolution: the ratio of external debt to gross domestic product climbed to roughly 87 percent in 1999 from about 37 percent in 1995. Russian economist Nodari Simonia (2002) argues that the IMF is primarily responsible for the bulk of Russia's foreign debt, because it forced domestic authorities to cover budget deficits and support the ruble within a framework of foreign exchange rates. In addition, starting in the 1980s, waste and inefficient credits and loans pouring into Russia brought that country to default status before the IMF advised additional borrowing to save the ailing ruble (Simonia, 2002).

Another criticism is that by keeping the ruble so overvalued, the IMF made it much easier for the most corrupt Russians who had already stolen money to buy more dollars with their overvalued rubles and then permanently ship all this badly needed hard currency outside of Russia. Russian convertibility of the ruble in international markets, which could have benefited Russian transition development enormously through greater access to international trade, was made even more difficult to achieve because of actions like these, which then created and magnified the dramatic reduction in living standards for most Russians. One more consequence of the IMF's and the West's refusal to support a lower ruble value was the growing demand by Russian consumers—because of the ruble's strength—for more imports to satisfy basic consumer needs. In this environment, it became impossible for Russian domestic productivity and manufacturing to generate long- or even short-term momentum, which would have created more employment in Russia along with higher wages and thus greater demand for Russia (Stiglitz, 2002).

The result was dramatic increases in Russian unemployment and general misery throughout the country, with the average Russian lifespan and living standards falling precipitiously for most Russians. When the IMF finally agreed to let the ruble fall, the much-feared inflation never appeared in what was left of Russian markets. However, although the West allowed the fall of the ruble to occur, the originally expected benefits that would have occurred had the IMF agreed much earlier to a calculated fall, were now much smaller. Putin inherited more stumbling blocks as the new Russians president in 2000 because of these dramatic situations, and the Russian financial collapse called for more dramatic—or, as the West would say, *undemocratic*—solutions to these increasing plights.

Western Financial Involvement

During Yeltsin's era, the IMF, the World Bank, and the European Bank for Reconstruction and Development approved about $60 billion in programs from 1991 to 2001, and slightly more than half were actually disbursed. Now, let's look at major loan initiatives that were supposedly intended to boost confidence in the country; a few statistical figures will help to clarify the logic. A number of loans and negotiations took place with the IMF beginning in the early 1990s. A $1-billion credit loan to Russia from the IMF was approved on August 5, 1992. A $3-billion Systemic Transformation Facility loan (established at the April 1993 Group of Seven meeting in Tokyo to empower the IMF quickly disburse loans) was approved on June 30, 1993. By April 11, 1995, a $6.8-billion stand-by loan was approved. In March 1996, a $10-billion loan was awarded, and in July 1998—before the August crisis—further loans for about $11.2 billion were approved. The IMF's executive board approved a stand-by amount of about $4.5 billion on July 28, 1999.

The financial involvement of the West has not protected the domestic political economy from intense external interference nor provided the basic requirement for the country to get the best outcomes for the country. It is important, however, to consider the expected costs of further deterioration that an economy would experience without a serious economic program strategy. On top of this complicated scenario, it was confidently expected at the IMF's headquarters that a new consensus would gain favor with new Russian reformers, but there were many troubles and much misguided advice. For example, three factors became visible during the first part of the 1990s. The period from February 1996 to mid-1997 saw inflation dip below 3 percent monthly and real interest rates fall sharply. The interest of foreigners in investing in the stock market and access to the domestic treasury bill market soared. The co-opting of oligarchs occurred through the support of commercial banks, energy companies, and other powerful private businesses. The government, however, was forced to find bargains to halt the upsurge in prices of energy through commodity credits—that is, shipments of fuel and fertilizers to farms would result in lower prices and limit economic growth in the spirit of the commitment to the IMF. An example is the bargain made with Lukoil that waived 1.2 trillion rubles in tax arrears in return for supplying farms and defense installations with fuel. Another deal was made with the seven "court" banks, the most influential commercial banks that were controlling the country de facto, to secure loans to the government in exchange for the best standing in the loans-for-shares auctions. Electricity prices were frozen in August 1995, as were the prices of gas and railroad transportation in October.

In fact, concern about the IMF's tactics was acute enough to have been a motive for reformulating strategies. While the archetype of the IMF approach and reformers' credo failed in effectiveness, the involvement of an international institution retains credibility as long as it comes under reformulated circumstances. The experience of the 1990s must prompt new forms of coordination between international and domestic actors; despite the fact that our views of the economic transition are now based on larger flows of news and empirical knowledge, we still might find it difficult to facilitate a painless transition despite the knowledge we have gained in hindsight.

Despite a constant requirement to keep inflation and budget deficits under control, during the Yeltsin presidency the IMF started pressuring reformers to consider policies—specifically, to uphold a common economic space at the end of 1991 and produce a vigorous banking bankruptcy law. As a qualification for Russia to receive loans, the IMF tried to impose a dynamic that would slash the government's deficit and decelerate inflation, but inflation first decelerated from 11 percent in 1997 to some 84 percent by 1998. The IMF was not working in partnership with domestic authorities at all.

By the mid-1990s, the IMF emphasized the need for structural reforms as well. To receive a large loan in 1995, Russia had to agree to increase domestic oil prices and to helping hand pro-market reforms in the economy. That very same year, the IMF asked Russia to increase tax revenues, thinking that taxation was the key Russian financial problem. Although top Russian officials reported that the country's domestic debt was very low by any standard applied in the

West, the Washington Consensus remained an important sticking point, but the Washington Consensus has not encouraged stability nor supported Russia's economic performance. At the time of the 1998 crisis, the Russian government agreed to tighten the budget policy, increase foreign exchange reserves, extend the maturity of its short-term debt, and approve legislation that enacted structural reforms. Unfortunately, the government continued to focus on the risk of macro-economics rather than the soundness of applying this policy inconsistently.

Michel Camdessus played the game on behalf of world political leaders. For instance, Camdessus led IMF delegations to Moscow (and he went in 1992) ten days before the Group of Seven summit meeting in London to smooth the difference of opinions between the IMF and Moscow over the conditional inflation target to consider as part of a $24-billion foreign aid package announced by President Bush. In the same year, Camdessus went to Moscow to facilitate an IMF disbursement of $1 billion before the Group of Seven's summer reunion in Munich, and for the second disbursement of the Systemic Transformation Facility loan in March 1994; he led the delegation and met directly with Prime Minister Chernomyrdin. A similar approach was taken for the $6.5-billion agreement in 1995. When Yeltsin's reelection was in peril in June 1996, Camdessus announced in Moscow that an extended $10-billion loan was soon to be released. No one wanted a collapse of the Yeltsin government—especially on the eve of the U.S. elections—and no one wanted Russia falling into a severe crisis.

The Failure of the One-Size-Fits-All Program

The actual recommendations made by Jeffrey Sachs (2005) as the lead foreign economic advisor to Russia during the early stages of the Yeltsin presidency might in hindsight have been much more relevant and ethical than his critics gave him credit for. As many, or most, of these critics were from the West, it seems even more obvious (retrospectively) that criticism directed against Sachs and other western economists was inaccurate and lacked clarity. In addition, William Easterly (2006) very effectively asserts that the western world failed to accomplish its ill-conceived plans because it assumed it knew what the best strategies and policies were for everyone involved, without the ground-level planning and conscious effort to consult with Russians other than corrupt politicians and self-congratulatory bureaucrats.

In the face of events leading to the crisis of 1998, it is clear that western criticism of Putin enjoys no greater degree of credibility concerning what Russia needs today than it did in the 1990s when Jeffrey Sachs and his team were first advising Yeltsin in the very early stages of the transition in Russia. Harsh criticism of the 1990s experiment should, therefore, be judged by the continuing lack of clarity concerning Russia's financial realities. Simply stated, the criticism of the 1990s and the long-term foundation of the logic emanating from the Yeltsin presidency must not confuse the means with the end.

Regarding means, Russia surely needed fully functioning and efficient democratic institutions, as defined by western standards, to increase living standards throughout Russia. Today, the country is already raising general living standards, helped greatly by very high oil and natural gas prices and buoyant export volumes. But while seemingly obvious, the lack of shared democratic development in Russia under Yeltsin led to an electoral democracy profoundly shaped by bandits, to the capture of state resources, and to powerful groups conflicting with one another—or as Stiglitz (2002) puts it, bribery, huge sell-offs, and corruption schemes initiated in the mid-1990s. The West, the IMF, and independent experts knew that one-size-fits-all programs to rescue Russia would not work without benefiting some more than others.

Actually, growing corruption occurred that coincided with nasty privatization tactics. These were not necessarily cultural factors specific to Russia, but more symptomatic of underlying poorly managed institutional problems (see also Shleifer and Treisman, 2000). Deputies loyal to oligarchs and influential groups of power blocked tax optimization programs and tax legislation unfavorable to oligarchs. This was what current Russia inherited from that past, caused by the West's incapacity to offer the right aid at the right time while at the same time overlooking—more or less consciously—the logic of it. This and other domestic mistakes caused the rise to power of significant criminal elements, and once they were in power, Yeltsin found it easier said than done to move against this negative force. Regarding the intended goal, Putin is achieving the ends much more successfully than Yeltsin, even though he has partially reversed the inspired western route of excessive and uncontrolled privatization of the 1990s.

The best way to illustrate this is with an example. The West should interpret Putin's attack on the deformations of the 1990s as a move toward a democracy, compatible with current Russian realities, rather than as a move away from democratic structures as western critics claim. I agree with Jeffrey Sachs who states that "Putin's attack on the oligarchs in 2003 and 2004 can be viewed as an utterly appropriate challenge to ill-gotten wealth. Alternatively, it can be viewed as an attack on the kind of independent wealth that could challenge the supremacy of the state. It is probably a bit of both, time will tell" (Sachs 2005: 145–146).

It would have been more logical to recommend other forms of economic assistance to Russia from the international community, such as the creation of a stabilization fund for Russia (which had worked well for Poland), an immediate suspension of Russian debt payments, and a new aid package and program that would focus primarily on the most vulnerable sectors in Russian society throughout the scope of transition. None of these was implemented primarily because of strong uncertainty about domestic Russian politics and business and reflected in the West's influence. The end results were tragic. If the West had offered Russian reformers effective support with the right domestic transition path, the reformers would have had a good chance of transforming Russia along a good track. Instead, the opposite occurred.

Stiglitz strongly criticized the IMF for its specific transition policy choices regarding Russia. What Stiglitz had to say is important here because, although he criticizes Jeffrey Sachs and the IMF overall, his criticism of Sachs offers further support to the views articulated here that western policy toward Russia was wholly unethical. Stiglitz asserts that the policy choices pursued by the IMF—while not knowingly intended by IMF policymakers—have dramatically taken a significant turn for the worse concerning the living standards for a vast majority of Russians. This certainly made it much more difficult for Putin, when he eventually came to power, to carry out the kind of programs expected by the unrealistic, and often uncomprehending, western media.

In other words, I agree with those few economists who believe that the West has to take considerable responsibility for the collapse of the Russian standard of living after 1991, which in contrast has improved under the last part of the Putin Kremlin. Stiglitz (2002) writes that the much-touted transition strategies of international agencies like the IMF were responsible for moving Russia and other transitional countries into poverty beginning in the very early 1990s; this is also a cause for concern. There are two parts to the underlying theme of experts' writing. On one side, Stiglitz cast doubt on the logic that the IMF followed in Russia. On the other side, George Soros (1992) believed that international economic agencies should have been kept out of the rescue attempt altogether!

That is, based on the belief that liberalization, stabilization, and privatization would have worked for prior paternalistic, communist-type governments, and that better-specified sequences and more social-domestic targeted options could ease the transition and facilitate a more effective recovery process, western economists moved so far as to advance criticisms concerning the methodology of past policies. János Kornai (2000) also felt that he had been too optimistic in his previous predictions of economic recovery. The cost of the transition was so high that small private garden plots supplied income to a large part of the population during the worst of the economic crisis. In the end, the IMF could be responsible for the Russian transition disaster which as Welfens said, is probably the first case in which "an international organization instead of solving a major international problem actually reinforced it" (Welfens 1999: 134).

Other respected international economists—e.g., Ravi Batra (2005)—have stated that Russia's problems as presented above and severely affected by IMF, the World Bank, and western policies, bring to mind another unethical aspect related to western policy. The corrupt Russian oligarchs, who were sending money to the United States with the help of the western-generated overvaluation of the ruble, were contributing to the even greater overvaluation in the U.S. stock markets, which eventually led to an even bigger stock market collapse that reverberated around the world.

One can state that western policies concerning Russia were even more inequitable when one realizes that making Russian elites and oligarchs wealthier increased the already grossly and unethically high rates of growing wealth disparity in Russia. When it came to economic policy for Russia, this represented the worst of all possible economic worlds. First, the transition caused some outcomes that no one could have predicted, because we lacked a precedent or similar experience on which to base evaluations of the situation. Second, Russia needed more than just comprehensive micro- and macroeconomic reforms. Everyday life in a system that has been shaped over many generations, and the vastness and the complexity of the region, would have required far more tailored policies to affect change and capability in the domestic arena. Turning a blind eye to certain spheres of the markets was a mistake. Neither international economic agencies nor the internal culpability of foreign advisers may allow us to gloss over their responsibility for the failure of the policies they announced as being able to deliver rapid revivals. But as a result, the shake up in January 1992, inspired by the new Russian kamikaze crew that employed radical economic reforms, pointed to macroeconomic stabilization and market price policy as a precondition for the next waves of privatization, but the policy was not too realistic then.

Perhaps the failure of some reforms was unavoidable because the transition was very demanding. Occasionally, when circumstances were right, the West did exactly what the model predicted—it tipped the balance of incentives, trying to favor a long-term strategy to reinforce the credibility of governments. The piece that was lacking was the uncultivated economic stimuli—people not responding to incentives, as Easterly pointed out (2001). International economic agencies were at fault when interpreting the economic transition without having accounted for those canonical incentives. The proposals from the IMF and other international economic organizations were not down-to-earth, as they rushed the privatization process and endorsed unrealistic adjustment programs through healthy public finances and monetary stability. All operational decisions were grounded on a few rigorous economic rules, which straightforwardly counseled the best ways of targeting exchange rates, the ideal method of privatization, and the optimal sequence of structural reforms. The need to heed an oversimplified approach and impose macroeconomic stability has been an obsession of the West. This does not prove that the IMF and the World Bank were mistaken when thinking about macroeconomic stability, but they were mistaken in the absolute belief that western principles would have worked for Russia quickly, painlessly, and without producing absurd social destruction. The proper timing and sequencing of reforms carried some weight, but all of the actors involved failed. Russians cherished the faith of western experts in the region, but the latter miscalculated the exact extent of policy choices even though great strides were taken toward achievement of results.

Does it all add up? Does it not drive us to understand the difference between what is ethical and what has to be done to combine these two values in a judicious setting? The commitment to establishing an acceptable base for ethical behavior had to prompt a set of policies aimed at achieving economic and financial stability and providing adequate economic resources to the poor. Tackling inflation and unbalanced public finances, promoting trade liberalization, creating governance, and strengthening financial systems contrasted in their realization with economic and political rationalizations to be made regarding policy making. Political explanations of IMF and western involvement needed a simple ethical validation. Concrete, substantive concerns about economic risks did matter and demanded fair-market stability.

In principle, targeted aid and debt relief often served as a springboard to self-sustained business groups and to their fighting each other to grasp state resources and to coerce governments to give away state resources. The inertia of entrenched domestic institutions and poor macroeconomic policies served to finance booming consumption by some groups as a replacement for the much wiser general economic growth, that is, without having a positive impact on the country's recovery. It is true that inflation projections and outcomes of programs supported by the IMF have systematically been missed in other countries' experience also. Summing up, Russia did not give any empirical confirmation of a positive role for IMF's role and did not have the features of superior steps into the economy if not a minefield for other corrupt practices.

While foreign advisers and international organizations did not have total knowledge of local markets, they forced fixed-format programs. The Russian people, who were the intended beneficiaries of international aid, had no real voice in how the money was spent or on the design of overall policy concerning domestic incentives and the accountability of domestic players, although the West much praised that kind of accountability and that pseudo-democratic system. Western experts started reflecting seriously on the poor only late in the game. Western economic advice to Russia was that Russia was pervaded by the wrong business logic in the 1990s. In light of this mounting debate, the West threw its weight behind reforms, but in a way that neither benefited the country nor gave greater influence to ordinary Russians.

Global demand for Russian exports—helped by a better-late-than-never fall in the value of the Russian ruble—was now even weaker, perhaps fatally so, with the great dropoff in demand for Russian exports. In this context, academics argue that the speed of reforms did not matter in explaining the poor performance in transitional economics. Although in terms of Hungarian transition reforms, János Kornai (1990) deemed transition to be a clean break to wipe out corrupt practices, with measures that could take place within one year of the new government's inauguration, he finally recognized that his prognosis of a painless transition was wrong and that his expectations had been overly optimistic (Kornai 2000). Or as Olivier Blanchard (1997) stated with the same unjustified optimism, that the "transition came with an often large initial decrease in output should be seen as a puzzle. After all, the previous economic system was characterized by a myriad of distortions. One might have expected that removing most of them would have led to a large increase, not a decrease, in output"(p. v). Several other economists were advocates of shock factor economic reforms in Russia (once on all, Anders Åslund, 1995). Others—Peter Boone and Jacob Hørder (1998), Andrei Shleifer and Daniel Treisman (2000), Vladimir Tikhomirov (2000), Jerry Hough (2001)—did not.

Western policy brought about the most likely unethical economic outcomes in Russian development and global economic stability. This was the state of Russian affairs when Putin took office and entered the new millennium. In light of the general instability, confusion, and lack of shrewd strategy, Russia had no real opportunities to develop any other way during the 1990s. Rationally and ethically, Putin was only able to choose from a very narrow offering of political and economic choices from which to elevate Russian living standards and stabilize the functioning of institutions. The effectiveness of this policy will be discussed in the next chapter.

Chapter Six

Russia's Manhattan Boys—Some of Them Fell into Disgrace

We have established that western analysts might impose a double standard or contradict themselves when they criticize Putin and Russia's citizens for requesting much stricter regulation and control over the business sphere of influence after the debacle of the wilder 1990s. Recognizing Russia's logic throughout Putin's eight years in office requires a real awareness of the ethical issues pervading the country's society during the 1990s and into the twenty-first century. To do this, we have to build a foundation of facts and analysis that allows us to see the moral paradox from a coherent perspective and to further demonstrate how business and politics in the 1990s forced Russians to call for new leadership and a U-turn in politics. Russians simply got irritated.

The new business leadership that grew up and expanded in Russia embodies the perspective of those years. The most powerful among this new class of business people were referred to as Russia's Manhattan Boys—*Manhattan* for their wealth, and *Boys* for their youth. Occurrences in Moscow did not happen on the basis of the best interests of the people. Frictions between social classes and groups of power were likely to advance in Russia. Because the government was actually uncommitted to the general interest, that triggered alarm among Russians, who feared that policy makers were not adequately addressing the problem of growing income disparity. The unethical drift and practices of the 1990s can be understood by the comparison between Moscow and the business center of New York; this comparison of Moscow and Manhattan highlights things that the public would not believe without proper explanation.

The comparison between Moscow and Manhattan needs to be made appropriately, considering that the western-based interpretation of Russia's experience has been problematic for the past twenty years. A group of Russians emerged from the collapse of the Soviet Union to become the owners of valuable oil, natural gas, and metal-deposit companies. By the 1990s, some of the new ultra-wealthy were living off of the majority of Russians, having made their billions from market-valued resources and former state-owned companies. Under the attempted free voucher policy, based on which the government started mass privatization, it was expedient to use companies' book values as they were fixed in January 1992, before the high inflation of the first kamikaze government, as the basis for the voucher auctions. During the first wave of privatization, insiders—i.e., directors and workers—were allowed to buy 51 percent of the voting shares of their organization at a nominal price—sometimes using the enterprise's own funds. In some cases, Boris Yeltsin even issued special decrees that excluded outsiders. Insiders were given vouchers, which could buy shares. Nevertheless, workers were too often unable to interfere with management and managers bought workers' shares before they had any market value. In the end, some insiders leeched cash, seized company ownerships, and put the profits into offshore accounts through the use of cooperatives, joint ventures, and later, offshore havens.

The government wiped out the savings of many Russians—seventy million accounts in the state-owned Sberbank alone—through post-1992 inflation and corrupt privatization. Especially after 1994, during the loans-for-shares scheme, the government sold off many state companies, in what Chrystia Freeland described in her book *Sale of the Century* as a "crude trade of property for political support" (2000: 169)

By the end of 1995, the government auctioned off twelve of Russia's most important companies, sold off several huge oil companies, and some buyers acquired the potential for huge fortunes by obtaining these companies for a fraction of their market value. When the Yeltsin administration initiated the loans-for-shares scheme, private bankers received stakes in still unprivatized state companies as collateral for the money they were lending to the government. Bankers knew, however, that the state would never repay such loans, and thus anticipated future ownership as they were allowed to sell the stakes, which they resold to themselves at knock-down prices. In the end, by auctioning off packages of shares in the most desirable enterprises, the government deprived hundreds of thousands of Russians of their savings and prevented the majority of Russians from becoming entrepreneurs. The IMF and western experts share equally in the intellectual responsibility for this.

Several cases of corrupt insider deals exhibited the methodology of a corrupted country that ran rampant in the 1990s. The Yeltsin government let the new capitalists take the companies from their directors to buy their support for Yeltsin as he stood against the communists, as everybody knows. The government could not repay the loans previously obtained by banks and the fresh banker-capitalists then sold the shares to themselves at very low prices, as repayment for the loans, through offshore companies. In the end, Russia was completely devoid of any kind of genuine corporate governance, at least of the kind that we expect in the West, and so degraded business and state companies amid what Freeland terms the "sale of the century" (2000).

A number of banks—originating from the former *pocket banks*—ran the auctions, disqualifying possible rivals and winning the bids in the end. This type of activity could occur through political evaluation of worth, discriminatory use of political clout, and some bank cash. The capitalists readily admitted that they paid fourty times less than the enterprises were worth. By 1997, five of those individuals were on the *Forbes* list of the world's richest billionaires.

Some of these oligarchs were accused of using their capitalist knowledge, learned during the 1980s: intimidation, political connections at top government circles, and occasionally violence.

A qualitative leap was made by the end of the 1990s when oligarch Mikhail Khodorkovsky donated a million dollars to the Library of Congress to start the Open Russia Foundation in support of educational and cultural projects. Dr. Henry Kissinger and Lord Rothschild, among others, were appointed to the board of this foundation. Just as Khodorkovski cleaned himself up and sought justification for his activities in the eyes of western analysts, Vladimir Gusinsky, another oligarch, transformed himself into a philanthropist by helping to fund the Library of Congress's collections of Russian documentaries. In sum, some of the oligarchs tried to rely on the sympathies of businesspersons and politicians like themselves in the West to look legitimate in the eyes of the world, and became respectable because of their impressive economic and political backgrounds; western institutions and intellectual clubs freely offered them their services. Almost no one, however, reckoned that these forms of sponsorship were designed to produce only the appearance of legitimacy, rather than an actual legitimate practice.

Because the extremely biased distribution of wealth to a single group of people is one of several pieces in the growing puzzle of the disparities and anomalies in noncommunist Russia, we must strip western awareness down to one basic piece of the puzzle. My reading of these occurrences is based on the episodes that developed from a transformation conceived as an alternative to communism by Gorbachev and rooted in what happened during the 1980s, when the *first vision* for a modern Russia was initiated, and was reinvigorated during the 1990s with the bureaucratic-managerial culture that a new class of entrepreneurs brought to light. Those periods witnessed Komsomol activists receiving privileges in businesses opportunities, controlling state apparatuses, and inspiring the epithet "the Komsomol is a school of capitalism," based on the well-known Leninist adage, "trade unions are a school of Communism."

A Tour of Moscow

What, then, does this have to do with Manhattan—the spirit of New York—the world's premiere financial center? And what do Russia's Manhattan Boys have to do with Moscow? Russia was reemerging as an international power; and some positive comparisons can be made between Moscow and New York that engendered feelings of grandeur within the Russian leadership as they became increasingly involved in the European and world affairs of this century.

First, just as people assume that the sheikhs from the Middle East are the only rich oil producers, many people also assume that most rich people live in Manhattan, along with the big companies listed on Wall Street's Dow Jones and NASDAQ. Regardless of the world's perceptions, we should be clear that Moscow is the home of an incredible number of billionaires and millionaires.

Second, Moscow is not, of course, literally like Manhattan, but it has many features in common with it and is comparable in a number of ways. Saying that Russia is home to an amazingly high number of millionaires—some who became so without any venture capital—and noting that this number is clearly larger in Moscow than New York, would sound like blasphemy to the casual observer. Certainly, in light of recent events, Moscow has become a very expensive town. *Forbes* magazine came to this startling conclusion in 2006, declaring that there were more extremely wealthy people living in Moscow than in New York City. Russia is home to thousands and thousands of millionaires and thirty three billionaires, gauged by U.S. currency. This may sound incredible, but it is true.

Second, comparing Moscow and Manhattan makes it easier to point out Russia's unusually and dreadfully unequal distribution of income and increasingly divergent reality for its poor versus its rich citizens. This is the result of the unfair allotment of wealth, different managerial qualifications, capitalist cultures, and skills accumulated during communism and the 1990s, and, more recently, the rising value of natural resources.

The comparison between Moscow and Manhattan can actually shed light on modern Russian ethical perspectives, as surprising as this may be to readers. Moscow has become a place of huge contradictions—home to the very rich and with a high cost of living. Comparing Manhattan and Moscow challenges conventional wisdom to arrive at an understanding of Russia and elucidate the contours of such an emerging puzzle. Besides the phenomenon of many rich men in Moscow, which is a novelty to many outside observers, another surprise comes from a recent cost-of-living survey from Mercer Human Resource Consulting (2006) that offers extraordinary data. Moscow now holds the title of the world's most expensive city for expatriate, or foreign, employees to live in, edging out Tokyo, which ranked first for four straight years and is 24 percent more expensive than New York. Moscow ranked fourth last year, according to the 2005 survey, but rose to the top of the list in 2006 for several reasons. First, the currencies of Tokyo, Osaka, and London—the top three cities in 2005—fell relative to the U.S. dollar, while the ruble remained almost stable. In addition, in 2006, the price of housing for expatriates in Moscow rose considerably. To give a concrete example of how much the cost of living differs in various cities, Mercer Consulting priced out the cost of a two-bedroom unfurnished apartment, a cup of coffee, a fast-food meal, and an international newspaper. Amazingly, the research showed that in Moscow an apartment would run $3,000, a cup of coffee $5.27, a newspaper $3.40, and a burger with fries $3.87. In international business, the cost of living for foreign workers is an important aspect to take into consideration.

On the other side, the latest sign of Russia's wealth explosion—a 5,000-ruble banknote—equates to $195 in U.S. dollars as of July 2007. This new 5,000-ruble banknote has been in circulation since July 31, 2006. The last time Russia had a 5,000-ruble banknote was in 1998, just before the ruble crash in August that year. With it, the Russian Central Bank wants to reduce the bulge in the wallets of the country's growing affluent circles and rising real incomes, and give Russia a currency commensurate with its superpower status. Another sign of strength for the ruble was that it was made fully convertible at the start of July 2006, six months ahead of schedule. In addition, the Central Bank has launched a competition to find a universally recognizable symbol for its currency—akin to the $ denoting the U.S. dollar. Muscovites seem to favor the *R* with two Euroesque horizontal lines running through the center.

Even critics of the Kremlin cannot disagree that Russians are becoming richer on average. As a not too surprising result, luxury items worth more than one billion euros were exported from Italy to Russia during 2006 alone and the import of new cars is expected to rise from over 300,000 in 2005 to over 700,000 in 2014.

Forbes and the Russian Billionaires

To correctly interpret Russia from an ethical perspective, we need to analyze the many and sometimes controversial obstacles that it faces, beginning with its billionaires. *Forbes* magazine is all about wealth. The way *Forbes* ranks billionaires is a realistic and useful way to begin to compare Moscow and New York. The much-renowned magazine is located in a building located along Manhattan's Fifth Avenue. It is home to journalists who inquire into and concoct the hit parade of the fortunes of the richest people in the world, as if building up enormous fortunes is nothing anomalous.

This publication helps us understand facts too relevant not to be explored here. The accumulation of wealth gives us a new perspective and new insight into Russian development. We recognize the new Russia—the one that has abandoned communism and is now emerging from a long period of fallacious expectations proffered to workers and ordinary people. However, what is the fallout in a system that—after enduring a seventy-year period of conservative and highly structured governmental regulation—has been driven toward a more liberal state of affairs by the communists themselves? Perhaps that class of communist *nomenklatura* formed since the 1960s drove a hard bargain during the late 1980s and early 1990s. If false democracy, deceitful social and economic equalities, and disruptive paternalism characterized the early years of noncommunist Russia, what can we expect from the modern Russia of Putin's era?

In *Forbes's* March 2007 ranking of a total of 946 wealthy people, there were 178 newcomers on the list. A number of Russians obviously knew which way to turn during the passage to noncommunist days, while others did not. They are worth a combined $3.5 trillion, calculates *Forbes*; the average billionaire is sixty two years old. Strong stock markets, rising real estate values, and higher commodity prices around the world contributed to this surge in wealth and the 178 newcomers. "Ingenuity, not industry, is the common characteristic; these folks made money in everything from media and real estate to coffee, dumplings and ethanol ... Of list members' fortunes, 60% made theirs from scratch," writes *Forbes* (2007). And Russia is not excluded from this method of creating wealth as nineteen newcomer Russians enter a list of fifty three. Suffice it also to say now that among the top one hundred richest people in the world, there are fourteen Russians whose ages range from thirty nine to fifty eight.

Moscow's RTS stock exchange resulted in an increase of 108 percent on strong gains in commodities prices. While the beginnings of such fortunes go back fifteen years (although only a couple of Russians were originally on the *Forbes* list), the surge in the stock exchange swelled the fortunes of some. In the *Forbes* list, the Russians exhibited a net worth of $172 billion this year, up from $91 billion a year before, based largely on oil and gas prices and the expansion of steel and bank markets. In contrast, China now had eight billionaires, four times as many as the year before.

In the world's top twenty, *Forbes* ranks Roman Abramovich exactly sixteenth. Abramovich, a fourty-year old Russian oil baron, governor of roughly 50,000 inhabitants of the Chukotka region, and owner of London's Chelsea football club, sold his stake in Sibneft last year to Gazprom for $13 billion. He currently has a net worth of $18.7 billion, up from $14.7 billion two years ago. Others in the top-100 list include the fourty one-year-old Suleiman Kerimov, thirty fifth. Vagit Alekperov (age fifty six)—the chief executive of oil giant Lukoil (Russia's largest private oil company)—ranks fourty eighth, with $12.4 billion in assets. Oleg Deripaska, fourty—known as "king of Russian aluminum"—is fourtyth in the list of world's richest men ($13.3 billion) and married Polina Yumasheva in 2001, Boris Yeltsin's step-granddaughter; he owns Russian car maker GAZ, the Samara-based Aviakor plane factory, the insurance company Ingosstrakh, the bus maker RusPromAuto, and Ruskii Aluminii (Rusal) company, the largest such company in Russia. Steel tycoon Vladimir Lisin (fifty) is ranked thirty sixth with $14.3 billion. Viktor Vekselberg—who co-owns the Russian-British joint venture TNK-BP and the big aluminum group, SUAL—places sixty first with $10.4 billion.

Oil industry magnet Mikhail Fridman, fourty two, is fourty fifth in *Forbes's* most recent rankings, with assets totaling $12.6 billion. Another important name is former Kremlin insider Vladimir Potanin, who was one of the biggest winners from the loans-for-shares privatization schemes of the 1990s. At the age of fourty six, Potanin is listed thirty eigthth on the *Forbes* billionaires list with $13.5 billion in personal wealth. Potanin is a major entrepreneur in the metal sector with Norilsk Nickel—the world's biggest producer of nickel and platinum—but his luck began in the banking sector. The tycoon Boris Berezovsky, sixty one, who has lived exiled in London since 2003, ranks 840th and has a fortune estimated at $1.1 billion. The only Russian woman to appear on the *Forbes* list in 2007 is Yelena

Baturina, the owner of a flourishing construction business, who ranks 279th with $3.1 billion. She is the wife of Moscow mayor Yuri Luzhkov.

Forbes dropped oil tycoon Mikhail Khodorkovsky (once Russia's richest man) from its top list after he was found guilty of fraud and theft and his company auctioned off. He is currently serving an eight-year prison sentence in an Eastern Siberia penal colony; however, his article and "rescue plans" to revive Russia, which I consider in the course of this chapter, along with the many westerners who voice his case, prove that his name is not cut off from outside world.

Oligarchs or simply billionaires are now using their fortunes and swelling bank accounts to internationalize and invest outside of Russia. In contrast to the 1990s, the goal now is not to put assets beyond the reach of the Russian authorities as some did or to work with some western institution on cleaning up their image and having an immaculate track record, but to invest whenever they find financial opportunities. In a world in which much bigger profits can be made by following aggressive international strategies, they are building up interests ranging from property to high-technology industry and some of their purchases represent the very first foray into new advanced businesses ever made by and in Russia.

The Broader Logic of This Story

The dramatic power of such events could not fail to affect the course of Russian history and became the backdrop for the disparities and disputes that currently plague Russian society. These facts about modern Russia are surprising to many people. Much of the astonishment lies in the fact that Russia was on the verge of an inescapable economic and political crash in the 1990s. In contrast with what people remember from the early years of the *first vision* of a modern Russia, Russia is once again a premier actor in the international panorama, enjoying a geostrategic visibility and voice at the table of world affairs. With Russia now looking stronger and more influential at the international level, however, ordinary Russians shoulder the burden of the unbalanced income distribution, unequal managerial skills, and diverse business opportunities in their country. These inequities are the result of what happened in the top political circles in Moscow in the 1990s. In many ways, the socioeconomic revelations coming out of Russia are some of the most important issues under analysis today. The way that Russian domestic affairs developed in the 1990s—with control of national resources and national enterprises in the hands of a few—became a dangerous situation in terms of social sustainability and the long-term credibility of Russian politics and society. This became progressively more frightening, both nationally and internationally.

Therefore, international comparison of capitalist culture can assist us in understanding the rationale of Russia's leaders during that period and help in identifying the socioeconomic troubles that have resulted from the absolutely right but ill-conceived and anomalous abandoning of communism. Instead of starting from the presumption that Putin's Kremlin has changed everything for the worse, we should focus on broadening existing knowledge rather than reacting with dismay and giving a misleading impression of a country that was in the 1990s much too vulnerable to pressures from powerful groups. The core of the issue is that we must understand the raison d'être of Vladimir Putin's politics, to understand why it therefore has gathered momentum, and this book aspires to offer a courageous perspective on Russia and Putin by relating these questions to moral principles, to the public, and to international observers who did not fully perceive the long-term risks of uneven wealth distribution and business opportunities.

The many connections between these factors and the manner in which these features interacted domestically, coupled with the new international dimensions of this boundless country, cause anxiety about Russia's political strategies and the future of its society. All said, the majority of western observers do not defend the illegal misbehavior of the oligarchs; they still do not seem likely to justify the Kremlin's methods of dealing with them. In fact, fears mounted that the Kremlin had possibly exaggerated the issue. In parallel, the press—intellectuals who were impressed by these good-hearted persons who were donating money to western institutions, although for unknown financial reasons—stepped up criticism on the new Kremlin policies.

People like Boris Berezovsky, Vladimir Gusinsky, and Mikhail Khodorkovsky have become well known in the West. These names, among others, and their legal cases have come to be known both by Kremlinologists and western media. While I concentrate here on three examples, I do not deal with the questions of legal principles arising from these cases nor do I offer any legal opinion or guidance. Cases are based largely on available information already subjected to scrutiny, sometimes leading to very severe conclusions by other scholars, and firm complaints by those were involved in these affairs. Overall, the arrest of these men or their forced flight into exile must remain within a pure legal sphere of analysis, which is beyond the scope of these pages.

Mikhail Khodorkovsky and the Yukos Affair

Mikhail Khodorkovsky was a member of the Komsomol, as were many other millionaires. He fleshed out a small bank charter for Bank Menatep, and become Russia's richest man. Khodorkovski was able to acquire more than 80 percent of the ownership of Yukos, Russia's second-biggest oil company, for little more than \$300 million, despite the fact that Yukos was apparently worth \$5 billion, writes Marshall Goldman (2003, 2004). This happened very simply—Bank Menatep won an auction by lending some \$159 million to a Russian government that was short on cash. This loan, as well the others made during the loans-for-shares privatization scheme of the mid-1990s, was secured by 45 percent of Yukos shares. In addition, a subsidiary of Bank Menatep (Monblan) won another bank note for 38 percent of Yukos shares on the same day. When the government formed after Yeltsin's reelection in July 1996 was unable to pay back the loans by the due date of September 1996, Bank Menatep became the majority owner of Yukos, and Khodorkovsky became Yukos's chief executive officer.

Bank Menatep was able to supply Khodorkovsky cash from Russians' savings accounts, and the bank was allegedly involved in the Bank of New York money-laundering scheme. The money-laundering scheme involved simply moving ill achieved gains through a series of bank accounts and a byzantine labyrinth of offshore corporations made such gains look like legitimate business proceeds. In the end, this served to move funds out of Russia without payment of customs duties and taxes. From 1996 to 1999, the Bank of New York (and its London offices) is alleged to have taken part in a money-laundering scheme in which Russia suffered billions of losses. It is also suspected that Russian organized crime may have siphoned hundreds of millions of dollars of foreign aid that had been pumped into Russia by the International Monetary Fund, funds originally intended to aid the country's economic efforts at stabilization.

A study conducted by the CIA on input provided by the Federal Reserve claimed that half of Russia's banks during the 1990s were controlled by the Mafia, and Bank Menatep was the only one named in the report, according to Goldman (2003). According to Goldman, Khodorkovsky diverted those assets to a subsidiary in St.Petersburg, well beyond the reach of ordinary Russian investors and creditors, and only provided some token compensation after the government intervened. Instead of helping depositors, "Khodorkovsky took whatever sound assets he could salvage and diverted them to a subsidiary in St. Petersburg, beyond the reach of his creditors" (Goldman, 2004: 37). In addition, Khodorkovsky was disloyal to big investors as well, including Amoco (later BP Amoco) that had invested money in an oil-producing subsidiary that Khodorkovsky seized and stripped of its assets, according to Goldman (2003, 2004).

Khodorkovsky was also accused of plotting an oligarchic coup before he was arrested on tax and fraud charges, and sentenced by the Meshchansky court of Moscow to a total of nine years in prison—eight of which will be spent in a cell in the Chita region, close to the Chinese border. Platon Lebedev, the chairman of the Bank Menatep and a major stock holder of Yukos, was accused of stealing shares of stock in the Apatit chemical plant in 1994—a charge he denied—and sentenced and locked up in the freezing Siberian region of Yamalonenetsk. When Khodorkovsky was arrested, the people's support for Putin rose from 70 to 80 percent. The majority of Russians perceived these sentences not to be a blow to a fresh, growing democracy and they accused oligarchs of bearing full responsibility for the ethical shift in Russia's politics and behavior. Such a very negative way of thinking about the nastiest aspects of oligarchy was remarkable coming from ordinary Russians and it underlined a real change in people's attitudes as well as widespread and mounting disappointment among Russian citizens who blamed oligarchs and 1990s political circles for having been driven to cement their business interests and dampening the likelihood of forging a genuine market economy in Russia. I could interpret this general feeling as a renewed pledge to stop the overwhelming power of certain business oligarchs in Moscow: the general feeling of Russians should not come as a big surprise to us in the West. The Russian Trading System Stock Exchange (RTS) index—established in 1995 and based on fifty of the most liquid Russian securities—fell after Khodorkovsky's arrest, but only temporarily.

But let us examine the Yukos case, which began in the autumn of 2003. Tax authorities have actually been accusing Yukos, its subsidiaries, and other companies of using illegal schemes to decrease tax payments by billions of dollars. Regardless of the fact that these firms intend to contest tax obligations, nobody can avoid the reality that leftover communist-era *nomenklatura* cheated Russians out of billions in resources and paid little to no taxes thereafter. According to tax authorities, Yukos had to pay a tax bill of only $3.4 billion in 2000 and $3.3 billion in 2001, and the Yukos daughter company, Tomskneft, was accused of tax evasion in the amount of $114 million in 2001—equaling almost $25 billion for both companies combined.

Interestingly, in October 2003 the merger of Yukos and Sibneft was announced: this merger would have created Russia's largest oil corporation and the fourth-largest oil company in the world behind BP, ExxonMobil, and Royal Dutch-Shell. In fact, a merger between these two oil companies was first attempted in 1998, but it failed because of disagreement over management issues. The merger idea was resuscitated, and the resulting company would have enjoyed a joint daily production of 2.3 million barrels. ExxonMobil—the world's number one oil company, out of Texas—would have purchased 40 percent of oil produced by the new company. The presence of a foreign company in a very powerful, controlling position was very worrisome to some Russians. Russian authorities thought that this implied that strategic reserves were being sold to foreigners. It was also argued that this step was intended to prevent a joint venture of the company with oil companies from the United States, because of the concern that collaboration would mean most of the benefit would go to foreigners rather than Russians.

Chevron-Texaco (the second-biggest oil company in the United States) was also interested in a 25 percent stake of Yukos. After the initial difficulties facing the Yukos-Sibneft merger as it was agreed upon in 2003, the antitrust minister authorized it. The Yukos fraud and tax evasion case, however, stopped that merger.

Yukos's main oil production unit, Yuganskneftegaz—which produced roughly 60 percent of Yukos's oil—was sold a couple of days before Christmas of 2004 to pay off the company's unpaid taxes. Russia's antimonopoly service managed the auction that was eventually won by the Baikal Finance Group. This was a little-known firm registered in the provincial Russian town of Tver, located in the same building as Gazprom, which bid on and bought 76.79 percent of

Yuganskneftegaz shares for $9.34 billion, even though the net worth of Yukos's shares was between $14 billion and $24 billion, according to various analysts. In this way, the Russian antimonopoly service took care of selling Yukos's key assets. Gazprom denied having any type of links to the Baikal Finance Group, but the populace quickly understood that the state-controlled gas giant or other state interests had had a hand in the winning bid.

Said auction came under suspicion because it could potentially hide two separate issues from view. First, there was the repeated injury of purchasing assets that were not at market prices. Second, it could have been a tactic to evade a temporary U.S. court ruling, in light of Yukos's defense of its bankruptcy application against arguments by Deutsche Bank that the Moscow-based company had no right to Chapter 11 protection in the United States. Yukos had only two bank accounts and Bruce Misamore—the expert chief financial officer who was hired by Khodorkovsky in 2001 in an attempt to bring western practices to Yukos—was based in Texas. In February 2005, however, Judge Letitia Clark dismissed the case, saying Yukos's limited presence in the United States was not adequate to qualify for Chapter 11 protection. The Russian gas monopoly Gazprom was named in the U.S. court order and was widely seen as a favorite to win the bidding war for Yuganskneftegaz, which would have put Gazprom in direct violation of the U.S. court, which had already prohibited Gazprom's plans to get funding for Yuganskneftegaz from a consortium of foreign banks, including Deutsche Bank and J.P. Morgan.

A broad Kremlin strategy was to make the three big companies—i.e., Gazprom, Rosneft, and Sibneft—into just one giant state company. The first step was the merger between Rosneft and Gazprom, which was established after the configuration of Rosneft's purchase of Yuganskneftegaz. But this did not go through. Simply put, Rosneft had acquired Baikal Finance Group, which had paid a $1.7-billion deposit to participate in the auction, for just 10,000 rubles, about $358. It is reported that Rosneft paid the balance of $7.65 billion for Yuganskneftegaz into Court Marshals Service accounts in MDM Bank on New Year's Eve. Investors and bankers said that other state banks—such as Vneshtorgbank and Vneshekonombank and possibly Surgutneftegaz, the country's fourth oil producer—might have helped to finance the Rosneft transaction.

Then state-controlled banks helped a state-controlled oil company purchase a controlling stake in Yuganskneftegaz, which was being sold by the state for tax debts owed to and defined by the state. We have no evidence of misdeeds by the Kremlin from a purely jurisdictional point of view, despite the fact that the chairmen of Gazprom's management commitee, Alexandar Medvedev, and Igor Sechin—who is deputy chief of Kremlin's presidential staff and became Rosneft's chairperson in the summer of 2004—are closely allied with Putin. Rosneft paid $7.65 billion through state-controlled Sberbank to take control of the Baikal Finance Group. After that, Rosneft agreed to a merger with Gazprom in 2004, but this endeavor ended in May 2005 due to difficulties in procedures and corporate management, and these reasons left Rosneft independent. Had this merger gone through, China National Petroleum Corporation would have acquired $6 billion in crude oil in advance for the following five years in exchange for supporting the financial cost of this acquisition.

Meanwhile the original Kremlin plan to merge Gazprom, Rosneft, and Sibneft into one giant state company partially failed as mentioned previously, and Gazprom was able to take out $12 billion in syndicated loans from a consortium of six western commercial banks—including ABN Amro and Dresdner Bank—in order to purchase Sibneft in 2005. This deal gave the Kremlin control over one-third of Russia's pumped crude oil as of the end of 2005. The Gazprom purchase of Sibneft was the largest transaction in modern Russian history and was thereby dubbed the "buy of the decade" and placed third on the list of cash acquisitions in the energy sector worldwide. Afterward, shareholders in Sibneft voted to rename the company after Gazprom purchased 72.633 percent of Sibneft for $13.01 billion in September 2005—Gazprom already held 3.02 percent of Sibneft through its banking unit, Gazprombank. In the end, Sibneft became GazpromNeft.

Nevertheless, Yukos had planned to sell about $10 billion of Russian and overseas iron-core assets to clear its remaining tax liability of $7.5 billion and bank debt of $1.3 billion. Rising oil prices and foreign sales activity reduced Yukos's actual debt to $6 billion. Yukos wanted to sell Mazeiku Nafta (which controls the Lithuanian terminal of Butinge, the only refinery in the Baltic States) and other overseas enterprises. Yukos management also claimed that the company owned 23 percent of Yuganskneftegaz and 20 percent of Sibneft—some $21 billion at market prices.

To have a clearer picture of events in this sector, it is important to note that the Moscow Appeals Court overturned an earlier Moscow Arbitration Court ruling that allowed western banks to pursue their $475 million claim against Yukos in Russia. Yukos was facing $12 billion in legal claims from Yuganskneftegaz, its former subsidiary acquired by the Baikal Finance Group/Rosneft, as I said. Yuganskneftegaz's former managers were also being investigated by law enforcement agencies in the autonomous Khanty-Mansiisk district for large-scale tax evasion of about two billion rubles. But as of August 2006, Russian authorities had declared bankruptcy, and all that remained of Yukos's old assets had to be liquidated, and proceeds from the liquidation of assets used to satisfy creditors. Russia's prosecutor general accused former Yukos managers of asset theft due to their alleged attempt to keep the company's overseas assets out of the reach of bankruptcy liquidators. While Yukos managers were claiming that the assets were worth in excess of $18 billion, the liquidators claimed that the company's assets were worth more like $15 to $16 billion. Russian and foreign companies jumped into this bidding. At this writing, it is expected that the liquidation procedure will last for more than one year and involve quite a number of shares, but what was once the country's biggest oil production company now no longer exists.

Putin's then-chief economic advisor, Andrei Illarionov, and the then prime minister Mikhail Kasyanov, criticized the judiciary action against Yukos. Notably Illarionov, speaking at a news conference in December 2004 and commenting on Russia's economic progress in 2004, openly declared that the sale of the core production asset of Yukos to the "mystical Baikal Finance Group" and the attempted activities on the merger of Gazprom and Rosneft were the "fraud of the year" (MosNews.com, 2004). Yet during the following year, the same Yukos case did not prompt any interest, even in Harvard circles (*Economic Newsletter*, No. 3, 2005). Besides the so-called Harvard scandal, a doubtful criticism arising even from top Russian circles exemplifies the complexity of the case and the several intrigues surrounding transition in Moscow which I illuminate throughout this book.

Despite his misfortunes, Khodorkovsky, through his followers, recently suggested a plan to revive Russia (MosNews.com 2005). According to him, Russia should enact a twelve-year plan of action to turn the country into a truly socialist and legitimate state and respond to the problems arising from society to prevent it from sliding it into authoritarianism. Astonishingly, he suggests that Russia should turn left toward its communist past. He does not explain the logic of this left turn, when the world knows how communism worked and what the transition period of the 1990s produced, nor does he touch on the issue of the profound economic and social distortions created by the class of tycoons of which he was once a major representative. Russia needs a president who is a moral leader and guarantor of the state's integrity, says Khodorkovsky. According to him, a strong parliament should have power over all economic and social programs to force a revival of federalism; should put an end to an oil-dependent economy by achieving a national structure where the knowledge industry accounts for some 40 percent, heavy industries for 40 percent, and farming for remaining 20 percent; should build a strong army; should revive the education system; restore the social security system; and more. While Khodorkovsky calculates that this long-term plan would require about $400 billion in government investment and roughly $500 billion in private investment, he does not offer any details of how to make it happen, nor does he address the contradictions of this plan when an external observer evaluates it in terms of what is actually going on in Russia today. Despite his legal case, which raises deep concerns about fairness, and despite the sympathies he enjoyed in the West, due also to his philanthropic giving, I have difficulty identifying him with these sorts of free-market policies.

Boris Berezovsky and His Many Businesses

The other well-known case that has been debated in the West is that of Boris Berezovsky. A former car dealer, Berezovsky had formed the LogoVaz automotive company by 1989, writes Paul Klebnikov (2000) in *Godfather of the Kremlin:*

Boris Berezovsky and the Looting of Russia. *Forbes*, in its December 30, 1996, issue, introduced Berezovsky as follows: "Is He the Godfather of the Kremlin? Power, Politics, Murder. Boris Berezovsky can teach the guys in Sicily a thing or two."

Berezovsky acquired several oil properties that he merged into Sibneft for some $100 million when the government sold 51 percent of Sibneft at the end of 1996 (along with his close partner at that time, Roman Abramovich, who recently sold his stake in Sibneft to Gazprom in 2005). It was widely accepted as true that the company's real value was much higher than the fraction that the new rich businessperson actually paid.

Also, Berezovsky used this windfall to acquire large stakes in state companies, including the car giant AutoVAZ, state airline Aeroflot (that Berezovsky acquired for an trivial sum when the government sold off the control shares of Aeroflot), oil properties, aluminum, and mass media, thus moving from obscurity to being the richest businessman in Russia and one of the closest members of President Yeltsin's inner circle.

Attempts to get control over state wealth came amid renewed signs of how important the creation of new commercial banks had become at that time in the pursuit of business schemes, to the detriment of general interests. Berezovsky founded a bank to finance the aforementioned operations and acquired several news media holdings, some of them from the state. For example, when Yeltsin privatized Channel 1, which reached all Russians, without the legally required auction, it was "acquired" by Berezovsky, whose capital actually was only a meager couple of million dollars.

All these activities provided support for Yeltsin's reelection in 1996, and after that, Berezovsky acquired further power. His political career was impressive as he rose up the ladder to serve as deputy secretary of the Security Council of the Russian Federation in October 1996, and executive secretary of the Commonwealth of Independent States (CIS)—which grouped twelve of the former Soviet republics in April 1998—before being dismissed by Yeltsin in March 1999 for exceeding the limits of his executive authority and for failing to implement the instructions of the chairman of the Council of the CIS heads of states. Berezovsky definitely fell out of favor, however, when Vladimir Putin gained the presidency in 2000, and he left Russia at the end of that year, after an investigation was launched accusing him of siphoning cash from Aeroflot and committing large-scale fraud in his LogoVaz car company.

Besides business activity, Berezovsky founded his own political party (Liberal Russia) in 2001 to oppose Putin and promote notions of free-market policies while putting what occurred in the 1990s in the past. Berezovsky also spent $10 million on funding opposition to Putin, and said he might invest his fortune in organizing a coup in Russia to "reestablish" the Russian constitution by 2008 (MosNews.com, 2006).

In March 2003, he was arrested in London but released on bail, and he sought and received political asylum in the United Kingdom in October that year. Meanwhile, his stake in Russia's major television company ORT—now First Channel and run by an alleged man from the FSB—was sold, and a ruling of the Russian Arbitration Court closed down his TV6 channel. Although extradition is technically possible, a British court rejected a Russian extradition request in June 2006 and, in fact, Britain has refused to extradite other high-profile Russians who continue to live in exile in London because of accusations that Russia's enforcement authorities allegedly resort to unfair practices and unfair trials.

In November 2006, Britain and Russia signed a memorandum of understanding enabling Russian prosecutors to cooperate directly with the UK Crown Prosecution Service when drawing up extradition requests. Although London has become an asylum for some Russians accused of several type of wrongdoing, this recent deal will probably change nothing about extradition requests for some exiles in London. In addition, accusations against the Kremlin continue: an alleged plot to kill the Russian tycoon was reported by British authorities in July 2007, and he promptly accused the Kremlin of being behind it, a charge denied by Moscow.

Vladimir Gusinsky and the Media

In 1988, in the wake of Gorbachev's authorization of cooperatives, Vladimir Gusinsky formed Most, a consulting firm that ultimately became Media-MOST. This enterprise ventured out in several directions, from construction to banking and media, speculating on foreign exchange and federal state securities. By 1994, a subsidiary of Most, Most-Bank, became one of the largest banks operating in Russia. Together with other well-known oligarchs, Gusinsky consolidated forces in the banking sector through mergers like that of Most-Bank, Bank Menatep, and Onexim Bank, to form Rosbank.

After Yeltsin won reelection in 1996, Gusinsky was given the country's first private television network, NTV, and became owner of the majority stake. His media conglomerate, Media-MOST, expanded to include a satellite communications network, a series of radio stations, and magazines. The western media treated Gusinsky's June 2000 arrest by the Kremlin's chief prosecutor on suspicion of embezzlement as part of a crackdown on Russia's independent media. Immediately following Gusinsky's arrest, seventeen other top businessmen signed a letter of protest, claiming that the Yeltsin type of immunity was at risk. The charges were connected to the purchase of a state-owned television station in St. Petersburg in the mid-1990s. The charges were denied by Gusinsky's media company, and he was subsequently released. He has lived abroad, according to Gusinsky's supporters, since the summer of 2001. Yet, most Moscow journalists claimed that a truly free press was largely lost when the tycoons took control of the national broadcasting and newspaper companies.

After Gusinsky fell into disgrace and in exile, Gazprom claimed the credit and seized NTV with the U.S. Capital Research and Management Group. A Russian court also ordered the liquidation of Media-MOST, and gave Gazprom 25 percent plus one share of all companies once owned by Media-MOST. Gazprom also took control of and closed Gusinsky's first newspaper *Sevodnya*, and fired and locked out the staff of the news magazine *Igoti*. Malicious rumors concerning the firing of NTV's director Evgenj Kiselev have been linked to the harsh, anti-Putin TV campaign during the presidential election in 2004, malicious voices said in Moscow.

We have seen that business groups have been at the center of a series of alleged cases of doubtful privatization episodes, money-laundering schemes, and the funnelling out of Russia of billions of dollars in funds. Capital flight schemes and money-laundering operations suggest that enormous amounts of money disappeared and overall some $350 billion in capital may have fled the country just during the 1990s, with the flow of funds having accelerated since the crash of the ruble in August 1998. If commercial banks were increasingly becoming a focus of investigation, elaborated games have become a dominant feature of Russia's 1990s and commercial banks sought to control the entire country. If Russian commercial banks might have became platforms for insiders seeking to move money out of the country or control national resources rather than intermediaries for domestic economic growth, the fear that the 1990s would be an obstacle to the process of democracy and market building moved to a new worry. Powerful, self-interested economic actors gained control over the state for their own advantage, to the enormous loss of the entire Russian society. If the West has always underestimated oligarchy and the game oligarchs pursued buying politicians and bureaucrats for their own interest, such private interests radically contradicted those of the society at large and of the country's economy, too. A partial renationalization of selected companies may be seen in this light in a larger battle over state stability. The role of the oil and natural gas industry is the next logical step of my analysis and the focus of the next chapter.

Chapter Seven

Russia into the 2000s: Oil and Gas Bonanza

Colossal crude oil and natural gas reserves have long been marvelous opportunities to improve any country's chances at economic growth. Ample reserves of these natural resources could turn out to be a bonanza. However, if a country becomes overly dependent on these resources, its economy may fall into the so-called "Dutch disease." This disease can be traced back to the discovery of natural gas off the shores of Holland during the 1960s and the subsequent adverse effects on that economy's manufacturing system—which was quite prosperous at that time—due to a high exchange rate that arose after the increased exporting of discovered gas. In the context of modern Russia, one could compare the Dutch situation with a similar situation in the non-oil-tradable sector that might endanger Russia's economic future should the country be unable to develop a more balanced economic growth.

In any case, wealth has proven to be a key resource in most of the cases of oil cartel OPEC and other oil-exporting countries. Likewise, wealth can be distributed quite unevenly and unfairly within a country, such as in the Arabic sheikdoms, or become a lucrative source for current governments that violently seize the resources, with military spending eating up most of the revenues, as the case of Sudan. On the other hand, some countries, such as Norway, find a proper natural resource equilibrium. Russia could conceivably transform the oil industry into a major growth and social engine for the betterment of the country.

Despite the fact that Russia has been a relevant crude oil producer for the past 130 years, oil production has not yet spurred much economic growth for the country nor affected Russia's overall international political power. Nor has Russia been clearly hurt by any "Dutch disease" or by the associated loss of competitiveness in the recent past, although these could still surface. That is, these natural resources did not turn out to be either a curse or a bonanza for Moscow. Yet, importantly, perspectives are much different today because Russia is a world player, giving the country an unrivaled stake, to say the least. Nevertheless, this crown jewel of oil production is a double-edged sword in Russia, as it resulted in huge complications during the 1990s, but it has ultimately served to reveal very positive consequences on the country's future.

In post-Putin Russia, world energy markets and the link between Russia's economic growth and oil and gas exports will depend critically on the continuation of good economic reforms. As hydrocarbons continue to be significant components of Russia's economic growth, the debate over this industry could eventually devolve into a discussion of the alleged hegemony of Moscow concerning the political use of these commodities. Without becoming too anecdotal, we must develop an understanding of oil industry growth in general as well as the Russian strategy—specifically, how Russia collaborates with foreign companies—to show that charges of isolationism or the image of Russia as closed to the rest of the world is wrong. Thinking that Russia might resort to stopping the piping of gas and oil at the flick of a switch is unjustified. This conjecture is economic nonsense, given the Russian economy's strong dependence on the revenue from these exports. Even if Moscow becomes an even stronger key player of gas reserves, and this is coupled with excellent geographical circumstances and more general political stability than exists in the Middle East, Russia's economic and political power in the coming years will not transform this industry into a political weapon. This oil bonanza still requires a prudent international strategy, a sensible domestic approach, and a shrewd use of resources for all.

If coal and atomic energy are the two largest sources of energy production, oil and gas will continue to have great impact during the next several decades, and transitioning away from them will not be easy or inexpensive. These realities are the start of the modern Russian strategic move into the gas and oil realms, and they provide relevant points of departure for analysis.

Two Reasons

Russia sits atop huge gas and oil reserves and the proper control of these commodities—as aforesaid—is of the utmost importance to Russia these days for two main reasons. First, the country has been reliant on oil and gas riches in the recent past. Russia shows one of the highest outcomes among producer countries of government budget and economic performance based on the export of these resources. Russia has benefited very much from the export of oil and gas. As the export indicators of crude oil and refined oil products accounted for roughly two-thirds of Russia's total export income in 2006, the relevance of this sector for the entire country is clear. Due to the steep rise in crude oil and gas prices, the effects on the country's budget have been exceptional, representing about 40 percent of consolidated budget revenue. And as the export and the inflow of investment and technology toward this industry are equally essential factors, Finance Minister Alexei Kudrin has recommended changing the overall budget structure, devoting larger shares for economic and social needs, limiting pressures on inflation, and developing legislation to limit the deficit in the non-oil budget. Kudrin's vision of how to handle Russia's oil dependence was right on the money; note that in the Duma-approved federal budget for 2007, the expenditure structure remains quite stable. In sum, this will be a hot issue for years to come.

To get a true picture of the situation, the second reason has to be understood well. This is the issue of diversification, which should continue to dominate both the economic and political landscapes. (Diversification means that the country cannot base its economic fortune and future on one source of income.) If oil and gas are two exceptional sources of revenues, realistically long-term growth has to be tied to a broader economic base, i.e., industry, SMEs, services, etc.

While control over this market and its collateral segments of the economy produced unethical chaos in 1990s, the exact impact of this market on Russian past and future policy choices deserves review. In present-day Russia, the Kremlin administration acts as a powerhouse through state-owned gas and oil companies, as well as through tax policy that governs the revenues from the industry's export activity. Russia is using those mounting tax revenues for national projects that aim to improve housing, education, and health care, etc., as well as to open up networking relationships with western and Asian governments and private companies.

To bring together the past and future of this industry in Russia, not least important has been Putin's 2006 State of the Nation address. Putin recently introduced the case for transitioning to a ruble oil-trading mechanism, that is, the creation of a national energy market that only uses rubles. According to Putin, Russia is now strong enough to consider this mechanism as a way of replenishing state finances. Moreover, if Russia originally had an interest in adopting the euro in light of the large amount of trade with Western Europe, Russia might now consider switching to the ruble along with China and Japan to facilitate trade with these countries, but this all fits in with Russia's ambitious agenda. This inspiration was presented to Russians only as a long-term project. Although the American dollar is the standard currency for the oil industry today—the two main oil exchanges are the New York Metal Exchange and the International Petroleum Exchange in London, and will remain so in the long-term—any potential devaluation of the dollar could put further pressure on Russian authorities to institute such an oil exchange. Although discussion of such a reality is premature, in theory it could provide Russia with a strong reserve status and benefit the Russian economy by using rubles instead of foreign currency—sparking new waves of foreign investment in Russian industries.

In this evolving context, the West continues to apply a double standard when accusing the Russian Kremlin of having a dissolute strategy for setting prices and a "strategic" export strategy, and monopolizing national resources.

The World of Oil

The past serves as a base upon which one can draw a vivid inquiry into Russian energy markets and challenges. The oil price crisis of 1973–1974 and 1979 resulted in a new geopolitical strategy on the part of the United States to control the oil supply in the Persian Gulf. These policies became a reality in 1975, when former secretary of state Henry Kissinger argued that the United States was prepared to go to war over oil. The sticker shock of previous years could have had a different impact on Russia's revenues and strategy. The world economy currently consumes about 85 million barrels of oil per day and consumption increased by 2.7 percent in 2005, with the strongest increase of 5.8 percent in the Asia Pacific region. Gas consumption grew by 2.3 percent, with the largest gains in China, but its consumption decreased in the United States by 1.5 percent. The market keeps growing despite signs of geopolitical risk.

The United States consumed slightly less that 20.6 million barrels a day in 2006 (-1.3 percent over 2005), and China was the world's second-largest oil consumer with 7.4 million barrels daily (Chinese consumption grew nearly 6.7 percent over 2005). Over the last ten years, global oil demand has gone from 70 million barrels per day to the current rate of 83.7 million in 2006 (BP, 2007). *The World Energy Outlook 2006*, published by the International Energy Agency—the Paris-based energy policy advisor to twenty-six member countries (more expected to join) in their effort to ensure reliable, affordable, and clean energy—expects that U.S. oil consumption could increase another 32 percent by 2025. It is possible that a general rise in oil and gas demand together with surging demand from China and India could keep the price of oil going up. Russia's prospects for feeding world demand for petroleum are incredibly sizeable but bring in ethical issues about how to manage these resources with wisdom. Michael Ellman's (2006) book, *Russia's Oil and Natural Gas: Bonanza or Curse?* sketches a number of viewpoints on this subject. But suffice it to say at the outset concerning the totality of oil exporters that their overall revenues from oil and gas exports exceeded $1,500 billion in 2006, quite a large sum on which to build economic growth.

Gas reserves in European Union countries account for about 1.3 percent of proven global reserves (BP (British Petroleum), 2007) and a relevant share of gas imports by Western Europe is provided by pipeline shipments from Russia. China holds only 1.3 percent of gas reserves, with India holding 0.6 percent and Japan holding none. As for petroleum, reserves in the European Union account for 0.5 percent, China 1.3 percent, and India 0.5 percent. Russia is the second major producer, and a leading exporter, in the world of petroleum. Another piece of key data in order to substantiate the logic of what is occurring in Europe is that Russia has a daily surplus, while the United States and the European Union have an energy deficit. Russia supplies gas to almost all Western European countries, where it has exported about 156 billion cubic meters in 2005. That is, roughly 60 percent of Russia's oil exports and half of its gas exports go to EU countries.

I want to bring in other actualities. One: the consumption of oil and gas will not be eradicated in the short and medium term, and will continue well into the next several decades—the International Energy Agency (2006) forecasts that the annual growth of energy demand should be about 4.7 percent in China and 2.2 percent globally. A second actuality is that these commodities are only relatively expensive these days because they are readily available and the cost of transportation is relatively low. For instance, transporting oil via tankers costs about $2 per barrel, but pipeline gas networks in Europe are on the increase as well. Unlike oil, natural gas is hard to ship over very long distances and the technology of liquefying natural gas is available nowadays, although it requires a huge investment. It consists of cooling gas to minus 360°F at a liquefaction facility—this technique reduces the specific volume of gas by 600 times—and then it is then loaded onto specially designed tankers for transport all over the world. Once the tankers reach a facility where the liquid can be changed back into gas, the liquefied natural gas is offloaded, heated, and fed into a traditional gas pipeline. This form of transporting gas could transform the presently regional-based gas market into an international one and become particularly important in the future as world demand is on the increase and new pipelines are not adequate to meet the overall demand. Between $250 and $300 trillion theoretically must be invested to upgrade and build the much-needed new pipelines

Although Russia is not a truly monopolist player in Western Europe, nevertheless EU countries still import at least a quarter of their oil and gas from Russia. Moreover, the above percentages are set to rise sharply in coming decades to meet increasing internal demand. Demand for gas, especially, will surely rise because it is a cleaner-burning fuel and western industrialized nations are quite concerned about global warming emissions. Therefore, the interdependence between Russia and the European Union in the energy sector is extremely noteworthy and must be taken into account, as it provides a critical new direction through which Russia can gain trade partnerships and access to markets in Europe, and negotiate new preliminary accords elsewhere in Europe.

A Bell-Shaped Curve?

Before elaborating on this key aspect of Russia's and the world economy's long-term prospects, it is important to consider whether the world crude oil production is now ready to peak or not, or even whether it has already peaked in the past. The issue arose from Marion King Hubbert (1956, 1962), a Shell Oil geologist who tried to come up with a simple way to predict the lifetime of a natural resource. Hubbert wanted to find out when oil output in the United States would peak—when about half the resource is gone—and then begin to decline thereafter. He gave his report to the National Academy of Sciences in 1962. The Hubbert Peak, which is named after him, describes a situation in which maximum oil production rates are followed by a few years of gentle rollover and then an abrupt fall. Hubbert realized that the trajectory of oil discovery in the continental United States could be represented by a classic bell-shaped curve for the decades from 1910 to 1970, and he also observed that there would be a second bell-shaped curve representing petroleum extraction. Few countries exhibit production in a classic bell curve, but Hubbert used what he knew in 1950 about the history of discoveries and consumption to predict production rates for 1970.

Since Hubbert's discovery, geologists have embarked on calculating peaks for world production as well. It would be disastrous if these resources dried up—which some believe will happen soon—before the world is prepared for an alternative. Speculations about the *doomsday* era are common today, as are forecasts about how the price of oil will rise dramatically when oil consumption exceeds production. Although the end of oil production was predicted three times in the past century, it has never occurred.

Although the worldwide situation is quite unknown, the world is not yet running out of these resources. Several examples of new oil fields in Russia are a clear sign that oil and gas fields retain more reserves than expected, and that there are still undiscovered reserves in northern and northwestern Russian regions. In general, improved exploration techniques, investment and upstream strategies, and growth in unconventional oils (include heavy oil, oil sands, gas-to-liquid, shale oil, etc.) will make the world look less and less close to the eve of a catastrophe, and will ease concerns about impending shortages. I trust that the world has high expectations for being able to maintain significant reserves; in fact, vast amounts of oil and gas remain underground, and in the past the systematic discovery of new oil and gas fields has forced experts to upgrade their calculations regarding proven reserves; it is difficult indeed to appreciate the exact amount of recoverable resources in Russia or in any other country nowadays, although I do not deny the fact that crude oil and natural gas will vanish at some unspecified time in the future.

Considering the world's current oil consumption of 1,000 barrels per second, it has been estimated that the world's petroleum production peak will occur sometime between 2000 and 2012. Authors such as Deffeyes (2005), Roberts (2004), and Kunstler (2005) suspect that the production peak in oil is already here. According to them, the world will be facing an oil supply crunch within five years or so, and as reserves start to peak, prices will shoot up to record levels. And there are prospects of even tighter natural gas markets at the turn of the decade, the International Energy Agency said, as Blas (2007) reported in the *Financial Times*. This is consistent with the recently released report of the National Petroleum Council—an oil and natural gas advisory committee to the United States Secretary of Energy. This report, *Facing the Hard Truths about Energy*, concludes that complex challenges and global uncertainties could seriously affect oil production as early as 2015.

Goodstein, in *Out of Gas: The End of the Age of Oil* (2004), forecasts that the age of fossil fuels will end sometime in 2010, and Peter Tertzakian's *A Thousand Barrels a Second* (2006) recently made the case that the end of oil production is near and will reach its peak during the next five to ten years, so that oil supplies are becoming harder to guarantee. Less pessimistic predictions concerned with keeping modern civilization running predict that the oil peak, which includes the supply of conventional oil—that is, oil from onshore and shallow offshore light oil, light oil from deep-sea fields, natural gas liquid, polar region reserves, etc., which represents 95 percent of current world oil production (unconventional oils make up for few percentage points of current overall supply)—will occur sometime in the next thirty years, and there is no sign of peaking today (Clarke, 2007). I am well aware that notable increases in oil and natural gas prices could become a matter of fact in light of the long-term finite supply of fossil fuels, signalling the end of the "oil and gas age." But I do not see any catastrophe around the corner, although it is prudent to think about alternatives, such as nuclear energy and additional capacity, in the coming years (see Herbst and Hopley, 2007).

Turning to gas resources to replace diminishing supplies of oil will only be a temporary solution because the Hubbert Peak for gas has been calculated to occur only a decade or so after that of the oil industry. Nevertheless, BP (2007) predicts that the world's known gas reserves will be 181.46 trillion cubic meters by the end of 2005, of which 26.6 percent will belong to Russia and 14.9 percent to Iran.

It is not certain, however, when the worldwide Hubbert Peak will actually occur, or whether the world's petroleum production is at its maximum right now. Nor do I want to deny that a peaking problem will never arise; however, I suspect that peak oil is not probable in the near future, and we do not know much about when precisely this problem will show up in the decades ahead. Still, the more pessimistic projections about dangerous declining global reserves today are baseless (Lynch, 2003). I have not seen any problems of scarcity or upcoming oil depletion, although several claim to find evidence of this. Industry observers suspect that Saudi Arabia, the country that tops the list with 21.9 percent of world total reserves and 66.7 year reserves-to-production ratio, simply exaggerates the country's figures. BP (2007) reports that the world's known crude oil reserves and oil sands are 1371.7 trillion barrels as of 2006, of which 6.6 percent will belong to Russia and 74.9 percent will belong to OPEC. If the world pumps out a given amount of barrels from the ground each year, the world would retain a 40.5 reserves-to-production ratio of consumption at rates as of 2006—not considering unproved reserves. As we know, the Hubbert prediction that U.S. oil production would peak in about 1970 and decline thereafter was not fulfilled, nor have followers of his theory found any support at the international level. Despite Hubbert's prediction and those of other experts who predicted the end of an oil-based economy society three times in the past decades, such very negative expectations never occurred.

Although scientists estimate that we had 2.1 to 2.2 trillion barrels of oil in the ground before we ever started pumping it (Goodstein, 2004), the total amount of crude oil reserves is apt to increase with time for a variety of reasons.

As a matter of fact, it is a worth expanding our angle of analysis; there are more oil and gas fields available to explore. And thanks to new exploration, drilling, and less archaic recovery technology, we are able to discover and extract oil at a cheaper cost. The cost per barrel of extracting oil has declined over the last twenty years, from an average of about $21 in the late 1970s to less than $6 in the late 1990s—around the same time that the recovery rate from world oil fields increased from about 22 percent in 1980 to 35 percent today. The starting quantities of today's proven oil reserves are only partially reliable; we should consider not only the proven reserves but also those that would be actually available but have not surfaced yet. For example, oil reserves were originally calculated at 770.4 billion barrels in 1985, and then reserves climbed to 1027 billion barrels in 1995 and escalated up to 1220.7 billion barrels by 2005. If proven reserves exceed one trillion barrels as it is well possible these days, the world would retain more than three trillion barrels of recoverable oil resources at the same time as the yearly consumption persists in the 30 billion barrels level today. As for the proven gas reserves, they were calculated at 99.54 trillion cubic meters in 1995, rose to 143.42 in 1995, and were then estimated to be 181.46 trillion cubic meters in 2006 (BP, 2007). Therefore, increasing knowledge about specific deposits and advances in technology for recovering the oil will lead to discoveries of additional reserves in the near future. Pessimism regarding these resources' current and future consumption and unfilled reserves is completely unjustified.

Recent discoveries as well as improved oil and gas recovery techniques will make it possible to invest in new fields and allow for easier extraction. One recent example of the use of advanced technology is a huge new oil field that Chevron found in the summer of 2006 out in the Gulf of Mexico—430 kilometers southwest of New Orleans and around four miles below the ocean floor. This new deepwater oil field could produce between three billion and fifteen billion barrels of oil, which would boost the United States' current reserves by some 50 percent in the most optimistic case.

Although the need to develop alternative resources and enhance energy efficiency is a good way to benefit the environment, the concerns that have built up due to Hubbert's Peak are exaggerated. At the very least, such panic is remature when it is applied to the world situation and Russia specifically. A more complex and plausible scenario for Russia is to replenish petroleum reserves through exploration of Siberia and other regions, which are essentially untouched due to accessibility problems but have become worthwhile prospects in light of rising oil prices. In this context, Russia could play a huge role in ever-changing oil and gas policy. Without considering the aforementioned new technology and the capacity to explore additional fields, let us bear in mind that the country has huge proven reserves—6.6 percent of world oil, 26.3 percent of world gas, and 17.3 percent of world coal (BP, 2007). Russia supplies these to Western Europe and Asia, and manages strategic partnerships with western companies that own advanced technologies.

The West Blames the Kremlin

According to the West, Russia's strategy is geared toward becoming a monopolist player that artificially inflates prices to gain the most of its exports and leverages oil and gas domestic availability as tools to maneuver foreign policy. From this point of view, Russia would likewise seek access to European gas distribution and retail markets and collude with other oil and gas producers. The rationale behind the accusation is illogical. Russia's progress as an energy exporter has given rise to concerns that it is a major contributor to turmoil in past years. However, despite Russia's economic growth and dependence on oil and gas production, Moscow is not a monopolistic player in the world market because its production and reserves are nowhere near majority status. As I said, Moscow is not a monopolistic supplier in the European context, although does enjoy a significant portion of its market. Supply and demand will always remain the cornerstone of setting prices because it is a universal law. As a result, Russia cannot determine the price in energy markets.

Russia, like many other countries, receives fair market value based on world market price oscillations that are affected by the demand on the world energy economy, political instability in the oil-producing Middle East countries of Iraq and Iran, and throughout the overall Middle East, that shows no signs of long-term stabilization, and events in Venezuela and other countries. Sometimes the discovery of new oil and gas fields simply shifts the available supply to a new high. In the specific case of gas, it is not traded in a global marketplace as is oil, and there is not yet an OPEC-like cartel: gas is simply sold and bought in a fragmented market in which it is almost impracticable to direct production and prices. Ultimately, the multifaceted market determines the price outcome.

The drop in oil prices, from almost $78 a barrel in July 2006 to slightly less than $60 a barrel as of autumn 2006 and nudging a $78.70 a barrel record by early August 2007—due to the abovementioned factors, which were beyond Moscow's control—represents oscillating prices that are not at all in Moscow's control. This is further evidence of the western double standard and hypocrisy regarding Russia. Suffice it to say that OPEC cartel representative members agreed to cut oil production by 1.2 million barrels a day during the Doha meeting on October 20, 2006 (OPEC's oil production averaged about 27.5 millions of barrels a day in September 2006), in order to direct production and halt the drop in world oil prices. Obviously, Russia has no power in this decision; still Russia—and not OPEC and other countries—has come under criticism in the West for using vast energy resources to influence market prices.

On the other hand, western gas and oil companies—most of them owned by national governments—do enjoy the monopolistic ability to set their own distribution prices for their respective national consumers. The profit margin between the cost to national distributors and the final cost to the public is huge.

What makes western criticism of Russia duplicitous is that oil companies in the United States, as well as elsewhere, use the same tactics to produce high profit margins, yet the West criticizes the Russian profits and the eagerness of the Russian energy industry to control a portion of the market. Does the West expect Russia to just throw such commodities away? Or to not try to make the most of domestic riches as every country does? It seems that the West and its oil and gas giants are cynical when they do not want to see beyond their noses and will not be happy with the situation until they find a way to make money from Russian energy markets, and that cannot happen while the Russian government controls those resources.

The Development of Energy Riches in Russia

The attractiveness of Russia's geological resources its proximity to western markets and good transportation infrastructure from the Black Sea, which was built in the 1880s, and the facilities being planned in present-day Russia have all had, and will continue to have, positive consequences. Europe was seeking an alternative to monopolistic regimes that were emerging then—such as Rockefeller's Standard Oil Company in the United States—and a means of coping with regional exogenous political events in the Middle East and events that were causing economic turmoil. The price of oil was vital to economic growth as well as cartels, embargoes, and politics (Barsky and Kilian, 2002). Before World War I, Russia was experiencing macroeconomic turmoil second only to that in the United States. After the Revolution in 1917, oil production fell significantly, and by the end of the 1920s, its recovery was used to provide hard currency. At the outbreak of World War II, Russia's oil production made it the second-largest supplier of oil to Western Europe. By the 1950s, it was not Saudi Arabia but the United States that was the world's greatest producer of oil, and the global price of oil was the price in Texas plus the cost of transportation to wherever it was sold. Russia has always ranked second in extraction.

Aggressive marketing strategies in selected countries led Russia to achieve notable market shares in Western Europe. After the second World War, when other oil fields were being developed while the country was diversifying its energy resources, the new areas together with the old ones "yielded well over 600 million tons of oil in 1982 and the Soviet Union is now by far the world's largest oil producer" (Odell 1983: 54). Despite the Central Intelligence Agency's speculation on the potential of real oil production in the former Soviet Union (Odell, 1983), Russia was acting as a leader, and as an intermediary in Iran, whose gas was to be exported through a new pipeline in Western Europe. Russian oil was gradually finding markets in Western Europe, which was likewise boosted by the Suez crisis in 1956–1957 and the Middle East conflict in 1973, and by a price dumping (the sale of a commodity on a foreign market at a price below marginal cost) that applied to western countries—up from three million tons in 1955, Russia exported more than fourty million tons in 1969 (Odell, 1983). To ensure success, new pipelines (in addition to those already functioning in the Black Sea, the Baltic States, and the Danube port of Bratislava) were constructed, helping to cut transportation prices and penetrate even deeper into Europe. That export strategy reminds us of the current endeavor in Russia to penetrate Western European markets through improving transportation lines.

Let us jump into late 1970s and early 1980s in Russia. Due to large gas reserves discovered in Siberia, in the Urals, and in the Volga region after the 1960s, the Soviet Union reinforced its image as a major gas producer. During communism, gas exploration, development, and distribution were centralized in a state ministry. Mikhail Gorbachev, however, combined the ministries for oil and gas as part of his economic reforms in 1989. Moscow was endeavoring to build a long-term strategy and exploit export potential.

After the breakup of the Soviet Union, the state-owned Gazprom lost a large part of its assets outside of Russia, but when Boris Yeltsin appointed Chernomyrdin as prime minister in December 1992, the influence of Gazprom increased markedly. With the government committed to economic reform, Gazprom began to be privatized in November 1992, under the voucher methods of privatization. After the scandals of the mid-1990s that touched almost the entire privatization process, and the firing of Prime Minister Chernomyrdin in March 1998, the government demanded billions of dollars in back taxes from Gazprom. For example, in 1995–1996, Gazprom paid $3.5 million in taxes on $2 billion in earnings. This is an example of tax evasion, or rather a very friendly tax system and the possibility of circumventing it almost legally. When tax prosecutors began to seize Gazprom's assets, the company gave in and paid. The company's records started showing a loss for the first time. Due to these factors, as well as Gazprom's dubious transactions with foreign-based companies and corrupt management, Putin pursued a comprehensive reform of Gazprom early in the new century. Meanwhile, a lot of abuses were becoming evident within Gazprom, including large-scale nepotism, corruption, and shifting corporate assets towards "private hands." These led to the resignation of Gazprom's chief executive director Rem Vyakhirev, head of Gazprom since 1993, and thereby corporate reforms were enacted: Alexei Miller, former Deputy minister of energy, was appointed the company's new chief executive officer in 2001, and Gazprom quickly became a powerful economic instrument of Putin's administration and Russia's economic growth. Although the Russian government held less than a 39 percent stake until 2004, it enjoyed a majority on the company's board of directors. The Kremlin plan was to make Gazprom, Rosneft, and Sibneft (renamed GazpromNeft after Gazprom finalized its controlling stake in 2005) one big state company. If Gazprom was thwarted in its attempt to merge with Rosneft, the Russian government increased its involvement in Gazprom and became a majority stakeholder, making it the major state company responsible for gas production, distribution, and sales.

It appears that the Kremlin administration decided to reinforce its position in the natural resources and energy sector, as it had been so corruptly privatized during the 1990s. With immense resources and a spectacular increase in the Russian Trading System Stock Exchange (RTS) index and St. Petersburg market, Gazprom soared from 78.3 rubles to 343.82 rubles in May 2006. Gazprom now ranks third in the world in terms of capitalization with over $300 billion market capitalization, behind ExxonMobil with $387.2 billion and General Electric with 365.5 billion. This period is proving to be very advantageous for Gazprom, and the question is whether the momentum can carry into next years to achieve a market capitalization of $1 trillion dollars "in a period of seven to ten years," Gazprom's deputy chief executive Alexander Medvedev disclosed recently. By now Gazprom eclipses companies such as Microsoft and British Petroleum and is valued at a fourteen times higher price-earnings ratio (called P/E, it is the quoted price of shares divided by a year's earnings—a company with a good earnings expectation might exhibit a ratio of 15/1 or more, while a poor record drives the ratio well below that that) than companies such as ExxonMobil, which is valued at some eleven times higher P/E. In sum, Gazprom grew over 200 times its original size after the early 1990s, cashed in on the oil and gas boom, and became a conduit for international firms operating in this field.

Nowadays, the Russian gas industry is a monopoly run by the Gazprom group (the Duma voted to give Gazprom the exclusive right to export natural gas), which controls more than 95 percent of domestic gas production and owns the largest gas reserves in the world. Gazprom's corporate structure comprises a very long list of subsidiary companies engaged in hydrocarbons production, processing and refining, and transportation—Gazprom's transportation and storage of gas is performed through its Unified Gas Supply System, the world's largest high-pressure trunk pipeline complex. If the majority of Russia's gas and oil was exported to Eastern Europe by 1991, since then Russia has sought to diversify its exports geographically. Gazprom's marketing strategy is likewise aimed at participation in the whole value chain to capture attractive margins in the trading and distribution segments of the energy business in Western Europe, by which it is pursuing a path toward becoming a strategic global energy company and diversifying activities into projects involving the production of liquefied natural gas and synthetic liquid fuels as well as electricity power generation.

To summarize, a strategic and extensive partnership in hydrocarbon policies is a novelty in Russia's history. Russian fields hold immense quantities of these commodities, and Russia should be able to draw from its oil and gas resources just as countries around the world have done for years, and continue to do. We are inclined to forget that the country lost up to $60 billion in revenues between 1985 and 1989 and experienced an economic setback when oil prices fell from roughly $28 to $10 per barrel nine months after Mikhail Gorbachev took power in Moscow in 1985. Yet there is no reason that Russia should ignore the incredible wealth hidden away in its many regions. Russia has been a major world actor on the global stage of oil and natural gas resource production since the twentieth century and continues to be well into this century. Russia should be recognized for its role in the export of these commodities even if it is still commonly believed that most oil and natural gas is exported from countries located in the region of the Arabic Peninsula. Spectators of Russian affairs have seen oil and natural gas company owners in Moscow and the cold reaches of Siberia, or billionaires and millionaires making their fortunes on natural resource ownership. People hear much about the oil exporting sheikhdoms of the Gulf and nearby countries, and assume that the world's oil barons are Middle Eastern men of power.

Russia's Partnerships in the Oil and Gas Industries

The Russian government approved the *Main Provisions of the Russian Energy Strategy to 2020* in November 2000 and a revised plan in May 2003. As a result of joint action plans with Western Europe, Japan, and China as well as consultations with other countries in the region, Russian leadership is well aware that the energy sector accounts for a sizeable percentage of the country's GDP and state budget revenues. The development of an extensive network of pipelines as well as control of supply and distribution are becoming increasingly indispensable to the success of the entire strategy. Diversifying energy supply, promoting extraction from new fields located in Eastern Siberia, the Far East, the Arctic, and the Caspian region—these are areas of tremendous strategic exploration for their potential reserves—and intensifying a move to speed up the extraction of endless resources should all be part of a strategy for Russia.

Within it, Russia's strategic plan is to team up with all the aforementioned markets, which are, in fact, trying to link firmly with Russia. A continued effort is underway to expand the pipeline network because the existing infrastructure has decayed, and to fill the financing and technical gaps with support from foreign countries and investment. Taken as a whole, networking with foreign investors could provide much-needed money and other markets. Gazprom is redesigning its export policy to optimize gas transit costs to Western Europe, to better access the end-consumer and maximize export revenues. Currently, Gazprom is selling its gas at the border of importing countries to local distributors in Western Europe, who then supply the product to consumers and exploit the huge difference between the end-user price and the cost to distributors. Examples of this are numerous in Western Europe, and a couple of notable cases help shed light on the entire policy of partnerships with foreign companies.

Most Russian reserves are located in deep-sea areas within remote latitudes, and this requires huge efforts to cope with upstream investment to back the complexity of recovery and then reach distant end-users. Russia now has to expand extraction capabilities and distribution networks in the West and East. This will require a huge investment in the exploration of new fields and hard-to-explore areas, as well as investing in modern western technologies. Teamwork, and not control by foreign big companies, is the best strategy for developing Russia's huge gas and oil fields. The construction of new pipelines to replace old rail routes to export crude oil to East Asia, new tankers shipping oil from the Black Sea Novorossiysk to the Mediterranean and Asia ports, and reviving aging fields would allow access to multiple markets in Western Europe, Asia, and North America, as well as tap new fields in remote areas.

One cannot dismiss the importance of these facts and the associated costs regarding investment and upgrading this sector's technology. For example, technological advances in the oil industry are important, but need cooperation and investment. It is clear that experimental methods for extracting oil from heavy oil fields could increase recovery costs from 6 percent to around 40 percent, according to Saudi Arabia's petroleum minister Ali Naimi and Daniel Yergin, chairman of the Cambridge Energy Associates. Frontier deepwater drilling is now at 11,000 feet and it was only at 600 feet in 1978, as reported by Sheila McNulty (2006) in the *Financial Times*. In reality, Japan and China have been investing large amounts of money, and international consortiums with major world oil companies are now a reality. For example, from 2001 to 2030, it is estimated that a cumulative energy investment of $1.05 billion and $2.253 billion, will come from Russia and China respectively, according to International Energy Agency's *World Energy Outlook 2006*.

Estimated investments could total in the hundreds of billions to develop six gas projects and three oil projects in the Isle of Sakhalin—one-fourth of Russia's oil reserves and 6 percent of its gas reserves are in the Sakhalin offshore fields. Several additional projects are being developed under production-sharing agreements. One is being run by the French oil company, Total, in the Kharyaga field of Russia's autonomous Khanty-Mansi district, and is being developed under a production-sharing agreement between Total (50 percent), the Norwegian state-owned company, Norsk Hydro (40 percent), and the Nenets Oil Company (10 percent). Another project is the Sakhalin 1, whose participants are Exxon Neftegaz Limited, that is a subsidiary of ExxonMobil (30 percent), Rosneft (20 percent), India's ONGC (20 percent), and Japan's SODECO (30 percent).

The Sakhalin 2 LNG project, the world's largest project for the production of liquefied natural gas, was controlled by British-Dutch company Royal Dutch Shell (55 percent), with Japan's Mitsui and Mitsubishi holding 25 percent and 20 percent, respectively. Gazprom finally signed a deal with Royal Dutch Shell for obtaining a majority interest in the Sakhalin Energy Investment Company on December 21, 2006, in exchange for $7.5 billion and a 50 percent stake in the Zapolyarnoye-neokom oil field in Western Siberia. While the Sakhalin Energy Investment Company will continue operating the project, the three original partners will dilute their stakes by 50 percent, with Royal Dutch Shell retaining a 27.5 percent stake, Mitsui and Mitsubishi holding 12.5 percent and 10 percent stakes, respectively.

Surely, such cooperation in upstream development could benefit the North American market for the ease of transportation. The Yamal Peninsula in northern Siberia alone, for example, retains more gas than all of North America. But let us probe into developments in selected geographical areas.

Western Europe

Russia does not view Western Europe through the lens of an ever-increasing demand for these resources. Building up an extensive network of pipelines with virtually all countries in Western Europe is less a factor of isolating and more of cooperation. Nevertheless, those huge financial revenues represent a major element in Russia's existence and its primary means of funding is a matter of fact.

In the recent past, the Druzhba (friendship) line has served the West and is the largest Russian export pipeline to Europe today. Beginning in Samara (in the southeast part of Russia, near Kazakhstan) and spanning over 2,500 miles, it collects oil from Western Siberia, the Urals, and the Caspian Sea and heads to Mozyr (Belarus), where it forks for Belarus/Poland/Germany (so-called Northern Druzhba) and Belarus/Ukraine/Slovakia/Czech Republic/Hungary (Southern Druzhba). But new and unique projects are underway and when realized will give the European Union greater confidence in gas supplies from Russia and secure full and uninterrupted deliveries. Gazprom's goal has been to bypass Ukraine, Belarus, and Poland in supplying gas to Western Europe.

First came blueprints for the North European Gas Pipeline, or North Stream, which would run under the Baltic Sea from the coast of Russia to Germany. The offshore pipeline will cross territorial waters of Finland, Sweden, and Denmark, thereby bypassing the three neighboring Baltic States and Poland, which often have tense political relations with Russia. The former German chancellor Gerhard Schroeder agreed to become the chairperson of the shareholders' committee (i.e., equivalent to a board of directors) of the Gazprom-controlled North European Pipeline consortium. This appointment occurred less than four weeks after Schroeder formally stepped down as chancellor in November 2005, without any cooling off period, and it brought about vast speculation, especially among German commentators. The remaining 49 percent was split among German electric power generators, the distributor of gas E.ON Ruhrgas (20%), and BASF (20%)—the world's largest chemical company—and the N.V. Nederland Gasunie (9%). The $5-billion or so investment will be fed from the huge Yuzhno-Russkoye field and additionally from fields in Yamal Peninsula and eventually the majority of gas produced at the Shtokman field would be sold to Europe (and that is the first ever German-Russian joint venture in Russia's gas upstream)—with an annual transmission capacity of approximately 27.5 billion cubic meters of gas. The final project involves laying two parallel transmission pipeline legs: the first leg by 2010 and the second one in 2012. The first gas delivery is slated for 2011 with annual transmission capacity of 27.5 billion cubic meters per year for each leg. The jointly built, roughly 1,200-kilometer-long pipeline will pass under the Baltic Sea, will connect at Vyborg (located near St. Petersburg), and go under the Baltic Sea through Greifswald (provisionally earmarked as landfall) into northeast Germany. It will then potentially continue into Britain, bypassing the three Baltic States and Poland, and thus more closely anchoring Russia to Europe without having to pay transit fees or barter gas to countries through which transportation is needed.

President Putin prospected a major partnership role with the West and Germany. During his visit to Dresden in October 2006, Putin anticipated that Russia could double the quantity of gas actually sold to Germany, with added furniture of some fifty five billion cubic meters, in such a way that Germany could become a distributor of Russian gas for Western Europe.

The Blue Stream pipeline is another major project with both Russian and Western European actors. Measuring 1,213 kilometers in length and costing approximately $3.5 billion, it has been built in mutual participation with the Italian Eni (the Italian giant hydrocarbon company and the world's single largest customer of Gazprom, as roughly 25 percent of Italy's gas imports come from Russia, and could reach about 33 percent during the next ten years), with legal paperwork signed in the late 1990s and construction started in the very early 2000s. The Blue Stream is intended to supply gas from the Izobilnoy gas plant in southern Russia directly to Turkey, going across the Black Sea bed to the Turkish port of Samsun. The Blue Stream project was officially inaugurated at the Samsun-based Durusu gas metering station in November 2005. The designed capacity of the pipeline transports up to sixteen billion cubic meters of gas per year and is intended to be used to export 311 billion cubic meters of gas to Turkey before 2025. More than twelve billion cubit meters of gas have been transported since the pipeline was launched, and eight billion cubic meters of deliveries are already contracted for 2006. When the Blue Stream was inaugurated, Putin recommended building a second Black Sea pipeline that could raise the transportation capacity from 3.7 billion cubic meters to around thirty billion cubic meters.

Other significant agreements were signed with Eni in June 2006, when Gazprom and Eni identified an initial upstream agreement—similar to the type already signed with the German BASF—through which Eni will be allowed a 25 percent quota to exploit the Siberian Yuzhno-Russkoye gas field, which contains approximately 600 billion cubic meters of gas. In September 2006, Gazprom and Eni agreed in principle to reinforce their strategic partnership, and the two companies in fact worked out a final broad strategic partnership signed on November 14, 2006, agreeing to establish an international alliance for the next thirty years involving joint projects both downstream and upstream and in technological cooperation overall, both in Russia and outside of Russia. This reinforced strategic partnership increases the likeliness that Gazprom will enter the Italian distribution market and through this agreement, starting from 2007, Gazprom would sell directly into the Italian market increasing volumes of gas, building up to about three billion cubic meters from 2010 for the entire duration of the long-term supply contract.

Moreover, talks between Gazprom and Eni concerning a tentatively named Blue Stream 2 ended on June 23, 2007, when the two companies signed a preliminary agreement concerning an extension of it and finally named the project South Stream. Unlike the North Stream that runs on the Baltic seabed, the South Stream cannot avoid land transit. But Gazprom has chosen to work with the Greeks and Bulgarians, who have been culturally close to Russia for centuries; Bulgaria and Greece will welcome the chance to open Europe's southern gates to Russian gas, and are especially looking forward to an additional flow of foreign investment that the project could almost certain pour in. Construction on the pipeline, estimated at $14.6 billion and potentially clearing the way for an annual capacity of thirty billion cubic meters, may begin in the next two years after feasibility studies are completed. However, experts have not ruled out the possibility that the project will be found unprofitable. Under the plan, more than 560 miles of pipeline would be placed from the Russian Black Sea coast underwater to the Bulgarian shore, where it may eventually split off in two directions: one north through Hungary to Slovenia and Austria, and possibly additional offshoots to Italy; the other south through Greece (the route will probably lie parallel to the Burgas-Alexandropoulis oil pipeline, which Russia is involved in building) and eventually under the Adriatic Sea to the Italian port of Otranto, near the southeastern tip of Italy.

Nevertheless, the South Stream could call into question the Nabucco Gas Pipeline project, which for approximately $5.8 billion is conceived to transport Caspian gas to Europe through Turkey. The Nabucco Gas Pipeline Company, a European Union-backed project, was established on June 24, 2004, to project a gas pipeline connecting the Caspian region to Europe through Turkey, Bulgaria, Romania, and Hungary, with Austria and further on, with the Central and Western European gas markets. The pipeline's length will be approximately 3,300 kilometers, starting at the Georgian-Turkish and/or Iranian-Turkish border respectively, connecting near Erzurum with the Tabriz-Erzurum pipeline, and with the South Caucasus Pipeline, and connecting Nabucco Pipeline with the planned Trans-Caspian Gas Pipeline. Once completed, it would allow transportation of natural gas from producers in the Middle East and Caspian region such as Iran, Azerbaijan, and Turkmenistan to Western Europe and to the countries along its path, reaching Baumgarten in Austria, from where it could be further transported through Austria to the Central and Western European Countries. (The Nabucco pipeline will almost overlap the South Stream pipeline starting in Bulgaria, where the South Stream splits off in two directions, and the Nabucco will overlap the pipeline that goes to the north.) According to market studies, the project will start operation and marketing of the pipeline in 2013, with an initial pipeline capacity up to eight billion cubic meters per year, while the construction of the rest of the pipeline will be finished in parallel by 2017 to transport a maximum amount of thirty one billion cubic meters per year.

The network of partnerships has been expanding considerably. In early February 2006, Russia's foreign minister Sergei Lavrov held talks between the Greek gas utility Depa and the Turkish Botas in Athens to involve Gazprom in a new Aegean gas pipeline—a seabed pipeline across the Marmora Sea. Due to be completed in 2009, it should represent an alternative route for gas supplies to Western Europe that bypasses Ukraine. A few days before the Athens talks, Alexei Miller, Gazprom's chief executive, suggested that Gazprom could take an equity stake in the Aegean pipeline project and that its participation could increase the capacity to more than ten billion cubic meters of gas annually (it should be noted that the original project launched at the beginning of this decade was expected to carry two billion cubic meters, at most) as well as representing an additional improvement to West Europe's energy security. While Greece would become a regional hub for gas and oil supplies to Western Europe with the support of Russia, Russia endeavors to expand its strategy in the Balkans by reviving a 100-kilometer pipeline between Nis in Serbia and Dimitorvgrad in Bulgaria by the year 2007. This project would involve Yugorosgaz—an originally 50-50 percent joint venture founded in 1996, and now a 75 percent-controlled Gazprom subsidiary—and although uneconomical, it converted unpaid bills worth more than $235 million from the late 1990s into equity in gas-related projects.

Gazprom and other private Russian companies are seeking direct access to retail markets in Western Europe and in the former Soviet bloc countries. Gazprom expressed interest in Britain's Centrica, the owner of British Gas, in May 2006. Although no official talks were started, it had the potential to raise gas supply from three billion to four billion cubic meters per year. The government, however, was not convinced that this was a good deal, and the government certainly has the final say. Direct access to Western European consumers was recently gained through the German E.ON, with which Gazprom has agreed to swap a stake of 25 percent, minus one share, in the Siberian Yuzhno-Russkoye gas field, in exchange for E.ON's roughly 50 percent shares in two Hungarian gas companies.

The geographically distant Portuguese market could be direct involved with Russian companies as well. Gazprom could enter the Portuguese market by becoming a partner in Americo Amorim's company, Amorim Energia. Through his company, Amorim becomes one of the shareholders of Lisbon-based Galp Energia—an oil, gas, and electricity company. Galp Energia belongs in portions to Amorin, the Italian Eni, and the Portuguese government. Should the deal between Amorim and Gazprom go through (which was under evaluation during the summer of 2006), Gazprom could secure gas supplies for Galp Energia.

As for direct access to other retail markets in the former Soviet bloc countries, six oil refineries in Ukraine—four of them owned or controlled by Russian companies and all operating on Russian crude oil—hold an aggregate 90 percent share of Ukraine's oil production market. The two private companies, Lukoil (Russia's biggest private oil company) and TNK-BP (an Anglo-Russian oil venture), are by far the largest suppliers and refiners, and they control a critical mass of retail outlets. Gazprom and other Russian companies—whether alone or in partnership with Western European companies—hold large percentages of national transportation and gas trading companies in Bulgaria, the Czech Republic, Estonia, Latvia, Lithuania, Moldova, and several other countries.

Likewise, Gazprom has offered the Dutch gas firm, Gasunie, a stake in a pipeline linking Russia and Germany, in exchange for a Russian stake in the Dutch pipeline to Britain.

In addition, Gazprom is trying to develop the Shtokman gas field in the central part of the Barents Sea and to construct a gas plant there by allowing foreign company involvement as contractors and owners of the resulting operating company, as well as to link this field's upstream to North Stream, too, although for this purpose a new pipeline has to be built from the field through the Kola Peninsula.

Gazprom has received nine bids from foreign companies to develop a gas field that is located 550 kilometers northeast of Murmansk—beyond the Arctic Circle. Today, experts estimate its reserves at 3.2 to 3.7 billion cubic meters of gas and thirty one million tons of condensate. Three American, two Norwegian, two Japanese, one English-Dutch, and one French company have expressed attention to detail and would like to be involved in that business. Gazprom is currently choosing between those international companies to involve in the development of this vast field, and between this field and the Yamalo Nenezk field, which is expected to begin production by 2015; the appeal to international investors is intense. If companies such as ChevronTexaco, ConocoPhilips, Total, Norwegian state-owned StatOil and Norsk Hydro, and Royal Dutch-Shell are available to invest and be involved in the development of this project, as they are already doing in other locations in Russia, and Russia is open to this partnership, it will be enough to restrain specious Western criticism.

The Baltic pipeline system is geared to transport crude oil from the Timan-Pechora region, Western Siberia, and the Tyumen-Pechora oil basins westward. Construction of new port terminals in St. Petersburg and in new ports in Luzhsk Bay, in Batarejnaya Bay, and the port of Primorsk on the Russian Gulf of Finland are underway.

Other projected lines could carry oil to Murmansk (despite its current economic infeasibility) or Indinga (although it ices over during the winter) on the Barents Sea, enabling tankers to reach the United States in less than ten days, faster than importing from the Middle East for the United States. Liquefied natural gas facilities in Murmansk and Arkhangelsk have been proposed to tap into the lucrative North America market.

The oil pipeline system Eastern Siberia – Pacific Ocean is being developed in accordance with Energy Strategy of Russian Federation for the period until

2020, and in order to meet the long-term forecasts of demand of the Asia-Pacific region. Tomskaya oblast and the Khanty-Mansy Autonomous district in Western Siberia as well as oil provinces of Eastern Siberia form the resource base for the new oil pipeline system. The route of the designed pipeline will go through territories of seven Russian Federation entities. They are Irkutsk, Tchita, Amur regions, the Republic of Buryatiya, the Jewish autonomous district, Khabarovsk, and Primorsk territories.

The Adria line, which was completed in 1974, was once used to move oil from the Middle East and to pipe crude oil northward to Yugoslavia and on to Hungary from Croatia's deepwater port terminal of Omishalj. While reversal of the Adra pipeline has been under consideration since the 1990s, in 2002 Transneft originally proposed the Druzhba-Adria project that is considering the option of reversing the flow of crude oil from the East to the West. In light of the Adria pipeline's interconnection with Russia's Southern Druzhba system, it has been considered the option to reverse the Adria pipeline's flows to give Russia an important and strategic outlet on the Adriatic Sea. Six countries that should be involved in a route that would have the length of more than 3,000 km are Russia, Belarus, Ukraine, Slovakia, Hungary, and Croatia. In December 2002, these countries signed a preliminary intregration project but negotiations over tariffs and environmental issues have been slow. While Croatia in 2005 determined that a clear and definitive environmental impact study of such a reversal was not available—or at best it was incomplete—thereby postponing a final operative agrement, Hungary is said to be able to technically reverse its portion of the pipeline within one month, at most. At present, the Druzhba-Adria Pipeline Integration Project has made little progress so far; it could allow exporting fifteen million tons annually.

The full Yamal-Europe pipeline, currently under construction, should carry gas from Russia's Yamal Peninsula to Western Europe. By now, roughly 17 percent of Russian gas is already flowing to Poland and Germany through the Yamal-Europe pipeline via Belarus.

On April 4, 2007, EniNeftegaz, an Eni (60 percent) and Enel (40 percent) consortium (Enel is Italy's largest power company), won an auction for the second lot of assets belonging to the bankrupt Yukos oil group; this included a 20 percent stake in Gazpromneft (Gazprom's oil arm and Russia's fifth oil company) by Eni, gas producers ArcticGaz and Urengoil, and minor assets that will be sold or liquidated. The assets were acquired for $5.83 billion, which is the third largest foreign acquisition in Russia's oil and gas sector to date. The assets included 100 percent of Arctic Gas Company, Urengoil, and Neftegaztechnologia. These companies own five oil and gas fields and condensate fields, and parts of three other fields in the Yamal Nenets region, the world's largest gas-producing region. Combined, the companies have approximately five billion barrels of oil and gas reserves. However, Gazprom has obtained the option to acquire a 51 percent interest in the three companies within two years, and in this case, the assets will be operated through a joint venture between Gazprom and Eni. Moreover,

Eni has given Gazprom the option to purchase the 20 percent stake in Gazprom Neft at any point over the next two years, at a price of $3.7 billion.

Rosneft has emerged the victor and has furthered its primary role in the market following the acquisition of main production units from the Yukos confiscation and sale in lieu of back taxes. Rosneft has bought the last good extraction wells owned by Yukos for $6.43 billion, as well as those of subsidiary Samaraneftegaz and three refineries in the Volga region: this allows Rosneft to assume an import role in the refinery process. In December 2004, Rosneft paid $9.4 billion to buy Yuganskneftegaz, Yukos's biggest production unit. The takeover has seen Rosneft shift from the nation's eighth-biggest oil major, worth about $6 billion in 2004, to become the country's biggest producer with a market capitalization of more than $90 billion. Rosneft plans to produce a record 101 million tons of crude in 2007, more than one-fifth of the country's production, and become a leader in the retail market in Russia. Tomskneft and Samaraneftegaz, which Rosneft acquired from Yukos at auctions, will be included on Rosneft's balance sheet in the second half. Note that with this goal in mind, Rosneft tried to rise between $9 billion and $12 billion (about 15 percent of the company) in an initial public offering (IPO) in July 2006. Finally, 14.8 percent of Rosneft was sold to private investors, netting almost $11 billion. The state still controls around 85 percent of the company, which is estimated to be worth around $70 billion.

China, Japan, and Central Asia

Japan ranks second in the world in its dependency on the oil and gas industry. It is currently tied to Middle East supplies, but has supported the extension of the pipeline from the Russian city of Angarsk (in Southeast Siberia, around Russia's Lake Baikal) to the Daqing pipeline (being in this strongly supported by the Chinese government) to pipe Siberian oil reserves to China, with one-third of the pipeline to be built within the Chinese territory. China would invest billions in the Russian infrastructure and energy sector. But Japanese Prime Minister Junichiro Koizumi and President Putin met in St. Petersburg in May 2003 to discuss a line from Angarsk to the port city of Nakhodka, in the Sea of Japan. Then Russia reportedly gave up the Angarsk-Daqing route, and decided to construct the Angarsk-Nakhodka line instead. China and Japan appeared to be engaged in a bidding war and contesting access to Russian rival pipeline routes. As Russia did not want to lose the huge Chinese market, by February 2003 Russian Minister of Energy Igor Yusufov introduced a compromise solution to combine the two pipelines into one, though giving priority to the construction of a branch line to Daqing. This provided the embryonic form of the current Tayshet-Nakhodka route. Building the China pipeline first, and then exporting oil to Daqing and the whole Asian-Pacific region, was a more attractive option, allowing Russia to avoid relying too heavily on only a few customers. Meanwhile, the Russian government gave the green light to the

4,130-kilometer Tayshet-Nakhodka pipeline project in December 2004. The total construction cost is estimated at between US$11 billion and US$16 billion, but the cost could easily go up as the project gets underway. It is not clear what the actual contribution from Japan or China will be, but the Japanese did propose to contribute up to $5 billion to finance construction and $2 billion for further oil development.

This option was significantly more expensive than the alternative route to China's Daqing due to greater distance and more investment, but the Angarsk-Nakhodka route could open up new opportunities through the Pacific port, from which Russian oil exports could be shipped by tanker to other Asian markets and possibly even North America. Russian executives realized there was no need to rush exports to the United States, but it is an option in the long term. The construction of the first stage of the Tayshet-Nakhodka oil pipeline was planned for 2006, and a branch line from the main pipeline to China's Daqing will be put into use first. The first-stage pipeline, from Tayshet in central Siberia to Skovorodino sixty kilometers north of the border with northeast China, will be operational by November 8, 2008, with an annual oil transmission capacity of thirty million tons. Cost of construction is estimated at around $6.5 billion. The first phase of the 960-kilometer pipeline, which joins the Alataw Pass-Dushanzi pipeline in northwestern Xinjiang, has been completed, with a designed annual oil transmission capacity of ten million tons. Its second phase is expected to be finished in 2010, creating a delivery capacity of twenty million tons.

Gazprom and other companies have become very active. BP has been offered a cooperative venture in liquefied natural gas and needs support from Gazprom to develop a gas field in Kovykta, Eastern Siberia. The Kovykta gas field could also acquire a pipeline financed by TNK-BP, the South Korean Gas Corporation (a state-owned company), and the Chinese National Petroleum Company, to pipe almost half of Kovykta's production to China and the rest to the Pacific coast of Russia, headed for South Korea. This project could be of major importance to Russian domestic markets along its route, facilitate regional development, and activate more investment in exploring additional gas fields in Eastern Siberia and Yakutia.

Together with other planned pipelines, a pipeline system is being discussed that will spread out along the Chinese border and create export oriented branch pipelines to the Chinese markets. Russia pledged to build two natural gas pipelines to China by 2011—one of these routes has already sparked an environmental controversy because it would inflict irreparable damage to the high-mountain plateau Ukok, through which the pipeline is supposed to be laid. This project would raise gas exports to China from both Eastern and Western Siberia, up to thirty to fourty billion cubic meters of gas a year from each region. Major gas exports to China would require construction of a new pipeline, the Altai, which would stretch almost 2,700 kilometers and cross the Yamalo-Nenetsk and Khanty-Mansi Autonomous Areas, Tomsk and Novosibirsk oblasts, Altai Territory, and the Republic of Altai, and continue through the western

Russian-Chinese border. In the territory of the Republic of Altai, the pipeline is to cross the Zona Pokoia Ukok Natural Park. The $10-billion pipeline project could become operative in 2011.

In March 2006, India agreed to Gazprom involvement in a pipeline from Iran and Turkmenistan, a country enjoying immense reserves of gas, to India via Afghanistan. Uzbekistan has also found a strong ally in Moscow recently. As a result of this agreement, Russia will purchase gas from these countries and resell to other neighboring countries. In the same broad area, Gazprom has had to face strategic competition in the region from an oil pipeline running from Atasu in central Kazakhstan to China's western border and the Baku-Tbilisi-Ceyhan (BTC) oil pipeline. The BTC cost roughly $4 billion for 1,770 kilometers of pipeline and was been inaugurated in July 2006 to transport oil from the Caspian Sea to Turkey (Ceyhan), and from there to Southern Europe and the Mediterranean. This pipeline, sponsored by the United States and the United Kingdom, goes around Russia from Azerbaijan's Baku to Georgia (Tbilisi) and then to Turkey, and provides competition for Russia (especially the export program from the port of Novorossiysk).

Algeria

Gazprom and Algeria's Sonatrach (Europe's third gas supplier) signed a memorandum of cooperation in gas prospecting, recovery, and production on August 4, 2006. The memorandum opens new opportunities for expanding cooperation between the two companies. Algeria's proven gas reserves total 2.5 percent of the world total as of the end of 2006 and the second largest reserves in Africa after Nigeria (2.9 percent). Egypt is the continent's third largest oil producer and controls 1.1 percent of reserves of the world total (BP, 2007).

Out of the many possible joint projects, Russia and Algeria could be looking at expanding cooperation in the liquefied natural gas and pipeline construction industries. A relationship between Gazprom and Sonatrach has been in the works since Putin made his first official state visit to Algeria in March 2006. During that meeting, Putin wrote off nearly $5 billion in Algerian debt to Russia. Sonatrach can offer a strategic partnership in liquefied natural gas strategy. Russia would love to get its hands on this technology, which has been elusive so far, because the technology would allow it to export gas all over the world, and it could begin exporting to markets such as the United States and Southeast Asia.

Nevertheless, just as international observers systematically interpret Russia and Putin in a negative light, there are those who criticize the Gazprom-Sonatrach memorandum of cooperation because they believe that the two companies will collaborate to artificially use their big market share to set gas prices high. In response to recent rumors that the Russian Natural Resources Ministry initiated proceedings against French oil company Total, claiming that development of the Kharyaga field violated the license agreement, President

Putin dismissed the case as "greatly exaggerated" while meeting with French President Jacques Chirac and German Chancellor Angela Merkel in France in September 2006.

While concerns of collaboration are reasonable, there do not seem to be any concrete risks from leaving much of Europe at the mercy of these two large gas suppliers. Fears, especially in European circles, are often explained by the methodical (although illogical) criticism of Russia's strategy—and other times by the fact that Russia and Algeria are the largest gas suppliers to Europe. Although many people believe that the European Union could become 80 percent dependent on gas imports by 2030, with demand rising by 60 percent, this is not enough to spark fear in light of Russia trying to get the most out of its energy riches by working internationally to lift production synergy and share technology.

The Environment, the European Union, and the Kremlin's Doubts

Meanwhile, the European Union is pushing Russia to sign the Energy Charter Treaty (ECT)—an international agreement that came into effect in April 1998 and aims to strengthen the rule of law on energy issues and minimize the risks associated with energy-related investments and trade—through which a legal framework could be created to assure and manage dependence on imported supply from Russia, open up the Russian market to western companies, and give independent gas producers access to its pipelines—but the Duma voted to increase the monopolistic power of Gazprom instead. Talks continue, however, while Russia has signed but not ratified this treaty.

At the end of September 2006, a quarrel erupted between the Kremlin and Shell concerning the new upstream activity the oil giant was running in Sakhalin—the Sakhalin 2 project. The Natural Resource Ministry threatened to cancel Shell-led Sakhalin Energy's environmental license because of complaints about the ExxonMobil, Total, and TNK-BP project. Yet the case in question uncovered the issue of the respect for Russian and international environmental standards. Oleg Mitvol, the deputy head of the Russian Natural Resources Ministry, environmental watchdog, has protested Shell's environmental pollution, and damage has come from the development projects. Russian authorities gave Shell a deadline to fix purported environmental violations before revoking its environmental license with the allegation that the $20-billion project was causing $50 billion of damage to the environment. International observers—who have been writing endlessly about the oil giants (how they have stolen natural resources and cavalierly destroyed the environment all around, while doing too little to suck pollutants out of the ground) now redirected criticism to Gazprom's strategy and work to safeguard the oil giants' advantage. I have no definitive legal knowledge of the situation, however; perhaps the amount of the damage has been inflated or the legal case is an excuse to control the field, but it is undeniable that oil giants spill millions and millions of resources and then they take years and years—if at all—to mop up the environment. The issue of the TNK-BP's license has come under debate. The Kovykta gas field (in the Irkutsk region in eastern Siberia) has come under regulatory pressure, and Gazprom and TNK-BP reached a deal over Kovykta in June 2007 that puts an end to the quarrel by giving Gazprom more control over Russia's natural resources. According to the agreement, TNK-BP will pass majority control of the above project to Gazprom. BP and TNK-BP have also signed a memorandum of understanding on creating a strategic alliance with Gazprom for investing in long-term strategic projects or asset swaps across the globe. The deal cements state-controlled Gazprom's control over the Russian gas sector and resolves a long-running standoff with BP's Russia venture. TNK-BP is to cede its 62.89 percent holding in Kovykta to Gazprom, but has been given the option to buy a stake of 25 percent plus one share in Russia-Petroleum, the license holder of the Kovykta field, at a market price. The option is to be activated once agreement is reached on international projects. Gazprom is paying TNK-BP between $700 million and $900 million for the Kovykta stake and a half-share of a local company that is building gas infrastructure in Eastern Siberia. The exact sum will be set subsequently. According to Tony Hayward, the new BP chief executive, this deal could lay the groundwork for powerful cooperation between BP, TNK-BP, and Gazprom.

This incident has to be reinterpreted. The West, or rather big western groups, obtained upstream licenses at low prices to resell (arguably) the oil at a high price but not to disrespect environmental rules. While this was going on, the West was accusing Russia of irrational behavior. The issue of whether or not Shell and other companies have complied with environmental rules must be left to the Russian authorities. It is true that the Russian foreign minister Sergei Lavrov has invited all to talk with each other to avoid any further clashes. Some speculate that licenses to big foreign firms like Shell, ExxonMobil, and Total—that is, the operators of the country's three production-sharing agreements in Sakhalin—will be revoked or that the Kremlin is behind the challenges so that it can come within reach of Sakhalin 2's immense resources (by 2006, Russia enjoyed a direct participation only in the Sakhalin 1 project) or change the licenses to give the state a bigger slice of the profits.

ExxonMobil's Sakhalin 1 project also came under fire from the head of another watchdog group, the Federal Service for Ecological, Technological and Atomic Inspection, who accused the operator of gross violations. Fears in the West over the issue of respecting environmental rules and the licensing of western companies to access upstream activities in Russia are one side of the recent dispute. We can get a better grasp of this complex issue by looking at the recent dispute between the European Union and Russia over the call for Putin's Kremlin to agree to binding rules on energy relations. This issue is actually very strategic for both sides, as Western Europe is increasingly dependent on the import of these commodities and Russia is dependent on export revenues. European leaders gathering in Finland reinstated this same concept on October 20, 2006. While Putin's Kremlin is confident that both sides will find common ground on trade and investments in oil and gas, he has said that the specific issue of signing the Energy Charter Treaty will require further analysis. As Russia and the European Union start negotiation on a new strategic partnership, these issues will have to be put back out on the table.

According to the Kremlin, Russia is not against the principles of the charter, but there are certain provisions herein which should be better defined if the European Union truly wishes to develop a common approach with Russia. The rule of reciprocity should be respected, and while the investment of foreign gas and oil companies in Russia is included in the agreement, there is little opportunity for Russian companies to gain access to Western Europe's distribution markets. Of course, full reciprocity would be best for both sides.

A Kremlin Misstep over a Ukrainian Gas Dispute

A disagreement has developed as a result of the Russia-Ukraine dispute over gas supply and its payment. It started over gas that was sent to Europe and allegedly stolen in Ukraine. Ukraine was accused of drawing more gas than the country paid for off of the pipeline. Already in 2000, then president Leonid Kuchma admitted that Ukraine siphoned thirteen billion cubic meters of gas out of the pipeline. Gazprom filed a suit requesting reimbursement for European-bound gas of more than a billion cubic meters for the year 2001 alone. In the first months of 2004, Ukrainian police discovered more than 150 holes in the nation's oil distribution system. The controversy recently increased when it was revealed how much Kiev has to pay for Russian gas. In addition, observers saw Putin's strategy as a way of punishing Ukraine for establishing tight ties with western powers, especially following the November 2004 Ukrainian Orange Revolution that Viktor Yushchenko won.

Gazprom announced on December 30, 2005, that it would cease fuel exports to Ukraine unless it could implement a price increase of $230 over market price by the beginning of 2006—that is, four times what the country was paying for Russian gas in 2005. If this deal was not finalized, it would create a risk for the gas supply to Western Europe—western Siberia's gas traverses Ukraine, and approximately 80 percent of Russia's gas exports flow through it—and would mean that Ukraine would not receive gas and would experience up to a 5 percent drop in GDP, which would force inflation pressures up to 30 percent annually. The price was set at $50 per 1,000 cubic meters (several of Russia's former Moscow allies are paying this price as well; however, $260 to 265 is being paid by Western Europeans). In the midst of the crisis in early January 2006, Russia interrupted supply for three days, but on January 4, the two countries' state-run gas companies, Gazprom and Naftohaz, seemed to agree on resuming the gas supply to Ukraine under a new deal in which

Russian and Asian gas would be sold to Ukraine by Gazprom through a trading company for $230 per 1,000 cubic meters. In fact, they secured a new agreement for Ukraine to pay $95 per 1,000 cubic meters (up from $50), but this rate might fluctuate with the market.

The result is that Ukraine will buy gas through the purposefully created RosUkrEnergo—jointly owned by two banks (Gazprombank and the Austrian Raiffeisenbank)—which will charge Ukraine only $95 per 1,000 cubic meters. RosUkrEnergo can afford the much lower price because it receives cheaper gas from Turkmenistan, Uzbekistan, and Kazakhstan. (These three Caucasian countries will supply some two-thirds of Ukraine's gas needs). The pipeline that runs through Ukrainian territory brings gas to Ukraine as well as to Western European countries. Gazprom will pay $1.60 per 1,000 cubic meters every 100 kilometers (it used to be $1.09) for the transit fee through Ukrainian pipelines.

Besides the political intent of forcing Kiev back in the face of the political influence of Moscow, Putin has been able to tie several former satellite countries to the same mind-set, at least for the next few years. Originally, it was not known if the Russia-Ukraine deal was a compromise, a diplomatic masterpiece for Putin, or a setback for the Kremlin. Or perhaps this could have been a Kremlin misstep, a harsh stance over a country that was under the West's observation. The fact that all these countries are much more unified now than they were before is undeniable. RosUkrEnergo and Ukraine have been able to negotiate a $95 per 1,000 cubic meters price that applies until the end of 2006, and will replenish depots with 24.5 billion cubic meters. This is the result of a meeting held in the Black Sea town of Sochi on July 16, 2006 between Putin, Russian Prime Minister Mikhail Fradkov, and Viktor Yanukovich (the political elections that took place in Ukraine on March 26, 2006, led to the formation of a government run by Yanukovich, Yushchenko's former political adversary during the presidential election in 2004). Future prices for gas will be set according to the status of the relationships between the two countries and the role of Turkmenistan, who has been tempted to raise its selling price to some $100 per 1,000 cubic meters.

Nevertheless, this gas deal is having an impact, and the state-run oil and gas company, Naftohaz, is rapidly falling into arrears for gas delivered by Gazprom through RosUkrEnergo. The growing indebtedness exposes Naftohaz and the country to the risk of losing control over the gas transit pipeline system. Naftohaz has incurred just under $600 million in debt to RosUkrEnergo for gas received during January – April 2006. In addition, Naftohaz owes $85 million to the Gazprom-devised joint venture UkrGazEnergo. These debts add up to $680 million that is owed to Gazprom's proxies after only four months, without even considering the subsequent months and the hundreds millions in bank loans that have to be repaid. Meanwhile, Gazprom went through the motion of billing that amount to RosUkrEnergo, who in turn presented the bill to Naftohaz. In June 2006, Gazprom gave Naftohaz until July 15, 2006, to repay the debt in full.

The process will not accelerate as long as the price of gas sold to Ukraine stays below the market price (i.e., roughly $230 per 1,000 cubic meters).

By the end of October 2006, Ukrainian President Yanukovich announced that Russia and Ukraine had come to a general accord concerning gas supplies for 2007. The price has been set at $130 per cubic meter for 2007 and RosUkrEnergo reported that for this price, Ukraine would be entitled to receive an overall supply of fifty five billion cubic meters. In light of this, Gazprom would probably gain approximately $7.2 billion. Russia is now a major player in world energy markets as it enjoys more proven natural gas reserves than any other country in the world. Exporting energy resources has been a major driver of Russia's economic growth and the country is very dependent on it. Moscow already supplies sizeable amounts of natural gas to several countries in Europe. Besides Western European countries, China, Japan, and South Korea are seeking access to the vast energy resources of eastern Siberia, as those countries strive to meet their increasing energy needs while reducing dependence on the Middle East. Russia's profitability for state budget revenues relies a lot on exports and the expectations of economic growth abroad. North Stream, South Stream, and other important pipeline investments are audacious plans to meet the gap between Europe's and Asia's gas supply and demand and to secure supplies to emerging countries overall. Bolstering spending on the energy infrastructures signifies increasing cooperation between countries in terms of financial and technological involvement as Russia needs foreign companies' modern oil and gas extraction technology. Also, reinforcing common strategic goals is generally affordable and guarantee availability of energy resources for all involved actors through a network of new pipelines or through expansion of existing export pipelines across all countries and regions. Besides transit risks and countries that have threatened to block supplies because of pricing disputes, in fact several governments support these projects, as does the European Union.

Nothwithstanding, there is no reason to blame Russia too much for its role as an oil- and gas-exporting country. International observers believe that Russia has used the potential of its energy resources as political and economic leverage. Several policy choices in the recent past with Ukraine, Moldova, Belarus, and Georgia over contracted volumes have not been characterized by overaggressivity because most of the economic leverage was finalized to exploit favorable conditions on the international markets and the associated higher prices are quite logical when applying the West's capitalistic logic. Perhaps the general fear over Russia's actions is quite exaggerated, given that it is in Russia's long-term interest to be more cooperative with the West.

Chapter Eight

A Divided Society

The preceding chapters have provided a glimpse of the economic inequality in modern Russia, which is the most unequal industrialized society in the world—much more so than the United States or Mexico. Estimates concerning the distribution of income also provide a sense of this very negative force by looking at preliminary data regarding the 1990s. The Gini coefficient is a number that assumes any value between 0 and 1, where 0 means perfect equality in the distribution of wealth (everyone would have the same level of income) and 1 stands for perfect inequality (where one person holds all income and everyone else has absolutely nothing). To put it another way, the Gini coefficient measures how much income distribution deviates from an equal distribution, with a coefficient above 0.40 being a warning sign of unequal income distribution. In Russia income inequality remained relatively low until 1991, but thereafter the Gini coefficient doubled between 1991 and 2001, moving from 0.26 in 1991 to 0.45 in 1996 and rising perilously to 0.52 in 2001. The coefficient increased by more than 50 percent in several members of the Commonwealth of Independent States (CIS)—the successor of the Soviet Union—with Georgia registering at the top end of the scale with a Gini coefficient of 0.55. In total, Russia and the other CIS countries are approaching the levels of inequality typical of Latin American economies.

From a different perspective, the poverty line peak was reached in 1992 when 33.5 percent of the population was below it, and the ratio fell to 20.7 percent by 1997, rose again to 29 percent by 2000, and came back down to 17.8 percent as of 2004 (Russian Federal State Statistics Service). A number of factors have contributed to Russia's economic decline, which was followed by the rise in income inequality during the 1990s. In most cases, the biggest economic declines have occurred in countries that initially had the largest macroeconomic imbalances, were the most industrialized, had the smallest previous experience with market institutions, and implemented only limited reforms in less than effective ways. Incomplete market reforms, high levels of bureaucratic corruption, and the theft of national wealth by powerful business elites accounts for crucial and growing differences in poverty and inequality outcomes.

These factors created a split in Russian society, made up of the poor and the new rich Russian elite. Income distribution became so unevenly distributed that only 7 percent of the populace had an income above $2,000 per month and much less than 10 percent earned between $1,000 and $2,000 per month. In the 1990s, the largest percentage of Russians were living in very poor conditions, and the population that was earning less than half the average national per capita income increased from 11 percent to 32 percent between 1990 and 1998. While the average monthly wage in Russia was 5,221 rubles during the first part of 2003, 2,137 rubles constitutes today's minimum monthly wage according to the Russian government. This, however, is simply the real poverty threshold, according to experts.

Since Putin came to power, the standard of living indicators have certainly shown signs of improvement. The portion of the population living with incomes below subsistence levels has steadily decreased since 2000: real disposable incomes increased 9 percent in 2000 and 6 percent in 2001. This gives us an idea about how big the change in the real disposable income of Russians has been since the early 2000s. The share of population living at the subsistence level decreased from 29 percent in 2000 to 28 percent in 2001. Pensions also increased approximately 20 percent in real terms over the same period.

Even today, the Committee of Social Politics of the Council of the Federation reports that about one-fifth of Russian citizens still live on or near the poverty line, while the Russian Federal Statistics Service claims that the number is less than 18 percent. This is the result of improved disposable income, which increased by an average of 11.25 percent from 2002 to 2005. In practice, according to the distribution of population by per capita average income, the share of the population living with less than 4,500 rubles is diminishing, while the percentage of the population living with more than 4,500 rubles is increasing. Two examples suffice to demonstrate this. First, the portion of the population living with an average per-capita monthly income below 1,500 rubles was 17.3 percent in 2002 and only 3.2 percent in 2005; and second, the portion of the population enjoying more than 12,000 rubles monthly was 17.7 percent of the total in 2005, up from 2.9 percent as of 2002. The final consumption by households (i.e., consumption of final goods) also increased by 8.48 percent over the same period. In contrast, independent observers calculate that approximately 65 percent of Russians are disadvantaged and unable to provide for themselves (i.e., 30 percent of the population is poor and 35 percent earns a meager income), because the 2,137-ruble minimum monthly wage is considered adequate to satisfy basic needs.

Looking at statistical figures from a comparative perspective, one finds that average monthly wages were approximately $150 by the end of the 1990s and are now above $400 as of the summer of 2007 (Russian Federal State Statistics Service and Central Bank of Russia). These facts provide evidence of an improved financial ability and an improvement in the lives of Russians at least to some extent, but the same evidence does not conceal the fact that only a tiny number of Russians are wealthy or very rich, as the Gini coefficient demonstrates.

Other Indicators of a Divided Society: Health, Life Expectancy, and Mortality

A highly divided society is evident when one looks at several other indicators. In fact, another factor that has been developing since the breakup of the Soviet Union is the dramatic decline in general health of Russians, along with a corresponding decline in population due to a natural slowing of the birthrate and migration. Life expectancy is a frequently utilized and analyzed component of demographic data that represents a person's average lifespan, and is used as an indicator of the overall health of a country. Life expectancy can decrease due to problems such as famine, war, disease, and poor health. Life expectancy for men in 2006 is expected to be lower in Russia than in India and Egypt, decisively lower than in high-income countries where average life expectancy at birth is seventy-seven years. The average lifespan of men in Russia decreased from 69.7 in the early 1970s to 66.1 in the late 1990s. By 1998, the life expectancy for both sexes had recovered about half of the decline, and the gap had narrowed to 11.6 years before falling again following the 1998 collapse of the Russian ruble. By 2000, male life expectancy had fallen to 59.0 years and female life expectancy to 72.2 years, with the gap increasing to 13.2 years—nearly back to their levels at the height of the Russian mortality crisis. This unusually high mortality rate was well above its natural rate, which emerged in all its negative consequences in the mid 1990s, although no doubt high mortality rates were a feature of the Brezhnev period also.

Epidemic heart disease as well as other health crises and accidents caused death rates to more than double in the last decade. The mortality crisis of the 1990s, which Susan Shapiro (1995) called a social crisis of transformation through mass psychological stress, along with deteriorating health services and living standards and nutritional deprivation, reached its peak in 1994, attenuated from 1995 to 1998, and then worsened again in 1999 and during the current decade. The largest contributors to this aggravating social trend during the current decade are heart attacks and strokes, for which the main risk factors in Russia include unhealthy diet, excessive consumption of alcohol, and cigarette smoke. Russian men and women are among the heaviest smokers in the world.

The recent World Bank (2005) report, *Dying Too Young: Addressing Premature Mortality and Ill Health Due to Non Communicable Diseases and Inquiries in the Russian Federation*, shows that male life expectancy has plummeted to fifty eight years, twelve years shorter than in the United States, twenty years less than in Sweden, and thirteen years less than in Poland; in Sub-Saharan Africa men's life expectancy is around fifty years. Russia is one of the few middle-income countries in the world where life expectancy is falling. Overall, Russian men live an average of sixteen years less than men in Western Europe, and fourteen years less than Russian women. The alarming population decline in Russia—mainly owing to deaths from heart disease, traffic accidents, and alcoholism—translates into a current life expectancy for men and women that is significantly below that of their counterparts in a European Union country. Russian men are particularly at risk and the male-female gap in life expectancy in Russia is the widest in the world, suggesting that the dramatic drop in men's life expectancy and specific gender behavioral factors are important, rather than simply external factors such as environment or health care. The World Bank report calculates that if current levels of ill health and disability continue, the healthy life expectancy of Russian males will fall to fifty-three years, even worsening the current Russian population structure which shows the lowest ratio in the world of males to females—at this writing 88 males per 100 females (the gender imbalance is absent only at age thirty six but increasingly pronounced in older age groups). This appalling scenario could hamper economic growth and have a negative socioeconomic impact by shrinking the adult workforce. Policies aimed at reducing deaths from noncommunicable diseases and road accidents to Western European levels by 2005 (Russia ranks first in the world for road accidents, with twelve accidents for every 10,000 vehicles) could confer socioeconomic benefits equivalent to close to 30 percent of the 2002 Russian GDP, the World Bank says.

It seems logical that, despite recent economic growth and healthy public finances, Vladimir Putin still has plenty of big problems to solve. The Russian Ministry of Health and Social Development has been developing a federally targeted program to prevent and control early death, ill health, and disability caused by these killers but much more needs to be done to mobilize sufficient resources. The country is still facing population decline, due in large part to deaths from heart disease, cancer, traffic accidents, and alcoholism. Between 1992 and 2005, the Russian population declined by six million people to an estimated 143 million. If current trends in low fertility and high mortality rates continue, Russia will lose approximately another eighteen million people by 2025, as calculated by experts at the World Bank.

Premature mortality, combined with an aging society and a shrinking workforce, is the worst combination for sustained economic growth and widens inequalities—especially in Russia's poorer rural areas, where a vicious cycle of alcoholism, absenteeism, and unemployment are associated with households that remain locked in poverty with a substantial and significant reduction in disposable income. This has destabilized families, resulting in a large number of divorces in 2005 (467 out of every 1,000 marriages, although lower in comparison with the 700 in 2000), which has increased regional disparities and put national security at risk.

Another bit of good news is that Russian authorities are beginning to notice the severity of other aspects of Russian life—above all, the demographic crisis that is shrinking the overall Russian population. This is a multifaceted issue, however. On one side, one might consider the dramatic health crisis in Russia. President Putin, in his 2005 State of the Nation address, referred to this crisis, stating that the problem could not be resolved through the prohibition of alcohol. Each young person must realize that leading a healthy lifestyle means success—his or her own personal success—said Putin. Although a prohibition campaign was one of the very first policy measures implemented by President Mikhail Gorbachev in the mid 1980s and temporarily reversed mortality trends, it proved extremely unpopular, and Russia had to consider more sophisticated approaches to deal with this issue.

A study by the World Bank (2005) estimated that reducing mortality from noncommunicable diseases in Russia to Western European levels by 2025 would bring economic benefits equaling about 5 percent of the 2002 Russian GDP when valuing a year of life at one GDP per capita. While since the late 1990s, the burden of chronic illness on families is estimated to have contributed to an annual loss of 5.6 percent of per capita income per year, catching up with the European Union countries in terms of life expectancy would require a reduction in Russia's annual mortality of 4.6 percent per year for noncommunicable diseases and 6.6 percent for injuries. If these results were achieved, this would translate into an increase in per capita GDP of between US$2,856 and $9,243 by 2025, calculates the World Bank. Even greater benefits, as much as 30 percent of the 2002 Russian GDP, could be achieved when measuring the contribution that improved health makes to a person's standard of living (World Bank, 2005).

A related aspect is the issue of fertility. The total fertility rate declined from 2.19 children per woman in 1987 to less than 1.2 in 1999. (This measures the rate at which couples replace themselves in the population). In the 1980s, the birth rate was externally stimulated by various factors that allowed women to accelerate their fertility. These factors included extended and paid maternity leave, easier qualification for housing, and other benefits. After peaking at 2.19 children per woman in 1987, the total fertility rate fell by more than a child per woman to 1.17 in 1999. These birth rates are low in any comparison with other countries. This, together with low fecundity rates, has a potentially negative impact on macroeconomic performance.

Therefore, the Russian population has been decreasing since 1992 by an average of 700,000 people every year. Until 1998, migration into the country compensated for over half of the natural decrease, but the population decrease still required attention and new ways to cope with increasingly negative trends. The most recent data (April 2007) show that the birthrate has increased by 8.5 percent and the death rate has decreased by 9.5 percent, and these facts mark very positive news for Russia. In his seventh annual address to the Federal Assembly on May 10, 2006, President Putin announced a new action plan to focus on these issues. Gorbachev also publicly supports the goals set by Putin in his 2006 annual address because Putin's Kremlin has the opportunity to implement those goals within twelve to eighteen months and thereby beef up expenses for economic and social needs while keeping an eye on the overall economic policy goals of protecting the economy from inflationary pressures and additional strengthening of the ruble, as well as showing concern toward the people.

Among others things, Putin stated that child care benefits should be increased to support women who have a second child because those women are often out of employment for a long time. Russia must stimulate families to have a second child, adding that concerns about housing, health care, and education are prompting many families to stop at only one child. President Putin declared that couples should receive significant help, worth approximately $50 a month for eighteen months for the first child and $107 a month for two children, despite the fact that this was dubbed reminiscent of the Soviet era in Harvard's *Economic Newsletter* (2006, No. 9). It is smart politics, however, and sends clear messages to counteract a negative trend.

In reality, boosting the birthrate actually seems dependent upon a establishing a consensus in society. The Yuri Levada Analytical Center—the private polling agency originally named VTsIOM-A—surveyed Russians and found that they would be happy to have more children if they were in a financial position to do so. The Yuri Levada Analytical Center report that is quoted in the *Economic Newsletter* (2006, No. 8), shows that those interviewed would be prepared to have another child if their income increased (26 percent), if they had more confidence in the future (22 percent), or if they had better housing (20 percent). The Putin administration is trying to answer these needs, as the aforementioned State of the Nation speech of 2006 suggested.

The Roots of Economic Woes

As I have already suggested, the roots of these maladies are in the system and the distortions that the 1990s created and systematically amplified. Two additional aspects of the 1990s must be considered—income dispersion and non-monetary transactions.

Income dispersion declined substantially in Russia from 1960 to 1989, following the beginning of consecutive wage reforms and an increase in minimum wages. The inequality of disposable income distribution in Russia decreased into the late 1970s, but increased moderately during the mid to late 1980s. The increase in income differential was the direct result of wage reforms introduced by Gorbachev and the increase of the informal economy that was beginning to grow. Therefore, there were no negligible differences in income concentration prior to the transition from communism to a free-market economy. The markedly different institutional evolution, however, may explain the variation in inequality trends. The sharp rise observed in income inequality was also due to the development of labor institutions and the concentration of assets. It developed into a sharp increase in both earnings and disposable income for those who already had money because ordinary citizens were unable to mobilize resources, labor markets became distorted, and asset concentration became more pronounced following the covert privatization process. In turn, unequal income dispersion contributed to increasing instability and Russian discontent.

Non-monetary transactions had been taking place in Russia since its early transition years. The unique effect of bartering on the economy is a tendency to overproduce low-quality goods, substituting money as a means of exchange and restricting trading networks. In addition, credit shortages do not cause a fall in the price of goods because either the debts create external issues between creditors, or credit constraints are distributed asymmetrically. This phenomenon led to an unwillingness to restructure and improve production and, in turn, allowed the quality of bartered goods to deteriorate.

One explanation for why the economy was drawn to a barter system can be found by reviewing the development of inflation during this time. By the mid-1990s, the Department of Finance was not in control of the strong inflationary pressures that were affecting the economy. And although the high inflation in Latin America did not force the appearance of a barter system comparable in size to that in Russia, bartering in Russia kept increasing on all levels until the mid-1990s.

Daily life has been affected by this phenomenon. By 1992, the barter economy accounted for 5 percent of enterprise transactions. By 1997, it had increased to at least 47 percent. Overall, estimates placed the barter turnover range at between 30 and 80 percent of inter-enterprise transactions. At its peak in 1998, over 50 percent of industrial transactions took place in barter form (Guriev and Ickes, 2000). Demonetizations became so widespread that the health of the entire system was threatened and required serious attention from the authorities. The effects have been destructive to the economy's ability to work smoothly. Bartering and counter-trade activities in the West increased during the 1980s because of the international debt crisis and global reluctance to finance imports to developing countries. Although the bartering system increased as a domestic phenomenon up until 1998, the year of the financial crisis, it decreased in popularity afterward due to better economic conditions overall.

A growing barter economy, a lengthy and deep economic slowdown that occurred in the 1990s, the uncertain creditworthiness of firms, and the banks' unwillingness to provide credit to firms correlated with the banking sector's ability to reconcile the need for sound banking policies, which were burdened by a high volume of nonperforming loans as banks' portfolios were still exposed to nonrestructured corporate finance. The lending behavior of banks with weak balance sheets could not have affected the response of bank loan policy. In the absence of an efficient banking sector, individual enterprise incentives were inconsistent with profit maximization, which was extremely costly for the economy as a whole. The failures of the banking industry and capital market imperfections prevented the disbursement of capital to Russian enterprises. Some of those imperfections included the cost of searching for market alternatives, the emergence of natural monopolies, lagging restructuring, both tax and credit incentives for firms and state fiscal and quasi-fiscal institutions, and the development of survival mechanisms in the face of sales and production difficulties. Amid the chaos of the 1990s, the barter system was used to pay taxes to local, regional, and even federal governments. In addition, wages were occasionally paid by bartering, thus affecting real household monetary income.

Another negative factor was that of wage payment arrears. Although this phenomenon has almost disappeared in the wake of economic recovery, wage payment arrears accumulated and characterized the economic reality of Russia after 1993. Companies postponed payments to federal and regional governments, pension funds, and employees themselves. By the second half of the 1990s, only one-third of the workers received wages in full and on time. Roughly 30 percent of Russian workers had to wait for months to be paid. Although wage payment arrears were uneven and differed greatly from region to region—Eastern Siberia and the Far East suffered most—the phenomenon created huge social problems. In 1998, outstanding debt ranged from a month's wages in Moscow and St. Petersburg to five months of pay in Western Siberia, creating huge economic burdens and general unhappiness among the population. This problem prompted families to create survival mechanisms such as interfamily transfer (parents helping children, and vice versa), living off of savings while waiting for paychecks, home production of goods for both consumption and sale, and the sale of family assets. Discontent was highly visible within the country's social fabric.

Academic Division over Russian Unfairness in the 1995

Scholars seem to fall into one of two groups when trying to determine why the serious economic inequalities in Russian society continue to persist. One group tends to be critical of the way the transition was conducted, asserting that it created more trouble than any of the other policies that could have been put in place. This group blames either domestic or external factors. A second, smaller, minority group obstinately insists that transitional Russia does not show evidence of social disaster (e.g., Åslund, 2002), yet the outcomes of the transformation have been negative and uncomfortable to both western consultants and international economic agencies.

Nevertheless, because Russian society became so largely divided, the growth of regionalism and separatism greatly hampered Russia's development. In addition, Yeltsin was coerced into pursuing contradictory policies by shifting power and financial revenues to regional leaders who had a tendency to conceal potential tax revenues for the benefit of local oligarchs and business groups. This created additional regionally distorted economic interests that were noticeable to all, and Putin had to counteract this situation by strengthening the unity of Russia. Although commentators and experts believe that Russian inflation and economic issues during the Yeltsin years have altered the dynamics of voters, the support for Putin has a different explanation. With charges of election fraud against Yeltsin only of minor importance—it is difficult to believe that election fraud accounted for more than a few percentage points of Yeltsin's victory (Hough, 2001)—Putin's electoral support has been much, much less controversial. Putin was promising a different plan than Yeltsin, and even Gorbachev, had offered. Putin offered strategies for reducing the attempt to control the country's enormous natural resources and the growth of the previous bureaucratic-capitalist classes' transition into an oligarchy.

What has emerged in Russia is not surprising considering the past, and one must reinterpret the outcomes of the 1990s to truly understand their patterns and the relevant need for leadership that unifies the country. The paternalistic epoch governed by the former Soviet Union ignored the private accumulation of wealth, but the system itself created a class of state managers. This group of former state managers and people from the newly created class of private businessmen were not acting as modern Schumpeterian innovators—named after the economist born in Moravia, which is today part of the Czech Republic, and who then moved to Harvard in 1932—who have managerial skills enough to produce technical advancements and express business creativity. Yet, state managers and youth communist members acquired managerial or political skills over time that they could capitalize on during the transition to a free market. This supports another relevant truth that the transformation process originated in the murkiness of previous political and social realities. The passage from one system to another was accomplished through the transformation of technocratic state managers and top officials into savvy market capitalists (Sergi, 2004). The ensuing Russian institutional chaos and nonexistent middle class led to overt oligarchy and the striking phenomenon of large new fortunes.

During these developments in Russia, a fresh, middle-level management class emerged (in contrast to a traditional middle class). It possessed a political and cultural capital developed over decades of paternalism. Therefore, what has surrounded oligarchs has been a concentration of political and cultural human capital developed during communism, which the oligarchs used to take control of the economy. This form of predatory activity was often the case during the 1990s. Politics and financial operations were not simply Schumpeterian creative destruction; they were predatory wealth redistribution efforts, and the losers in this situation were the nascent middle class, which had been led to believe that their jobs were secure and that Russian rubles were real money. The degeneration of the system resulted not simply in the transformation and adaptation of a new social class to the new state of affairs, but also in the complexity of a market experiment that reformers quickly created and that the intelligentsia supported for a long time to allow them to use their inherited wealth. The experiment used the ideology of the monetary approach as well as that of the Washington Consensus. A new market-oriented approach imposed measures that promoted price stability and attempted to achieve macroeconomic stabilization. If developments cemented the diverse functions of the elite into a hegemonic bloc, reformers implemented monetary policies and budgetary restraints favored by international economic organizations and preferred economists.

These aspects illuminate why Russia was searching for a new social reality, improvement in living standards, and more stable and effective institutions. The results could be seen in new groups of elite capitalists and in the application of strong measures of capitalist regulation. Nevertheless, the transition from one social situation to another has not been easy and has produced far-reaching distortions. One strong statement made here was about the emergence of a group of new managers and reformers. This statement, however, must be clarified. The technocratic component of the new elite was only somewhat accustomed to western-type practices and negotiation techniques, but symptoms of corporate-gang capitalism appeared during Brezhnev's era.

As it happened, some powerful people lost favor to a group of young communist technocrats who created a form of managerial capitalism using state property. They obtained their power through political and cultural dominance, preserving some 80 to 90 percent of their positions in economic and land management. They simply did not squander political and economic gains and found enough power to maneuver things in such a way as to control important resources and cultivate support within the political establishment through reciprocal benefits.

It would be an exaggeration, however, to claim a complete absence of capitalists during the era of communism, for two reasons. First, the transformation did not occur abruptly, and the regime allowed some private enterprises during the 1980s. Second, the class of state managers and young entrepreneurs can clearly trace its origins to the previous paternal structure. The class of new managers formed a vital component in today's society, although the chaotic situation of the 1990s may have transformed political and managerial capital into a hegemonic oligarchy of corruption and inequalities. In truth, these were also significant in an early stage of capitalism in Europe as well as in the United States, where the robber barons of the nineteenth century resorted to violence but built businesses and factories and reinvested their profits at home. The transformation as it played out in Russia and the policy choices adopted by competing groups heightened already serious social consequences, and resulted in major rearrangements within society to fit the new economic context, with some groups gaining power and others not. The resulting oligarchy has not created an economic base of factories, steel mills, and railroads, as the robber barons did in their countries. Instead, oligarchs captured the wealth of the country and exported profits and capital abroad, producing a society that now struggles to find equilibrium in the sphere of economic reform and social groups. Putin's Kremlin, therefore, was searching for a new socioeconomic structure.

When voters welcomed the new democratic vision, they were inclined to accept some economic losses as an inevitable part of the transition. Rapid privatization was indispensable in reducing the power of the Communist Party, and citizens wanted this program to succeed. Yeltsin's privatization policies, however, produced unenthusiastic results. These post-1991 events in Russia can be explained via a fivefold hypothesis, which was made most convincingly by Amartya Sen (1999). Owing to the removal of restrictions, socioeconomic development is a process of intensifying political freedoms, economic facilities, social opportunities, transparency guarantees, and protective security—all of which serve the development model equally. Development should remove all the restrictions that prevent people from being able to "shape their own destiny and help each other" (Sen 1999: 11). In such an endeavor to remove obstacles to certain freedoms, a forward-looking policy-making strategy must not hamper the functioning of the markets but instead enforce equitable rules of the game. In this framework, access to both market opportunities and all relevant information ought to be made available to everyone. Private initiatives would prompt economic growth from one side, while the government would continue to enforce institutional achievements and fair play on the other. Gorbachev initiated a timorous season of partial liberal reforms, but nothing resembling a wise government of the type described by Sen was achieved during the Yeltsin era. Wise and forward-looking policies will be the measure of Putin's legacy.

Sen and others offer excellent insight into the nature of development as both an economic and social construct. Others, like Joseph Stiglitz, state that the successful transformation of any economy requires nothing less than complete transformation of the society as a whole. These excellent concepts are innovative, ethical, constructive, and, above all, timely. They share a common acceptance and understanding of the fundamental and universal economic laws. As all economists know, violation of this universal tenet requires a negative economic response that affects all of society. In the case of Russia, this was seen most clearly under Yeltsin's leadership. In other words, violation of the basic economic laws specifically means a rejection of the universal validity concerning growing wealth inequality—or growing wealth disparity—as the primary cause of all economic problems and their subsequent growth. The development of tremendous wealth disparity under Yeltsin was the most negative economic trend or pattern that contributed to the overall economic chaos in the Russian society following the collapse of communism in 1989. More importantly, Yeltsin and his team seemed to show no awareness of these particular problems as primary causes of all other Russian economic problems.

At this point, one is tempted to conclude that Yeltsin and his economic advisors deliberately avoided respecting these universal economic laws. The evidence would also appear to suggest that Yeltsin and his economic advisors deliberately did not sympathize with the need to respect simple rules of ethics and economic laws; the resulting discussion in the West over the logic of these events proves that not everything that occurred in Russia was well understood by most readers or even experts in major western media outlets.

Many examples of reform throughout the Yeltsin years would seem to substantiate this. Growing wealth disparity in Russia beginning in 1989 and the implosion of communism through the Russian economic collapse in August of 1998 clearly indicate the reality of a massive and unprecedented shift in the concentration of wealth away from the Russian middle and lower classes.

This shift placed the state's wealth under the complete, personal control of a significantly small percentage of already wealthy Russians. This massive increase in wealth concentration within the Yeltsin-supported inner circles deserves further investigation, because Putin's popularity with the Russian people thus far has been based on his ability to reduce this massive concentration of wealth in Russia since his election in 2000.

Public Expectations And Youth

In the post-1991 Russian environment, the aforementioned realities represented the most serious issues documented in the vast majority of official analyses. At some point, however, international observers started pushing the debate over Russia's problems toward a false conclusion. The obvious gap between expectations at the public level and the reality of unethical practices has been so overwhelming that the public has simply dismissed experts who still deliver the official analysis. In other words, post-1991 predictions and assessments have been so far from reality that the Russian people now assume a level of cynicism that is unparalleled elsewhere in Eastern Europe. This is why the public now demands a consensus of outcomes that meet the level of ethical considerations they expect.

One can no longer attribute the dramatic developmental failures in Russia to natural errors in the learning process of structural development; rather, those failures can be instead attributed to a corrupt system of privatization and state ownership, which had to be addressed by government officials in the 1990s and the overall phenomenon of privatization and corruption had to be managed appropriately and differently. A system of entrepreneurs stealing from the state has developed along a precise path since the 1980s with the complicity of top political leaders, yet former communists have continued to support a policy of privatizing state ownership—producing the paradox of a buddy system with minor clashes between power groups drawn from the same power base and evident political clout.

When Yegor Gaidar and Yeltsin's kamikaze crew adopted a harsh policy stance as part of the government's official goal of economic reform in the early 1990s, the Russian people widely and quickly understood that they would suffer serious economic loss. A well-defined, objective economic model has not guided reforms, however, and Gaidar's economic reforms involved a rearrangement of economic relationships among various interest groups in a way that resulted in the economic improvement of some at the great expense of others.

As a result, Yeltsin's government lost all credibility with the public, who subsequently sent word to Putin and Russian decision makers not to ignore this very powerful chain of events. This is now considered the greatest ethical failure yet witnessed and experienced by Russia's populace, which is why it is so important to interpret facts from an ethical perspective rather than just applying a traditional economic and political analysis. The public will now get a clearer vision of what is happening in Russia, which in turn will elevate to a new level the current debate over what went wrong in Moscow.

It seems that traditional analysis has partially failed to offer government leaders and advisors an appropriate framework for realistically assessing the broader implications of the overall policy choices available to Putin and other decision makers. In this context, overestimating the degree to which many intended or unintended consequences of the 1990s altered long-term policy initiatives is a less grievous mistake, with fewer negative ethical implications, than is underestimating such issues. However, it might now be impossible for Putin—who is directing development goals for the entire country—to achieve justice for the entire population. When a country's economy has to be improved for everyone, it is not easy to achieve a balanced economic justice for all, as some classes gain more than others. Still, the objective of improving the economic condition for the overall country is on the way to achieving justice for the entire population, something that all observers should acknowledge.

Criticism from inside Russia is not absent, either. The former chess champion Garry Kasparov—who leads the United Civil Front group, part of the opposition coalition, the Other Russia—joined several protests against the Kremlin during the 2007. Protesters accuse Putin of creating an authoritarian regime on one side; the Kremlin denies these charges and accuses the opposition of destabilizing Russia on the other side. After the street protests of pensioners in 2005, St. Petersburg University students began using Internet chat rooms to discuss the prospect of regime change in Russia. Even though St. Petersburg police arrested several Marching without Putin (an anti-Putin group) students, young activists played a key role in mobilizing student disapproval (Rodriguez, 2005). An anti-Putin youth group, called Nashi ("ours"), appeared on the scene as well. The daughter of former St. Petersburg mayor Anatoly Sobchak (who was also Putin's professor of law and his political sponsor in St. Petersburg) recently initiated a new pro-Putin youth movement called Vse Svobodnnij ("We Are All Free"). Despite these examples of recent youth movements against or for Putin, Russia's youth have generally steered clear of civic life, voting in far fewer numbers than other age brackets.

Political engagement is not that widespread. The fact is that protesters are minuscule groups of Russian citizens and do not represent the vast majority of the country. And apathy remains a problem. According to Russia's Levada Center, just 39 percent of Russians aged eighteen to twenty-four voted in the 2003 parliamentary election (Rodriguez, 2005). In the 2004 presidential election, youth turnout was 45 percent. "Apathy among youth has been a great obstacle, and it remains an obstacle," said Ilya Yashin, leader of a youth organization affiliated with Yabloko (Rodriguez, 2005). Although it is possible to witness irritation among Russia's young people openly displaying their concern with what is happening in the country or among pensioners taking to the streets to protest cuts in social benefits, apathy is, in reality, a major issue for young Russians, states Sarah Ashwin (1999) in *Russian Workers: The Anatomy of Patience*.

People's health, longevity, medical technology, and improved access to public health services are all among crucial pillars in reducing risks to Russian population and helping the country catch up with those more developed nations in this area. Although Russian is growing economically at quite high rates, much improvement is needed in people's health, public health services on Western European levels, the quality of the environment, and life expectancy, which is the most useful indicator that reflects a country's population well-being, although it is important to have realistic expectations about Russian development in the next few years. If the open protests recently encountered in Russia are to be taken into account, the truth is that protesters have not been able to involve the entire population nor large shares of it. Finding the right balance between expectations and financial capabilities is not always easy, but the Kremlin has to help move the process of betterment along and overcome any hurdles. The next topic of my excursus through Russian affairs is the phenomenon of corruption and how to interpret it.

Chapter Nine

Russia's Democracy and Russians' Attitudes

Because several authors take Mikhail Gorbachev's and Boris Yeltsin's new democratic initiatives for granted, Russian culture contains elements of dualistic concepts of democracy, where the idea of a strong state or authority has appeal and where short periods of transformation have been followed by periods of conservatism and stagnation. Peter I, Catherine II, Alexander II, the Bolshevik Revolution, and the 1980s perestroika are good examples of this. Because all these evolutions have been imposed from the top and not by the people, there is a distinct perception of democratic values in Russia that is not necessarily linked to the power of the populace. The emergence of pseudo-western democratic institutions in Russia and the distortions of the new class of politicians during the 1990s were sufficient to produce additional social and institutional uncertainties.

When discussing the issue of democracy and its advantages, we could argue that economic development correlates with democratic governance rather than authoritarian rule, and that democratic countries are less likely than authoritarian countries to encourage threats to security. No one, however, is willing to consider that electoral democracies do not automatically establish a wide, respected consensus of accountability and responsibility. Real democracy was something different and hard to establish overnight in Eastern Europe, and an artificial electoral freedom did not preclude unjust outcomes—it can change the mix of policies that accomplish long-term good governance. Russia has been a notable example of elites trying to manage the electoral process at the federal and regional levels.

Minimal Electoral Democracy

To take further appropriate steps in this analysis, we must first consider two facts. First, the Russian system has undergone several failures and several transitions accompanied by reactionary regimes, reforms, and many kinds of reactions over the years (Sergi, 2004; McDaniel, 1996). Second, western-style democratic elections are quite new to Russian society, and very different from the previous communist era. Designation of the highest political personnel and members of Parliament have only occurred democratically, to some extent, since the 1990s. The free presidential elections, although not the country's first vote to directly elect the president, were clearly one of the first signs of the new electoral attitudes taking place in Russia—although in very narrow measures (through the minimal lens of the universality of electoral principles accompanied by moral justice) after Gorbachev began reforming the country in the mid-1980s. The concept of minimal electoral democracy was true as well throughout Yeltsin's grotesque political years, which he himself enforced during the 1990s, although the full and coherent concept of democracy and moral values were not coming together in the late 1980s and 1990s.

Despite these seemingly serious semi-democratic developments, many do not believe that Russia has any typical western standards of fairness, and this belief was felt particularly concerning presidential elections held in 2000 and 2004, according to many observers. Free elections, no matter how flawed they may seem, are not futile and are important for many reasons. The fact of the matter is that the Russians picked a former KGB man in 2000, backed him unenthusiastically, and four years later reconfirmed that appreciation. A few weeks after Russians reelected Putin in 2004, they were again encouraging him to steer the country toward a new state of affairs. The Russians showed perseverance, and praised Putin because they perceived him as capable of reaching the goals they had been chasing for some time now. Russians called on President Putin to reinforce this stance. Many poor Russian citizens had suffered many wrongs, and because their expectations had never been realized, they wanted a strong person in charge at that time.

Thus, Putin won the Kremlin by popular support and not by revolution. Nor did the new Kremlin win by consensus, but rather through elite support and control of the electoral process at all levels across Russia, as had occurred with Yeltsin. Although Russians do not want to go back to the days of communism, their expectations of Putin may have been colored by their experience of earlier leaders, and Putin may have felt the need to live up to the example of his predecessors, who were strong communist revolutionaries, but without pushing the country back to communist economics and politics. Putin gave his word that he would guide his country through an unparalleled path of modernization and steer the populace toward better times—exactly what Russians had been promised for a long time. And according to widespread consensus in Russia, no one after 1985 has accomplished these goals as well as Putin thus far. Resorting to opinion polls can make this difficult subject more accessible and exhibit the exact attitudes of people on political issues and society.

Public Opinion Polls

Professor Yuri Levada, the first to teach sociology at Moscow State University, led the way to using this method of analysis. In reality, sociology was not taught in Russia as a separate discipline because it was perceived as a threat to Leninist Marxism and the party's monopoly on information and social guidance. At the end of the 1950s, amid the excitement over its new leadership, the new Communist Party Secretary General Nikita Khrushchev allowed Professor Levada to carry out limited surveys of public opinion. By 1968, the Institute of Applied Social Research had been established in Moscow and sociologists considered it a serious tool for managing and interpreting their society. Sociologists and segments of the liberal intelligentsia were formulating concepts that reflected western thought.

Nevertheless, the Communist Party cried out that this kind of research could touch off trouble for the system, so Khrushchev's successor Leonid Brezhnev stopped the experiment and purged Yuri Levada from his position in 1972. When public opinion polls demonstrated that the Soviet invasion of Czechoslovakia in August of 1968 and the suppression of the economic reforms introduced in the 1960s had led to a decline in Russian popular support of the regime, the Institute and the sociologists were accused of deviating from communism's mainstream. Most of the dynamic experts working at the Institute and in the field of sociology were forced to leave, split up, or move on to other disciplines. By 1974, a regular sociological journal reappeared and the institute was renamed the Institute for Sociological Research.

Professor Levada could not restart his work, however, until the beginning of Gorbachev's glasnost. In 1987, the All-Union Center for the Study of Public Opinion was opened, and then renamed the All-Russia Center for the Study of Public Opinion (VTsIOM) after the end of the Soviet Union in 1991. Yuri Levada was part of this change. The Center became much respected, and although VTsIOM was a state-owned agency, it received no budget funds from the Kremlin. VTsIOM's work was funded with private-sector polling contracts. By September 2003, the government appointed a new board of directors. Professor Yuri Levada stated that the Kremlin was trying to silence public opposition to the Chechen war and, because of this, he and some of his colleagues quit VTsIOM and started a new private polling agency called Analytical Service (or VTsIOM-A), which was renamed the Yuri Levada Analytical Center in March 2004.

I disagree with a reading of Russia done on the basis of the country's history; instead I deem that the generalized and widespread discontent of Russians about what was going on in their vast country, and a few examples of people's perception concerning past and contemporary leaders, can be of absolute significance. Simply put, Russians showed significantly greater dissatisfaction with certain characters of the present rather than the past. In 2006, 40 percent of Russians deemed Stalin the best communist political leader in their history, as evidenced by recent polls on the subject (Johnson's Russia List, 2006). However, of 1,500 opinions taken by the agency Bashkirov and Partners in Moscow during the winter of 2005, 60 percent said they would not live under Stalin's leadership again, but 31 percent would not object to his return to power. Moreover, 47 percent of respondents weighed Stalin's role in the country's history as generally positive, while 43 percent feel it was generally negative. Overall, respondents aged sixty and over praised Stalin (69 percent), while young people between eighteen and twenty-nine were the least excited (37 percent).*

The Yuri Levada Analytical Center conducted another poll gauging people's feelings about building a monument to Stalin for the sixtyth anniversary of the end of World War II. While 37 percent of respondents opposed the idea, 29 percent backed it and 28 percent were indifferent. In a recent poll of 1,600 adults conducted by VTsIOM, 52 percent said that modern Russia does not need a politician like Stalin, while 42 percent said it does.

Let us draw another comparison. In a 1997 survey of 2,200 people, roughly 40 percent responded that they would like to live in Brezhnev's era, but only 11.6 percent of those wanted to live with Yeltsin reforms, and only 3.4 percent wished to live in Gorbachev's system. A recent public-opinion poll conducted after twenty years of transition and conducted by VTsIOM-A was held in 100 Russian cities, towns, and villages in March 2005 and 1,600 people were questioned; the results showed that Russians generally disliked perestroika. As published by the *Russia Journal Daily* (2005a), 61 percent of Russians dislike it, and only 14 percent of respondents approved of it. In reality, 45 percent of respondents disliked Gorbachev himself and only 23 percent believed Gorbachev wanted to reform the system. Yet, 24 percent of Russians believed that Gorbachev wanted to move Russia toward a capitalistic system, and 37 percent believed that he had no specific model to implement other than solving everyday problems. In 2006, 56.3 percent of Russians said they regretted the disintegration of the Soviet Union, according to a survey by the Bashkirov and Partners consultancy, as reported by Granma, the Cuban Press Agency.* Many in Russia today consider the roles played by Mikhail Gorbachev and Boris Yeltsin to be part of a conspiracy to destroy Russia as a superpower.

Russian support of Putin's policies is quite robust, although it has probably declined in some measure recently as was suggested by Professor Levada. Putin's economic programs and policies have benefited many more Russians than occurred under Gorbachev, and have broken through the people's distrust following Yeltsin's noncommunist vision. These facts explain the Russian support of Putin's *new vision*. It is nearly impossible to exaggerate the distinction in Russians' minds between Putin and other former Russian and Soviet leaders, if for no other reason than that traditional western analysts have always been so inconsistently willing to apply the same ethical standards to themselves that they do for Putin and Russia.

Also, most recent public opinion polls comparing the perception of official bribery during the pre-revolution era, communism, Gorbachev's years, Yeltsin's years, and now Putin's tenure show that the period with the least amount of rampant bribery is Putin's era, and the period with the most was Yeltsin's.

*See http://www.cdi.org/russia/johnson/9027–26.cfm

*See http://www.huffingtonpost.com/blake-fleetwood/56-of-russians-regret-fa_b_35939.html

In keeping with my own classical liberal credo, I consider government intervention on the energy sector to be a cure rather than a curse. Expanding government control over these resources has proved not to be detrimental to economic growth at all, and eventually has helped prevent more corruption from emerging and hurting the country definitively. Consequently it should not come as a surprise if Russians have expressed the perception that rampant bribery has been lower under Putin's Kremlin than in previous experiences; and the perception of the Kremlin as guarding a sort of credibility as corruption fighter. Although corruption has not been contained fully in Russia, the attack on the Kremlin's new progression was one of disbelief but was carried out in an empty way, and, perhaps what worried pessimists, as a sign of envy by groups of interests over the control of the country's resources.

In the end, it may well be impossible for the West to realistically assess the true benefits of Putin and his policies toward the Russian people without examining at the feelings of Russian society about past political leaders and the recent Kremlin administration's record of accomplishment on political, economic, and broader societal issues.

Are Russians Depoliticized?

Although the literature has presented Russia and Russians from an unfair perspective, mistaking the ruling elite classes for ordinary people, much less effort has been made to explain how Russians are, to a remarkable extent, depoliticized—this is not without its challenges. Russians often believe that ordinary people cannot have any influence over their government, which they view as a closed corporation of officials who look out for their own interests. This was the effective result of the reforms of the 1990s, but Russians do not blame the type of democracy they initiated. Russians do not reject democratic elections and procedures as inherently fraudulent. What matters to them is that their government did not reflect their preferences. A government's function is to preserve stability and enforce the laws of the land because the cause-and-effect relationship starts with order as a prerequisite to other activities, and this is not much different from what happens in the western world.

When pollsters ask Russians what is more important, order or freedom, three-quarters of Russians pick order, apparently assuming that the two choices are incompatible. This does not change our previous points, however. A factor that encourages an unbalanced understanding of Russian behaviors and their aspiration for good government is that Russians often do not trust one another. Mutual trust, which is essential to the functioning of a civil society, is in short supply in Russia to some extent, but this feature is present in other countries as well. Except for their families and close friends, Russians tend to view one another as antagonists or competitors, which may demonstrate the need for a government and institutions to be active and stable. Russia's recent past, and not

Russia's history, represents a good grounds for people to express dissatisfaction with Gorbachev's and Yeltsin's politics, a dissatisfaction which is visible among certain categories of citizens. Both of these experiences were seen by common Russians as utterly negative. The people's primary concern was that they needed new leadership capable of both stabilizing the country and taking action against the risk of a complete oligarchization of Russian society during the 1990s; I read and interpret this belief under this light, rather than historically. This perception may also favor strong governments because most Russians rely on the authorities to protect them, but it is completely fallacious to extrapolate that Russians would enthusiastically endorse autocratic governments. That modern Russians seem depoliticized is one aspect of the larger picture, but accusing them of being preferential to unusual forms of government is quite illogical.

We must recall that Russia today, as in the past, consists of several tiny enclaves to whom the 1990s government felt no responsibility. Assuming that only a mere 10 percent of Russians (who mostly live in large cities) hold western views of the powers and duties of government based on voting results or expert analysis is inaccurate. In reality—and this is another western hypocrisy—the West does not have one exclusive model of democracy and government to offer to Russians, nor to any other citizens around the world. The West has a Scandinavian model of social welfare, the U.S. model, mixed models of paternalism with incentives for business activities, and an Asian business model. When Russians were asked about what model they preferred, they exhibited a preference for western countries as a potential pattern of development for Russia, and a VTsIOM public-opinion poll taken in 1996 showed that roughly 70 percent of respondents preferred such a model, with high marks for the Swedish pattern indicated in a 1998 VTsIOM poll. Intellectuals in Russia often seem more disillusioned with western values than do ordinary Russians.

If Pipes and other experts believe that the cause of the disillusionment is, in some measure, the deliberate refusal of the new leadership to make a clean break with the Soviet system (put into simpler words, that Russians did not fully embrace the West), then this could only be applied to the mid-1980s experiment, not to what occurred afterward. In reality, clear signals that Russians did not like and continue to dislike communism and any other kind of authoritarian regime are clearly expressed in several of the public opinion polls highlighted in this book. The results of these polls, although vague at times, show that Russians are not in favor of autocracy.

Rather than just write about the Russians from our own distorted western perspective, we should reflect on modern Russian culture. Any analysis of Russia should start from a very simple focus: perhaps experts confuse each other and misinterpret Russians' quest for a strong government—in the West, we would call it a stable and trustworthy government—or at least a solid substitute for a communist government.

Western analysts should strive to not misinterpret or overlook these facts. Except for the two capital cities of Moscow and St. Petersburg, the relics of the communist era can be seen everywhere. Although there are countless statues of Lenin still scattered throughout the country, and streets named after well-known communist events and heroes, it is also true that top Communist Party officials announced the removal of the names of communist leaders, such as Brezhnev, from streets, plaques, signs, and monuments at the end of 1988. Therefore, criticism by some who consider the Russians to be tied to autocracy by historical predispositions has little to do with the recent democratic aspirations of Russians. If there is a conflict between the exact extent of western-style modernization and neotraditionalism, and the interest in having a stable government and political institutions, it does not imply any wish to return to a nondemocratic system. President Putin's government recently adopted the old Soviet national anthem, although with different lyrics, as the new national anthem of Russia, and in February of each year, the country celebrates the founding of the Red Army of 1918. But these are celebrations of historical events and prove nothing against the Russia's clear move toward democratic values and notions. The symbols of communism were destroyed by the end of 1980s and permitted Russia to move toward a noncommunist society without bloodshed (Sergi, 2004). Even though some opinion polls showed that one out of every three Russians, most likely residents of rural districts and small towns, were not aware that the Soviet regime no longer existed, this was a limited reality in the early 1990s, but not of the present.

Even the most uncertain opinion polls could not herald long-term trouble concerning Russia's relations with the outer world. Because of booming economies in several world regions, it is a fact that energy resource supply and demand have to match and this turned attention in Russia to the necessary ubiquitous cobweb of pipelines and other means of transportation in order to guarantee adequate supplies where productive systems need them most. As long as managing this new productive reality has become a central issue for Russia in the regional and world context, this fact hints at more international ties than blockades because even a small amount of discouragement of Russian exports could be economically and politically troublesome and could affect the country significantly. If Moscow, St. Petersburg, and other regions in Russia have seen their own economies propelled and seen inhabitants benefit from the energy and related service-sector expansion, and as Russia entered into wide oil and gas networks with companies and governments across Western Europe and other regions as well, the growing influence of imports from the West steered us toward a more open reading of Russia. Some 85 percent of trade is conducted with countries outside of the Commonwealth of Independent States, and only about 11 percent of Russia's foreign trade takes place with Ukraine and Belarus—the two countries most closed to the concept of Russia's new identity. These statistical figures should be adequate to alter the inaccurate perception that Russia is closed to the outside world. With roughly 40 percent of Russia's GDP being generated in Moscow and St. Petersburg—the two most western-oriented towns—it is difficult for mainstream critics to blame Russia for being inclined to isolationism and alienation. The international energy market is a tool of the country's transformation because it helped set in motion robust financial support for its current social national programs. This may prove a blessing for Russia in the future, too, provided the Kremlin plans the use of resources and rebalances the composition of national income, leaning toward an effort that relies not only on energy to generate income. Still Russia's economic fortune is increasingly tied to the global economy's growth. In contrast, Russia would become an absolute loser and thus much less a beneficiary and very vulnerable should the Kremlin's political establishment redraw and undo the country's numerous international partnerships.

The theory that neither the Russian government nor the Russian population at large are able to establish a workable relationship with the international community is equally false. If Russians feel they are unique, and that their enemies deny them their rightful place in the global affairs that affect their huge nation, it may be because the authorities encourage these feelings to help create a bond between the government and its citizens that might otherwise be difficult to develop.

Do Russians Feel Nostalgic for the Past?

At this point, Mikhail Gorbachev's leadership must be linked directly to what went awry afterwards, and most importantly, to what is currently occurring in Russia. For instance, many believe that a substantial section of the liberal intelligentsia is nostalgic for the Yeltsin era because they are disappointed by the policies and methods of the Putin administration. While this is utterly untrue and muddies the real Russian reality, the liberal intelligentsia's social alienation did lead to nostalgia for the Yeltsin period in the same way that people were nostalgic for Gorbachev once Yeltsin was in office. With every socio-economic transition, the country experienced a feeling of nostalgia for what they had before—a natural reaction when faced with the uncertainty of what lay ahead. What is occurring now, however, is not a culture looking backward to better times, because Russians were well aware of the negatives associated with communism. This time, they are searching for a better model of political governance.

These issues bring us to a question: What kind of governance were Russians looking for? Political governance refers to a combination of governmental stability and economic prosperity and freedoms. The paradox is that Russians experienced political stability during the era of communism but could not enjoy economic freedom. The period begun by Gorbachev initiated political instability and clashes among groups of competing interests, but it also offered much more economic freedom than that experienced during communism. As a result, we observed nostalgia for Brezhnev's years of general well-being—at least nostalgia for old benchmarks such as security in their old age, universal literacy, a good technologically advanced educational system, universal health care, and so forth. After Yeltsin took office, we also observed some nostalgia for the era of Gorbachev's perestroika.

This work does not share the views expressed by those who do not recognize or understand the phenomena of Russian nostalgia. In light of this nostalgic focus on past leaders, Putin's reelection in 2004 was surprising, but not necessarily irrational. Russians chose a candidate whom Yeltsin labeled as the most moderate of all possible candidates because the Yeltsin leadership was colliding with regional elites and aggressive business interests. While government officials in Russia's various regions gave tax breaks to big businesses and delayed the payment of wages and stipends, the oligarchies began to provoke strikes by workers and miners in an attempt to compel the government to tailor policies to the interests of the businesses. Experts express sharp critiques of Putin's personality and the Kremlin's attempt to become a visible stable institution as a break from Yeltsin's injudicious path, yet this move is not a change in principle for the Russians. That Putin emerged as a prime candidate among Yeltsin's potential successors, and then got the support of the people, is neither an irrational phenomenon nor the negation of democracy or Russians' preconceived notions of absolutism.

There are many episodes that Russia and Russians have gone through over the course of the last fifteen years that help us better comprehend the recent internal evolution and potential future challenges. These factors contrived to allow Russia to support a person who could push the nation toward much-needed achievement, which is in line with the recurrent theme that Russians were asking for stability rather than insecurity. At this point in time, there were no other candidates in the elections of 2000 or 2004 who could compete against all that Putin offered.

Only time will tell if the phenomenon of nostalgia will also occur for the Putin years. Still, sentiment favoring the Mikhail Gorbachev and Boris Yeltsin periods has almost disappeared in Russian society today.

Chapter Ten

Clamping Down on Corruption—Is It Legitimate or Not?

Interpreting and sorting out ways to take steps against the corruption that was and still is plaguing Russia is not a simple undertaking, given the issues at stake and the critical level plainly observable all across the country. The tolerance of the level of corruption was getting close to a critical point where the Russian citizens were not going to take it any more. I am not alleging that the phenomenon was a typical Russian one, because it has also appeared in other transition countries and in some advanced countries too. But corruption going well beyond a critical level was primarily responsible for Russia's loss; this is a clearly observable fact, but still the West quite overlooked it. It is one of several factors that played a negative role on the country, and continuing to apply standard western perspectives would be shortsighted.

Putin came to office wanting to strengthen governmental control over Russia's economic system, as his detractors maintain, who mistakenly said that the process of demanding back taxes would create a lawless country, would harm Russia's investment climate, and would possibly cause a resumption of capital flight from the country. Certain businesspersons, however, have done much harm and have behaved unethically. Shady groups that divert money abroad, establish their own dubious security services, and block the development of a liberal market economy—as Putin warned of on July 8, 2000—must be kept under control. Even if only a portion of the business community used illegal schemes to conceal bills by rerouting billion of dollars abroad—which could also have happened when the IMF backed huge loans to support the ruble before the August 1998 financial crisis—strong speculation was certainly justified about the misuse of, and profiting from, billion of dollars for nonofficial purposes.

In this atmosphere, perfecting the political system was possible and categorically necessary. Statistical data for the past is revealing. Observers in both the West and Russia should have been optimistic about Russia's prospective economic growth under Putin, before embarking on unfounded criticism and disparagement at the beginning of the 2000s, as most economic indicators for Russia at the end of Putin's term are favorable. The role of sufficient and improving competition within the country is positive. Consider that capital flight was some $20 billion a year in the mid-1990s, but reversed to $2.3 billion in 2003, thus showing that the approach of Putin's Kremlin to fighting this phenomenon—although unsuccessful—was much less harmful to the country's well-being than his detractors believed.

Instead of officially defending the tight control of Putin's Kremlin administration and supporting a clear reversal of Yeltsin's poorly managed reforms, Kremlinologists did just the opposite. While a clear-cut state response to corruption and dishonesty would be quite normal if it took place in the West, the West itself denied this was going on in Russia, not only not endorsing what was going on in Russia or simply understating the fundamental risk to the country embedded in the phenomenon, but also being very critical. Despite this error on the West's part, the West has been unable to prove unlawful behavior on the part of the Russian government.

Russians Demand More Efforts against Corruption

The main issue at stake is the Russian populace's call for more concerted efforts to focus on those who stole—or acquired at little to no cost—state assets and the country's natural resources. Actually, the country's natural resources scrambled the race for wealth, transforming the country in an immense battlefield for control of resources, but corruption was so widespread that these resources were almost given away to beneficiaries who did pay a small sum for the ownership of natural resources, and created unfair business opportunities and advantages for themselves. This approach has proved devilish to the country overall. Far worse is that these corrupt interests illegally used the state to avoid paying taxes, and as a result, millions of such oligarch dollars have left the reach of the state while parts of the populace starve.

We must remember that Putin's tenure began after the economic crisis had become evident, following the disastrous reforms of Yeltsin in the lack of growth and uneven distribution of income and resources. When Putin took office, he had to make crucial ethical choices. One was to assure international investors that though previous Russian privatization schemes were undertaken in completely distorted and unlawful ways, the Kremlin would not to go back and renationalize what had been privatized before. Another decision was to tackle the inequity in income distribution created by the unlawfulness of the 1990s, and provide help to the large number of people living in either poverty or economic trouble, who expected the president to lead them to better times. Finally, Putin needed to apply ordinary rules of law in the same way as we intend adherence to law in the West.

The recent intensification of activity regarding the Prosecutor General's Office scarcely indicates a softening approach by Putin, if it does not raise doubts about the exact extent to which cases of anti-corruption were prosecuted on a selective basis or not and whether this new anti-corruption drive has acted as a hedge against more corruption. This is not a criticism of the authorities, however. Personal advantage involved in the unlawful privatization activities and the logic of corruption in the business sector were and are large, by western or any other standards. The Russian people have witnessed socioeconomic troubles, though diminishing in absolute value, but still have one of the most discriminatory economic systems in the world. The fact that companies and predatory elites in Russia made the bulk of their fortunes by capturing state wealth, controlling state policies, enhancing cronyism, and creating ambiguous boundaries between the society and top institutions during the 1990s has been well described (see Hellman, 1998; Kryshtanovskaya, 1998). Likewise, rescheduled tax payments to the state's arbitrary tax administration required strong, ethical counteraction by Putin's Kremlin, as did those who had billions of dollars of debt with the state in the 2000s. Denying this necessity would be irrational. Considering Putin's actions to have the business sector pay taxes and move against tax evasion or to invoke the sale of assets to pay back taxes as undemocratic or unfair is entirely incorrect as long as state policy is not proven to be illegitimate.

Putin began running the country when corruption had so pervaded the country's business activities and top institutions that strong, decisive action had to be taken immediately. Putin was obliged to intervene in a severe manner, and despite outside criticism of his actions, not everyone in Russia is convinced that his strict interventions were enough to curb this phenomenon. Besides criminal behavior, the capitalist logic in the Russia of the 1990s created parasitic companies and banks whose profits were divided amongst themselves and used to perpetuate additional morally corrupt business activities. Anatoly Chubais—head of the State Privatization Committee before becoming Yeltsin's first deputy prime minister in charge of economics and finance and chief of the Russian presidential administration in 1996—said in 2003 that Russia's capitalists were stealing absolutely everything and that it was impossible to stop them (Goldman, 2003). These new capitalists began their exploitation in the 1990s by taking advantage of opportunities to acquire Russian businesses, whose internal worth was quite low in comparison with high world market prices. Gas, oil, gold, and other precious metals were the main speculative fields, but they also profited from negative real interest rates and speculation against the ruble.

Widespread Corruption as a Frightening Obstacle

Many still feel that corruption is a daunting obstacle in Russia, even after Putin's most recent steps to curtail illegal business practices. Discontent has been growing even against the United Russia Party (the pro-Putin party), and has resulted in some social criticism of Putin and street protests over current policies because the protesters think the state administration's fight against these negative phenomena is not harsh enough. Mid-level bureaucrats who had been on the receiving end of the policy changes are now increasingly disappointed with Putin and his damaged reputation among those who have suffered the most from painful benefits reforms. These reforms angered many of his traditional supporters and prompted street protests all across Russia. In fact, Professor Yuri Levada, the founder of the eponymous center, claimed that after his policies were put into effect, Putin's apparent approval rating was considerably lower than it actually was; in fact, overall support for him was considerably higher.

An *Ekho Moskvy* radio poll (Kupchinsky, 2006) conducted in the wake of Putin's seventh State of the Nation address, however, revealed that 93 percent of respondents expressed doubt that the president was serious in his stated endeavors to root out corruption. That is, the expressions of uncertainty over the effectiveness of state corruption prevention efforts, as extrapolated from the latest public opinion polls, can be interpreted as Russian acknowledgment that corruption is an unpleasant fact and something that could never be eradicated after the chaos of the 1990s. Russians want their law enforcement agencies to be resolute in the fight against corruption. It should be clearly understood in the West that there was and is widespread discontent among some Russian groups regarding certain economic reforms implemented by the Kremlin before 2004 that severely weakened the government's credibility and led to the replacement of Mikhail Kasyanov's government one month before the presidential election of 2004. This reality is coupled with clear discontent with corruption among all Russians, who believe that Putin's government and state agencies must move against corruption at all levels.

A survey conducted in January 2004 by the private polling agency VTsIOM-A (*Economic Newsletter*, No. 9, 2004), sought to answer the question as to what levels of government were most corrupt, and whether corruption in upper governing levels had improved in 2003. The results indicated that 48 percent of respondents believed corruption was endemic at both upper and lower levels, while 35 percent believed it was worse at upper levels. Only 11 percent thought corruption was worse at lower levels.

Concerning the second question, whether corruption in upper governing levels had improved in 2003, 45 percent said there was no change, 30 percent said it had increased, and only 13 percent said it decreased. Despite the fact that several polls recently showed a slightly diminishing approval rating for Putin, his personal approval ratings were quite high and in January 2004, 65 percent of respondents said they would vote for Putin again. Even more recently, the All-Russian Public Opinion Research Center conducted a poll to determine Putin's success and the level of popular confidence in major Russian politicians (*The Russia Journal Daily*, 2005b). Putin remains the most trustworthy elected leader of the modern era, with a 64 percent approval rating. An understanding of Russia and Putin himself requires a realistic, holistic analysis.

Transparency International (2007), the Berlin-based global civil society organization that leads the fight against corruption and ranks countries in terms of the perception of internal corruption, has regularly updated the annual report on corruption perception index. This is an analysis of eighteen polls reflecting the perceptions of the people in a given country. The picture of corruption in Russia is a large one, infiltrating both everyday and business activities. According to the generalized perception of respondents, Russia is deeply affected by corruption and the country's corruption level remains extremely high in 2006. Russia turned out at 127th place among 163 countries, having a rate of 2.5 points (2.8 in 2004) out of 10 maximum and minimum 0, as Transparency International's twelveth annual report since has made clear. Russia has been included the same group with Central African states and the poorest Latin American countries. According to the report, corruption remains one of the insurmountable obstacles in the struggle against poverty, both in Russia and in other countries. In the realm of leading institutions, the Russian Central Bank was also said to be home to enormous corruption, at least through Gerashchenko's leadership, according to Boone and Horder (1998).

The sixth and latest publication of *Worldwide Governance Indicators* by the World Bank Group, authored by Daniel Kaufmann, Aart Kraay, and Massimo Mastruzzi (2007)— which measures six components of good governance: voice and accountability, political stability and absence of violence, government effectiveness, regulatory quality, rule of law, and control of corruption—shows that Russia did not make much progress in improving governance and fighting corruption between 1996 and 2006. This is not encouraging at all, given that good governance and corruption control are fundamental for Russia's long-term growth and social consensus. Although the report says that it would be possible to make significant governance progress in a relatively short period, this has not occurred in Russia. The Kremlin failed to make a breakthrough in this respect, despite a high-profile campaign since 2000. For a nation that has always taken a long view of history, time is quickly running out and attempts at curbing this phenomenon seem to be thwarted, which is why it is very disheartening to read the findings of this prominent report.

According to the report by Transparency International, corruption remains one of the insurmountable obstacles in the struggle against poverty. Business corruption, administrative corruption, and widespread recourse to kickbacks have created considerable wealth for some. Transparency and protective security are necessary to stop the upheaval in the protection services—or *krysha*—caused by the Russian mafia or even by business authorities and elites.

According to several other surveys, unbridled corruption continues to increase—an awkward reality felt by a majority of Russians. A survey by the *Information Science for Democracy Russian Foundation* (INDEM 2006)—an NGO founded in 1990 that conducts extensive efforts to measure bribery in Russia—reports that the average size of bribery payments rose from $10,200 in 2001 to $135,800 in 2005. As long as bribes are frequently paid to ensure placement in educational institutions, in real estate, in municipal services, to obtain a driver's licence, to secure medical treatment and the like, the INDEM Foundation estimated that Russians paid more than $3 billion in bribes annually over the surveyed period. From a different angle of analysis, the INDEM study reports on the aggregate dollar amount of bribes paid per firm per year. The bribe index measures the share of annual revenues paid in bribes, and the study implied an approximate increase in the volume of bribery of nearly 900 percent. As was noted by Russian Deputy Prosecutor General Alexander Buksman, the country's bureaucrats take in approximately 125 billion British pounds in bribes every year, which is a level very close to equalling the state's entire annual revenues, as Tom Parfitt (2006) reported in the *Guardian*, and in 2005 the business corruption market exceeded federal budget revenues 2.66 times (INDEM, 2006). This figure implies a fourfold increase of the corruption market measured by revenues of the federal budget. As reported by Transparency International (2007), 8 percent of respondents admitted that they or another person in their household had paid a bribe in 2005.

Even before most the recent years, in 2002, Valeria Korchagina of the *Moscow Times* reported that Russians paid out $36 billion in bribes and other unofficial sums equaling 12 percent of Russia's GDP that year. However, another revealing public opinion poll conducted by INDEM and reported in *Economic Newsletter* (2005, No. 9), indicated that the perception of official bribery (i.e., bribery by government officials) was more rampant during the Yeltsin era than at any other period, with 58 percent of the public and 57.3 percent of business people interviewed believing that such bribery takes place. The poll also indicated that only 14.3 percent of the public and 11 percent of businesspeople named the Putin era as having the most rampant bribery—which is significantly below the percentage of people who believe that the Soviet era was the worst (22 percent and 14.1 percent).

It goes without saying that Putin's Kremlin also needs to continue reforming the huge bureaucracy, as the size of the bureaucracy has been on the increase. In 2000, there was one government employee for every fifty six people employed, but the ratio has now increased to approximately one government employee for every fifty employees. In light of the latest options pursued by the administration, some say (and ordinary Russians fear) that the removal and firing of certain employees from government jobs, even at the top level, may indeed target corrupt individuals, but does not tackle the problem of corruption itself. As long as the Kremlin is not able to destroy the entire phenomenon of state corruption, single cases of top officials being fired will not be enough to turn the Russian state bureaucracy into an efficient apparatus adhering to the law throughout the country, which is necessary to transform Russia into a full-fledged *normal country*. It is enough to say that on a scale of one to five, where one is "not at all corrupt" and five is "extremely corrupt," respondents gave the Russian police a rating of 4.0 and the legal system and judiciary a rating of 3.9 (Transparency International, 2007). Should the Kremlin be able to deal with corruption, which is a serious and pervasive problem, it would improve the country's credibility greatly.

In this overall negative scenario, significant socioeconomic impact on a large segment of the population, and pervasive corruption became chronic features within Russian life. Apart from recurring corruption scandals and doubtful privatization schemes during the 1990s, real GDP continued to plunge until the financial crisis of 1998. The current income distribution was so uneven that less than 10 percent of the populace had an income above $2,000 a month, and 10 percent earned between $1,000 and $2,000. It is true that Russia is home to billionaires and millionaires, and uneven income distribution is common everywhere in the world. The less wealthy sector has recently shown adequate income (although not comparable to that enjoyed by the wealthy); however, the West has deliberately misread recent Russian progress, asserting the existence of a large enough new middle class in Russia with moderate income but failing to recognize that there are still many poor Russians. Because this part of the population was often ignored, the inability of the state to increase the regulation of back tax payments or to modernize the economic system increased the risk of anarchy and another social implosion in Russia.

This was a matter of fact during the 1990s. The options pursued by the current Kremlin administration and various state departments to claim back taxes and fire top officials from government jobs represented and still represents a major hurdle in tackling the overall problem of corruption. This is how Russians feel. If the Kremlin is unable to rid the state system of all corruption, single cases of firing top officials will not be enough to turn the Russian state bureaucracy into an efficient apparatus. The causes of this corrupt system are rooted in the past and were strongly reinforced during the Yeltsin years. Taking definitive steps against this overall phenomenon was a difficult task that helped produce the paradox of western interpretations overall.

When western interpreters miscalculated the truth that Russia had to face a growing tide of dishonorable behavior in the spheres of bureaucracy and business, this left them with a primary question: what does the Kremlin administration have to do to stop corruption? While western intellectuals were using western-style analysis and their limited knowledge of Russian realities to intentionally disapprove of Putin and close their eyes to Russian wishes, they also transformed their unjustified criticism into a paradox whereby they sounded as if they would have been happier if Putin had not taken any action. The West looked into uncertain profiles of Russian legality and, never having found any examples of misbehavior by the state, acted as if it was better to not curb any illegal activities. The paradox is accentuated by the fact that the misplaced understanding of Russia by western observers creates a situation where any harsh policy reaction by the Kremlin automatically labels the Russian leadership as authoritarian without any systematic analysis of the basic facts. This paradox has never appeared in the West.

It is a matter of fact that a large number of Russians (77 percent) recently expressed fears about privatization, and that something should be done to revise policies that regulate it. The poverty that most Russians experience explains their anger toward the business environment and privatization, clearly demonstrating what privatization has done to their living conditions.

The country was experiencing a crisis of confidence. Putin chose Mikhail Fradkov, fifty three, to replace Prime Minister Mikhail Kasyanov (dubbed the last of the Yeltsinians, having been Yeltsin's former finance minister, first deputy prime minister during Putin's acting presidency, and then cabinet chief during Putin's Kremlin) until February 2004, when Kasyanov was dismissed. Fradkov, Russia's envoy to the European Union in Brussels, was appointed just before Russian voters went to the polls on March 14. Fradkov was with the Russian embassy in New Delhi in 1972, and then he joined the Russian government in 1992 when he was deputy foreign trade minister in the Yegor Gaidar government. He served as trade minister for less than a year in 1997, and was named foreign trade minister two years later. He lost his job when Putin was elected president in 2000, but was made head of the tax police in March 2001 and given the goal of ending Russia's massive tax evasion. The agency was disbanded during a government reshuffle in 2003, and Fradkov was sent to Brussels.

Putin was attempting to achieve the efficiency that the country was still lacking and to normalize Russia's relationship with the European Union. Putin certainly saw Fradkov as dependable, but the choice was based on more than just logic; the reason is evident in the party opposition choices during the elections held in 2004. Communist leader Guennadi Zhiuganov left the job of representing his party to the lackluster Nikolai Kharitonov, ultranationalist Vladimir Zhirinovski abdicated his candidacy to his bodyguard Oleg Malyckin, and the liberal Grigory Yavlinski simply boycotted the elections. Other minor candidates were running, but they were not in a position to contest the elections.

Observing these developments from a traditionally faulty western perspective rather than through Russian perceptions would definitely put Putin in a negative light. Seeing him as a captain driving the boat against oligarchs, jailing them, putting natural resources back in the hands of the state, and being controlled by KGB personnel would be logical observations to western interpreters, but this is the wrong conclusion. If these viewpoints were accurate, it would be logical to see him as more authoritarian than democratic.

However, considering that Putin has, in fact, achieved such strong popular support—especially in the 2004 presidential election—and that the pro-Putin party witnessed a major victory in the Moscow city Duma elections in December 2005, should inspire Kremlinologists to be concerned about all possible aspects of reality and democracy in Russia. It's true that the pro-Kremlin United Russia Party took roughly 47 percent of the vote in an election that witnessed a turnout of around 35 percent of the 6.9 million registered voters—note that the opposition was disappointed about what it claimed were numerous violations. Nevertheless, strong support is visible and the country's voters are sensible about the new democratic wave bashfully begun by Yeltsin. Given the evolutionary process of Putin's decision-making during his eight years in power, it would be inaccurate to judge his decisions as illegal and illogical or to simply lay blame on everything being done in Moscow without suggesting realistic alternatives.

Academic Experts on Corruption

While the real battle to capture the country's wealth was well underway during the 1990s, commentators were looking at the formal electoral situation while missing the Russian desire and need to have free elections and order at the same time. Richard Rose and Neil Munro's (2002) *Elections Without Order: Russia's Challenge to Vladimir Putin* argues that resorting to free elections was creating a functioning modern state where a formal electoral democracy was less important that making the state the guarantor of public interest.

Several other books have been published in the West to analyze different aspects of this phenomenon. Incredibly important is Paul Klebnikov's story—the editor-in-chief of the Russian edition of *Forbes* wrote an extraordinary book entitled *Godfather of the Kremlin: Boris Berezovsky and the Looting of Russia* (2000). This title itself contains two key words signifying the real inconsistencies and crimes in Russia: *godfather* and *looting*. The book is about the fortune acquired by Berezovsky. Unfortunately, while Klebnikov was energetically describing the missing moral principles in today's noncommunist Russia (in July 2004), he was killed by a Chechen hired gun. (Note that after 2000, investigative journalists were being murdered in Russia, and Klebnikov was one of those victims.)

Klebnikov's book is interesting because it explains how six people who had little or no money were controlling the economy during the 1990s, building up fortunes on pyramid schemes, and shaping electoral outcomes to the extent that they almost guaranteed Yeltsin's reelection in 1996.

Another book whose publication complemented *Godfather of the Kremlin* is *Kapitalizm: Russia's Struggle to Free Its Economy* by Rose Brady (2000)—*Business Week*'s Moscow bureau chief from 1989 to 1993—which tells the anecdote of a widowed pensioner lamenting that "we were just beginning to live when it was Brezhnev's time." This revealing story exemplifies how Russians were becoming unhappy with the new course, or at least with how Yeltsin's government had managed it.

From a different perspective, Peter Baker and Susan Glasser's (2005) *Kremlin Rising: Vladimir Putin's Russia and the End of Revolution* offers an important look at Russian society. The two authors, *Washington Post* correspondents in Moscow from 2001 to 2004, offer a hard-hitting examination of the new Russia over a relevant period to examine Putin's political accomplishment. They believe that Putin has always abused his authority in trying to achieve full control of the country, and that he is destabilizing Russia and demoralizing future generations as well. But this comes as a paradox, as all critics of Putin's Russia tend to think that Russians are naturally prone to authoritarianism, which does not fit into the derisive picture of this frightening future generation!

Interestingly, western observers compare Stalin's rhetoric as he industrialized the country to Putin's quest for economic growth and a strong state, his removal of all obstacles (Project Putin) such as television networks, his jailing of Mikhail Khodorkovsky, the repossession of Yukos, and his firing of Prime Minister Mikhail Kasyanov three weeks before the March 14 presidential elections. Putin temporarily replaced Kasyanov with Deputy Prime Minister Viktor Kristenko, and finally appointed diplomat Mikhail Fradkov in March 2004 simply because Kasyanov would have become president temporarily if the election turnout was less than 50 percent, rumors in Moscow said.

Baker and Glasser maintain in their book that Mikhail Fradkov was totally unknown to most Russians: this is untrue, or rather only partially so if we consider the large public. The degree of visibility of a new political leader is meaningless in our analysis, and I do not understand why certain experts bring it up. In actuality Mr. Fradkov began his career in the diplomatic service in New Delhi in 1973, working through the ranks to become the deputy minister of foreign trade, and finally the trade minister in 1997. Dismissed from this post after the financial crisis in 1998, Fradkov was appointed chairman of the state monopoly insurance company, Ingosstrakh, and then reappointed as foreign trade minister in 1999. He was dismissed in May 2000 and appointed deputy to the National Security Council. He was then put in charge of tax policy in March 2001, and subsequently appointed Russian ambassador to the European Union in 2003. In reality, he was not well-known politically; however western diplomatic and economic circles expressed a positive regard for him. Thus, the West did not disapprove of his appointment as prime minister, despite Baker and Glasser's view (2005).

Several other books on Russian criminals and criminal events were published around 2000 (e.g., Volkov, 2000; Shleifer and Vishny, 1998; Satter, 2003; Handelman, 1994; and Hoffman, 2002). The simple fact that books were being written or published while many of the more despicable activities of the 1990s were taking place, with Russians simultaneously supporting the new Putin presidency, was not mere coincidence. Western observers had another reason at that time to better interpret Russia and not look at it through a narrow western prism.

Russian business elites were divided into a number of warring clans, and whenever one clan became too strong; the other would unite to bring it down, according to Lilia Shevtsova (2005). This scenario produced further turmoil among business groups and conceivably contributed to what Rasma Karklins describes in *The System Made Me Do It: Corruption in Post-Communist Societies* (2005)—a system believed to be so comprehensively corrupt that most people feel they must play along because the system itself compels them to do so.

Silvoviki and the Kremlin

When Kremlinologists and intellectuals missed the observable fact that Russia was facing a growing tide of dishonorable behavior—even at top levels—and mounting private corruption, this left them with an important question: what has the Kremlin administration had to do to stop corruption? While intellectuals were using western-style analysis and their unclear knowledge of Russian historical events and their development to intentionally criticize Putin and ignore the wishes of ordinary Russians, they transformed their unjustified criticism into the much-discussed paradox whereby they sounded as if they would be happier if Putin had left well enough alone.

Due to indistinct analysis or weak understanding of Russian realities, western-style debates have not concentrated on facts and have operated from narrow and even distorted perceptions of Russian business practices. The West systematically continues to paint state actions as unlawful, and it appears that western intellectuals have lost their independence, becoming more receptive to accusations that Putin's Kremlin is dictator-like. In contrast, Putin embarked on a necessary, heavy-handed state counter-response. Russian realities continue to convince Russians that the Kremlin should be even more empowered now to assault the remaining niches of criminal and corrupt behavior.

One serious aspect of what happens with this Kremlin is much criticized in the West and by some Russian journalists. They feel quite skeptical about the growing role of former KGB members in the state administration, as this would be part of the general centralization of power under Putin. Nabi Abdullaev and Simon Saradzhyan's article in the *Moscow Times* (2006), an authoritative and independent newspaper published in Russia, noted that Olga Kryshtanovskaya, head of the Moscow-based Center for the Study of the Elites at the Russian Academy of Sciences, reported that 50 to 70 percent of the Putin Kremlin staff belonged to *siloviki*—the hard-line inner circle of aides to Putin in the Kremlin. Although Kremlinologists are inclined to read this fact as a return to communist practices, *siloviki* are not proponents for going back to communism, however, as Kryshtanovskaya correctly maintains. She also gives the same figures since the early 2000s, and her findings show that slightly less than 80 percent—up from 26 percent—of current political leaders and state administrators in Russia had reported serving in the KGB or its successor agencies. It is true that at the topmost levels of the Putin Kremlin, the number of officials drawn from the KGB or the armed forces soared above their modest quotas under the late Soviet era. Composing roughly 5 percent under Gorbachev, there is no doubt that *siloviki* are encroaching on the business sector; they occupy a large share of the highest posts at the Kremlin and head the largest state companies quoted on the stock market. Even though the exact final percentage relies much on Kryshtanovskaya's (2003) research methodology, this piece of evidence should not draw readers into quickly seeing what *siloviki* do as misguiding interests of the state for unlawful personal enrichment a priori, without providing evidence of their misbehavior and corruption. It is true that the influence of *siloviki* has been growing and that a deep structural national transformation could have swayed former KGB and army officials in favor of establishing business activities. However, if condemning them a priori is right, we should equally condemn any other current KGB or any other country's secret policy affiliate who jumps into business or politics.

There is no basis for interpreting these actions as Putin's way of strengthening his own control over the country, because he does not need to do so. Observers in the West had to officially defend the tight control of the state in certain sectors and justify the Kremlin administration's purposeful methods, as the 1990s were not moving the country from communist economics to market economics but to nowhere, that is, to chaos. No one in the West could prove the unlawfulness of the Russian government's robust response or of the judiciary system's actions, and no one in the West has been sincere enough to assert that it was a necessary step toward moving Russia into the modern era. Instead, we should have disentangled the gross social injustice that conditioned Russian expectations and Putin's policy response on behalf of the Russians. It is true that the Kremlin administration must move Russia toward a definitive *normal country* status, but western views should not negatively affect that passage or misrepresent Russians' desires.

Specific Kremlin Anticorruption Steps

Most recently, Putin has strived to clamp down on corrupt practices and inefficiencies. In 2006, Putin removed Prosecutor General Vladimir Ustinov, who was initially associated with Yeltsin and nominated as prosecutor general by Putin himself in March 2000, shortly after Putin won his first presidential election. Ustinov was loyal to Sechin and Ivanov, two leading *siloviki*, and he played a prominent role in the legal case against Yukos. The Federation Council—the upper house of parliament—voted by 140 to zero (with two abstentions) to remove Ustinov from his post. The vote was added to the chamber's agenda at the last minute after legislators received a letter from Putin asking them to remove the prosecutor general from office. In reality, Putin's letter accompanied Ustinov's own letter expressing his desire to step down, as both were sent to the Council late in the day on June 1. Neither of them gave clear reasons for the change and the circumstances surrounding the dismissal are murky. Ustinov had served as chief prosecutor for more than six years—during Putin's tenure. The preceding year, the Upper House had voted to give Ustinov another five years in office upon Putin's recommendation. Russian financial markets were unchanged upon hearing the news of Ustinov's departure.

This dismissal was a tactical victory for moderates over hardliners in a Kremlin power struggle, analysts in Moscow reported. The fact that Ustinov's dismissal dealt a blow to the *siloviki* could support a point of view that the *siloviki* clan is weakening in the Kremlin, which favors extending Putin's powers beyond 2008 and strengthening the faction that endorses managed presidential succession. Alternatively, some theorize that First Deputy Prime Minister Dmitry Medvedev—a Putin confidant and possible 2008 contender—may also have initiated the Ustinov departure. The rivalry between the factions could become intensified because Putin has to step down in 2008. Another possible reason for this dismissal may include Putin's frustration with the prosecutor general for acting on his own and making public statements about government corruption.

The shakeup at the prosecutor general's office follows several other firings, including those of security and law enforcement officials, a likely part of increased efforts to beef up Russia's law enforcement bodies, to ensure law and order in the country, and to intensify the fight against corruption. The prosecutor general's office took the unprecedented step of arresting Alexei Barinov, the governor of the autonomous Nenets district. The arrest and ensuing investigation into some owners of shares in the Transneft pipeline monopoly showed excessive independence of the general prosecutor's office, as some interpreted this in Moscow.

Ustinov's dismissal and his tendency to pontificate prompted him to publicly lament the prevalence of corruption and organized crime in Russia. Criminals are becoming increasingly impudent and gaining strength, Ustinov reported to a gathering of senior law enforcement officials on May 15, 2006 (Abdullaev and Saradzhyan, 2006). This sermon came a few days after Putin made the fight against corruption a central plank in his 2006 State of the Nation address, pointing to the damaging impact of corruption on the country's economy, calling it a national threat, and pledging to rid Russia of it for the last time. Putin called on the government to dig up official corruption, saying that a number of state officials had enriched themselves at the expense of the majority of citizens and that it had to stop.

Kryshtanovskaya considers Ustinov's remarks outrageous in light of Putin's rebuilding of Russia's international image. The public expected a large law enforcement effort by the Putin administration, and before Ustinov other important dismissals took place. Several senior officials in Ustinov's office were fired in a purge of law enforcement agencies two days after Putin's speech. Major generals Yevgeny Kolesnikov and Aleksandr Plotnikov, both deputy heads of two influential units in the FSB (they worked for the Department for the Protection of the Constitutional System and the Fight against Terrorism) were let go, as was Lieutenant General Sergei Fomenko (who headed the section battling contraband and narcotics trade, as well as the Department for Economic Security).

Through orders issued separately, Putin, the prime minister, and Interior Minister Rashid Nurgaliyev fired other officials responsible for fighting terrorism and drug trafficking at the FSB, a first deputy Moscow prosecutor, several top police officers, and various customs officials. President Putin picked Justice Minister Yury Chaika to become the next prosecutor general. He is loyal to

Putin and independent of the Kremlin clans, and his work on prison reform has won praise from nongovernmental organizations. All thirteen deputies in the Russian prosecutor general's office submitted their resignations on Chaika's first day as prosecutor general, at his suggestion, and he decided which members of the old team would continue to work in the office under his management.

Despite the fact that corruption has worsened in recent years, we do not know the exact magnitude of the corruption market. The anticorruption crusade improved from 2001 to 2002 but then worsened by 2004, and overall attempts to curb it did not undergo any specific alterations other than a relevant increase in overall size. It could be quite a complex process to catalog because an increase in the authorities' direct pressure on citizens and citizen willingness to resort to bribery has been witnessed. Unfortunately, in the overall biased business situation created during the wild 1990s, state agencies were and are often helpless.

The Kremlin sponsored new legislation in February 2002 to ease the creation of new businesses and reduce the number of administrative steps needed to set up a business, and lowered the cost of obtaining such licenses. Putin and his administration also reformed the tax administration, lowered corporate and income tax rates, and widened the tax base in 2001. Despite Russia's current political and economic stability, the Kremlin has had to reinforce its reforms continuously and create more definitive and more effective steps against the inertia of this phenomenon. I might also point out that from 2000 to 2005 anticorruption policy reforms suffered from ineffective implementation of such reforms in practice. Recently, while the State Duma ratified the United Nations Convention against Corruption on February 17, 2006, in October of the same year the Duma's Anti-Corruption Commission, the Council of Europe, and the European Commission announced a joint initiative to develop legislation and other measures to fight corruption in several areas. Also, thousands of criminal investigations were launched in connection with allegations that officials had grabbed budget money in the agroindustrial, real estate, educational, and in health-care sectors, among others. The government simply launched a new anticorruption drive, planned to set up special anticorruption units in all public offices, to create a network of informers in the public service, and to educate public servants by having them attend ethics classes, reports Osborn for the *Independent* (2007).

If new efforts and such a shakeup resulted in the removal of several people, including top state officials such as security and law enforcement officers, these actions were lawful although only the years ahead will confirm their effectiveness.

Is It Rational to Describe Putin as a Mere Dictator?

Recent news, propagated in the West by western intellectuals and academic experts, revealed that several oligarchs had been imprisoned or exiled with no trial and no evidence whatsoever. The West was also informed that growing classes of *siloviki* who are believed to be in the thousands are speaking for Putin from the Kremlin and governing major companies. It is accurate information that *siloviki* are encroaching on the business sector and are members of Putin's cabinet. However, western critics sound as if they would be happier if Putin had not taken any action. Would it have been better not to curb any illegal activities for fear that such a policy reaction would automatically incite observers to label Russian leaders as despots without any systematic analysis of the facts? Western misinterpretations of Russian realities have inspired much of the hostility between the West and Putin's Kremlin, because Putin is seen as a fledgling dictator who allegedly runs the risk of driving the country into poor economic growth, further business arrests, repression, and the like. Nevertheless, there is yet another false western charge against President Putin, that he bears resemblance to a jailer.

For instance, President Carter's former advisor Zbigniew Brzezinski (2004) drew a comparison in the *Wall Street Journal* between Putin and the fascist regime of Benito Mussolini in Italy during the 1920s and 1930s. Although a better comparison might have been with the early and post-Leninist periods of the early Soviet era, rather with than with Mussolini, Brzezinski finds strong parallels between Putin and Mussolini, and Putin's Kremlin would be much like that of Mussolini, as both, according to this argument, used fear to reach their goals, broke the rules of democracy, created scapegoats, and so forth. Although Brzezinski suggests that future generations can probably overcome this anomaly, Mussolini and Putin do exhibit some common characteristics, such as the hesitation to exalt national glory and nationalism, a heavy emphasis on secret policy, and a strategy to strengthen the economy by destroying oligopolies, says Brzezinski. Yet this comparison does not stand up to scrutiny. In a similar vein, Goldman, writing in *Foreign Affairs* (2004), voiced fears about the future of the business community in Russia and whether the arrest of Khodorkovsky is the forerunner of what will happen to his business colleagues. However, Goldman's fears have not materialized at all during the years that followed.

Another view comes from Moises Naim, editor of the very respected quarterly, *Foreign Policy*, who wrote in the *Washington Post*, "Today the war on corruption is undermining democracy, helping the wrong leaders get elected, and distracting societies from facing urgent problems" (Naim, 2005). Naim who does not refer to Russia specifically, approaching the issue theoretically and on a global scale—states that the war on corruption is risky and argues that concentrating on corruption does not always produce effective results. An obsession with eliminating corruption crowds out debate on other crucial problems, thus creating political instability, says Naim. He is absolutely right that prosperity has coexisted with significant levels of corruption in selected countries, as well as that launching anticorruption campaigns can distract a government from other equally important commitments; these are apt points with which I wholly agree. However, Naim surprisingly argues that a war on corruption definitely undermines democracy and helps the wrong leaders get elected.

That fighting corruption weakens democracy is a viewpoint I do not agree with; that an anticorruption crusade might help the wrong leaders be elected could, in and of itself, be correct, but definitely not at all times. However, these are beliefs largely based on experience occurring in selected countries, and we cannot extrapolate from specific cases a definitive rule that would apply everywhere else, Russia included. In the specific Russian case, political instability, chronic corruption, and the business delinquency of the 1990s fully explained the Kremlin's strong awareness and understanding that it had to do something to counter the phenomenon spreading so dangerously throughout the country and increasingly becoming a problem—and Russians supported the Kremlin.

If some experts simply say that anticorruption campaigns are right in principle but badly managed at the national level, in actuality these scholars should consider the following three points. First, the ethical reasons for fighting corruption, which often undermines the poorest citizens, must be considered as important as any other problem facing the country. Ranking issues in terms of their importance can be successful from a purely theoretical perspective, but to establish a ranking of priorities is wrong, especially in a country in transition. A government must be able to address several public issues simultaneously and systematically—that is, take care of education, public works, health care, foreign policy, and of course, all levels of corruption. A second equally important concern, absent from most scholarly viewpoints, is that governments must also avoid the tendency for business- and bureaucracy-related frauds to become chronic features in their country. Finally, yet most importantly, denying that corruption may have a potentially disruptive impact on economic growth potential for GDP is another serious error. When news is announced that China—and other countries where corruption is perceived as pervasive—is recording economic growth, observers willingly ignore the opposing problem of explaining how a corrupt country like China can grow with corruption.

Therefore, Russia had to use a precise legal strategy to counter the synergy between corruption and unethical outcomes. There is no doubt that a government must embrace the law, but one also must not deny the importance of the task at hand or advance inexcusable and meaningless priorities in place of real solutions. Theft and bribery affect the country by squandering millions and billions of dollars, which is a lot of money even by western standards. Unfortunately, it is a fundamental problem in governments today around the world. Focusing on corruption, however, should not prevent the government from taking steps to address other equally important aspects of public life. Denying this reality would be an oversight.

How Would the West React?

Vladimir Putin had to set goals for making all the players willing to accept and enforce judicious rules. The experience with the West demonstrates that the progress Russia is making to reform the judicial system is extremely important. There is no doubt that complex and controversial legal case issues are and were taking place in Russia, which is why Putin's administration could not remain idle.

Two issues need to be raised. First, no critics of President Putin have been able to prove that judges behaved dishonestly. Secondly, critics should be able to offer a clear alternative to simple disbelief in Russia's administrative policies. In other words, why did critics pick on Russian judges without any proof of wrongdoing? Would forceful state judicial reaction over corruption cases be assessed differently if it happened in the West or in Russia? All this speculation could cast a pall over the responsibility of the Russian judicial system, or simply label the Russian system unfairly, which is an inequitable judgment of real facts.

It is true that a stronger, more independent and reinforced judiciary system is good for the country and could strengthen it over time, but at another time or in another country, this same variety of scandal could bring forth a stout reaction from the state without it generating criticism or receiving the praise of citizenry. For example, the Enron Corporation case and the savings and loan debacle in the United States are two good examples to compare with what is happening in Russia. The Enron scandal erupted in December 2001. It was one of the biggest business scandals in U.S. history, costing investors roughly $70 billion and destroying over 4,500 jobs. In brief, Enron Corporation's chief executives Kenneth Lay and Jeffrey Skilling—two of the world's top business leaders—were found guilty in May 2006 of lying about the company's poor finances. Kenneth Lay—founder and chairman of Enron—was convicted of six counts of conspiracy and fraud and faced a maximum of forty-five years in prison, although he died of a heart attack before he could be sentenced and the criminal charges against him were vacated post-mortem in October 2006. Skilling was found guilty of nineteen counts of conspiracy, fraud, insider trading, and making false statements, and subsequently sentenced to 24.4 years. Skilling, however, was acquitted on nine counts of insider trading.

In a separate bench trial, U.S. District Judge Simeon T. Lake III found Lay guilty of fraud charges for illegally using money from $75 million in personal loans to buy stock; each of the four charges carries a maximum of thirty years. Lay paid off the loans and the lenders suffered no economic damage. Skilling remained free on a $5-million bond, while Lake required Lay to post a $5-million bond and give up his passport to stay out of jail until sentencing. Overall, these two recent convictions brought to nineteen the number of Enron executives who pleaded guilty or have been found guilty of crimes.

This catastrophic collapse of the Enron Corporation and others prompt consideration of a specific aspect of the U.S. savings and loan scandal of the 1980s. William Black (2005) details this in his book entitled *The Best Way to Rob a Bank Is to Own One*, which ties into the phenomenon of pocket banks and the use of bank loans in Russia in the 1990s. In his book, Black seeks to learn how top managers deceived everyone into believing their companies were spectacularly successful when, in fact, they were massively insolvent. Black lays bare the strategies that corrupt managers used to defraud companies for their own personal gain, taking advantage of a weak regulatory environment to perpetrate accounting fraud on a massive scale, which he calls control fraud. Black's book is an act of courage as it portrays the unethical management and resulting collapse of certain savings and loan banks in the United States. In Russia, similar schemes took place in the 1990s when, before Russia declared a moratorium on its debt in August 1998, most Russian banks closed their doors, depriving Russian citizens of their savings.

Enron's demise raised questions about the quality of corporate oversight and was followed by similar scandals in companies such as HealthSouth, WorldCom, Global Crossing, and Adelphia. After Enron, however, the U.S. Congress passed the Sarbanes-Oxley Act (2002), toughening financial and auditing requirements for publicly owned companies. Besides the tough sentences that have been handed down to the actors in these scandals, this scenario serves to help interpret the ethical realities behind what is going on in Russia today.

Another parallel to the United States' experience with corporate scandals is the public's distrust of giant business trusts. These giant business trusts dominated manufacturing and mining markets during the late nineteenth century. Corporate giants such as John D. Rockefeller and J. P. Morgan were able to fix prices in a way that forced potential competitors out of the market, thus endangering competition and negatively affecting consumers. By the 1880s, abuses by the trusts were so sizeable and widespread that growing demand for reform led to the Sherman Anti-Trust Act of 1890, which was the basis for antitrust law, including the amendments added to it at various times until 1950 by the U.S. Congress (e.g., the Clayton Act of 1914 and the Robinson-Patman Act of 1936). The Federal Trade Commission Act of 1914 created a regulatory agency to administer and enforce antitrust regulations, as well. Most importantly, in 1885 the U.S. Supreme Court inadvertently created the impression that corporations and related trusts would, from that time forward, have the same rights as persons under the larger meaning of the newly passed Fourteenth Amendment of 1867. This amendment officially gave all freed slaves (freed after the Civil War) the same rights as others enjoyed before the Civil War in any U.S. court of law. Simply put, corporations were now persons beginning in 1867. What happened in 1885 led to much greater corporate trust power at the expense of individual rights, which in turn led to weaker individual rights. This was followed by the previously mentioned Sherman Anti-Trust Act of 1890, which was unfortunately unable to stop the powerful post-1867 trend away from individual rights and toward unparalleled growth in the power of corporations—and this continues to this very day. Corporate trust power and growth now completes its dominance by the development of corporate trusts over several aspects of U.S. government under the U.S. Constitution—a truly negative development for the world today.

Insincere Western Critics and Lobbying to Influence Politics

Despite the lack of interest in the Yukos affair that recently emerged in Harvard circles, the shift in the focus of Russian critics from the functioning and efficiency of the whole system to the alleged monopolization of the oil sector should be reinterpreted. A dishonest government's behavior cannot be taken for granted, and debates over the appropriate extent of the Kremlin's involvement in the national economy and its socioeconomic impact on poor Russians must occur. The geopolitical choices must likely remain the interest of scholars, students, journals, newspapers, and all concerned persons well into the future.

Most notably, it is time for Russia and President Putin to take a renewed aggressive stand against criminal behavior. Much must be done on this front. Putin is under obligation to Russians to modernize the country and to continue to implement legality and economic effectiveness while refuting a risky return to either absolute rules or anarchy. Consequently, these efforts could help in improving our interpretation of Russia and its relationships with neighboring states.

It is not ironic that Putin casts a shadow over the credibility and worthiness of fighting corruption and tax evasion. Taking whatever action is necessary against legal violations is a standard operation all over the world. Observers notice a significant risk of backsliding into communist-style politics and because of that, they blame Putin for allowing Russia to lose its democratic culture and democratic institutions. It is possible that Putin has been perceived as moving Russia away from a more democratic culture initiated by Gorbachev and the events of the 1990s. But Russia has not lost its democratic flavor, and it is not on the fast track to nondemocratic ideals either. It is also not clear that Russians are inclined to accept authoritarian leadership to clear up problems (Shevtsova, 2005). It is certain that the 1990s in Russia created colossal problems that required a mighty response from the state, but I cannot fail to differentiate between a strong response to corruption and a return to Soviet authoritarianism.

To put it in a different light, most people who live in these societies understand well that corruption is widespread, and that they must play along because the system compels them to do so (Karklins, 2005) as long as the state is not able to escape this negative reality. Therefore, Russian failure to embrace western-style democracy does not have its roots in an exaggerated economic reliance on oil, too little economic liberalization, or a very weak national legislature (Fish, 2005). Instead, the astonishing results of the democratic 1990s are that those events forged a political system that knowingly liberalized the economy too much and too fast, relying on artificial private capitalists and irrational laws to let small minorities capture state resources and deprive ordinary Russians of their expectations. These were, and are, the right perspectives from which to decipher Russian reality and uncover western insincerity regarding proper democratic ideals in Russia.

Perhaps all these critics fit Steven Rosefielde's (2005) *Russia in the 21st Century: The Prodigal Superpower,* which portrays a country that intends to reemerge as a superpower before 2010, challenge America and China, and potentially threaten a new arms race. That Russian goal is within the Kremlin's grasp, but the cost to Russians and global security would be immense, posits Rosefielde. The reasons, though, for describing Russia and Russians as systematically predisposed to authoritarian leadership, both domestically and internationally, are wide of the mark. Karklins's observation that ordinary Russians were coerced to adopt unethical practices in an effort to survive the appalling events of the 1990s is quite different from most western "interpretations," depicting a more accurate reality in Russia that easily destroys the earlier belief that the initial democratic system was developed for the well-being of all Russians.

Many observers become confused by the difference between fighting corruption and property nationalization. This concern by international observers has led to a systematic review of the state's pursuit of some billionaires for unpaid taxes and other rule violations, but not to a discussion of the core issues of tax fraud and other dishonesties that are sometimes ignored by western writers. This is not a minor issue, but a major component of an intelligent analysis of Putin. In contrast, confusion over the exact extent of these negative events is passing with very little opposition, or even none (Goldman, 2003). Confused western critics of Putin are simply miscalculating the reason why the government had to react to curb crooked billionaires. Instead of appreciating this, critics described any involvement of the government as ethically dubious.

It is absolutely true that Russians do not want Putin to bring true liberal western freedom, because similar transgressors of the 1990s were encouraged to rob the state and restart liberal economic reforms and a pragmatic orientation in foreign policy—and they do not want to be party to a long debate about a priori pro-West or pro-East orientations. A comparison of the "Chair of the Gang"—as *Time* magazine described Khrushchev in January 1958, who did not enjoy absolute power over the country at that time—and the gangs of Russia's political and business elites fighting to dominate and control Russia during the 1990s (Volkov, 2002), suggests that harsh criticism of Putin for taking radical action against unethical activities should be issued with caution. If Putin had not seriously contended with gang activity during the early years of the new millennium, the violence and bullying of criminals and the outrageous activity of certain powerful business groups, substantial credibility and a chance to get the country back on a proper democratic pathway would have been compromised.

All of the above and the recent news disseminated in the West describing a country where oligarchs have been taken into custody or exiled by representatives of the KGB who work for Putin in the Kremlin and govern major companies are quite off the mark. When Putin came under attack by numerous thought-provoking western observers who saw in him the risk of Russia becoming a dictatorship again, western readers would think President Putin is a cross between a tyrannical ruler and a very simple thinker, incorporating the worst features of both. Nevertheless, this is an inaccurate portrayal of Putin, as was Brzezinski's (2004) comparison of Putin's leadership to Mussolini's fascist regime. Goldman (2004, p. 41) echoed Brzezinski's view, writing that although it is difficult to defend most of the oligarchs, it is "equally difficult to justify the methods Putin used against them [and] the machinations of the *siloviki* have been particularly aggressive." Although Brzezinski suggests that new generations in Russia can probably overcome this comparison, he also posits that there will always be common characterizations between Mussolini and Putin—such as the tendency to exalt national glory and nationalism, heavy dependence on secret policy, and overall control of the economy. The existence of such "machinations" has never been born out, nor has the comparison between fascism and modern Russia been fully demonstrated.

Because ethical behavior should always be a welcome outcome for and by any government and jurisdictional system, identifying with those who see some risks of an undemocratic rift is nevertheless a worthwhile undertaking. Unfortunately, most existing analyses have focused on a limited and forceful perspective rather than inquiring about the complexity of the legal aspects under analysis. Reprimanding someone like Putin—especially when such a leader has to have tremendous patience while searching for feasible ways out of Russia's problems, by labeling Putin and the Kremlin administration as an "axis of evil" is spurious for its simplistic approach and unethical foundation.

Goldman does rightly accuse oligarchs in Russia, and finds no realistic basis to defend most of them, writing, "Two senior Yukos executives have been charged with murder and attempted murder, and the mayor of Nefteyugansk, where Yukos's major producing unit is headquartered, was murdered after criticizing the firm's failure to pay taxes" (Goldman 2004: 36). In spite of such evidence, based on plenty of observable facts, the West misconstrued events and experts distorted views about how those years and events should have been conducted. These inaccuracies occurred to such a distorted extent that authors such as Guriev and Rachinsky (2005: 147) actually described the Yukos affair as "[i]ronically … crushing Russia's most transparent company." Yet, it is hard to understand why the West did not ask Russian authorities to take action and be more actively engaged in eliminating the nastiest phenomena of the 1990s, or at least launch deep inquiries into these and several other cases.

In contrast, there is at times something to be said for expecting from Putin the unachievable, as western experts sometimes did—that is, they ignored the distortions and mistakes introduced in the 1990s, which moved Russia toward a complete fiasco created by and from spectacular theft perpetrated by members of the *nomenklatura* and high political circles, yet expecting Putin to strengthen western-style democracy in Russia. In this context and in light of the very complex situation and the risk of a definitive social collapse, it is possible that a dictatorship could emerge during the early part of this century in Moscow. Criticisms of Putin's methods seriously overstate the risk of dictatorship, however, from both legal and real perspectives, and inaccurately describe the warped logic of the 1990s. Readers should be more attentive to the period in question—i.e., the 1990s—which is accurately considered the best example of the most complete moral, economic, and political fiasco ever faced by Russia. General political elections and the ensuing Putin presidential appointment—which is still characterized by constant support from the population despite Putin's eight years in power—guaranteed that the passage from the *reputed democracy of the 1990s* to Putin's alleged dictatorship has not happened. That is, the conjecture that the 1990s represented the highest rung of democracy in Russia is false, as is the description of Putin as an utterly illogical autocrat.

The evidence as presented clearly supports the conclusion that reforms and opportunities initiated by Gorbachev instead produced bankers and certain communist functionaries that transformed the country into unjust oligarchy. These wealthy Russians built their practices during the era of communism while creating very invasive actions and interference in Russian politics, negatively affecting the state and Russian citizens as a whole. After having trusted Gorbachev and Yeltsin, Russians asked Putin to take resolute action, as any other option would have been a mistake for Putin at that point. Putin's activism was the best news Russians had heard since the fall of the Soviet Union, as a failure to proceed against tax evasion and other forms of fraud would have been a double injustice for the citizens of Russia. It would have perpetuated the strength of the illegally created oligarchs, and would have been an insult to disadvantaged Russians, who were the majority.

It is true that Putin gathered the oligarchy at the Kremlin to ask them to step back. It scarcely matters whether western observers were surprised by this tactic because it could have been the most painless and fruitful attempt to address basic issues—aside from the several and evident cases of unlawful behavior. This initial approach by Putin was not strange or eccentric, and all the evidence available from that period points to the fairness of the initial diplomatic attempt to reconcile with the oligarchs. The oligarchs were not prepared to step back and start down a judicious path because this would have implied an admission of guilt. They—or rather some of them—acted in response and began sponsoring politicians and political parties openly hostile to the Kremlin by resorting to practices used in the West. where are there are already debated risks, resorting to spending millions and millions of dollars – or other national currencies – to lobby to influence national politics and grease the corridors of power.

Some other oligarchs participated in similar activities to undermine Putin and his chances of being reelected in 2004. The enormous flow of money spent on political retribution against Putin was very suspect in terms of origin and intent, as was the expenditure of money by part of the newfangled *nomenklatura* and western circles on fueling media campaigns and political opposition both in Russia and in the West. Even more shocking misrepresentations were heavily supported, thus providing the means to spread the nastiest falsities about the reversal of Yeltsin's programs. This was not a move along an egalitarian course. A genuine democracy in the mid-1990s in Russia was a labile notion, and the result of elections was determined largely by money to bribe—or to shape the electorate. The Greek historian Plutarch wrote about this same phenomenon during the Roman Empire and that system collapsed in 49 BC. But the entire West and most of the Kremlinologists overlooked Russia's electoral phenomenon in the 1990s and the causal effect on the 2000s.

A Failure in Stopping Psychiatric Hospitals and Abuses?

In addition to the much-discussed cases of corruption, the disparaging of business, the unfair atmosphere of the 1990s, and misconstrued policies of the past, one specific issue surrounding modern Russia and Putin needs to be resolved. This is the problem of the label of insanity—a means used during the Soviet era to get rid of political opponents who needed to be watched closely or completely stopped. Critics of Putin use this issue to accuse him of wrongdoing, but it should be examined more carefully.

The phenomena of paranoia, insanity, mental disorders, and psychiatric hospitals have a long story in the Soviet system. After Vladimir Lenin theorized the use of this system as a political means, which was implemented under Stalin and Yuri Andropov (the longest-serving KGB chairman and after Brezhnev general secretary of the Communist Party), it would have been officially stopped by Mikhail Gorbachev. To take notice of some observers, we learn of cases of people who were forced to check into these hospitals for psychiatric treatments. The post-Putin Kremlin is certainly expected to get involved and learn more about these abuses and take strong and resolute action against these injustices, should these facts be true, of course.

A recent newspaper article by Kim Murphy (2006), published in the *Los Angeles Times*, describes the issue of people reportedly hospitalized without being convicted of any criminal charge, and mentions several cases of such abuse. One of those cases is that of Albert Imendayev, a businessperson eager to run for the legislature in the fall of 2005 in Cheboksary—a city of 420,000 people located about 650 kilometers east of Moscow and the capital of the Republic of Chuvashia. Former Justice Minister Nikolai Fyodorov had governed Cheboksary since 1994. One day before Imendayev completed filing for his candidacy, an investigator from the prosecutor's office met him at the courthouse with three police officers. He was locked up until a judge could be found to sign an order requiring him to submit to a psychiatric evaluation. He was released nine days later, but the election filing deadline had passed and he was out of the race. Another case involved Igor Molyakov, an opposition deputy in the regional parliament of Cheboksary who spent six months in jail on libel charges in 2004. A third case was economist Ivan Ivannikov, who lectured for thirty-eight years at the State University of Economics and Finance in St. Petersburg before being "hospitalized" at the city's local psychiatric ward in December 2003 after a protracted dispute with a well-connected contractor over repairs to his apartment. An influential state psychiatrist signed the recommendation for Ivannikov's commitment without ever meeting him, wrote Murphy (2006).

The practice of detaining people in psychiatric hospitals for medical treatment until doctors believed they no longer posed a risk to the public was normal during former Soviet Union years. Allegations hinted at mental illness or something similar, and this punitive psychiatric practice continues in Russia today, according to some sources. While this tactic was used during the Soviet period as a means to control political dissidents, its use may take a different form nowadays. Citizens today can fall victim to regional authorities in localized disputes, or to well-connected private rivals who have the means to bribe their way through the courts. The theory that patients are being forced to sign their own consent forms is seemingly extensive now.

Abuses are on the rise, says Yury Savenko, president of the Independent Psychiatric Association, which has pushed for mental health reforms in Russia (Murphy, 2006). Responsible doctors warn that accusations of abuse should be issued with caution because there are truly cases of legitimate mental illness that must be treated, as is the case all over the world. Murphy's article, however, correctly points out only those individuals who deny that abuse is occurring in Russia. Doctor Alexander Kozlov, for example, swears that not one dissident ever received treatment of this sort, or was diagnosed with schizophrenia, or was sentenced to compulsory treatment in his hospital (Murphy, 2006). Is he right, or is he protecting himself, his hospital, and his relationships with powerful citizens?

Abuse has become so pervasive in Russia, according to aforementioned sources, that there may be sufficient evidence of systematic repression of dissenters through the use of unorthodox mental health system practices. The Kremlin should threaten strict penalties to prevent these practices from happening. Putin should have taken strong action against this unlawful practice—if it exists—of punitive psychiatric activity by ordering further investigations into how many people have passed through these hospitals and what happened to them, then reinforce the current legislation as required. With the Kremlin's record of firm leadership and acquired stability, it should be only a matter of time before the administration tackles this problem and enacts rules that would prevent such abuses.

Pieces of Truth

It is clear that the main purpose of western comments concerning the 1990s and 2000s emanate from a strong deformation of what actually happened, or at least from strongly biased pieces of the truth. A biased approach, due either to incomplete awareness of complex Russian events or misrepresentations blaming Putin, has since become a major topic of analysis. The West has consistently misunderstood Putin and the Russians, as well as built a genre of criticism based on an evidently self-contradictory argument. The West was probably no more nor less unconsciously involved in this line of interpretation of Russian affairs following the Cold War. The West, however, cannot continue alleging Putin to be a novel criminal and dictator, and to blame Russians for expressing support for him by agreeing to have a powerful man ruling the country from the Kremlin, while it continues to interpret Russia through standardized western rules of thumb.

To restate what is now obvious, the damage produced in the 1990s was long-term in nature, and its existence instantly became Putin's reality. What is striking, and what points to purposely biased information from the West, can be found in several episodes, although it has been essential in this article to mention only a few. The West has reported that several oligarchs have been sent to jail, are awaiting trials, or have been otherwise discredited. Apart from the unspecified methods—perhaps extreme in nature—involved with the expropriation of oligarchs' wealth and the return of property stolen from people and given back to them, Putin should be seen as a matter-of-fact leader who dealt with these issues in a practical way. Although the West saw those raids as exhibitions of arbitrary executive decisions that would prevail over the rule of law, Russians and the financial market viewed these state actions in a completely different way.

Anyone looking at the 1990s should cultivate awareness about how some people acquired assets that they did not have to pay for with the complicity of state and regional authorities that made such acquisitions possible. This is a fact, and those who do not see these truths through Russian eyes and continue to draw on traditional western analyses are doubly hypocritical because western leaders, in similar situations, would act resolutely against bribery and unpaid taxes. If Putin's administration is deemed undemocratic, this is a logical consequence of the West's distorted analysis of Russia and typical western hypocrisy as it pertains to selective interpretation.

If we believe the western interpretation of modern Russian events and yet understand that the new path in Russia has strong popular support, I should regard the elections as entirely falsified or be forced to believe the country is a slave to madness, which would be even worse. Despite the criticism of Putin's overall policies as part of an evolutionary undemocratic process, one must rely on a much better and wiser analysis of current circumstances in Russia to be able to make suggestions. Ultimately it would be disingenuous to simply accuse Putin of wrongdoing without proving that a crime was committed by the Kremlin and without suggesting doable lawful and ethical alternatives.

Anticorruption measures, based on an assessment of their effectiveness, do not seem to have been a triumph for the Kremlin, however. I have to describe corruption as a cancer on Russia, and perhaps the energy invested in the anticorruption drive has failed to reduce average levels of corruption in Russia.

If some observers are concerned that the Kremlin has done only the minimum necessary to persuade voters that it is serious, it is true that there has not been much improvement on average. I can simply challenge the Kremlin's forecast as overly optimistic and a bit vague, lacking concrete measures to embrace the whole phenomenon, but I cannot deny that a campaign of some sort was and is underway by the Kremlin. Still, I do not fear that it is a case of too little too late. As I have said, an unchanged level of corruption in Russia has been tracked by surveys of the perceptions of knowledgeable people, and it confirms the huge costs and potential development results of the anticorruption fight. World Bank researchers and others showed that small cuts in the level of corruption in a country could multiply its per capita income by two to three times, reduce infant mortality, and increase economic growth and foreign direct investment. Therefore, further progress in Russia could not be achieved without improved governance and a reduction of corruption with increasing vigor.

I am well aware that there is no single solution to fighting corruption, nor is it possible to rely on one single agency when endemic corruption is the norm; still, the post-Putin government in Russia should continue with economic restructuring, cut back on bureaucratic interference, and reinforce property rights and investor protection. If past anticorruption measures have not generally been successful, it is necessary to signal the implementation of new laws and procedures to comply with international standards and spell out terms for increased international cooperation and for the recovery of the proceeds of corruption. It is difficult to understand why some experts criticize the Russian government for being heavy-handed on one side and for being incapable of focusing on fighting terror and speeding up overall reforms on the other. The Kremlin has initiated a resolute shakeup at the prosecutor general's office and other offices, resulting in the removal of several top people and state officials; thus, the core question is not whether the government is harassing the business community and affecting investor confidence, but whether the jurisdictional system is acting lawfully or lawlessly.

Extensive literature has been written about costs and benefits of an anticorruption campaign in ensuring fairness and stability, while allowing some flexibility. I argue that the idea of a clear-cut policy of stabilization that has been initiated in Russia in the past is still worth considering, because worsening chaos would not be compatible with the country's sustainable competitiveness and resource allocation.

Chapter Eleven

Toward Russia's Next Kremlin

Modern Russia has based its evolution upon communist politics and economics for almost seventy years. In light of this, global political players and western commentators must fully understand the logic of the passage from a communist system to a noncommunist capitalist economy in a way that helps identify the nature of the latest Russian events. The dishonesty and downfall that emerged during the first stage of the transition in Russia was not surprising given how the passage was initially conceived and managed. Observers of Russian affairs should have recognized that the mistakes and illegalities of the 1990s did not appear from nowhere or materialize suddenly overnight in the mid 1990s. The logic of the events I have interpreted and explained here was actually conceived during the initial planning stages of the transition, and I would say starting in the 1980s. Readers should have a clear understanding of the Russian economy, as well as of capitalism, democracy, the intricacies of the oligarchic society of the 1990s, and the difficulties of combining rational acts with ethical effects.

Putin came to power at a time when the Russian state was in a great decline after fifteen years spent attempting to rebuild and renovate the country shaped by Gorbachev and Yeltsin. The Putin era was initiated in 1999, and has been characterized by a Kremlin administration exerting growing control over natural resources and endeavors to curb corruption realities that were, and still are, pervasive and visible to the naked eye. Western observers did not completely see or understand the core essence of a society pushed toward oligarchy and, even worse, a society split into two disproportionate economic classes. These economic challenges had a simple explanation: a general lack of fairness. The previous class of political administrators was not abiding by ethical standards and did not recognize where ethical conflicts could arise. Ethical behavior was in the interest of the country but the political class caused significant harm to those ordinary Russians who had no connections with top decision makers. Not withstanding this, the western-style approach that became visible after the involvement of western theorists spawned an ill-conceived economic recovery program that did not provide business ethics for the developing Russian economy. Macroeconomic stability was definitely important, but Russians did not need technical programs. Russians did not need a simple macroeconomic framework to apply to their situation. They needed to see a new strategy—one that would create a middle class and develop a new, wise approach to public life and socioeconomic justice.

Nevertheless, one aspect of modern Russia is no doubt extraordinary: the growing number of millionaires. It is true that there were a couple of millionaires by the 1990s who found themselves millionaires many times over. Yet there has been a spectacular increase in the number of millionaires who are not linked to oligarchic logic of the 1990s, and they are reshaping the country and Russia's prospects. The new Kremlin will have to support this new course, as well as support globalizing the economy and encouraging competitiveness.

Changing the Appalling Direction of the 1990s

Undoubtedly, certain groups in power had believed anarchy would rule in the new Russia. Moreover, the West failed to recognize the exact extent to which this harsh business phenomenon born in the 1990s was driving Russia toward becoming a permanently oligarchic and insecure political system, and why a turnaround was necessary. Instead of looking at Russians' aspiration for a stable country and more evenhandedness, political analysts and several academic specialists have portrayed the Russian people as unconsciously inclined to dictatorship because of Russia's history and the alleged attitude toward authoritarianism among Russians. In addition, Putin's detractors described him as a predatory, irresponsible, and undemocratic leader, and some have predicted that Russia is definitively close to economic impoverishment. Just as the West's rhetoric represents China as weak and even on the verge of economic collapse despite the fact that since 1978, its economic development has been the fastest-growing one in the world, so it has propagated funereal news about Russia (on China, see e.g., Chang, 2001; Shirk, 2007).

The 2000s desperately needed some way to curb the appalling direction in which events had steered the country by the end of the 1990s, when it became obvious that the two previous visions for a modern Russia—i.e., the efforts by Mikhail Gorbachev and Boris Yeltsin to transform Russian society—had failed. A dilemma that no one explained to western readers was that ordinary Russians trusted the modernization visions of the 1980s and 1990s, but neither vision accomplished a traditional credible market economy or democratic institutions. Amidst oligarchization, academic experts and intellectuals ignored that risk of a society that was quickly transforming into a permanent oligarchic system, and instead drew on an effortless rhetorical western logic to analyze macroeconomic stability and the new market economy's financial fragility. Unfortunately, discussion of financial technicalities characterized this debate, in which western experts were truly experts. Technicalities may be complex, both in design and in meaning, as they help to identify basic grounds for stability and well-being. They are essential and serve as valuable reference sources for complex, modern capitalist systems. This situation was not much different in Russia, yet the Russian composition was not addressed in enough detail. When the system took measures to add control, which included mere ratios, percentages, and so forth, it created a smoke screen that prevented the West from spotting the ethical issues surrounding Russia's passage from the recent past to these days. And when each of the measures made by top authorities was examined separately, numerous surprises were revealed that concerned the overall effectiveness of such steps. In the late 1990s there was growing concern that the system could burst, as it did. The financial system unquestionably lacked modern safety nets, such as deposit insurance and a serious and responsive lender of last resort. The economic system became completely vulnerable to panic, and the unfolding crisis proved to be nearly impossible to stop: once panic started, it lasted until the financial crisis in August 1998 and beyond. The banking system collapsed even before that August of 1998, and bankruptcy and economic gloominess ruled the day and impoverished ordinary Russians. Still the West did not grasp why reforms failed and were only benefitting a few.

From the 1990s Enthusiasm to the Prediction of Doomsday

Despite the appalling direction of the 1990s, academic circles and intellectuals in the West enthusiastically welcomed Yeltsin's political experience, a bizarre electorally managed democracy, and deceitful economic reforms and privatization; these were the same intellectuals who embarked on the increasingly negative hobby of expecting the worst in economic and social sectors when Putin was elected. Soon after Putin took the top chair at the Kremlin, two different lines of criticism began to influence the world, each feeding into the confusion of the other. One side condemned Putin immediately, based primarily on his former KGB association; this may have occurred because academia, central banks, and trade unions are the usual sources of credible political personnel in the West. In any event, Putin's KGB link produced a nasty reaction in the West. What makes this amusing is that Putin had been an aide (in charge of international relations) to a vice president of Leningrad State University after he returned to Leningrad (now St. Petersburg) in the 1980s. Even giving detractors the benefit of the doubt, criticism in this area was unfounded because no one had enough information by the year 2000 to find sensible reasons to attack him politically, or to attack the Russian people for electing him. The initial Putin-KGB link was just an excuse to condemn him. And some oligarchs' donations to a competitor's political campaign fund may have been orchestrated in an overall crusade to demonize Putin and fuel the attacks from both the West and part of the Russian groups. (As I cannot believe that they were behaving like certain captains of industry who systematically give their fortunes away to educational and scientific institutions for the improvement of mankind, I do not rule out the possibility that they have made donations since then in to benefit other groups of power as well.)

The second line of criticism appeared in books published on the most corrupt aspects of Russian business and the plague of rampant frauds. Although not numerous, authors we have seen in previous chapters secured a minimum knowledge of what was really going on in Moscow in the 1990s. Nevertheless, the dichotomy between these two different perspectives, and an absolute incapacity to bring them together has emerged, demonstrating a lack of sincere interest in Russian realities and a misunderstanding of the plight of a society that was in the middle of becoming a complete oligarchy. Because Russians did not want rule by oligarchies and called for policies that would create a more resolute and fair society, the new Putin administration undertook certain steps against instability and business fraud. Scandalmongers prophesied a fall in real GDP, a decrease in investment from abroad, and restrictions in freedom for businesspeople. Such nasty prophesies and incoherent interpretations were released to westerners to such an extent that westerners became very worried about them. The recurrent prophets on Russian affairs saw further setbacks for economic growth, a growing and definitive state control over means of production, a plummeting decrease in disposable income for ordinary Russians, and diminishing interest from big oil and other international groups on investing in Russia. A government inspired by repressive ideas and with no interest whatever in ordinary citizens would close down political institutions, put an entire class of businesspeople behind bars, banish writers, and end international relations. Putin's detractors have predicted all these occurrences.

The Experts' Predictions Have Borne No Fruit

Yet, nothing of what they have written has turned into reality. The predicted doomsday never occurred. Russians went to the polls regularly, and even the Russians' search for a minimum of national identity and prestige did not prove to be so outlandish. Helped by a rapid growth in oil and gas exports, and coupled with rising world prices, economic growth in Russia has been robust from 2000 to the 2007. The real economy has averaged an annual growth in excess of 6 percent, in contrast to the 1990s when it trended downward, and Russia's economy has more than quintupled when measured in dollar terms to over $1,200 billion during Putin's Kremlin. The IMF stated in its 2007 *Economic Outlook* that it expects the GDP will swell by as much as 7 percent in 2007 and 6.8 percent in 2008 (roughly flat with 2007). Although these statistics of economic growth are not at all surprising, the good news is that the IMF has revised its previous forecasts upward. The escalating real GDP growth benefited ordinary Russians, and real private consumption soared to roughly 9 percent in the first decade of the new millennium. Household consumption increased by 11 percent in 2005, and it should continue to increase—perhaps at a faster pace—in the coming years. Luxury imports are also showing sustainable upward trends, and the economy shows a positive "twin surplus" of the state budget and the country's current account. (Economists refer to the so-called "twin deficits hypothesis" to describe a particular relationship between a country's simultaneous government budget deficit and current account deficit.)

International investors, both public and private, kept searching for good business opportunities in Russia. Although they concentrated primarily on the oil and gas industry, they have recently targeted other productive sectors. The investment atmosphere in Russia has been slowly improving over the 2000s. Risk has somewhat improved, and total investment has grown by approximately 10 percent annually since 2000. International investors rank Russia sixth in the world for attractiveness and have viewed the country as one of the most attractive in the region and as a top foreign investment recipient. The number of billionaires and millionaires increased, and despite predictions to the contrary, the country did not nationalize Russia's means of production (except for a reinforced position of the state in the energy sector, which had been unscrupulously privatized during the 1990s). The Russian Kremlin is now playing an active role in the country's economy and social sector, but this slightly increased government ownership in the oil and gas industry has not resulted in negative consequences for Russia's untainted business sector, nor has it impeded economic growth. Political isolation also did not occur, as the West often predicted, and despite the West's wrong approach to Russia, which is part of their complete misunderstanding of Russian affairs.

Russians are predicting a time when the ruble will become an international reserve currency equal in prestige to the dollar or the yen. The recent 5,000-ruble banknotes that have been circulating in Moscow since the end of July 2006 no doubt serve this purpose. Since the financial crisis of 1998, when the country defaulted on foreign debt and devalued the currency, the government has reinforced its citizen's view of the ruble. Russians are now more confident in their country because the foreign cash that they hold has depreciated by $10 billion during the past three years, while savings held in rubles in commercial banks has increased in value more than five times to $50 billion (since the 1998 default).

Russia Needed an Uncompromising Reaction

Then why do Putin and his administration attract so much harsh criticism from major global players, especially the western political and cultural elite? Why do international observers label modern Russia as a post-democratic system in which the Kremlin administration makes the decisions and the Parliament merely rubber-stamps their endorsement? What can be said about several books published at the turn of the century that shed a negative light on state resources and the squandering of state money, or the several business groups (or gangs) and their ringleaders enveloping the country in corruption?

Russia needed an uncompromising reaction from someone like Putin to offer strong institutional stability and restrain the corrupt practices of the 1990s. The powerful electoral principle inaugurated several years ago in Russia and the initial trust Russians gave to Yeltsin in 1991 are important here. Some consider a simple legal democracy with lukewarm popular support legitimate, yet the trustworthiness of people in political leadership is also important, or the democracy might fall into a substantial crisis. Russian citizens did not give up democracy and democratic control over policy making when they asked the Kremlin for firm action against corruption and distortion. When opinion polls show dissatisfaction concerning the exact extent of Putin's steps against corruption and illegality, the respondents simply doubt the real ability of Russia's government to curb the phenomena they wished to end, whereby they then ask for even stronger measures to fight the corruption. This truly is democracy in action, not authoritarianism or electoral madness, as some suggest.

Even if Russia is too big, too complex, or too historically disheartened to be judged simplistically, current Russian distrust of certain economic outcomes are signals that citizens want more resolute responses from the Russian government. This state of affairs stands out against what international experts have long interpreted when looking only at the general aspects of the Russian system, and centering only on efforts to introduce a market-based ideology. These dimensions, sometimes in comparison with those in the major industrialized countries, appear composite today, as the issue was always the passage from one status to another being completely fashioned by a recycled *nomenklatura*.

The Russian population's loss of confidence and faith in both Mikhail Gorbachev and Boris Yeltsin, who kept the populace's difficulties suppressed and unaddressed, naturally led to a form of democracy unique to that country. The West has always interpreted the concept of democracy in Russia, and in all transition countries, from the perspective of a representative democracy, but has always ignored the intimate and important link between a decision maker's leadership and the approval of the population. In reality, this is far more important in countries moving to democracy now than in those countries that embraced democracy long ago. The rising complexity of modern societies prevents us from ignoring this truth, and as modern Russia calls for ample and incredibly complex reforms, observers must weave western thinking with Russian thinking and consider the astonishing effects of postcommunist events. From this perspective, it is clear that Putin has yet to cause complete upheaval in his country and drive it toward a postrevolutionary setting, in which the exact relationship between the oligarchy and Russian society has to be presented in a way that is more informative and effective and that spurs attentiveness. Cultural elites must consider important factors, such as the institutional authority and prestige of the country and the spread of poverty among certain social classes during the 1990s, before they can offer an overall diagnosis of reality in Russia.

Surviving the complex realities of Russian society is not easy, however, because fighting against such realities can make policy making too strong or aggressive.

All political and cultural spheres have to weigh in on any intelligent analysis of what is necessary, how the targeted solution will work, and how to prevent or repair side effects. Political institutions affect political dynamics today. When they operate in a post-transition, consolidated democracy, they can profoundly shape the system instead of working behind the scenes in a supportive way. Transitional players change their strategies, according to Olga Shvetsova (2002), thereby supplying some of the instability and expectations about the nature of transitional political interactions. Such political strategies enforced by Putin were in alignment with actual Russian realities.

In Russia, a significant difference from the past is revealed by the formation of new social groups, which replaced the old system of *nomenklatura*. Putin has undertaken the difficult task of reducing the power of oligarchs. Because former members of the *nomenklatura* and high-ranking bureaucrats captured big business for themselves, Putin should focus on the oligarchy and subject its members to principles, social interests, and an economic rationale that harmonizes capitalism with Russia's social issues—that is, he should make oligarchic groups work for the country.

Radical Changes in Tax Policy

As discussed in previous chapters, the Russian tax system had worked inefficiently, enabling a corrupt system for most of the 1990s. What's more, the failure to collect taxes threatened to throw the state into bankruptcy once again. The farraginous way taxes were being collected and the common interest of federal and republic level leaders to conceal revenue, as well as tax avoidance overall, had to be put to an end.

On January 1, 2001, Russia launched a truly radical tax initiative, completely disregarding the Washington Consensus – inspired stringent advice from the IMF, which was meant to cut government deficits by raising government revenues through the implementation of a new tax code. Putin's Kremlin introduced several new chapter tax reform initiatives. After part I of the Tax Code came into force in January 1999 and contained basic principles and definitions, part II of the Tax Code was signed on August 6, 2000, to take care of collection difficulties that had plagued Russia for most of the 1990s.

A notable policy of the new administration was introduced through a new personal flat income tax with a rate of 13 percent, which replaced the former three-bracket system, which spanned from a minimum rate of 12 percent to a top rate of 30 percent.

New tax rules that covered flat income tax, social taxes, excise taxes, and the value-added tax were being introduced systematically into the system. Effective January 1, 2002, the state Duma approved chapter 25 of part II of the Tax Code,

"On the tax of profit of organizations," initiating a 24 percent corporate flat tax rate (many in the state Duma had favored a 23 percent rate), which was down from 35 percent. This was an essential measure to bring more business-friendly changes to the business community in Russia, and it was estimated by the Finance Ministry that the enactment of this new law on profit taxes could reduce the tax burden by 1.1 percent of GDP. Since January 1, 2003, small business enterprises have been granted either a 20 percent flat tax on profits or an 8 percent flat tax on revenues. Small business enterprises have also been exempted from value added taxes, sales taxes, property taxes, and social insurance taxes. The international business community working in Russia at the beginning of the 2000s reacted quite positively to the new tax stance; 2001 tax reforms were simply "Napoleonic," said German Gref—the minister in charge of economic development and trade during a speech to the U.S.-Russia business community on April 3, 2001. The truth of the matter is that Russia suddenly jumped into the rate-cutting race in Eastern Europe, showing among the lowest marginal tax rates in all East-Central Europe (Sergi, 2007). These new tax incentives permitted greater consistency, encouraging common Russians and businesspeople alike to optimize their consumption choices and operation decisions respectively, as well as providing stimuli to the economy's advancement.

The budget impact on new reforms has been quite positive. Results have been achieved with Russian government tax revenues soaring from 9 percent of GDP in 1998 up to over 20 percent by 2001, and further efforts to streamline the tax system will produce further results. Yet these recent efforts need to be continued, as tax evasion schemes were still being endured as late as July 2003, when more than half a million of the 3.4 million legal businesses registered in Russia had either not submitted tax statements at all, or had reported themselves as owing no taxes and paid none (Sergi, 2004).

In an effort to be aggressive and courageous about the new tax policy, both Putin and the Prime Minister Mikhail Fradkov were seriously considering, as of September 2006, introducing tax breaks for oil companies to encourage the exploration of new fields.

A Bonanza from Gas and Crude Oil Resources

At the beginning of this decade, the share of oil profits going to oligarchs was greater than that in industrialized countries—roughly one-half in Russia versus one-fifth in industrialized countries. The Putin Kremlin government created new tax models, changing the policies from the 1990s when deputies loyal to oligarchs blocked any tax optimization and unfavorable tax legislation. The new Kremlin-sponsored tax structure, which replaced the original flat tax on oil extraction, varied according to the quality of the field, so that the fields with easy access would face heavier taxation in recognition of their higher profits.

As of August 2004, a new system of oil export duties went into effect. It included 1) no tax on oil exports when the price for the Urals-grade is below \$15 per barrel, 2) a 45 percent tax rate when the export price is between \$20 and \$25 per barrel, 3) a 65 percent tax rate for prices above \$25 per barrel, and 4) an increase in the mineral extraction tax on oil from 347 rubles to 400 rubles per ton starting in 2005. Another change was introduced for the regions that encouraged investment by full or partial tax exemption, under which the enterprises that enjoy the highest tax exemption paid a 6 percent profit tax to the federal government. By this time, the federal budget was benefiting so strongly that it posted a 7.5 percent surplus both in 2005 and 2006, and revenues are expected to increase.

In his seventh State of the Nation address on May 10, 2006, Putin recalled that extraction taxes on oil would be set according to world prices until 2015. He encouraged the search for development of, and investment in, oil and gas fields and dealt with an increasingly heavy tax burden on extraction companies whose taxes reached more than 50 percent of their valued added in 2005. Putin also made the case for letting participating regional budgets share in larger portions of tax revenues from this sector. In reality, most tax revenues are going to the federal budget—the entire amount of gas extraction taxes go to the federal budget as well as 95 percent of the revenue taxes from other hydrocarbon resources.

The importance of this resource flow was put forward under a different line at a cabinet meeting in the summer of 2006, when the draft 2007 federal budget was approved before the final approval by the Duma in its fourth reading in November 2006 (the 2007 budget expects an average price for Urals-grade oil of \$61 per barrel, compared to \$40 in 2006). Finance Minister Alexei Kudrin showed that without the income from the export of oil and gas, the budget could not be balanced during fiscal period 2007 to 2009. The budget deficit would be 5.4 percent of the GDP in 2007 without that income, which is why Kudrin had taken to proposing measures dictating that budget expenditures financed through the export of these commodities be limited to 2.8 percent of the GDP. Such a 2.8 percent limit on "petrodollar" spending would be the right balance of the extent of independence from oil and gas income and to give strength to the proposal also suggested by Kudrin that limits should be set by legislation. Skepticism accompanied Kudrin's proposal and other ministers' comments seemed less than enthusiastic overall.

Exceptionally high state revenues, which were accumulated over the past years due to strong oil, gas, and other raw-material exports, helped the government achieve record surpluses and pay down external debt, and inspired the Kremlin administration to accumulate revenues. The latter strategy is based on income from oil exports, which have allowed the establishment of an ad hoc stabilization fund to harvest windfall revenues and finance social welfare programs—funds are held by the Central Bank of Russia, but the Ministry of

Finance is in charge of administering the stabilization fund's assets. The fund is financed by oil export tax revenue when the price of the Urals-grade oil is above the threshold price of $27 per barrel. Considering that the average price of the Urals brand was $64.46 per barrel during May and June 2006 and taxes were high, one can easily understand how much money the fund has been accumulating over the years. In contrast, gas tax revenues are not funneling income into the stabilization fund despite Finance Minister Alexei Kudrin's suggestions that this be done. Unfortunately, his point of view seems unpopular among Russia's other ministers.

The stabilization fund's assets equaled roughly 3 percent of the GDP by the end of 2004 when the fund started accumulating money. The fund accumulated $18.9 billion in 2004 and amounted to more than $80 billion by November 2006. It could come close to 10 percent of GDP as of beginning of 2007, roughly $100 billion. Moreover, the Ministry of Finance predicts that the fund could hold up to $160 billion by the end of 2007 if the funds are not used before then.

The Central Bank, therefore, invests them according to instructions from the ministry, even though the law stipulates that sums can be spent only after 500 billion rubles (equivalent to approximately $17 billion in 2006) have been accumulated—the threshold had already been achieved by the end of the fund's first year of existence.

While these resources can be invested in government bonds in fourteen countries with the highest possible credit ratings by the three major rating agencies—Fitch, Moody's, and Standard & Poor's—part of the fund's assets were converted to foreign currencies for the first time in late July 2006. Approximately $15 billion of the fund's resources were converted to U.S. dollars (45 percent), another 45 percent to euros, and 10 percent to British pounds. In general, Finance Minister Kudrin feels that the country should not relax budgetary discipline and invest public sector surpluses in swelling the stabilization fund money for the moment to avoid fueling inflation, which is picking up to two digits (roughly 12 percent) while the Central Bank's target for the 2007 was 7–8 percent and real wages in the economy are growing by roughly 20 percent and productivity slowing somewhat.

Russia's approach stands in contrast to the cases in other countries, where billions in oil revenues have prompted leaders to delay any type of reform. Russia is reaping the benefits of oil revenues, trying to be like Norway—the European country that turned into an oil nation after the remarkable discovery of the Ekofisk field in December 1969—where the Norwegian Petroleum Fund has accumulated resources that exceed 50 percent of the country's GDP—financed by part of its offshore oil profits. This helps the country to sustain a high standard of living and a welfare-state model made of investment in infrastructure and education. This is achieved through investment in government bonds; in fact, between 50 and 70 percent of Norway's stabilization fund has been invested in government bonds.

Other positive effects from a flood of positive cash flow in state finances include restructuring the country's debts to the Paris Club. The debt was restructured in the 1990s (after disagreements with other neighboring countries, especially the Ukraine, about how to split Soviet debt and property) and two additional major restructuring efforts were completed in 1996 and 1999 when Russia failed to keep to its agreed payment schedules. By 2001, Russia again asked for another debt rescheduling. This time, however, the sharp rise in oil and gas revenues engineered a big improvement in the country's ability to pay those debts faster than scheduled. In 2004, Russia offered to prepay part of its debt and concluded a first prepayment agreement in May 2005, which led to the prepayment of $15 billion of debt during the summer of 2005. Russia had been due to pay off the debt between August 2006 and August 2020 (Germany, the biggest creditor, had allowed the debt to remain unpaid until 2015). While negotiations were difficult, with Paris Club members insisting on a premium and Russia seeking a discount, Kudrin proposed another round of early payments to the Club because Russia could afford early amortization of its debt. Russia wiped the slate clean of foreign debt after successfully negotiating an early repayment of all its debt with the Paris Club on June 15 and 16, 2006. On June 30, 2006, Russia and the Paris Club of creditor nations signed a multiparty agreement allowing Russia to pay its remaining debt of $21.3 billion—the largest prepayment ever made to Paris Club creditors. The deal involved a $1 billion premium for early repayment to compensate the creditors for lost interest, and Germany received the lion's share of $700 million.

Vneshekonombank (which takes care of state's foreign creditors) started repaying over 1 billion in euros to the Paris Club of creditor nations on August 15, 2006, as the first installment in the early debt repayment agreement, and made the last payment on August 21 in U.S. dollars. After the August monetary payments, Russia will have $3 to $4 billion remaining in restructured Soviet-era debt to Paris Club countries that will be paid in products and services.

Note that Russia also owed money to the London Club—an informal group of commercial banks. The Club's banks held $32 billion worth of Soviet-era debt on which Russia defaulted in the financial crisis of 1998. This debt was later restructured, and in February 2000, Russia and the London Club finalized the repayment schedule for $31.8 billion of debt, resulting in a considerable reduction in the total debt owed. As of 2006, Russia's London Club debt is less than $21.2 billion.

The keystone of Russia's debt strategy thus far is understood as the settling of default obligations. After this clearing of debt to the Paris Club and other early repayments to the IMF, Russia is left with obligations to the World Development Bank and the European Bank for Reconstruction and Development, plus smaller obligations of "new Russian debt." The early debt repayment allowed the federal budget to save roughly $1.2 billion on interest in 2007, $1.1 in 2008, and $1 billion in 2009. These savings will beef up the newly created investment fund that is primarily focused on important infrastructure projects on one side and the prevention of inflation on the other. And after settling the Paris Club debt, Russia will theoretically be ready to grant loans to other Paris Club nations, although this is not expected to take place over the next two years, in accordance with Russia's debt strategy for 2007 and 2008. Meanwhile, the previous payoffs, the most recent payoffs, and the government's stable fiscal policy have exerted a positive effect on Russia's sovereign long-term, foreign currency-denominated debt ratings. Starting last year, all the key credit rating agencies raised the Russian government's debt rating. Moody's current long-term rate for Russian debt is Baa2, up from Baa3. Standard & Poor's now rates it BBB+, upgraded from BBB–. Fitch, the other big rating agency, upgraded the country's rating in the summer of 2006 to BBB+. Russian sovereign debt has now been granted investment grade status by all of the big three ratings agencies. This factor will remove the restrictions for many international funds that can only invest in a country in which sovereign bonds have investment grade status from all three agencies.

Last, but not least, in light of the recent Fitch rating, Standard & Poor's and Moody's could well grant Russia an additional upgrade, thus improving Russia's credit rating and giving Russian entrepreneurs and business groups access to cheaper loans.

Russia Should Unleash Modern Russian Entrepreneurial Fervor

We must not interpret geopolitical linkage and its larger economic importance from a narrow perspective. Stronger financial ties and economic cooperation with business implies formation of a class of Russian capitalists that can innovate and take advantage of the current international dimensions of business and politics. With Russia increasingly tied to both the West and the East, and operations of all firms mutually linked and interdependent at the present stage of international economic integration, the country offers immense resources and, in perspective, offers an array of new strategic opportunities for big corporations and joint ventures.

Beyond its bigoted views of Russia, the West's assumption that Putin's interest in modernizing Russia is unscrupulous and unlawful at times is shortsighted at best, and dangerous at worst. Other countries around the world have also experienced large gaps between rich and poor due to small groups of elites acquiring and controlling most of the wealth. This stolen wealth clearly represents the greatest threat to these countries and their ability to raise living standards for their regular citizens. This phenomenon should be obvious to any objective observer analyzing Russian events.

The West should not, in good conscience, try to coerce Russia not to use natural resources for the good of the country. Russia is a leader in the extraction and export of hydrocarbons. These resources are incalculable in their importance for Russia, because they geographically enhance Russia's influence, which coincides with Russia's interests. No other country can ask Russia not to pursue its own best interest. What the West has asked President Putin and Russia to undertake in terms of becoming democratic does not seem to pertain to Russian business advancement. Western criticism is extremely unfair and hypocritical because the West creates geopolitical alliances with Kazakhstan and Azerbaijan without any criticism whatsoever, despite these countries' lack of democratic progress by western standards.

In the political arena, Putin may have tried to move the country toward an international consensus of economic interests while leaving big business and related interests operating on a larger and ampler scale, correctly striving in fact to adapt to and grasp global interconnections, which serves Russia's interests. The Kremlin's increasing economic activism and its impact on Russian business is most welcome. Russia's burgeoning state revenues and international reserves are having positive effects on the country's internal strategic projects and external debt repayment. The Kremlin's technological modernization and completed national projects in the areas of education, health, agriculture, and the construction of new houses and access to affordable housing indicate yet another positive step toward social policies that should favor all Russians, rather than just a few, as was the case under Yeltsin.

Interestingly, to strengthen the Russian role internationally, Putin and government officials kept negotiating early repayment of all the country's debt. The recent agreement with the Paris Club makes Russia no longer a debtor but a prospective major creditor country. Russia has also regularly repaid the disbursements received from the IMF through 1999. In addition, the Russian government recently approved amendments to national currency regulations to make the ruble convertible. While the Fradkov government planned for full convertibility starting January 1, 2007, Putin called to remove the restrictions by July 1, 2006, making the domestic Russian debt market more attractive to foreign investors and hopefully a very desirable investment in world markets. This is all good news for Russia and the Russians.

International Business Activism

President Putin could not pass up the opportunity to get back on track with a stable political and business modernization process. Doing so could allow the country to move toward a definite exchange from its prior directive government (above all in the oil and gas industry), which has been inescapable considering business skirmishing and social deformations in the 1990s, for one that unleashes the zeal of both Russian public and private groups. Private businesspeople are and should be even more welcome by the Kremlin when they push Russian businesses internationally.

One key case is the corporate governance in the oil and gas industry, which has been the cause of ungrounded criticisms from the West. The Kremlin's pressures on oil and gas companies (forcing them to pay more and to give up tax law loopholes) are not contrary to the entrepreneurial spirit. Activities in this industry are partially in line with global trends, which are observing a concentration in production and actually complement the Kremlin's efforts to jump in the market and reduce the distortions of the 1990s.

Much in this spirit, during his seventh State of the Nation address in May 2006, President Putin made the case for Gazprom to have more influence on an international scale. While it has been decreed that up to 40 percent of the stake of Gazprom could be sold to large foreign investors (while at least 51 percent would remain in the hands of the Russian state), other state and private companies are welcome to do business on the international markets. Private investors bought around 15 percent of Russian oil company Rosneft stock in the summer of 2006—Gazprom acquired a controlling stake in Sibneft, in October 2005—and the market reaction has been a success in terms of netting billions and billions of American dollars for the company and improving investors' credibility in the Russian marketplace.

We need to make two points in this context. First, the recent letter to the *Financial Times* by former Soviet leader Mikhail Gorbachev (2006) compared the Rosneft case to positive privatizations in Great Britain in the 1980s. He stated that Rosneft's IPO would raise the confidence of Russians and investors in Russia's consolidation of its capitalist system (the Russian government plans to privatize 100 percent of state-owned oil company Rosneft over the next couple of years or so). Gorbachev says that with this move, Russia would consolidate its capitalist system. This would mark a big difference from the sale of state assets in Russia under Yeltsin's leadership, in which a few were enriched while the majority of the population was impoverished—another lesson westerners should learn from modern Russia. Whatever works for the Russian government and general society should be accepted by the West rather than criticized.

In the face of western admonishers, who purposely misinform the West of the risks of Bolshevik-style nationalization, prophets for the worst voiced their concerns about a complete renationalization of oil and gas companies but were systematically hushed by positive economic statistical figures and the fact that a definitive nationalization has not yet materialized in the oil sector in Russia. Instead, a vast network of private gas and oil companies from Russia and abroad is visible in upstream and midstream operations with foreign companies and is becoming realistic in downstream development in selected European countries, too. We are observing a soaring number of joint ventures and important partnerships with foreign companies, which are often in the hands of foreign governments. In addition to private foreign companies that hold stakes in state-owned Russian firms, private oil companies such as Lukoil (one of Russia's top oil producer), the Russian-British joint venture TNK-BP (Russia's second-largest oil company group in terms of crude oil production), the Surgutnefteaz, and several others are, and will remain, in the private Russian domain. Following the successful Rosneft IPO, the Russian government planned to privatize Rosneft to create a mixture of state and private economy and markets in the natural resource sector and disavow those who only saw the risk of completely nationalizing the country's means of production.

For President Putin and Russia, this is an unusual combination. It is unique because, in other countries such as Norway (one of the world's major oil exporters) and other OPEC countries, the state controls the oil sector, which strangely solicits no global or western criticism. This may seem confusing because the West criticizes Putin for increasing government ownership over this specific industry (not over the entire economy!) despite the fact that Russia has one of the largest numbers of billionaires and millionaires in the world. Despite fears of nationalization that did not materialize in recent years, the West should now support whatever works for Russia and Russians and not overlook the reality. That is, the Kremlin activism in oil and gas industry (and tax collection from this sector) was the indispensable step to cut back the wild capitalism and unethical practices of the 1990s. Western hypocrisy increases when we fail to spot this very sensitive issue in Russia and at the same time do not criticize Norway, the world's third-leading exporter after Saudi Arabia and Russia. In Norway, the oil industry is state owned, operating well, and does not come into conflict with the country's economic growth. The West already supports Norway's complete government control of hydrocarbon industry through the state-owned StatOil (71 percent is state-owned) and Norsk Hydro (44 percent state-owned), which has clearly worked well for Norway because of its Petroleum Fund (renamed the Government Pension Fund – Global in 2006) and extensive export revenues that finance a high standard of living and investment in infrastructure and education. Moreover, StatOil agreed to buy the oil and natural-gas division of Norsk Hydro for nearly $30 billion and the merger proposal was announced in December 2006, in a deal that gives the government control of 62.5 percent of the new group, which will enjoy control of over about 70 percent of the country's petroleum production. This not only will create the largest offshore rig operator in the world but will also give StatOil (renamed StatoilHydro after the merger) more strength in the global oil market for competing more effectively in upstream activities beyond Norway's borders. Financial markets reacted well to this news, as did the media, trade unions, and the government, which reacted enthusiastically to a project that was seen as strategically justified.

More recently, no one has reacted negatively to the possibility of French government-run corporation control over the proposed merger of Gaz de France and Suez SA (a French state-controlled gas company and a Franco-Belgian utility, respectively), which the new French president Nicolas Sarkozy would like to and probably will implement. Such a merger—which could be completed in 2008—would protect Suez SA from foreign buyers but also create a major natural gas and energy supplier in Europe. GDF Suez—the probable name of the new company—will become the largest buyer and seller of natural gas and also the largest importer and buyer of liquefied natural gas in Europe, among others. Although the merger could imply a partial privatization of Gaz de France, the deal also gives the state indirect control of the new company. Western hypocrisy toward and criticism of Putin's Russia has reached its pinnacle!

Overall, whether or not a state monopoly in oil and gas production is best for productive and efficient corporate governance is a subject that belongs to several spheres, especially the economic one. The theory that effectiveness in this industry is higher under private rather than public management is entirely ungrounded. In addition, having the Russian government keep this industry under control should not endanger its efficiency and competitiveness, jeopardize the country's economic growth, nor raise fears regarding the future business dynamism, as the economic growth in Russia of the past seven years proves.

Other Strategic Examples of International Activism

Two big foreign acquisitions became apparent by the mid-2000s. Lukoil acquired the Canadian Nelson Resources for a $2 billion deal value in September 2005, and CTF Holdings-Alfa Group bought 13.5 percent of the Turkish Turkcell for $1.6 billion in December of that same year. These notable cases opened the most recent international activism by big Russian groups abroad, with deals of up to $13 billion in 2006 from slightly more than $1 billion in 2002. Russia became the third-largest foreign investor among developing countries by 2006, with a cumulative stock of investment overseas of some $120 billion, after Hong Kong ($470 billion) and the British Virgin Islands ($123 billion).

There are additional cases. Alexei Mordashov, forty-one years old and fifty fourth in the *Forbes* ranking with $11.2 billion in estimated wealth, is the owner of the powerful steel company Severstal—one of Russia's largest steel makers with iron ore and coking coal mining divisions. Located 400 kilometer north of Moscow in Cherepovets, Severstal is a steel basin with Soviet roots employing approximately 34,000 people. Mordashov tried to merge his giant steel company with the French-Luxembourg company, Arcelor (the second-largest global steel company). Mittal Steel kept Arcelor, however, and Mordashov lost his bid. President Putin, however, blessed this move by a Russian domestic company in foreign markets. Such a merger would have created the first steel company in the world with an annual production rate of seventy million tons (in comparison, U.S. Steel produces about 19.3 million tons annually) for a value of $46 billion and expected gross trading profits of roughly $9 billion. That merger did not materialize.

Severstal still intends to achieve better corporate governance. Among others, Mordashov announced plans to list global depositary receipts on the London Stock Exchange by the end of 2006. A small part of Severstal is already listed in Moscow, and although at the time of the announcement in October 2006 there were no official details of the size of the float, Severstal is expected to list between 10 and 15 percent of its equity, with a market capitalization between $10 billion and $20 billion.

A large Russian commercial bank, Vneshtorgbank (VTB Bank), 122nd among the world's thousand largest banks by capital, according to the *Banker* magazine, and controlled by the government (which is its major shareholder with 77.5 percent shares control), purchased slightly more than 5 percent of the European aerospace and defense colossus, EADS, which also controls Airbus, in August 2006. This step poised Russia to win control of EADS in the end, and raised fears of the impact Russia's stewardship could have on the integrity of the company as well as of the possibility that Russia might meddle in sensitive European issues. The two EADS cochairmen stated that they would not contemplate Vneshtorgbank's representation on the board, and probably for this same fact Germany has proposed in the summer of 2007 to create "golden shares" in the company to give Berlin and Paris a veto over EADS' strategic decisions. Due to VTB Bank's international strategy and efforts to expand international networking, it became the sole owner of a 100 percent stake in CJSC VTB Bank (Armenia), its subsidiary bank in the Republic of Armenia, on July 25, 2007, by acquiring 30 percent minus one share from Mika Armenia Trading Ltd.

In connection with the aforementioned case, it is worth recalling that Russia is developing ambitious strategies involving the aerospace industry. In past years, Russia has been a producer of both civil and military aircraft, and the demand for Russian military aircraft has notably increased recently. Today, Russia would like to expand its presence in the civil aircraft industry as well, and a giant venture, United Aircraft Building Corporation craft manufactures, was established, to bring together private and state manufacturers, in November 2006. The deputy prime minister, Sergei Ivanon, who also holds the new company's chairmanship, unveiled the ambitious share of up to 12 percent of global civil aircraft sales by 2015. In addition, and in the spirit of international cooperation, the Russian Sukhoi Aviation Holding and Alenia Aeronautica (of the Italian Finmeccanica) agreed to sign a strategic cooperation accord to construct a new generation of regional jets capable of competing with the Canadian Bombardier and the Brazilian Embraer. A so-called Superjet 100 with ninty five seats and two possible options with seventy five and 110 seats is a reality now, and deliveries should start by the end of 2008; aircraft projected for business, cargo, and military segments could follow. The total investment should amount to roughly $1 billion. In addition, oligarch Oleg Deripaska would enter into partnership with Bombardier—the world's third-largest aircraft maker—through his company Aviakor.

Another case in the summer of 2006 was the move by Evraz, the largest steel producer in Russia, to buy Oregon Steel Mills (United States) for $2.4 billion in August 2006, another move that had a big effect in Russia and on the international market. Two big Russian aluminum companies—SUAL of Viktor Vekselberg and RUSAL of Oleg Deripaska—joined to form one of the world's biggest aluminum conglomerates with Glencore International AG, the Swiss aluminum group and the world's largest supplier of commodities and raw materials to industrial consumers. This move also had Putin's blessing. (*Forbes* 2007 ranking lists Vekselberg sixtyfirst and Deripaska fourtyth in terms of overall wealth, and they are fourty ninth and thirty ninth with net worths of $10.4 and $13.3 billion, respectively.) As part of a larger and more ambitious plan, SUAL and RUSAL set the stage for further development to form an alliance with Glencore and a merger agreement with Glencore was signed in October 2006 to become the United Company RUSAL—a true global leader in the aluminum industry. Under the terms of the share-for-share deal (RUSAL's shareholders own 66 percent of the new company, SUAL's shareholders own 22 percent, and Glencore owns 12 percent), the three parties' merger concluded on March 27, 2007, to became the world's largest aluminum and alumina producer—ahead of the U.S.'s Alcoa and Canada's Alcan—employing more than 110,000 people in seventeen countries on five continents, and accounting for an estimated 12.5 percent of global aluminum sales and 16 percent of global alumina production, respectively.

An additional case in point of international cooperation is that of the diamond industry, consisting of the state-controlled (the state and Yakutia—about 23 percent is privately held) diamond and gold producer ALROSA and the South African De Beers rough diamond producers—the second-largest and the world's largest producers, respectively. They signed a memorandum of understanding in 2006 because they foresaw the possibility of teaming up on diamond prospecting and exploration activities in Russia and around the world. ALROSA may also have an interest in the gold and platinum business of Norilsk Nikel, and conceivably in the oil and natural gas industry in the medium term.

Putin's May 10, 2006, State of the Nation address drew media attention not simply because he referred to social breaks as nefarious aspects to concentrate on, but also because he made the case that the overall oil and natural gas industry should be active internationally and become, more than ever, linked with foreign companies. State-controlled Gazprom, the world's largest natural gas producer, is already engaged through cooperative agreements with foreign companies, especially in the West. As for Rosneft (the giant state-controlled oil company with production activities that spans from Sakhalin Island to Siberia and to southern Russia, with shipping and pipeline interests), fresh private capital has been sought. Rosneft raised some $11 billion (by floating 14.8 percent of the company's share capital while being listed on the Moscow and London stock exchanges) in an Initial Public Offering (IPO) on July 14, 2006. News of other offerings spread across financial markets, showing that big Russian companies are increasingly involved internationally.

This is not the first case of Russian companies that have conducted IPOs, as they started to do in the mid-1990s. With the number of IPOs up from fifteen in 2005, Russia was expected to witness some sixty IPOs during the period between 2006 and 2008, and other Russian companies are expected to become public in 2007. This long-awaited Rosneft IPO, as a state company, was the largest initial public stock offering ever in Russia, and the fifth-biggest worldwide.

It raised a very sizeable sum of money, created a market capitalization of as much as $70 billion for the company, and increased the credibility of the Russian economic environment for international investors.

The credibility of Russia in its entirety will be at issue with raising private capital for private and state-owned companies. It is well known in economic circles that Russia has built its economic fortunes on crude oil and natural gas riches. While this increasing dependence has been an important step in an overall pro-growth strategy, a long-term durable policy is obliged to build on a variety of sectors in view of the fact that an economy overly dependent on only crude oil and natural gas economy could develop the "Dutch disease". Likewise, other productive and service sectors such as finance, information technology, various manufacturing branches, and skill-intensive industries need an attentive policy and abundant investment and resort to main sectors of competitiveness to nourish the country's long-term strategy. The fact that the economy has benefited from a high degree of unused capacity since the mid 1990s which has helped the country to grow over the past seven years despite a low level of investment is a compelling case for the country to create a program of large investment policy approach to be maximally effective.

Moving to implement investment stimuli rather than waiting until this necessity has been explicitly established by an economic slowdown is imperative. The fact that international financial markets have reacted quite positively to these offerings shows another facet of the double standard that western analysts and companies apply with respect to Russia. After seeing the failure of many malevolent prophesies about a country on the verge of collapsing again (after the big collapse in August 1998), several foreign companies—and foreign state-controlled entities as well—are openly interested and willing to take part in business investment in Russia. Lots of money has been invested thus far, and this trend will continue, as the business community is expressing further interest in other investment opportunities. Additionally, there has recently been a specific attempt to raise private capital in connection with another sensibly strategic state company, the electricity monopoly Unified Energy Systems of Russia (RAO UES), which is launching a drive to attract $79 billion in investment, mostly from private investors, to upgrade Russia's overstretched electricity sector.

In the face of western critics who purposely misinform western citizenry of the risks of Bolshevik-type nationalization, we are catching sight of a soaring number of joint ventures and important partnerships with foreign companies that are often in the hands of foreign governments. In addition to big private stakes in state-owned firms, private oil companies such as Lukoil, the Russian-British joint venture TNK-BP, the Surgutnefteaz, and several others are (and will remain) in the private domain, as was initially suggested by German Gref. This change will, therefore, create a mixture of state and private economy and markets in the natural resource sector and disavow those who saw too many risks in a complete nationalization of production.

For President Putin and Russia, the oil and natural gas industry has been and will continue to be an unusual combination. It is unique because in countries such as Norway and other OPEC oil-producing countries, the state controls the oil industry, which strangely generates no global or western criticism. This may seem confusing because the West criticizes Putin for increasing government ownership over the economy, which is clearly false, considering that Russia has an increasingly large number of billionaires and millionaires. Nationalization did not materialize in recent years, and the West should support whatever is pragmatically working for Russia and Russians instead of criticizing it.

Russia's Luck

With the facts above, we can see more clearly the realities concerning Russian reform then and now. Putin's Kremlin certainly has exhibited partial contradictions, and the Kremlin has not been without lapses in effectiveness. Still, the post-Putin Kremlin administration needs to reinforce an effective process for modernizing the bureaucracy, fighting corruption more strenuously, curtailing distortions and inefficiencies in the productive system, and creating stronger foundations for economic development. This is an overall strategy that requires time, however, as Russia had to face a thorny situation and make responsible choices in the policy area when Putin took over the Kremlin.

One move was to assure international investors that previous privatization and private property rights were guaranteed against fears of Bolshevik-type changes. The other was to tackle massive disparity in income distribution and offer specific solutions for large sectors of Russia's population who were living in poverty and asking the president to steer them toward better times. He could not back away and leave those Russian needs and hopes unanswered.

When Putin appointed Gref as minister in charge of economic development and trade (Gref then became one of the key architects of the economic policy of the Putin Kremlin), Putin asked him to draw up a long-term strategy for economic reform. The western media enthusiastically endorsed Gref's program—a "bold economic blueprint," wrote Michael Wines in the *New York Times* (2000). Although Putin support for Gref's program appeared to be dwindling, Gref was asked to incorporate certain changes. What happened next was a bit surprising. Gref's program was diluted only slightly, and he gained wide support and Putin's backing in the end. The government approved only an eighteen-month version and not the long-term strategy, and all measures touching on deeply reforming the state were removed from it. In an effort to move Russia toward the goal of economic liberalization, and through the work of "ultra-liberals" like Gref and Illarionov, Putin's Kremlin issued its long-awaited plan to overhaul Russia's vacillating economy. Based on "the very model of modern Western economic theory," wrote Wines, the plan was "considerably bolder than almost any plans that most Western nations have ever tried to push past suspicious voters and hardened special interests." Although the plan did not pass in its entirety, the West could not have approved it. Since then, Putin has demonstrated that there is no valid economic alternative to a market course, although Putin had little sympathy for the original shock therapy ideas, and Gref's main program points were effective private land ownership, deregulation, and enhanced competition.

The 2006 state budget surpluses and new budget directives are seemingly in the spirit of Gref's early plan, with an increasing share of social transfer. Also, in the most recent federal budget, 2007—which records huge revenue streams that keep the country's budget completely in the black, and which the Duma approved at the end of November 2006—revenues were expected to rise 13 percent and expenditures 23 percent in nominal terms; the budget surplus could be 4.8 percent of GDP. While the 2007 federal budget set defense and security expenditures up 10 percent in real terms, most main expenditure categories received nominal extra funds ranging from 20 percent to 40 percent; transfers to regions and general administration would receive an increase in real terms of more than 15 percent. Allocation to social expenditures would receive a 3 percent increase in nominal terms; although a decrease in real terms, transfers from the federal level to regions should more than compensate for those losses.

Certainly, Russia is extremely rich in natural raw materials, with a sizeable quantity of petroleum, natural gas, coal, and other natural resources. Russia has roughly 26.3 percent of the world's natural gas in proven reserves (77.8 year reserves-to-production ratio), and 21.3 percent of world production. Russia's coal resources contribute 17.3 percent of world reserves, the UK oil major BP quantifies in its bulletin (2007). To put this in historical perspective, Russia produced slightly less than 6.3 million barrels per day in 1995 and 9.7 million in 2007 (domestic consumption of 3 million and 2.7 million barrels per day, respectively)—an increment in the production of more than 50 percent.

This mounting production has fueled the export of an abundance of oil and other raw material reserves not only for the benefit of Russia's state finance, but also for the balance of payments record surpluses and the buildup of foreign reserves. With over $400 billion of foreign currency and gold reserves as of the summer of 2007 (this sum corresponds to roughly twenty months of goods and services import), Russia is ranked third in terms of reserve assets, behind China with very close to $1 trillion and Japan above $850 billion. As the gross external debt is below the amount of gross official reserves as of the summer of 2007, Russia has become a net creditor to the rest of the world!

Also, thanks to this stable financial situation, the country could witness a policy toward more substantial social sector outlays as well. In addition, this facet of the Russian transition helped push the Kremlin administration to create a financial stability policy through a growing stabilization fund (note that only oil revenues, and not gas revenues, are funneling income into the stabilization fund). This fund is accumulating sizeable reserves which were $121 billion as of the summer of 2007 but that could increase to 13 percent of the gross domestic product by the end of 2008 if the funds are not otherwise used. What is more, in 2007 the Duma passed a scheme to split the oil fund into a so-called Reserve Fund, which is intended for macroeconomic stabilization, and a so-called Fund for Future Generations.

In addition, the Russian government adopted new budget parameters in March 2007 on the first-ever three-year federal budget (for the 2008–2010 period) to submit to the lower house of Russia's parliament before April 30, and which was actually approved in a first reading at the end of May and the final by the summer. This new approach envisaged the government to move to a new stage of developing a budget-forming ideology through a so-called non-oil-and-gas budget, in order for the government to toughen control of budget spending, streamline revenues and expenditures, and diversify the economy as much as possible. It is well known that the recent strong growth of the Russian economy might not be sustainable for a long time, in case better macroeconomic management were espoused (e.g. Hanson, 2007) and this should be reflected in the government budget in line with the worries expressed by both Prime Minister Mikhail Fradkov and Finance Minister Alexei Kudrin.

No doubt, luck has been on the side of the Russian economy and budgetary capabilities. Had oil and gas prices not been so high and exports not so buoyant, Russia's gross domestic product growth rates would have been negative instead of positive since 2001, and the country's budget would have been in a deficit instead of the surplus it now enjoys. With global oil prices slightly above $22 to $23 per barrel a couple of years ago, and well above $70 a barrel in 2007, the momentum for Russia should continue. Crude oil had its first close above $78 a barrel in New York in the last day in July 2007, and closed at $78.21, up $1.38. The price of crude oil is heading up to $100 per barrel but also high oil prices could spur drilling, the discovery of new fields, and prevent a crisis of confidence and a medium-term-oil-supply crisis

Talk was that crude might hit $80 a barrel amid worries that domestic demand would outstrip supplies; it was up 10.7 percent for July and up 28 percent for the year. Therefore, it is conceivable that the trend toward such revenue increases might continue.

Higher export duties on natural gas, and higher fees for natural gas and crude oil extraction also contribute to higher revenues. Thus, some people consider luck to be an important part of Russian development; the recent success, in this view, is not just based on exclusive government participation in the economy, even though the Russian people are much better off under the current Russian government-directed approach. The small business climate has improved, a better capacity utilization strategy is driving industrial growth, and the registration process for setting up new businesses has become less bureaucratic to some extent, despite the increasing number of bureaucrat personnel. While increased pay to civil servants, ministers, and so forth are measures against corruption, the Kremlin administration has considered cuts in the growing bureaucracy (although the success of this is questionable so far) that has soared to roughly one and a half million employees in 2006—up from roughly one million in 1994. While these numbers don't include military and security personnel, the number of bureaucrats in Russia is now larger than in the entire Soviet Union in its heyday; even the United States has a smaller ratio.

According to Andrei Illarionov, the country's bureaucracy has not worked for the general improvement of the country, but for personal achievement instead. In support of his view, we know that the Russian bureaucracy has not brought about responsible economic policy to the fullest extent possible, even though it is much better under Putin. In other words, while Illarionov provides a proper analysis of the mistakes made in the 1990s and the negative role of public administration officials, he and others fail to acknowledge that the new Russian political administration had to jump in and take a leadership role in helping Russian citizens improve their lives.

Under Putin, Russia had to assume that there were risks in stemming the tide of unethical behavior, which means Putin had no choice but to move resolutely. The West, along with the rest of the world, must understand the significance of recent years and find ways to properly interpret the country. The West is increasingly adopting a disgraceful double standard in dealing with Russian affairs; formulating such an interpretation through application of western standards is a mistake.

Russia and the World Trade Organization

Only recently, in November 2006, Russia and the United States signed a bilateral deal removing the last major obstacle in Russia's thirteen-year-old bid to join the World Trade Organization (WTO), the very influential organization that is supposed to insure free trade among continents and countries. Russia's minister in charge of economic development and trade, German Gref, and United States Trade Representative Susan Schwab, signed the agreement on the sidelines of the Asia-Pacific Economic Cooperation summit in Hanoi. Obstacles in this regard were financial services, copyright issues, and agriculture—and especially U.S.—but not E.U.—reluctance regarding Russian membership. Still, definitive WTO participation might result in real economic benefits for Russia over the long term, as it is it a powerful stimulus for the development of the economy, increased the inflow of investment, and development of the agrarian sector. In fact, because current events in the region and their global impact are now more important than ever, the process of globalization itself continuously imposes new dynamics on all forms of development. This requires the Kremlin's administration to understand how globalization's intended and unintended consequences permanently alter the development process ethically for better or worse. Previous crises and distortions at the national level, and in neighboring countries, should warn Putin and other political leaders about appropriate steps to take as they move forward.

In the future, robust economic growth could shield Russia from financial crises. Export revenues, which could continue to be a major driver of economic growth in Russia, are playing a strong function in replenishing state revenue and the country's foreign reserves. In this context, export revenues that allow mobilization of resources for the least fortunate citizens of Russia could well be the most important determining factor concerning Russia's development.

Meanwhile, Putin has criticized the WTO and other international organizations, defining them as "archaic" and "nondemocratic." According to Andrei Illarionov, the country's bloated bureaucracy has not worked for the general improvement of the country and even represented a serious deterrent to inward investment during the 1990s and to the inception of serious market reforms.

Some structures that had been designated to be run by a few active actors did not succeed in insuring much equilibrium these days, Putin said to the economic forum celebrated in St. Petersburg in June 2007. Old decision-making methods simply do not work, and all of us can see the outcome in the WTO's paralysis related to the Doha negotiations, Putin added. The protectionism arrives from the developed economies these days, and it would be necessary to envision the creation of an institution of free commerce in Eurasia to stimulate trade and investment flows, Putin also said.

Better Outcomes Ahead but Russia Has Not Become the Nth Wonder of the World

In examining arguments of political economy, much positive data can be found, and this general data is understandable even for those without economic backgrounds. To take stock of the situation, the most notable trends in Russia's economic performance in 2006 (compared to 2005) concerned government revenue, which stood at 23.6 percent from 23.7 in 2005, therefore mounting from the data achieved during the 1990s and early 2000s. Meanwhile, the real GDP increased 6.7 percent in 2006, and was expected to record a 7.8 percent to 8 percent by 2007, according to major forecasters. Russia's current account surplus posted $94.5 billion at the end of 2006, up from depressing levels such as $-0.1 billion in 1997 or a meager $29.1 billion in 2002. The unemployment rate showed a 6.9 percent decrease at the end of 2006, down from 7.7 percent a year earlier, and the rate was expected to lessen to approximately 6.5 percent by the end of 2007. A jump in the ownership of mobile phones and increased use of passenger cars are also signals improvement in Russians' standard of living during the 2000s. The composition of what consumers are purchasing also shows increased retail trade consumption and a higher share of imports—including luxury goods—in the Russian household's inventory. In addition, the number of pensioners per 1,000 Russian citizens of working age has been increasing significantly—from 202 in 1962 to 323 in 2005—and it is expected to grow to 464 by 2026 (*Economic Newsletter*, No. 9, 2006).

Real GDP, market capitalization, and booming real estate markets—the three primary drivers of wealth generation in Russia—grew rapidly in the country through 2006 and helped to increase the total number of millionaires, according to the latest Merrill Lynch and Capgemini (2007) survey. Those with at least $1 million in investable assets in 2006 increased quite a lot, and Russia was among the top ten countries with the fastest-growing number, increased by 15.5 percent.

Finally, if we look at this issue from a different perspective, statistics report that there are 585 passenger cars per 1,000 inhabitants in the European Union, while only 160 cars exist per 1,000 people in Russia (*Economic Newsletter*, No. 3, 2006). If experts feel we should not compare Russia with Western Europe in terms of income spent on passenger cars per se, then we can at least consider expectations concerning increased disposable income and the growing demand that has prompted foreign car manufacturers such as Daimler-Chrysler, Ford, GM, Hyundai, KIA, Renault, and Volkswagen to consider Russia as an expansion market. One of the latest achievements by German Gref has been an agreement with Nissan Motor Company. to build a car factory near St. Petersburg that will start production in 2009.

Foreign investors are targeting Russia in several other sectors, as well, with investment soaring to $13 billion in 2005 (accumulated investment approximately $50 billion), up 40 percent over investment activities in 2004, reports the Russian Statistical Office.

Despite all this, Russia is not a paradise or the nth wonder of the world. The country is not without its problems. While it is true that Putin launched an anticorruption campaign, it still needs to be realized in its entirety. Russia should now more than ever commit to holding bureaucrats and entrepreneurs accountable at various levels of responsibility, and reinforcing the credibility of the banking sector. Entrepreneurs will have to operate in all sectors without any government interference or careless commitment, and the lengthening list of billionaires and millionaires shows that the country is heading in the right direction. The rationale of a modern capitalism and large domestic enterprises must now definitively work for the betterment of the country and comply with accounting norms. Forcing business people to clean up suspect past practices, introducing new ethical norms, and retraining the bureaucrats to stop soliciting bribes or participate in other forms of corruption will all be additional signals that the country finally wants to and could become a *normal* one.

A post-Putin Kremlin could move the country toward carrying even more weight in the international arena. Today's new scenarios show that Russia can interact with the West and competently engineer the long-term mission of catching up with the opulent West or fast-growing Asia-Pacific region.

The government will need further incisive courses of action, grounded in wisdom, to shape the future of Russia. Post-Putin Russian leaders will have to take additional steps to insure that good ethics merge with rationality. While western intellectuals report that the institutional stability achieved by

Putin came at a dear price—and this is a piece of information that is as yet unconvincing—they have actually neglected the exact combination of effectiveness and rationality that the Kremlin administration used to plan and accomplish the best results for the whole country. If the Kremlin has encountered challenges trying to introduce a minimum of ethical business behavior, or the market fell victim to predatory disputes of one kind or another, further analysis will be necessary. We must at least be conscious of the current debate between the public and western specialists in response to the complexity and paradox of Russian society.

The Russians and Putin simply begged each other for stable and more efficient state institutions and a less-distorted economy than the one bequeathed to them by political leaders in the 1990s. The two have asked each other to agree to a more politically and economically symmetric game, as in the economists' parlance. After being cheated repeatedly in the past, the Russians wanted a policy pointed toward a fairer society. A modern scenario would exhibit a business environment in which both the state and businesspeople can fully express themselves and their needs. When President Putin's tenure began at the end of the 1990s, the poor performance of the 1990s had already occurred, with terrible results witnessed by the entire world. The country was headed in the wrong direction, the society was pervaded by a significantly negative socioeconomic impact, the largest part of the population was suffering, chronic poverty was rife and visible, and national income was unfairly distributed, as we have seen before. This scenario exacerbated social difficulties far more than was originally believed, and this contributed to inherently disequalizing results. Russians were not sharing equally the unavoidable costs of transforming the country. The economic benefit accrued only to a very small cluster of businesspeople, and all this with no end in sight.

After two rounds of visions for the country—Gorbachev's and Yeltsin's—with their associated mistakes and foolish socioeconomic choices, President Putin initiated profound changes in this tense situation in an effort to remold and better meet people's expectations in the wake of Yeltsin's fiasco. Russians are still demanding additional changes and a definitive move toward a viable democracy. Yet, a priori critical judgment of Putin was widespread shortly after he came to power and continues today. This is quite shocking when we consider the West's irresponsible magnification of both Gorbachev and Yeltsin when they surged to power, despite the fact that they had grown up within the Communist Party—Gorbachev himself had been the party's general secretary with KGB support.

Instead of striving for more realistic assessments of Putin by first discussing the rationale that Gorbachev brought in, scrutinizing the Yeltsin era, and then examining the overall ethical impact of actions on Russians, commentators seemed to turn a deaf ear to the harsh realities that faced Putin and the overall state of Russian affairs. International observers have reported inefficiencies and illegitimacies surrounding Putin, yet not everyone has observed those issues.

When non-Russian theorists seem to observe wrongdoing in the political and business realms of Moscow and the Kremlin administration, the majority of them have consistently failed to contextualize Putin's available options and the feasibility of any actions he has taken in light of the limited choices he could make.

For that reason, the complexity of Russian economic affairs must be relayed to the public wisely and fairly, and in recognition of the fact that Russia is now a global player. The way the new system worked and the extremely uneven distribution of income, however, were specific strategies of the political bureaucratic apparatus during the 1990s. It is true that wealth and income inequalities grew in the United States during the twentieth century, as well as in other rich countries that emerged from World War II. The prevailing situation in Russia, however, is inherently different from the one that emerged in the United States. Economic and financial crises, coupled with rising public discontent in Russia, produced a crash because the public believed and supported what Gorbachev and Yeltsin envisaged and promised. Unfortunately, the broken promises that have been constant in Russia's history have resulted in significant public malaise.

Chapter Twelve

Russia and the International Community

Russia's strategic links with Western Europe, China, Japan, and even the United States, through geography, natural resources, and politics, are too numerous and significant to be ignored. In previous chapters, we have seen the geographical perspective from a historical point of view and have reviewed the export of natural resources and the networks of strategic companies. Still, one must look at Russia from various perspectives, particularly in the international context. In the West, we tend to look mainly at facts and figures when evaluating Russia; however, we must also take into consideration ethical and moral norms and equitable business behavior.

At present, many businesses are flourishing as part of the remarkable economic growth that is taking place throughout the country, despite the fact that in Russia's recent past, democratic ideals were endangered by dishonest behavior, the mafia, and business corruption. Nevertheless, we must keep in mind similar cases in the West of dishonesty, bribery, corruption in top political circles, misconduct in international politics, and uncertain alliances with countries of dubious democratic reputation; to ignore these is a definitive mark of the West's double standards and insincerity when dealing with modern Russia.

There are several ways that the West could initiate a shrewd strategy with the new Russia. In light of similar approaches to issues of international securities, Western Europe has nothing to fear from Russia's aspirations, as Putin correctly points out in the *Financial Times* (2006). While the end of the Putin Kremlin is approaching, it is time to talk about Russia from a more politically coherent perspective. An encouraging approach toward Russia would help us to recognize the numerous contradictions of western political leaders.

Western Europe

The starting point is Western Europe. The basis for Russia's relationship with the European Union is the Partnership and Cooperation Agreement of 1994, which went into effect in December 1997 and reached the end of its initial ten-year period in 2007. The partnership established the institutional framework for bilateral relations as for principal common objectives and dialogue. Key policy areas are trade, economic cooperation, and the environment; research and education cooperation in science and technology; political dialogue, freedom, and justice; and external security. Overall, Russia and Western Europe were already strong partners in international affairs and have similar approaches to issues of international security and Europe, as Putin himself has pointed out (2006). The two sides are currently working on a new document concerned with the future shape of this partnership and cooperation. Russia and the European Union must explore all options for a more effective relationship and a common future as partners and allies, and forget anachronistic stereotypes and the "obsolete mould of 'friend or foe'," writes Putin. If the most important issues are cooperation in the energy sector and in the export and distribution of gas and oil, such a partnership is now becoming mature and well-structured, says Putin (2006).

The European Union is among the largest providers of economic and technical assistance to Russia, and the two entities have concluded a number of specific agreements on trade, science, and technology. Such technical linkages provide for an overall policy framework in the priority areas of consolidation of democracy, rule of law, and public institutions; integration of Russia into a common European economic and social space; stability and security in Europe and beyond; and common challenges on the European continent, including environment, crime, and illegal immigration.

Western Myopia

Surely, Russia has the capacity to revitalize the West's interests, and the West has to deal with Russia in a more intelligent manner. Whatever negative perceptions the West holds toward Russia are unjustified, and need to be dispelled if a true working relationship is to flourish. One such negative western perception was recently expressed at senior political levels, such as when U.S. Vice President Richard Cheney, during a speech in Vilnius in early May 2006, called on Russia to cease trying to leverage natural gas and oil exports as tools of intimidation or blackmail in the region, and to return to democratic reform. Demanding that Russia return to "democratic" reforms implicitly and unwisely condones the dissolute and dishonest business environment that emerged during the so-called "democratic" years of Boris Yeltsin.

We do not have to look far to understand why Mr. Cheney's comment, or any such similar comment from another western leader, is unwise. It is very important to understand that Russians see Belarus and Ukraine as a single country, with the history of Russia entwined with that of Ukraine as far back as the tenth century. This perception is validated by surveys taken at the time a Common Economic Space agreement was signed between the countries and presidents of Russia, Belarus, Kazakhstan, and Ukraine, in which most of the citizens in each country believed positive benefits could arise from such a future union. In such a context, the Kremlin administration described Mr. Cheney's speech as bewildering. Not least, the Russian people—whose opinions should be respected—disagreed strongly with Mr. Cheney's statement. Mikhail Zygar, writing in *Kommersant*, called it the "sharpest attack on Russia an American leader has made since the end of the Cold War" (BBC, 2006). Others also saw parallels between Cheney's speech and Winston Churchill's Iron Curtain Speech, delivered in Fulton, Missouri, in March 1946. Mikhail Gorbachev observed that Russians were calling Cheney's address "the new Fulton Speech" during his keynote address at the fifteenth Annual Russian-American Seminar held at St. Petersburg State University in May 2006.

Recent western views are skewed toward highly ungrounded and conservative interpretations of Russia, increasing the risk of initiating a new *Cold Peace* between Russia and the West. Many in the West forget that Russia has assisted with western interests, such as the establishment of several U.S. military bases in Kyrgyzstan, Tajikistan, and Uzbekistan after 9/11 in what was a great alliance against world terrorism.

Another recent example of western shortsightedness came to light in an incident involving an open letter issued by former Lithuanian president Vytautas Landsbergis on the eve of the recent Group of Eight summit in St. Petersburg on July 15–17, 2006, warning western heads of state and their governments about Putin's policies. By that time, the West's failure to understand the real issues in Russia and to understand the opportunity to establish new relationships had been both severe and disruptive; early signals of this came when the former Soviet empire collapsed. Landsbergis was unwittingly playing into the hands of West, trying to convince the West itself of the benefit of the creation of a Black Sea – Baltic Confederation, which had to include the three Baltic States together with Ukraine and Belarus. Had this idea have gone through, it would have created further instability as an anti-Russian entity. President Landsbergis's proposal did not succeed because of substantial problems among the participating states, but it signaled both a lack of diplomatic shrewdness in international issues and of long-run strategic vision. In 2006, Landsbergis—who was president of Lithuania from 1990–1992 and at this writing is European MP—organized the letter, which more than one hundred European members of parliament and others signed, warning the West that its current policies toward Russia were wide of the mark. The letter called on western governments and institutions to side with democratic forces in Russia, and oppose President Putin's undemocratic institutions.

Another example of the incredible shortcomings in western foreign policy—and of the incredible shortsightedness inspired by false moralists and self – interest—is the West's implicit criticism of Putin by referring to Mikhail Khodorkovsky as a political prisoner, with his trial interpreted as a "travesty of justice." All western observers should be much more cautious when talking about very sensitive Russian issues, including the completely immoral circumstances emerging in Russia during the 1990s that transformed someone from the corrupted oligarchy into a moneyed conspirator who directly threatened true democratic forces and impeded them. The Khodorkovsky case is a monumental example of the narrow-minded, self-serving, unethical western interpretations of Russian events that continuously rear their ugly heads.

An additional and recent western view has recently been expressed by the influential New York-based Council on Foreign Relations (2006). The Council published *Russia's Wrong Direction: What the United States Can and Should Do*—a report written by an independent task force, chaired by John Edwards and Jack Kemp, that centered on U.S. policy toward Russia. It stressed that U.S.-Russia relations were moving in the wrong direction, with Russia being less democratic under Putin than during the Yeltsin era. This is tragic nonsense if the United States wants a future strategic partnership in light of Russia's becoming steadily more authoritarian. According to the Council's report, U.S.-Russian cooperation is becoming the exception, not the norm. The report states that perhaps selective cooperation with Russia is possible, while keeping the Group of Eight as a viable international forum, but among other suggestions, calls for revival of the earlier influence of the Group of Seven to assume stronger coordination among democratic nations. The Council significantly notices recent economic progress in Russia in terms of the number of Russians living below the government's poverty line, where the number of people living in dire poverty dropped from forty-two million to twenty-six million between 2000 and 2004. Even more relevant to our discussion, however, is the report's official acknowledgment of the appearance of a middle class in Russia.

However, the Council's report misinterprets the notion of truly democratic events, especially when it compares the Yeltsin and Putin periods, and fails to understand the key events and the logic of modern Russia, as well as Russia's economic progress in income distribution and poverty reduction. This is truly the crux of this entire analysis regarding Russia under Putin. Could a middle class form and grow during the ever-changing economic and political instability of the 1990s—during the so-called democratic but tremendously unstable economic and political leadership of Yeltsin? Obviously the answer is no. Yeltsin and the growing oligarchic society would never have accomplished the necessary reforms because of his disastrous policies allowing entrenched and very powerful economic interests to have their way.

In the context of consideration of the upcoming 2008 elections in Russia, early, realistic, and explicit discussions of Russia by all interested observers would be far preferable to harsh, irresponsible, and meaningless critiques occurring on Election Day and the morning after. In Russia, electoral democracy has been in place since 1991, which the Council seems to have conveniently forgotten and does not mention in its report.

Last, but not least, innovations by individuals and by the civil society as a whole are now additional aspects to consider. Representatives of international aid agencies, charities, and other nongovernmental organizations met in Moscow two weeks before the recent Group of Eight summit in St. Petersburg, in July 2006.

Putin appeared at the meeting in Moscow, surprising most observers because in December 2005 the Russian parliament had passed a controversial new law regarding nongovernmental organizations which makes it extremely difficult for the groups to register—although the Registration Service estimates between 500 and 2,000 such organizations are operating in Russia. Ella Panfilova—general director of the Center for Anti-Corruption Research and Initiatives of Transparency International, and an adviser to Putin on civil society development and human rights—does not fault the situation because it is heading in the right direction amid the difficulties inherent in fighting widespread corruption.

Central Asia

Besides the West, Russia has identified Central Asia as another zone of vital national interest since the mid-1990s. Increasingly important are relationships with China and the entire Asian region. One cannot prohibit Russia from seeking to achieve peace and stability on all of its borders through integration, bilateral cooperation, and multilateral alliances. When Russia and China agreed in 2005 on definitive eastern boundaries in the region of Khabarovsk, thus ending a forty-year dispute over a mere 2 percent of their roughly 4,300-kilometer boundaries, this was good news for Russia, China, and the overall stability of the region. Even the various colored revolutions in Georgia (the Rose Revolution in November 2003), Ukraine (the Orange Revolution in November 2004), and Kyrgyzstan (the Tulip Revolution in March 2005) must be interpreted as stimulating all countries in the region to reinforce relationships with one another for the purpose of pursuing more insightful strategies that produce stable and growing cooperative solutions.

The Shanghai Cooperation Organization, for example, which incorporates Russia, China, Kazakhstan, Kyrgyzstan, Tajikistan, and Uzbekistan, began as a vehicle to settle border disputes in the region, but could evolve into a major political and military bloc with the potential to change the geopolitical situation in Asia. Members of these organizations met on June 15, 2006, to sign several agreements in economic, political, and military cooperation, and invited India, Iran, Mongolia, and Pakistan to the meeting. The Iranian President, Mahmoud Ahmadinejad, appears to believe this organization might gain strength over time at both regional and international levels. Although there are no doubts that Russia could become a major international actor, there are growing uncertainties in that region—also caused by the rude Ahmadinejad—and the international community's obligation to a secure Israel. These facts should compel the Kremlin to assume a more active role and work out a diplomatic strategy to move the entire region into stability, in light of the historical ties between Jerusalem and Moscow. Strong cultural, political, and economic linkages involve these two capitals and the many Russian Jews who have emigrated to Israel in recent years. Modern Russia could easily accomplish this strategy of safeguarding Israel and stabilizing the entire region; the West should be well aware of this. At the G8 conference of July 15–17, 2006, Russia was chair of this international forum and as the presiding country (for the very first time), Russia took care of discussing key international problems in global energy security, the quality and effectiveness of education, and health care, the main topics for the summit.

A New Shrewd Internal Consensus

To cope with challenging opportunities, a new, shrewd, internal consensus should address unequal endowments, increase educational opportunities for the poor, help Russia reinforce the need for trustworthy domestic institutions, and offer sound business opportunities to all. To this end, regulatory rules need to be tightened, and the discipline of national and regional institutions needs to be strengthened to increase wealth and welfare and improve the adequacy and strength of the polity. The public's expectations concerning Russia's development now demand nothing less than complete acceptance and understanding of what Russians want and expect from their leaders.

Russia is a country of mammoth natural resources, which, if used well, could help strengthen the country as well as lessen social contradictions and struggles among social interests and groups of power. A land of riches, still-hidden wealth, and excellent scientists in all branches of human knowledge, Russia is becoming an important player in the international context. Amid persisting contradictions and criticisms, this transition stands against ample and unjustifiable western criticism. Instead of fighting the misperceptions of its intentions and the rationale behind its more recent policies, Russia should be involved in an advanced stage of astute international partnerships.

President Putin is to step down in 2008, as the constitution has remained unchanged. Russia still has a way to go before its citizens and outside observers consider it a stable country. Russia and Russians are not hostile to the West, and involving Russia in western strategies would benefit the international community. Although Russia still suffers from asymmetries and reduced governance effectiveness, the West has to stop discrediting Russia and its citizens. A new western stance regarding Russian affairs and economic synergies would benefit both Russia and the West.

The new Russia that emerged in the 1990s stopped the country from sliding toward a greater and more definitive oligarchization of the society, established a minimum preeminence of politics over the country, initiated improvements for the benefit of the middle class, halted to some extent the unequally growing income distribution, and created the minimum base necessary for a more conducive corporate environment. We must acknowledge that the Russians are striving for better times and that they continue to call on the

Kremlin administration to more strenuously fight corruption and to create a better consensus among politics, big business groups, and the majority interest of Russian citizens to advance the country in the direction of more modern and judicious times.

Encouraging a New Attitude toward Modern Russia

If economic data show long-term potential for growth, critics of Putin and ordinary Russian citizens should work from a more intellectual perspective and cease their elaborate projections of potential threats to long-term Russian social stability that depict a pervasive state of decay and a judiciary system submissive to the Kremlin. The West has ended up having to search for a more cooperative approach toward Russia, seeking ever more international cooperation, instead of inspiring irrational hatred against Putin's policies. In addition, charges aimed at Russia and Russians of being isolationist and hating anything foreign constitute an entirely unjustified exaggeration and distortion of Russian realities.

Condemnations of Putin for oppressing civil liberties and moving the country to a new type of dictatorship or a scenario similar to past Soviet-type communist regimes are and will continue to be unfounded. Such analyses have been quite wide of the mark. Detractors have neglected the relationship and causal link between the corruption of the 1990s and Putin's policies. Contrary to any judicious perspective, Kremlinologists have taught readers in the West to take for granted that Putin is the cause of the corruption, and from that assumption, they have fostered other negative views of Russia in the modern world.

Intellectuals should be more sincere in researching their views now. Any negative perceptions at this point are based on their own emotions and misinformation rather than what ordinary Russians actually believe and what is truly best for Russia. As several public opinion surveys have indicated, Russians think differently about Russia than western experts do, and they now support a profound new political stance as well.

Western observers need to understand that the real causes of alarming corruption in the Russian system date back to the 1990s, when the country became embroiled in a complete institutional disaster. Putin cannot take responsibility for the causes of that institutional anarchy. While raucous critics represent Putin as having created a modern Russian state based on the abolition of free thought, this is not a precise and confirmed criticism. Western scholars and experts have completely misunderstood the Russian people, and therefore most western criticism of the stability and sentiment of Russian society is suspect.

Therefore, looking toward the future, I continue to see much possible cooperation between Russia and the West. My hope is that all western intellectuals will resist the calls for isolationism or continuous criticism of the Kremlin and the Russians. Nevertheless, recent occurrences also give us opportunities to think about what we can do with modern Russia, and to stop being afraid of Russian leadership. Western analysts and readers must rethink the Russian transformation and its aftereffects, and become aware of the true story that certain wealthy and powerful sectors strived to conceal. Despite the disputes and irrationality surrounding Russians and Putin, the West should get a full, coherent picture of the Russian story and of why a mighty response to the 1990s facts was necessary by going beyond detachment, insinuation, and the damaging and systematic condemnation of the Kremlin. We all should try to disentangle Russian problems by looking at the gross social injustice that conditioned the Kremlin policy response on behalf of common Russians, and we should be optimistic about a definitive passage toward a Russia where the state can correctly deal with a powerful monopolistic business oligarchy and meet Russians' expectations for state-run, efficient power structures.

In addition to the increasing western double standard in analyzing Russia's development and overlooking what the West has been doing for the past several decades, Russia is dangerously reliant on nuclear weapons to deter both nuclear and conventional attack, according to recent views. Stephen J. Cimbala and Peter Jacob Rainow argue in *Russia and Postmodern Deterrence: Military Power and its Challenges for Security* (2007) that Russia is facing an increased United States presence in adjacent territories, an increasingly assertive NATO, and a China that aspires to overtake Russia as the world's second-ranked military power in order to establish its hegemony over the Pacific basin. In short, Russia could confront a new political and military world order that would demand new deterrence and defense options for Russia. Cimbala and Rainow simply argue that Russia is to confront new political and military world affairs that are very different from the past. This new post – Cold War, post-Soviet panorama is changing radically and along with it the idea of deterrence based on nuclear weapons. Simply Russia should be inclined to readapt to new deterrence and defense thinking and if the country lacks modern technology for military purposes, Moscow could rely on nuclear weapons as its first line of deterrence against a military attack, either nuclear or conventional, the authors say. Unfortunately, Cimbala and Rainow focus only on the U.S. role, ignoring completely the increasing interactions of economic interests linking Russia, Western Europe, and China. The role of using armed force to support deterrence and crisis management, and a subtle interaction between military forces and diplomacy are important. The overwhelming force of the U.S. military intervention cannot explain the use of deterrence and military commitment and the U.S. policy emphasis toward preemptive and preventive attack, but it is important to ask under what conditions preemptive or preventive attack is worth considering as a response to perceived threats. The growing interconnections of market-based economies of Russia with China and Western Europe have formidable implications for policy makers and dilute threats of resorting to military actions in the next decades. The role of oil, natural gas, increasing trading links, huge investment, and other common financial interests are much too important to even consider this kind of nuclear attack. And even if Russia lags behind in leveraging modern technology for military purposes, resorting to nuclear weapons as its first line of deterrence against either nuclear or conventional attack is totally unfounded and unprincipled.

Moreover, western hypocrisy overlooks the fact that the scale of military spending and the scale of the defense industry have substantially shrunk from prevailing Soviet-era expenditures (see, for example, Charles Wolf Jr. and Thomas Lang, *Russia's Economy: Signs of Progress and Retreat on the Transitional Road,* 2006). Moscow is now spending some 5 percent of what the United States spends on its military (total spending on defense and non-defense ministries). Despite fears that Russia's official data might be distorted, the military burden as a percentage of GDP declined from 4.1 percent in 1995 to 2.9 percent in 2005, according to Wolf and Lang. I cannot foresee any military threat to the West or the United States from Russia: the new international context and modern economic realities make recourse to genuine war—nuclear or not—completely meaningless.

Nevertheless, I find another perplexing angle in the West's analysis reflected in the Bush administraton's paradoxical July 2007 plan to expand multibillion-dollar aid and weapons sales packages to friendly nations in the Middle East. Secretary of State Condoleezza Rice will soon announce proposed extensions and enlargements of foreign aid to Israel and Egypt and a prospective arms sale package to Persian Gulf countries—Saudi Arabia, among others. This proposed package of some $20 billion in advanced weapons for Saudi Arabia—the deal would include satellite-guided missiles, upgrades for fighters, and increase the capacity of their navy—has also raised concern in Israel and elsewhere. Because Saudi Arabia in particular is not trusted as a reliable partner in the fight against international terrorism and it is believed the Saudi government promotes militant Islam, say protesters in the United States, new weapons could be used for strikes on Israeli territory.

This is hypothetical, as Saudi Arabia has no apparent enemies in the region, but nevertheless, does it not present a paradoxical double standard? Besides long-standing U.S. commitments to Israel and Egypt, and besides two U.S. and western major allies in the region, the proposal would include asking the Saudis to accept restrictions on the range and location of the satellite-guided bombs, though it clearly is a paradox considering the West's growing concerns over what Russia does. The United States proposed an army deal with the Saudis and this has not caused much concern in the West. In contrast, the West expresses growing concern over Russia and Russia's weapon exports as well as against all Russia's military policies.

Although the plan to bolster Gulf nations' militaries is intended to contain Iran's growing strength in the region—and I do not argue with the importance of having a strategy on this issue resolutely implemented— a better and more realistic strategy could help even more. Even Mikhail Gorbachev severely criticized such western policies while speaking at a news conference in Moscow on July 27, 2007. Gorbachev voiced his disappointment, blaming the current low in Russia's relations with the West squarely on Washington, saying the United States was guilty of committing strategic mistakes that had thrown the world into a period of global disarray. We must avoid having the West and Russia fall away from each other in the direction of two equally extreme but opposite sides—from which the West "finds" criminal behavior at every turn and Russia turns its back on the West as it did during the reign of Nicholas I from 1825–1855, when discussing Russia's identity meant signifying to what extent Russia could steer clear of the West.

All this should inspire us to take a closer look at the West's foreign policy, a policy of double standards and uncertain benefit to all globally. Intellectual and scholar Robert Kagan, in his *Dangerous Nation* (2006), candidly describes the United States as a country with a continuing trend in its foreign policy—regardless of the alternate conservative and liberal White House administrations—feeling its mission is to change the world based on U.S. interests. Others have found it convenient to talk of a U.S. "benevolent empire" (Donnelly, 2005), through privilege because of the soft power of U.S. economy and culture (Nye, 2004). This indistinguishable stance of differing parties in the United States is subjected to criticism by George Lakoff (2006), who writes in his *Whose Freedom?* that the two U.S. political parties' ideals are quite different, and that they tend to think homogeneously within the same party, but differently from the other party's members and this may explain differing attitudes over foreign affairs and the United States' military and political supremacy. Kagan's *Dangerous Nation* goes so far as to say that the average U.S. citizen – not political parties – thinks the country needs the role of supremacy.

Does this attitude not signal a double standard, whether we talk about weapon supremacy or economic and cultural supremacy? We all want to have a realistic and mighty West, but when the same goal is pursued by Moscow—if it is at all—we start criticizing Moscow!

Alternatively, as John Gray (2007) put it in *Black Mass*, equally damaging is the rise of utopian politics in the West, a single model of political behavior that will become a worldwide norm and that, if necessary, will be enforced at gunpoint. All these views stand behind a risky partitioning of post-Soviet societies, and the creation two differing groups, one pro-West and the other pro-Russia. We do not need imperial states on either side of the world.

However, the West has confused its image of eastern societies by stating repeatedly our superiority—no doubt emphasizing its wealthier aspects—and western institutional and governing models, and by psychologically dividing these societies into groups of people in favor of and against modern Russia. In this context, we see what occurred during the Ukrainian Orange Revolution in 2004 and the arrest in Georgia of four Russian military officers—though later released—on spy charges, sparking a diplomatic crisis with Georgia. And does not the relocation of an aging statue of a Soviet-era soldier from a central location in Estonia's capital Tallinn to the city's Garrison Cemetery, which sparked protests in the streets of Tallinn and other towns by the end of

April 2007, remind us of a forced climate of enduring tension between East and West? There is no doubt about Estonia's patent right to do so, and no one can interfere in Estonia's internal affairs. However, to keep talking of Russia's belligerent intrusion into this democratic nation's internal affairs while not searching for lasting cooperation is a matter of short-sighted political vision in the West.

We have above three clear examples of the West's continued faulty approach to Russian affairs. At its heart, the West's plan has been to divide, and, even more troublesome, to connive with despotic dictators all over and in countries such as Kazakhstan in an unconventional and shameful political attempt to weaken Russia. Does this resemble a clear western paradox? I believe so! And this tactic is far from effective; instead of the West securing and cultivating stronger political ties with Russia, just the opposite has happened. This divisiveness is very wrong and wastes money on zealots who bring disunity to their societies. As Anatol Lieven and John Hulsman state in *Ethical Realism: A Vision for America's Role in the World* (2006), instead of splitting societies we should aim at using diplomacy and wise politics to spread economic prosperity all around, which is insolubly connected with economic interdependence (see also Mueller, 2006).

Taking a different stance, Amitai Etzioni's *Security First* (2007) seems concerned to address the future and what the United States can do to improve relations with the rest of the world. He asserts that basic security must be the priority in all foreign policy considerations, even ahead of efforts to democratize—good advice for the United States and for all countries. He sets out essential guidelines for a foreign policy that makes sense in the real world, builds on moral principles, and creates the possibility of establishing positive relationships with all nations. Etzioni's conclusions do not fall into black and white—that is, "liberal" and "conservative" categories—for he is guided not by ideology but by empirical evidence and moral deliberation. America should be more concerned about security and more understanding of the critical role of religion and moral culture in maintaining social order without violence.

The recent U.S. plans for a missile defense system in Central Europe to guard against Iranian and North Korean missiles could be quite divisive as well, though I do not forecast it sparking a new arms race. Putin fiercely opposed this, offering an alternative plan to President George W. Bush during the meeting at the Bush family's oceanfront compound in July 2007 (Putin was the first head of state to be hosted at the Bushes' Maine summer home). Though Bush called Putin's idea innovative, he said the United States still wants to anchor the defense in Poland and the Czech Republic. Does such a plan make sense today? What does it mean that the Czech Republic and Poland need to be an integral part of a system? Do they not belong to NATO? Basically, Putin had unveiled a proposal in Germany the month before to set up early warning radars in Azerbaijan and possibly modernize the Azerbaijan station as a substitute for the radar and interceptors the United States wants to place in Poland and the Czech Republic in order to monitor Iran's expanding nuclear-enrichment activities. While they seek to restart talks about the program with Tehran, diplomats say the Iranian government has not yet responded to the proposal. Washington has been clear in its doubts about the Azerbaijan facility becoming a substitute. In fact, it would be preferable to bring more European nations into the decision-making process about how the shield is structured and to incorporate a radar system in southern Russia or some other appropriate location. Putin suggested information-exchange centers in Moscow and possibly Brussels as a way to strengthen the Washington-Moscow national security relationship. "The relationship of our two countries would be raised to an entirely new level," Putin said. To paraphrase Gorbachev's recent statements at the fifteenth Annual Russian-American seminar at St. Petersburg State University in May 2006, the West displays a winner's complex, chilling relations into a conditions that some commentators have likened to the Cold War. Concerning Putin's recent decision to suspend Russia's participation in the Conventional Forces in Europe Treaty, Gorbachev claimed that it is an attempt to encourage talks on the amended version of the document, which Russia has ratified but the United States and other NATO members have not.

While the West continues to question Russia's return to world visibility through old-style power, murder, nuclear weapons, and so forth, it stands accused of running torture programs, according to Stephen Grey's *Ghost Plane: The True Story of the CIA Torture Program* (2007) and Trevor Paglen and AC Thompson's *Torture Taxi: On the Trail of the CIA's Rendition Flights* (2006), both of which provide details about such CIA programs. (I have no personal supportive evidence concerning this). These programs allegedly started during the 1990s, as the U.S. government chose to outsource its handling of terrorists for ease of mission and/or was unprepared to establish a proper legal framework within which to work. Secret directives prepared the way for that in the Bush administration, becoming known as the "extraordinary rendition," according to what their books convey. The Bush administration policy followed that of its predecessors, but this Bush administration has gone much further than any previous administration, writes Grey. The double standard in the West's treatment of modern Russia discussed in this book is also described in books relating to other geographical areas in the world, such as Noam Chomsky and Gilbert Achcar's *Perilous Power* (2007), which describes U.S. foreign policy in the Middle East.

The Rhetoric of Western Leaders

Currently, the West's long-term lack of approval for the feasible policy options undertaken by Russia's governments amid continuing socio-economic turmoil in the past decade illustrates how western critics of the current Russian leadership continue to see these issues through an ideological prism. The West has interpreted nearly all of Putin's policies as representing an ethical lapse when compared to the policies of previous presidents. This interpretation blinds western observers to the true nature of Putin's difficulties and the actual content of his overall policy. Failure to rectify western misperceptions causes more and more policy mistakes by the West with respect to the development of a noncommunist—and post-Yeltsin—Russia. While Russians supported reforms because they wanted to move forward, there seems to be a permanent mental block in the West regarding how to deal with any Russian leadership team that does not share specific leadership goals and concepts common with western thinking. The western failure to understand Russia and to offer shrewd lessons represents an essential part of this analysis. Most disturbing is the real possibility that the West has deliberately chosen not to assess Putin through anything other than the shallow, distorting prism it has always used. Western governments may well believe that this painful but true reality fits in too well with its overall historical policy objectives toward Russia and Putin, which were and are difficult for the West to defend on ethical grounds. Therefore, the West appears to believe that consistency regarding its policies with regard to Russia is more important than ethical improvement and change in overall policy objectives in Russia itself.

In light of this discussion, it is interesting to examine another western paradoxical approach to a couple of Russian events. One was the tragedy at the Beslan School—in the North Ossetia—on September 1, 2004, the traditional start of the school year, or the Day of Knowledge in Russian tradition. More than 1,200 children and adults were taken hostages by a group of armed Chechen separatists and Islamic fundamentalist rebels. There was subsequently a massacre in which 334 hostages (186 of whom were children) were killed after a three-day stand-off and a military rescue attempt. The suspicion was that the rescue operation was not conducted with care and contributed to the bloodshed. Another event was an assassination attempt on Putin himself in that same month of September 2004, an event that some detractors say never actually happened. Putin felt compelled to adopt a more rigid stance given these two events. Bold steps were required, but the West's approach was revealing. The West started criticizing Putin about these steps too. Also, the mismanaged rescue has been a reason to criticize Putin, but despite tactical errors, I do not see the opportunity of the West's reaction. Putin wanted and needed to increase government stability. Interestingly, former U.S. vice president Al Gore (cochair of the U.S.-Russian Gore-Chernomyrdin Commission of the 1990s intended to improve commercialization of Russian technologies by American companies) made comments on September 15, 2004, in St. Petersburg regarding Putin's reaction to the attempt assassination. As Gore recalled, President Bush and his cabinet took similar measures after the September 11, 2001 attacks on New York and Washington. Gore also stated that giving such powers to a president should usually be a provisional measure, not a permanent one, as reported in the *St. Petersburg Times* (2004).

U.S. senator Hillary Clinton, who says that she does not agree with torture in general, made a similar statement recently but assented to legal torture practices if a terrorist in custody is believed to have information on an imminent threat to millions of Americans. Despite Hillary Clinton's apparent opposition to torture, she rightly maintains that the practice is acceptable in some circumstances, although "there has to be some lawful authority for pursuing that." That is, Senator Hillary Clinton seems not actually against torture in all instances, but "in those instances where we have sufficient basis to believe that there is something imminent ... but ...[we must] have a check and balance [system]" (H. Clinton, quoted in *NewYork Daily* News, Oct. 12, 2006) This statement shows an appreciation of the tactics required to obtain necessary information to prevent events that could cause the loss of human lives even if the information is obtained while the prisoner is under duress. If western intellectuals think along those lines in the war on terrorism, they should be able to come up with similar interpretations concerning the logic of tough practices—if any at all—that were occurring after dramatic events in Russia.

Russia's corruption and business crime problems, the Beslan hostage drama, and the post-Yukos climate certainly created a September 11–like situation in Russia that the West should respect and understand. It is essential for observers, readers, and analysts to comprehend the very strong support Putin enjoys throughout Russia. Surprisingly, this has not happened, and the West continues to fail when interpreting and judging the Russian situation.

Epilogue

Misinterpreting Modern Russia, which has emerged from my exploration of the astonishing development of modern Russia, is a detailed study of the country's intense recent history. My aim in this book has been to provoke examination of and reflection on the perspective of everyday Russians about the passage of their country to noncommunist society through the three visions for modernizing the country from Mikhail Gorbachev to Vladimir Putin and his Kremlin administration. In as much as I follow a new coherent interpretative approach, I realize—beyond any doubt—that my analysis has been a long journey of wonder and discovery. Although Russia's current situation can seem disheartening and confusing, Russia is a country we will continue to watch well into the future.

Concerns Regarding Three Recent Murders

Sadly, however, as I was writing the last part of this book, reports of horrific murder came out of Moscow and London in 2006. Russian Deputy Central Bank Chairperson Andrei Kozlov, who was responsible for regulating the banking industry, was shot in Moscow on September 13. He died the following day. Then a very respected journalist, Anna Politkovskaya, was murdered on October 7. Finally, in London, a former post-KGB, FSB colonel, Alexander Litvinenko, was mysteriously poisoned at the Millennium Hotel and died after long suffering at University College London Hospital on November 22. The ample coverage of the latter two assassinations has brought back to the front page the specific issue of alleged erosions of civil liberties in Russia, as well as supposed Kremlin involvement. We observers in the West who focus on Russian affairs have not spent adequate time discussing Andrei Kozlov and his manslaughter case; there has not been enough recognition of his accomplishments, and nobody knows why there is such internationally unbalanced coverage.

Andrei Kozlov was forty-one years old and overseeing the central bank's policy against money laundering, the cancellation of banking licenses, and reform in the financial markets. As I have reported, a modern commercial banking system grew up in the recent past in Russia, and it is still developing in the direction of western standards. Small commercial banks (the so-called pocket banks) and eventually commercial banks pulling together to create political connections became an instrument used to the implement the criminal strategy of the 1990s. In fact, the wild rationale placed selected banks at the center stage of criminal behavior and widespread corruption during the passage from the Soviet era in the 1990s. This strategy operated through the phenomenon of pocket banks. Obviously, this bleak picture was not true of all newly created banks during the 1990s or of the commercial banks operating in Russia these days. However the observable fact of the establishment of hundreds of commercial banks was widespread enough to turn it into a modern experience with roughly half of these institutions performing true banking business, and with only a couple of dozen firmly sticking to western standards of financial stability requirements. In this context, Kozlov was actively fighting banks that still operated in an anomalous fashion.

Anna Politkovskaya, a forty-eight-year-old human rights journalist for the biweekly *Novaya Gazeta*, who wrote on the continuing bloodshed in Chechnya, accused both the Russian Army and Chechnya rebels of criminal behavior and also claimed that misbehavior was occurring at the Defense Ministry in Moscow. In addition, she denounced the continuing government abuse of the mental health system by using psychiatric hospitals as a political instrument, she said, although former president Mikhail Gorbachev had officially abolished such a network. Gorbachev correctly interpreted Politkovskaya's assassination—an attempt to poison her had failed two years earlier—as a crime against the country, while Putin assured the world that state agencies would endeavor to find the criminals behind her death, although the police have not made a definitive arrest in this case.

Alexander Litvinenko, a fifty-year-old British citizen, had been granted political asylum in the United Kingdom and lived in London with his family because he feared that he was a possible target. He had worked for Boris Berezovsky as head of security for ORT, the television channel once owned by the Russian tycoon. Before he died of radiation poisoning, Litvinenko accused the Russian government of his poisoning by direct order of Putin himself. Scotland Yard has launched an investigation and the UK Home Office concluded it had adequate evidence to ask for extradition of the Russian citizen, Andrei Lugovoi, for criminal proceedings. However, Russia's prosecutor general office considered the extradition request impossible to satisfy, alleging that Article 61 of the Russian constitution and Article 6 of the European Convention on Extradition of 1957 ruled out extraditions of Russian citizens to another country. Russian authorities repeated their offer to render assistance to Great Britain in harmony with international treaties in which both countries participate, but London cited inadequate cooperation from Moscow regarding charges against Lugovoi. On July 16, London forced four Russian diplomats to leave Great Britain in response to Moscow's reluctance to hand over Lugovoi. A tit-for-tat response ensued, and the case has resulted in expulsions of diplomats by both countries.

These developments emphasize a troubling turn for the Kremlin. Several concerns emerged from Anna Politkovskaya's and Alexander Litvinenko's murders.

The Putin Kremlin was caught in the storm. The West has debated these two cases in depth, expressing definitive and harsh conclusions about the Kremlin without taking into consideration the complexity of the cases. If there are cover-ups by the Kremlin, the public has to be informed; if the Kremlin or other state agencies have provided half-truths or have not adequately cooperated with investigations, this should be brought to light. Nevertheless, it is equally possible that these killings were purposely done to harm the Kremlin's reputation in the West, as part of a criminal stratagem to discredit the Kremlin. Predictably, these recent murders created a very serious image problem for Russia. No single authority had established a causal link with the Kremlin; one main snag is distinguishing an association from a cause. Nonetheless, speculation has fueled suspicions.

In addition to Andrei Kozlov, Anna Politkovskaya, and Alexander Litvinenko, Paul Klebnikov—the editor-in-chief of the Russian edition of *Forbes*—was killed in July 2004. Although these murder victims were working in different areas, they are all examples of uncomfortable truths: their killings also make it possible to spread awareness and increase everyone's sensibility about current affairs in Russia.

What I can affirm here is that the recent deaths of a central banker, famous journalists, and a former KGB man at the hands of criminals and criminal instigators were shocking murders of honest, hardworking people, and these murders have been denounced by both official and independent voices. They are the latest attacks on state-imposed legality, and Russians are anxious for a fairer and more equitable society that will truly succeed.

Speculations on Changes to the Constitution

In addition, another blow to the Kremlin has occurred around the same time as a ferocious intellectual campaign against Putin's Kremlin began and was reinforced during the last part of 2005 and 2006. There was speculation about having the 1993 Russian Constitution amended to enable Putin to legally run for a successive third term. This possibility forged discussions among Kremlinologists and Russian intellectuals—especially among the Kremlin's enemies. They voiced speculation that Putin was surely limited to two consecutive four-year terms by current rules, but was undertaking to prevent his term running out in March 2008. Adopting a new constitution would have required convening a constitutional assembly, where it was said to have unveiled a new draft to be ready for a vote by June 2007, before parliamentary elections in December of 2007. Western observers have blamed members of Putin's Kremlin staff for cheering on such constitutional evolution and weighing competing proposals for a new constitution, paving Putin's way to the presidential campaign in the spring of 2008. Some of the Putin Kremlin critics have contended that top aides to Putin used changes to the current Russian Constitution in a plot not to allow Putin himself to be reelected, but rather to have Putin's aides themselves stay in power following Putin's victory.

Technically, one option would have included several amendments entailing the establishment of a parliamentary republic headed by a figurehead president, who is elected by the parliament, and an active prime minister. Then, winning the presidential election would have been easy for Putin, given the popularity he enjoys in the country. A second specific option would have consisted of the unification of Russia and Belarus into a new single state, which echoes a pledge made by Yeltsin several years ago to reunite the two sister countries.

The Kremlin's draft constitution may be ready in time for a national referendum to be held to endorse the document in June 2007, Kremlinologists predict. Putin, however, has repeatedly sought to quash speculation that he would seek to stay in power past 2008 by using his patent influence over the parliament to change the country's Constitution. At this writing, none of this has occurred, and in my estimation, none of these predictions will come true.

Several Angles of Conjecture

It is from the above facts that this astonishing story has been transformed into a provocative one. Oddly enough, the problems that Putin's accusers have with him are that he is ex-KGB and that he has carried out certain initiatives against political instability and massive corruption. A mortified populace gave him the benefit of the doubt from the beginning in 2000, and this came from what citizens thought about him. Building a political furor against him based on his past job experience is anachronistic, yet the accusations have continued and are being reinforced over time. Nor do I believe that we should go back in Russian history and disparage the Russian people, who have yearned for a convincing, reliable, mighty president in the Kremlin. In the end, triumphs and failures occurred, and that is what this book is about.

Russians supported a former KGB official who pledged to refocus the politics and countermand the fashion of the moment, and Putin became the flagship of a new political course, even though many international spectators presumed he was unfit to lead the country: I see no reason to use Putin's work experience with the KGB to trigger dogmatic criticism of him.

Nevertheless, "intellectual convictions" are seemingly unshakeable today, with the instigation of a stinging attack on Putin's Kremlin, warning that the aforementioned murders bore the marks of Kremlin's direct involvement. Alternatively, there is no direct link of these murders with top Kremlin people, according to other Kremlin columnist censors. Nonetheless, although these others Kremlin censors do not accuse the Kremlin of having been behind these killings, these censors still blame the Kremlin for having tolerated the murders and following this logic, Putin would be morally and equally responsible for letting the elites tolerate murders used as a political instrument! I might not exclude in theory that the top Kremlin people were knowledgeable about this, but I cannot accuse anybody without a minimum of evidence, whether it be the Kremlin or its elites, especially when there would be and are several people interested in creating discontent with the Kremlin.

Out of these questionable accusations emerges another possible contradiction. Direct accusations against the Kremlin are not proved at all! However, attacking the Kremlin for having tolerated the murders is also a contradiction put forward by western writers because it is still hard to prove, perhaps even harder to prove than the first type of accusation. Moreover, while blaming the Kremlin for being directly responsible for these killings is legally nonsense (as we do not have any evidence at all), the second type of accusation, that of indirect moral responsibility, is morally wrong because we still fail to prove it, while trying to shield ourselves from accusing the Kremlin directly by moving the condemnation under a moral perspective: but this is morally wrong! We have no evidence whatsoever about either direct or indirect involvement! What we need is a fair-minded and truthful verdict from the judiciary system, not more guesswork.

As for the constitutional changes, the West does not favor any particular constitutional system. Notwithstanding, the West once again demonstrates its double standard. In certain western nations, including the United States, outgoing presidents cannot run for a third term in a row. What emerges from other democratic countries' constitutions is mixed evidence. In some places, running for a third or even more terms is not felt to be politically correct, and is thus forbidden; in other places, it is not ruled out at all. At this point, any hypothetical changes to the constitution allowing Putin to run for a third term would not be the catastrophe for the Russian people that western intellectuals and academic circles have believed it would be. Assuredly, such proposed constitutional changes to permit Putin to run again could be "politically incorrect," but not technically untruthful. Even worse for western critics would have been a Putin reelection, a devastating body blow to disbelievers of Russians' ability to choose a president electorally, especially if Russian constituents backed him by a large majority.

The issues above are only two of the latest topics of growing criticism over Putin's Kremlin. We have neglected several other angles, which have been lost in the debate. Powerful lobbies have blinded us to the events of the past decade in Russia and made light of everyday Russians' well-being. The West has glossed over a delicate subject: this story traces its roots to the 1980s and 1990s, and there are plenty of facets to rationalize, as in a mosaic. When the communist regime imploded in 1991, it was good news indeed, but a wild scenario replaced it in which some were able to operate in an illegal and violent jungle. Russia did not enjoy a jump into a bourgeois society, nor into a society mixed with a strange ethics of capitalism and unachieved virtues. An honestly ethical and well-thought-out rationale would have permitted Russia to become an exceptional player in a dynamic and varying world context during the 1990s.

If markets generate trust, as I do stalwartly believe, then the ethical benefits will emerge as long as ethics and virtues come together in a genuine market economy, but it was not Russia's time then. An efficient system, if implemented in Russia in the 1990s, would have been perfect for Russians, but the West intentionally overlooked that moral/ethical achievement in Russian society. No one cared about this in the West! Moreover, although the 1990s bred a Russia of unethical strategies and irrational political choices, the Russia of today is beginning to show signs of becoming a stronger, wiser, and more determined modern nation. It is important to keep this in mind.

The gap between rich and poor that emerged out of an outrageous plan represents a growing threat to long-term stability and that elusive goal we call democracy in the West. Long a favorite subject among certain spheres in economic literature, a growing income gap and its impact on the society were virtually ignored by Kremlinologists, and the results speak for themselves. Our overwhelming evidence shows that the massively growing gap between rich and poor during Yeltsin's pre-Putin presidency saw the largest, fastest-growing, and most destabilizing realities of wealth concentration occurring in the entire 1989–1991 context. The effects of Yeltsin's policy in Russia are without precedent anywhere in East-Central Europe, post-1989. This glaring discrepancy is the primary cause of my concern, and I rank it as the most important policy priority in Russia for the 2000s. Failure to elevate this issue as the primary cause of analysis risks alienating entire segments of the population. This growing disconnect between perceptions and the reality of the actual cause of larger political, economic, and social trauma makes a comprehensive solution all but impossible to achieve.

In the midst of all this, Putin has ascended to the Kremlin and has had to struggle with a post-Yeltsin political agenda of gloomy business infighting, growing corruption, and tense social injustice. During that period all the establishment around Yeltsin in the mid-1990s was supporting entrenched interests, some existing from actual communist days. Putin came into office promising to stabilize the political scenery and to clean up the despoiled system. The political staging is now more stable than it was in the past, but achievements in anticorruption and anti-dishonesty efforts have been only partially successful. True, many of the abuses were evident, and the consequences of the 1990s reforms caused increasing discontent among the Russian people. The West has displayed only an intermittent relationship with Russia throughout Putin's time in office. Also, I cannot agree with western scholars who have always pounced on the Kremlin administration's strategy and the judges' legal methods in general. Paying no attention to the unethical and unlawful 1990s while also paying too much attention to the state's harsh response at the same time is quite specious. Western scholars generally focus on the alleged unlawfulness of what Russia has been doing in the recent past, but not much else; however, we must not overlook the fact that Putin found himself in a very thorny economic situation when he took office.

Although the country was slowly recovering from a default on its debt in August 1998, Putin had to concentrate on that fiasco, the crime wave of the 1990s, and the continuing poverty of most of Russians. We can also attribute the business decadence that evolved during the 1990s to the same rationale pervading the Russian transformation to a free-market economy. The West observed the explosion of the banking sector in Russia as a problem with accountability or meeting financial requirements. Yet the West has neglected to understand it as a clear signal of the corruption bred during the 1990s. The West has also tread very lightly on the corruption phenomenon, providing no useful advice and even letting financing flow out of and into Russia during the 1990s, sometimes enabling such transactions, as with the case of the Bank of New York as discussed in an earlier chapter. The West's incoherent strategy at that time did not result solely from a misinterpretation of Russia's Kremlin and Russia's realities. The West has not gotten the full picture of the Russian transition, and failed to recognize the strong support for the new Kremlin's course among common Russians.

Putin and the Russian government found themselves somewhere between the West's standards regarding the Russian transition to democracy, now that they were *out of crisis mode*, and the actual reality of the Russian economy with yet thornier problems still needing to be confronted. That alone would have justified a resolute reaction from the government. Instead, pessimistic perception was customary among intellectuals who started depicting new Kremlin policies as authoritarian and dishonest per se. Those who accuse Putin and the Kremlin of not making efforts toward improving law enforcement agencies etcetera have to provide clear examples and bring evidence, too. But such evidence is still altogether lacking. But if we want to move from this angle of analysis to how efficient the Kremlin has been in making the system work much better, this is a legitimate question and in fact I talk about Kremlin's failures in several parts of this book.

The West is convinced that Putin—quite unknown to the larger public both in Russia and abroad in 1999—must be a pure dictator due to his KGB association. We in the West simply identified his crossover appeal in Russia with a supposition of that country's history of authoritarianism over centuries of czarism and then communism. Certain observers in the West who consider Putin's successful electoral record as legitimate still explain the tendency of Russians to support him because the country's historical inclination to authoritarianism would have pushed Russians to support an authoritarian man. I regard this as nonsense!

In the face of all the evidence, Kremlinologists want to focus on a purely historical interpretation of Russia today, but I see it differently: Putin and Russians have the same set of values and it was time that someone stepped in to fix the Yeltsin-era imbalances.

Corruption and fraudulent behavior under Yeltsin became extreme, and a few were able to manipulate whatever they could to the benefit of certain "investors," to the detriment of every Russian. Young communist bureaucrats and functionaries invented themselves as market-style entrepreneurs. Meanwhile, bankers made money through the previously created pocket banks or began overseeing the country's politics. In this environment, the responsibility of international economic agencies and *nomenklatura* capitalism greatly jeopardized Russia's economic recovery and the minimum degree of fairness. The Russians end up suffering more, providing a clear and troubling picture of how easy it was for certain oligarchs, during the 1990s, to capture the state and pose threats to the country's stability, while ordinary Russians were crying out for a real alternative so the country could offer something other than a face of corrupted business. We should not have treated this reality as an unavoidable byproduct of transition, but as something graver. As I noted earlier, certain oligarchs are becoming billionaires nowadays due to the stock exchange, real estate, etcetera Although we refer to all of them as oligarchs, only some of them gained immense wealth through the wild 1990s.

Nevertheless, Kremlin failures emerged to such an extent that Putin again made the fight against corruption a central plank in his platform during his State of the Nation address in May 2006, pointing to the damaging impact of corruption on the country's economy, calling it a threat to national security, and pledging to rid Russia of organized corruption. Putin called on the government to fight official corruption strongly, saying that a number of state officials had enriched themselves at the expense of most of Russia's citizens. Because of his speech, the public expected major law enforcement by the Putin administration, but there is no doubt it has not reached the original goals at all.

The Kremlin's failure is evident when one considers that Russia has not achieved much progress in improving governance and fighting corruption all through 1996–2006, according to the sixth and latest *Worldwide Governance Indicators* published by the World Bank Group and authored by Kaufmann, Kraay, and Mastruzzi. This is not good news in view of the good governance and corruption control that are much-needed to enhance Russia's long-term prospects and to normalize the country. While the World Bank says that it would be possible to make significant governance progress in a relatively short period, another regular annual report by Transparency International ranks Russia's corruption level high in its twelfth-year report (2007). Although that perception does not necessarily and adequately reflect the existing level of corruption in a country, Russia turned out at 127th among 163 for 2006, and is in the same group with Central African states and the poorest Latin American countries. As noted in the report, corruption remains one of the insurmountable obstacles in the struggle against poverty, and attempts at improving the country seem thwarted despite a high-profile campaign since Putin's Kremlin struggles to clean up the outrageously corrupted system. For a nation that has always taken a long view of history, time is quickly running out, and the post-Putin Kremlin has to address definitive anticorrupotion policy and the economy's diversification more resolutely.

Saying the Right Things

Of course, the top political elite have enormous responsibility to say the right thing and behave accordingly. Although I can only guess the exact extent of what could have occurred with Russia without Putin's U-turn, had no steps been taken toward stabilization at the end of the 1990s, surely the country would have done much, much worse and inflicted lasting damage to the country overall.

What happens when observers fail to have an evenhanded view of facts? What has to be done to comprehend one of the most profound changes of our time: the transformation of Russia and the end of Putin's presidency? Alternatively, should the West push for moving Russia back to the 1990s-like managed democracy and unethical business infighting? Putin's Kremlin seems to have been cursed in the recent past, and perhaps it has shown a lack of diplomatic tact. Poor economic performance would have increased pressure on Putin's leadership, but he has been quite lucky to achieve advantageous economic performance.

If these topics are among the most talked about these days, still they call for taking a step back from an unbalanced-interpretative approach and reinterpreting Russia by opening up new perspectives on the realities that conditioned the 2000s. I am thinking afresh about reconnecting the different facets of Russian development, and reexamining the Kremlin's triumphs and failures. I draw on interconnecting economics and politics at the center of a greater coherent interpretative picture, dissolving stereotypes and raising awareness of the logic of the 1990s and the need for a normal and stable Russia.

There are many questions to be asked: Should actions have been taken against political instability in Russia? How far and deep would western countries' legislation have gone to understand and contrast domestic instability and social chaos? Sure, the post-Putin Kremlin must work hard on this subject. One very important view is expressed in Alena Ledeneva's *How Russia Really Works* (2006); she refers to practices in Russia in the 1990s to capture the essence of post-Soviet systems. She notes the use of personal networks for breaking or circumventing official rules, for obtaining hard-to-find goods and services, and for bypassing the inefficiencies of communism as it continues to operate today. This is taking place under a new generation of informal practices—some entirely new, *kompromat*; others following traditional forms, *krugovaya poruka*—which are pervading the political nation and the society at large. In this context, I share the same view with Ledeneva that there is need for more formal law in a society where legality is a highly flexible concept.

What is more, what should an oil- and gas-rich country realistically do with this wealth? This has offered the West other angles for criticizing Russia. The oil and gas industry has been a powerful economic engine, responsible for economic activity such as taxes, economic output, and so forth, and industry providing an excellent chance for Russian policy makers to focus on the best route for building the country's economy and improving the quality of Russians' future. Losing or wasting these resources would be a devastating blow to the government and a detriment to Russia's economic vitality and growth.

However, the West has approached Russia's development demagogically, while at the same time taking no notice of what the West has been doing for the past few decades. Should Russia rely on dangerous nuclear weapons to deter both nuclear and conventional attack? I think not. However, if I consider recent views, such as Cimbala and Rainow (2007), Russia is facing an increased presence of the United States in adjacent territories, an assertive NATO, and a China aspiring to overtake Russia as the world's second-ranked military power to establish its hegemony over the Pacific basin. Russia would then confront a new political and military world order that demands new deterrence and defense options. Besides pointing out the active role of the Unites States in the "Russian backyard," and China increasingly influencing its own "backyard," Cimbala and Rainow unfortunately overlook the many economic interactions and interests that link Russia, Western Europe, and China.

Numerous conservative and Kremlin commentators should put less emphasis on Russian military might, or its so-called "hegemony," and focus more on other "ethereal" forms of power—e.g., economic and cultural—that are still ultimately linked with international cooperation. Oil, gas, traditional trade, and other financial common interests are too important for Russia to consider exercising a nuclear attack option. Russia lags behind in leveraging modern technology for military purposes: the idea that Russia would resort to nuclear weapons as its first line of deterrence against either nuclear or conventional attack is totally unfounded.

I assume that post-Putin Russia will take business advancement to a new high, avoiding falling into the trap of failing development, assuring oil and gas supply to neighboring countries, and avoiding western-like bad feelings and an even worse foreign policy. It is time that the West sees itself less and less as the beacon for the world and more open to interdependence and interactions.

I have provided a broad, though selective, perspective concerning the late 1980s and 1990s as groundwork for understanding the present situation and Russia's development, establishing the basis and actual content of important questions that the West apparently has never tried to ask, and put forward a specific rationale for preparing readers and observers to reach judicious and realistic interpretations regarding Russia. We should not heed a biased rendering of Russian realities. Russia was not on the way to becoming a *normal country* by western standards in the 1990s. Russia was instead a disorderly and unstable capitalist business country—distorted by greed and related negative politics. Nowadays, numerous economic indicators are confirming that Russia is on the right economic track, with a growing middle class and rich private Russians who add momentum to this development, although the government has rallied around a large part of Russian society that still lacks overall well-being. The Russian government must still think seriously about improving conditions for a large share of the society.

Russia will reinforce international networks for oil and natural gas through upstream and downstream activities by moving toward a transnational culture of entrepreneurial skills and effective competition and a leadership that is more attentive to global issues. The export of oil and gas represents a sizeable percentage of all Russian exports, and through either partial state ownership of these commodities or high taxes on exports, Russia is behaving as a powerful force in economic and political interactions with European and Asian markets. Growing exports and taxation helped the state budget transition into a surplus scenario and set up a budget stabilization fund that started accumulating money in 2004, officially insulating the economy against fluctuations in the price of oil and reviving real economic growth in Russia overall. The oil and gas industry, coupled with rising international demand, is certainly making Russia a powerful actor in the international arena.

I realize that the process of modernization is necessary and will require the strengthening of regional and international strategic alliances and the opening of domestic markets to foreign capital. I would also make the case for a social contract between the state, the class of billionaires, millionaires, and small entrepreneurs who are increasing in number and overall wealth—and are a vital component of Russian society—in an effort to create a fair and effective society, with wisdom in favor of long-term Russian growth and advancement.

The West should try to understand the basic rationale that guided Russia in its positive direction despite certain disappointments and failures. The West needs to acknowledge that Yeltsin was supported by predatory elites. The definitive goal for Russia now is to have a functioning bureaucratic apparatus and get business groups to work for the betterment of the country. In such situation, any well-meaning leadership would have been perceived as lacking something. Following the anomalies and deformations that western-inspired reforms produced in Russia, it was clear that a break with the 1990s era was necessary. In such a context, Russian political institutions had to become more effective, while business groups had to become more ethically and legally oriented. The country's generally poor legal record in the 1990s has led to chaos and centrifugal forces, which I have described in the book. With a different goal in mind, the attempt to uphold the country's unity, as acknowledged by Aleksandr Solzhenitsyn, was a strong, shrewd base upon which to build comprehensive support for making central Russian authority highly legitimate and effective in all or most areas. In addition, the recent signing of the Act of Canonical Communion on the feast of the Ascension of the Lord, which took place at the Cathedral of Christ the Savior in Moscow on May 17, 2007, is important to consider in this logic, as it symbolizes the return of the Russian Orthodox Church Outside of Russia into the fold of the Moscow Patriarchate—the schism occurred in 1927—and into the whole of the Orthodox world. Putin has described the signing as a truly historic national event. From a technical point of view, parishioners of the Russian Orthodox Church abroad, being part of the Mother Church, have the right to take communion at all of the world's

Orthodox churches from now on, and its clergy have the right to serve jointly with the hierarchs and clergy of all fifteen local Orthodox Churches. Moreover, the Moscow Patriarchate recognizes the Russian Orthodox Church Outside of Russia as a part of the local Russian Orthodox Church according to the Act of Canonical Communion, still independent in pastoral, educational, administrative, managerial, property civil matters, and remaining in canonical unity with the Fullness of the Russian Orthodox Church. Apart from the signing and the aforementioned consequences of the act, this event represents an additional step toward a strategy of restoring the unity of the country.

Current students of Russian history must consider the larger realities surrounding this issue. It would be foolish to believe that it is unnecessary to establish tough and structured institutions in a geographically large country like Russia. Any reasonable thinker would positively welcome a state that is strong enough to assure social stability and the rule of law.

I do not hesitate to declare that the future of Russia will lead to sensible interactions with the West. We should not be concerned about whether and how Russia will alter the regional *status quo* and exert a dynamic interdependent influence over international affairs. It is necessary to establish a stable, long-term foundation with the post-Putin Kremlin to maximize cooperation and mutual understanding. In sum, we cannot pull the wool over our eyes about this great and noble country. Putin will conclude his second term at the present, and I see a much brighter future for Russia and the Russians: they deserve serious reassessments and realistic appraisals by the West.

The End of an Astonishing Story or a New Beginning?

I hope you have enjoyed the journey through Putin's *third vision* experiment. This astonishing story both began and is ending in New York. It is August 3, 2007, and I am trying to rush and have the manuscript completed soon. This morning, international media in the United States and abroad are paying a lot of attention to Russia's deliberate decision to have one of its submarines plant a titanium flag slightly less than fourteen thousand feet deep, in the ocean waters of the North Pole. This happened yesterday. Some commentators argue that Moscow is attempting to throw a weight around the Lomonosov dorsal because of alleged energy competition involving the Arctic area's territorial disputes; supposedly, Russia would like to ascertain its rights on that area's potential reserves of crude oil, natural gas, and diamonds. Reserves would be up to ten trillion tons of oil; if this figure were accurate, they would represent a sizable percentage of world's oil reserves today. Whatever the usual critics say regarding the final months of Putin's Kremlin, I cannot fail to recall that international analysts are revealing that oil and gas reserves are close to peak and on the road to becoming too high-priced to upstream or conveniently extract, while oil and gas field equipment and services should led to greater investment in Russia to guarantee Russia's ability to expand its capacity to produce and to export energy products. They urge all of us to prepare for a post-oil society, which would certainly be a significant turn of events for everyone. In addition, there are doubts about the technical feasibility of extracting oil and gas from that Arctic region. Despite these two questions about the realistic availability of resources and their practicable exploitation, observers nevertheless seek to prompt the world to firmly reject the Kremlin's underwater land grab, believing it to be outrageous.

Lack of analysis pertaining to the portrayal of unstable Russia, which could represent a big blow to the need for stability in the West, was evident. Central pillars in the West have not been objective, rational voices informing the public opinion and the international community. However, nobody recalls the double standard we in the West have applied during the 1990s. Nobody is intellectually honest enough to recognize, for instance, that we would have gone into raptures over such a great technical, scientific success if western scientists had taken this expedition! At present, Russians are achieving this success and are met with accusations of imperialism and the like. The United States, Russia, Norway, Canada, and Denmark have filed claims on the area, which means we have increased the prospects for territorial disputes. However, a unilateral annexation of this region is impossible, for the simple reason that all countries must strictly abide by the United Nations convention regarding this region.

Biased talks and discussions will continue as well. During the following months, the parliamentary elections to the Russian state Duma take place on December 2, 2007, and these elections are taking place under new rules that have eliminated single-member electorates and raised the threshold for party representation from 5 percent to 7 percent of the vote. Those elections will be followed in March 2008 by the Russian presidential elections. We know that President Vladimir Putin will be ineligible, however. Over the past years, Russian oil production rose to an amazingly degree, as did as world oil prices. This type of growth has made the Russian economy dependent on oil and natural gas exports and vulnerable to fluctuations in world prices as well to the volume of the export of these commodities. True, the Russian government has moved to take control of the country's energy supplies and set up a stabilization fund to invest the proceeds of natural resources of the kind already functioning in the Middle East's and Asian countries. However, the country's reputation as a reliable energy supplier has not been scratched, as several announced agreements with Eastern and Western European governments and companies to build pipelines feeding Russian resources into a growing network of pipelines to Europe prove. Russia's investment climate has been improved, still more on a definitive property rights protection and a far more efficient government bureaucracy should become high in the future government's agenda. Hypocrisy will sculpt our discussions in the West.

Bibliography

Abdullaev, Nabi and Simon Saradzhyan. 2006. "Ustinov Fired as Kremlin Aides Look to 2008." *Moscow Times*. 5 June 2006. <http://pda.moscowtimes.ru/article.php?aid=168437> (6 June 2006).

Allison, Graham and Robert Blackwill. 1991. "America's Stake in the Soviet Future." *Foreign Affairs* 70 (3): 77–97.

Allison, Graham and Grigory Yavlinsky. 1991. *Window of Opportunity: The Grand Bargain for Democracy in the Soviet Union*. New York: Pantheon Books.

Ashwin, Sarah. 1999. *Russian Workers: The Anatomy of Patience*. Manchester, UK: Manchester University Press.

Åslund, Anders. 1990. "How Small Is Soviet National Income?" In *The Impoverished Superpower: Perestroika and the Soviet Military Burden*. Edited by Henry S. Rowen and Charles Wolf, Jr. San Francisco, CA: Institute for Contemporary Studies, ICS Press.

Åslund, Anders. 1995. *How Russia Became a Market Economy*. Washington, DC: The Brookings Institution.

—. 2002. *Building Capitalism: The Transformation of the Former Soviet Bloc*. Cambridge, UK: Cambridge University Press.

Åslund, Anders, Peter Boone, and Simon Johnson. 1996. "How to Stabilize: Lessons from Post-Communist Countries." *Brookings Papers on Economic Activity* 1: 217–313.

BBC News Online. 2006. "Cheney Rebuke Angers Russian Press." BBC News Online. <http://news.bbc.co.uk/2/hi/europe/4979932.stm> (6 May 2006)

BP. 2007. *BP Statistical Review of World Energy June 2007*. London, UK: BP.

Baker, Peter and Susan Glasser. 2005. *Kremlin Rising: Vladimir Putin's Russia and the End of Revolution*. New York: Scribner.

Baker, Raymond W. 2005. *Capitalism's Achilles Heel: Dirty Money and How to Renew the Free-Market System*. Hoboken, NJ: John Wiley & Sons.

Barnes, Andrew. 2006. *Owning Russia: The Struggle over Factories, Farms, and Power*. Ithaca, NY: Cornell University Press.

Barsky, Robert B. and Lutz Kilian. 2002. "Oil and the Macroeconomy since the 1970s." *Journal of Economic Perspectives* 18 (4): 115–134.

Batra, Ravi. 2005. *Greenspan's Fraud: How Two Decades of His Policies Have Undermined the Global Economy*. New York: Palgrave MacMillan.

Belkin, Victor. 1989. Kontseptsiia rynka i pozitsiia banka. *Izvestiia*. 30 January 1989.

Black, William K. 2005. *"The Best Way to Rob a Bank" Is to Own One: How Corporate Executives and Politicians Looted the S&L Industry*. Austin, TX: University of Texas Press.

Blanchard, Olivier. 1997. *The Economics of Post-Communist Transition*. Oxford, UK: Clarendon Press.

Blas, Javier. 2007. "World Will Face Oil Crunch" "in Five Years." *Financial Times*. 9 July 2007.

Bombardieri, Marcella. 2005. "Harvard, Teacher, and Lawyer to Pay US $30m." *Boston Globe*. 4 August 2005.

Boone, Peter and Jacob Hørder. 1998. "Inflation: Causes, Consequences, and Cures." *In Emerging from Communism: Lessons from Russia, China, and Eastern Europe*. Edited by Peter Boone, Stanislav Gomulka, and Richard Layard. Cambridge, MA: MIT Press.

Boyko, Maxim, Andrei Schleifer, and Robert Vishny. 1995. *Privatizing Russia*. Cambridge: MIT Press.

Brady, Rose. 2000. *Kapitalizm: Russia's Struggle to Free Its Economy*. New Haven, CT: Yale University Press.

Braguinsky, Serguey and Grigory Yavlinsky. 2000. *Incentives and Institutions: The Transition to a Market Economy in Russia.* Princeton, NJ: Princeton University Press.

Braithwaite, Rodric. 2002. *Across the Moscow River: The World Turned Upside Down.* New Haven, CT: Yale University Press.

Breslauer, George W. 2002. *Gorbachev and Yeltsin as Leaders.* Cambridge, UK: Cambridge University Press.

Breton, Paul, Daniel Gros, and Guy Vandille. 1997. "Output Decline and Recovery in the Transition Economies: Causes and Social Consequences." *Economics of Transition* 5 (1): 113–130.

Brown, Archie. 1996. *The Gorbachev Factor.* Oxford, UK: Oxford University Press.

Brzezinski, Zbigniew. 2004. "Moscow's Mussolini (How Putin Is Creating a Fascist State)." *Wall Street Journal.* 20 September 2004.

Central Bank of the Russian Federation. <http://www.cbr.ru/eng>.

Chang, Gordon G. 2001. *The Coming Collapse of China.* New York: Random House.

Chomsky, Noam and Gilbert Achcar (edited with a preface by Stephen R. Shalom). 2007. *Perilous Power: The Middle East & U.S. Foreign Policy: Dialogues on Terror, Democracy, War, and Justice.* Boulder, CO: Paradigm Publishers.

Cimbala, Stephen J. and Rainow, Peter Jacob. 2007. *Russia and Postmodern Deterrence: Military Power and its Challenges for Security.* Washington, DC: Potomac Books.

Clarke, Duncan. 2007. *The Battle for Barrels: Peak Oil Myths & World Oil Futures.* London, UK: Profile Books.

Clinton, Hillary. 2006. <http://blogs.nydailynews.com/dailypolitics/archives/2006/10/clinton_on_tort.php> (12 October 2006).

Colton, Timothy J. and Stephen Holmes, eds. 2006. *The State after Communism: Governance in the New Russia.* Lanham, MD: Rowman & Littlefield Publishers.

Conason, Joe. 2007. *It Can Happen Here: Authoritarian Peril in the Age of Bush.* New York: Thomas Dunne Books/St. Martin's Press.

Deffeyes, Kenneth S. 2005. *Beyond Oil: The View from Hubbert's Peak.* New York: Hill and Wang.

Desai, Padma. 2006. *Conversations on Russia: Reform from Yeltsin to Putin.* New York: Oxford University Press.

Donnelly, Thomas. 2005. *The Military We Need: The Defence Requirements of the Bush Doctrine.* Washington, DC AEI Press, c2005.

2001. *The Elusive Quest for Growth: Economists' Adventures and Misadventures in the Tropics.* Cambridge, MA: MIT Press.

—. 2003. "Can Foreign Aid Buy Growth?" *Journal of Economic Perspective* 17 (1): 23–48.

—. 2006. *The White Man's Burden: Why the West's Efforts to Aid the Rest Have Done So Much Ill and So Little Good.* New York: Penguin Press.

Edwards, John, Jack Kemp, and Stephen Sestanovich (eds.). 2006. *Russia's Wrong Direction: What the United States Can and Should Do.* Independent Task Force No. 57. New York: Council on Foreign Relations.

Ellman, Michael. 1994. "The Increase in Death and Disease under Katastroika." *Cambridge Journal of Economics* 18 (4): 329–355.

Ellman, Michael and Vladimir Kontorovich. 1992. "Overview." In *The Disintegration of the Soviet Economic System.* Edited by Michael Ellman and Vladimir Kontorovich. London: Routledge.

Etzioni, Amitai. 2007. *Security First: For a Muscular, Moral Foreign Policy.* New Haven, CT: Yale University Press.

The European Bank for Reconstruction and Development (EBRD). 1998. *Transition Report 1998.* London: EBRD.

Fish, Steven M. 2005. *Democracy Derailed in Russia: The Failure of Open Politics.* New York: Cambridge University Press.

Forbes. 2007. *Special Report: The World's Billionaires*. <http://www.forbes.com/lists/2007/10/07billionaires_The-Worlds-Billionaires_Rank.html> (10 March 2007).

Freeland, Chrystia. 2000. *Sale of the Century: Russia's Wild Ride from Communism to Capitalism*. New York: Crown Business.

Gaddy, Clifford G. and Barry W. Ickes. 2002. *Russia's Virtual Economy*. Washington, DC: Brookings Institution.

Gaidar, Yegor. 1997. "The IMF and Russia." *American Economic Review (Papers and Proceedings)* 87 (2): 13–22.

Garcelon, Marc. 2005. *Revolutionary Passage: From Soviet to Post-Soviet Russia, 1985–2000*. Philadelphia, PA: Temple University Press.

Gavrilenkov, Evgeny and Koen, Vincent. 1994. "How Large Was the Output Collapse in Russia? Alternative Estimates and Welfare Implications." International Monetary Fund Working Paper. No. 94/154. <http://ssrn.com/abstract=883913>.

Goldman, Marshall I. 2003. *The Piratization of Russia: Russian Reform Goes Awry*. London: Routledge Press.

—. 2004. "*Putin and the Oligarchs*". *Foriegn Affairs* 83 (6): 33–44.

—. 2004. *Out of Gas: The End of the Age of Oil*. New York: W. W. Norton & Company.

Gorbachev, Mikhail. 1985. O sozyve ocherednogo XXVII sjezda KPSS i zadachakh s ego podgotovkoi i provedeniem. *Pravda*. 24 April 1985.

—. 1987a. *Perestroika: New Thinking for Our Country and the World*. New York: Harper & Row.

—. 1987b. *Socialism, Peace and Democracy: Writings, Speeches and Reports*. London: Zwan Publications.

—. 1995. *Mikhail Gorbachev: Memoirs*. London: Bantam Books.

—. 2006. Rosneft Will Reinforce Russian Reforms. *Financial Times*. 12 July 2006.

Goskomstat. 1987 onward, various issues. *Narodnoe khoziaistvo SSSR*. Moscow: Statistika i finansy.

Gray, John. 2007. *Black Mass: Apocalyptic Religion and the Death of Utopia*. New York: Farrar, Straus and Giroux.

Green, Mark. 2002. *Selling Out: How Big Corporate Money Buy Elections, Rams through Legislation, and Betray Our Democracy*. New York: ReganBooks.

Grey, Stephen. 2007. *Ghost Plane: The True Story of the CIA Torture Program*. New York: St. Martin's Press.

Gros, Daniel and Alfred Steinherr. 1995. *Winds of Change: Economic Transition in Central and Eastern Europe*. London: Longman.

Guriev, Sergei and Barry W. Ickes. 2000. "Barter in Russia." In *The Vanishing Rouble: Barter Networks and Non-Monetary Transactions in Post-Soviet Societies*. Edited by Paul Seabright. Cambridge, UK: Cambridge University Press.

Guriev, Sergei and Andrei Rachinsky. 2005. "The Role of Oligarchs in Russian Capitalism." *Journal of Economic Perspectives* 19 (1): 131–150.

Handelman, Stephen. 1994. *Comrade Criminal: The Theft of the Second Russian Revolution*. London, UK: Michael Joseph.

Hanson, Philip. 1992. *From Stagnation to Catastroika: Commentaries on the Soviet Economy, 1983–1991*. New York: Praeger.

—. 1998. "Foreign Advice." In *The Destruction of the Soviet Economic System: An Insiders' History*. Edited by Michael Ellman and Vladimir Kontorovich. Armonk, NY: M.E. Sharpe.

—. 2007. "The Russian Economic Puzzle: Going Forwards, Backwards or Sideways?" *International Affairs* 83(5): 869–889.

Hedlund, Stefan. 2005. *Russian Path Dependence*. London, UK: Routledge.

Hellman, Joel. 1998. "Winners Take All: The Politics of Partial Reforms in Postcommunist Transition." *World Politics* 50 (2): 203–234.

Herbst, Alan M. and George W. Hopley. 2007. *Nuclear Energy Now: Why the Time Has Come for the World's Most Misunderstood Energy Source*. Hoboken, NJ: John Wiley & Sons.

Hessler, Julie. 2001. "Postwar Normalization and its Limits in the USSR: The Case of Trade." *Europe-Asia Studies* 53 (3): 445–471.

Hewett, Edward A. 1988. *Reforming the Soviet Economy: Equality versus Efficiency*. Washington, DC: The Brookings Institution.

Hill, Christopher J. 2003. "Russian Defense Spending." In *Russia's Uncertain Economic Future*. Edited by John P. Hardt for the Joint Economic Committee, Congress of the United States. Armonk, NY: M.E. Sharpe.

Hoffman, David E. 2002. *The Oligarchs: Wealth and Power in the New Russia*. New York: Public Affairs.

Holmes, Leslie. 1997. *Post-Communism: An Introduction*. Durham, NC: Duke University Press.

Horvath, Robert. 2005. *Soviet Dissident and Russia's Transition to Democracy*. New York: Routledge-Curzon.

Hough, Jerry F. 2001. *The Logic of Economic Reform in Russia*. Washington, DC: Brookings Institute Press.

Hubbert, M. King. 1956. Nuclear Energy and the Fossil Fuels. *Spring Meeting of the Southern District of the American Petroleum Institute, March 7–9*. San Antonio, Texas: American Petroleum Institute.

—. King. 1962. *Energy Resources: A Report to the Committee on Natural Resources of the National Academy of Sciences, National Research Council*. Washington, DC: National Academy of Sciences–National Research Council.

Illarionov, Andrei. Quoted in http://www.weforum.org/pdf/Russia_Meeting_2001/Russia_Report_2001.pdf

—. 2004. "Kyoto's Smoke Screen Imperils Us All." *Financial Times*. 15 November 2004.

Information Science for Democracy Russian Foundation (INDEM 2006) This is INDEM's web site: <http://www.indem.ru/en/index.shtml>. The preliminary report, published in 2005, is found at <http://www.indem.ru/en/publicat/2005diag_engV.htm>.

International Energy Agency. 2006. *World Energy Outlook 2006*. Paris: International Energy Agency.

International Monetary Fund. <http://www.imf.org>.

—. 2007. *World Economic Outlook: Spillovers and Cycles in the Global Economy*. Washington, DC: International Monetary Fund.

Intriligator, Michael D., Serguey Braguinski, and Vitaly Shuydko. 2001. "Human Capital." In *The New Russia: Transition Gone Awry*. Edited by Lawrence R. Klein and Marshall Pomer. Stanford, CA: Stanford University Press.

Jack, Andrew. 2004. *Inside Putin's Russia*. London: Granta.

Johnson's Russia List. 2006. <http://www.cdi.org/russia/johnson/9079-26.cfm> Moscow. (4 March 2006).

Kagan, Robert. 2006. *Dangerous Nation*. New York: Knopf.

Kagarlitsky, Boris. 2002. *Russia under Yeltsin and Putin: Neo-Liberal Autocracy*. London: Pluto Press.

Kaiser, Robert G. 1992. *Why Gorbachev Happened: His Triumphs, His Failure, and His Fall*. New York: Simon & Schuster.

Kapuscinski, Ryszard. 1994. *Imperium*. New York: Knopf.

Karklins, Rasma. 2005. *The System Made Me Do It: Corruption in Post-Communist Societies*. Armonk, NY: M.E. Sharpe.

Kathryn W. and Shelby Cullom Davis Center for Russian and Eurasian Studies. Various years. *Economic Newsletter*. Cambridge, MA: Harvard University.

Kaufmann, Daniel, Aart Kraay, and Massimo Mastruzzi. 2007. *Governance Matters, 2007: Worldwide Governance Indicators 1996–2006*. Washington, DC: World Bank.

Khanin, Grigorii. 1988. "Ekonomicheskii rost: al'ternativnaia otsenka." *Kommunist* 17: 83–90.

—. 1992. "Economic Growth in the 1980s." In *The Disintegration of the Soviet Economic System*. Edited by Michael Ellman and Vladimir Kontorovich. London: Routledge Press.

Klebnikov, Paul. 2000. *Godfather of the Kremlin: Boris Berezovsky and the Looting of Russia*. New York: Harcourt.

Kolodko, Grzegorz W. 2000. *Post-Communist Transition: The Thorny Road*. Rochester, NY: University of Rochester Press.

Kontorovich, Vladimir. 1992. "Technological Progress and Research and Development." In *The Disintegration of the Soviet Economic System*. Edited by Michael Ellman and Vladimir Kontorovich. London: Routledge Press.

Korchagina, Valeria. 2002. "Study: Bribery a $36 Bln Business." *Moscow Times*, 22 May 2002. <http://www.themoscowtimes.com/stories/2002/05/22/001.html> (28 May 2002).

Kornai, János. 1990. *The Road to a Free Economy: Shifting from a Socialist System: The Example of Hungary*. New York: W. W. Norton.

—. 2000. "Ten Years after 'The Road to a Free Economy.' The Author's Self-Evaluation." *World Bank Annual Conference on Development Economics*. Washington, DC: World Bank.

Kotkin, Stephen. 2001. *Armageddon Averted: The Soviet Collapse, 1970–2000*. Oxford, UK: Oxford University Press.

Kryshtanovskaya, Olga. 1994. "Rich and Poor in Post-Communist Russia." *Journal of Communist Studies and Transition Politics* 10 (1): 3–24.

—. 1998. "Smert' oligarkhii: oligarkhiia soderzhala gosudarstvo v litse ego kliuchevykh chinovnikov." *Argumenty i fakty, November 11*.

—. 2003.<http://www.hro.org/editions/control/11_03/19-1_11_03.php> (25 September 2006).

Kuhrt, Natasha. 2006. *Russian Policy toward China and Japan: The Yeltsin and Putin Periods*. London: Routledge-Curzon.

Kunstler, James Howard. 2005. *The Long Emergency: Surviving the Converging Catastrophes of the Twenty-First Century*. New York: Atlantic Monthly Press.

Kupchinsky, Roman. 2006. "Russia: Anticorruption Drive Touches The 'Untouchable' FSB." *Radio Liberty*. 2 June 2006. Radio Free Europe. <http://www.rferl.org/featuresarticle/2006/06/96d07d35-7728-41c8-a327-d7bb8a12e623.html> (5 June 2006).

Lakoff, George. 2006. *Whose Freedom?: The Battle Over America's Most Important Idea*. New York: Farrar, Straus and Giroux.

Layard, Richard and John Parker. 1996. *The Coming Russian Boom: A Guide to New Markets and Politics*. New York: Free Press.

Ledeneva, Alena V. 2006. *How Russia Really Works: The Informal Practices that Shaped Post-Soviet Politics and Business*. Ithaca, NY: Cornell University Press.

Lewin, Moshe. 2005. *The Soviet Century*. Edited by Gregory Elliott. London: Verso.

Lieven, Anatol and John Hulsman. 2006. *Ethical Realism: A Vision for America's Role in the World*. New York: Pantheon Books.

Lipton, David and Jeffrey D. Sachs. 1992. "Prospects for Russia's Economic Reforms." *Brookings Papers on Economic Activity* 2: 213–265.

Lynch, Michael C. 2003. "The New Pessimism about Petroleum Resources: Debunking the Hubbert Model (and Hubbert Modelers)." <http://www.energyseer.com> (15 October 2004).

Malia, Martin E. 1994. *The Soviet Tragedy: A History of Socialism in Russia, 1917–1991*. New York: Free Press.

—. 1999. *Russia under Western Eyes: From the Bronze Horseman to the Lenin Mausoleum*. Cambridge, MA: Belnap Press of Harvard University Press.

Maugeri, Leonardo. 2006. *The Age of Oil: The Mythology, History, and the Future of the World's Most Controversial Resource*. Westport, CT: Praeger Publishers.

McCarthy, Daniel J., Sheila M. Puffer, and Stanislav V. Shekshnia, eds. 2004. *Corporate Governance in Russia*. Cheltenham, UK: Edward Elgar Publishing.

McDaniel, Tim. 1996. *The Agony of the Russian Idea*. Princeton, NJ: Princeton University Press.

McNulty, Sheila. 2006. "Energy Leaders Seek to Diversify Resources." *Financial Times*. 9 February 2006.

Mercer Human Resource Consulting. 2006. *Worldwide Cost of Living Survey 2006–City Rankings*. <http://www.mercerhr.com/pressrelease/details.jhtml/dynamic/idContent/1142150;jsessionid=QN31H2M4FPL4SCTGOUGCHPQKMZ0QUJLW> (26 June 2006).

Merrill Lynch and Capgemini. 2007. *2007 Annual World Wealth Report*. <http://www.merrill-lynch.com/index.asp?id=7695_7696_8149_74412_79272_79918> (27 June 2007).

MosNews.com. 2004. "Putin's Advisor Calls Yuganskneftegaz Sale 'Fraud of the Year.'" 28 December 2004. <http://www.mosnews.com/money/2004/12/28/illarionov.shtml> (30 December 2004).

—. 2005. "Khodorkovsky Suggests 12-Year Plan to Revive Russia." 11 November 2005. <http://www.mosnews.com/news/2005/11/11/mbkhfollowup.shtml> (15 November 2005).

—. 2006. "Notorious Oligarch Berezovsky Reveals Plans for Coup in Russia." 26 January 2006. <http://www.mosnews.com/news/2006/01/26/berezrevolution.shtml> (30 January 2006).

Mueller, John. 2006. *Overblown: How Politicians and the Terrorism Industry Inflate National Security Threats, and Why We Believe Them*. New York: Free Press.

Murphy, Kim. 2006. "Political Dissenters Are Deemed 'Crazy' Again." *Los Angeles Times*. 31 May 2006. <http://pda.moscowtimes.ru/article.php?aid=168337> (1 June 2006).

Myers, Steven Lee. 2007. "The Cynicism Has Been a Hallmark of Mr. Putin's Presidency." *New York Times*. 27 May 2007.

Naim, Moises. 2005. "Tunnel Vision on Corruption." *Washington Post*. 20 February 2005.

National Petroleum Council. 2007. *Facing the Hard Truths about Energy*. Washington, DC <http://www.npc.org/> (18 July 2007).

Nye, Joseph S. 2004. *Soft Power: The Means to Success in World Politics*. New York: Public Affairs.

OECD. 2003. *The PISA 2003 Assessment Framework – Mathematics, Reading, Science and Problem Solving Knowledge and Skills*. Paris: Organisation for Economic Cooperation and Development.

Odell, Peter R. 1983. *Oil and World Power*. Harmondsworth, UK: Penguin Books.

Odom, William E. 1998. *The Collapse of the Soviet Military*. New Haven, CT: Yale University Press.

Oppenheimer, Peter and Brigitte Granville, eds. 2001. *Russia's Post-Communist Economy*. Oxford, UK: Oxford University Press.

Oppenheimer, Peter and Sergiy Maslichenko. 2006. "Energy and the Economy: An Introduction." In *Russia's Oil and Natural Gas: Bonanza or Curse?* Edited by Michael Ellman. London, UK: Anthem Press.

Osborn, Andrew (2007). "Russia Launches Crackdown on Corruption." *The Independent*. March 1, 2007. <http://news.independent.co.uk/europe/article2314214.ece>.

Paglen, Trevor and A C Thompson. 2006. *Torture Taxi: On the Trail of the CIA's Rendition Flights*. Hoboken, NJ: Melville House.

Parfitt, Tom (2006). "Corrupt Bureaucrats Cost Russia £125bn A Year, Prosecutor Says." *The Guardian*. 8 November 2006 <http://www.guardian.co.uk/russia/article/0,1941743,00.html>

Pasternak, Boris L. 1958. *Doctor Zhivago*. New York: Pantheon.

Peet, Richard. 2003. *Unholy Trinity: The IMF, World Bank and WTO*. London: Zed Books.

Pipes, Richard. 2005. *Russian Conservatism and Its Critics: A Study in Political Culture*. New Haven, CT: Yale University Press.

Politkovskaya, Anna. 2005. *Putin's Russia: Life in a Failing Democracy*. New York: Metropolitan Books.

Popov, Vladimir. 2001. "Russia: Inconsistent Shock Therapy with Weakening Institutions." In *Transition and Institutions: The Experience of Gradual and Late Reformers*. Edited by Giovanni Andrea Cornia and Vladimir Popov. Oxford, UK: Oxford University Press.

Putin, Vladimir. 2006. "Europe Has Nothing to Fear from Russia's Aspirations." *Financial Times*. 22 November 2006.

Reddaway, Peter and Dmitri Glinski. 2001. *Tragedy of Russia's Reforms: Market Bolshevism against Democracy*. Washington, DC: United States Institute for Peace Press.

Roberts, Paul. 2004. *The End of Oil: On the Edge of a Perilous New World*. Boston, MA: Houghton Mifflin.

Rodriguez, Alex. 2005. "Anti-Putin Youth Movement Draws Wary Kremlin's Notice." *Chicago Tribune*, 21 March 2005.

Rose, Richard and Neil Munro. 2002. *Elections without Order: Russia's Challenge to Vladimir Putin*. Cambridge, UK: Cambridge University Press.

Rosefielde, Steven. 2005. *Russia in the 21st Century: The Prodigal Superpower*. Cambridge, UK: Cambridge University Press.

Russian Federal State Statistics Service. <http://www.gks.ru/wps/portal/english>.

Russia Journal Daily. 2005a. "Polls Show Russians Mostly Dislike Perestroika." *Russia Journal Daily*. 11 March 2005.
—. 2005b. "Confidence in Putin Still High." *Russia Journal Daily*. 3 March 2005.
Sachs, Jeffrey D. 2003. "Institutions Don't Rule: Direct Effects of Geography on Per Capita Income." NBER Working Papers, No. 9490. Cambridge, MA: National Bureau of Economic Research.
—. 2005. *The End of Poverty: How We Can Make It Happen in Our Lifetime*. London: Penguin Books.
Sachs, Jeffrey D. and Wing T. Woo. 1994. "Structural Factors in the Economic Reforms of China, Eastern Europe, and the Former Soviet Union." *Economic Policy: A European Forum* 9 (18): 101–145.
St. Petersburg Times. 2004. "Gore Sees Sense in Boosting Power." 21 September 2004. <http://www.sptimes.ru/index.php?action_id=2&story_id=1621> (25 September 2004).
Sakwa, Richard. 2002. *Russian Politics and Society*, 3rd edition. New York: Routledge.
Satter, David. 2003. *Darkness at Dawn: The Rise of the Russian Criminal State*. New Haven, CT: Yale University Press.
Sen, Amartya. 1999. *Development as Freedom*. Oxford, UK: Oxford University Press.
Sergi, Bruno S. 2003. *Economic Dynamics in Transitional Economies: The Four-P Governments, the EU Enlargement, and the Bruxelles Consensus*. New York: International Business Press.
—. 2004. *Communist Economics in Russia*. Budapest: Akademiai Kiado.
—. 2006. "Economic Agents, Ethics and International Economic Organisations." *Managing Global Transitions* 4 (1): 63–78.
—. 2007. "Central and Peripheral Regions in the Wider Europe. Could Tax Competition Attract Foreign Direct Investment Forever?" *Journal of Transnational Management* 12 (2): 3–21.
Shapiro, Judith. 1995. "The Russian Mortality Crisis and Its Causes." In *Russian Economic Reform at Risk*. Edited by Anders Åslund. London: Pinter.
Shevtsova, Lilia F. 2005. *Putin's Russia* (translated by Antonina W. Bouis, rev. and expanded edition). Washington, DC: Carnegie Endowment for International Peace.
Shirk, Susan L. 2007. *China: Fragile Superpower*. New York: Oxford University Press.
Shleifer, Andrei and Robert Vishny. 1998. *The Grabbing Hand: Government Pathologies and their Cures*. Cambridge, MA: Harvard University Press.
Shleifer, Andrei and Daniel Treisman. 2000. *Without a Map: Political Tactics and Economic Reform in Russia*. Cambridge, MA: MIT Press.
—. 2005. "A Normal Country: Russia After Communism." *Journal of Economic Perspectives* 19 (1): 151–174.
Shvetsova, Olga. 2002. "Institutions and Coalition Building in Post-Communist Transition." In *The Architecture of Democracy: Constitutional Design, Conflict, Management, and Democracy*. Edited Andrew Reynolds. Oxford, UK: Oxford University Press.
Silverman, Bertram and Murray Yanowitch. 2000. *New Rich, New Poor, New Russia: Winners and Losers on the Russian Road to Capitalism, 2nd edition*. Armonk, NY: M.E. Sharpe.
Simonia, Nodari A. 2002. "Global Finance and Civil Society Deficit in Russia." In *Civil Society and Global Finance*. Edited by Jan Aart Scholte with Albrecht Schnabel. London: Routledge.
Smith, Adam. 2002 [1759]. *The Theory of Moral Sentiments*. Edited by Knud Haakonseen. Cambridge, UK: Cambridge University Press.
Smith, Hedrick. 1976. *The Russians*. New York: Quadrangle/New York Times Book Co.
Smith, Kathleen E. 2002. *Mythmaking in the New Russia: Politics and Memory during the Yeltsin Era*. Ithaca, NY: Cornell University Press.
Smith, Rodney A. 2006. *Money, Power, and Elections: How Campaign Finance Reform Subverts American Democracy*. Baton Rouge, LA: Louisiana State University Press.
Solzhenitsyn, Aleksandr. 1990. "How to Revitalize Russia." *Komsomolskaya Pravda*. 18 September.
—. 1991. *Rebuilding Russia: Reflections and Tentative Proposals* (translated and annotated by Alexis Klimoff). New York: Farrar, Straus and Giroux.
Soros, George. 1991. *Underwriting Democracy*. New York: Free Press.
—. 1992. "A Cold-Cash Winter Proposal for Russia." *Wall Street Journal*. 11 November 1992.

Spulber, Nicholas. 2003. *Russia's Economic Transitions: From Late Tsarism to the New Millennium.* Cambridge, UK: Cambridge University Press.

Stent, Angela E. 1999. *Russia and Germany Reborn: Unification, the Soviet Collapse, and the New Europe.* Princeton, NJ: Princeton University Press.

Stern, Nicolas. 2003. "The Future of the IMF and World Bank: Panel Discussion." *American Economic Review (Papers and Proceedings)* 93 (2): 48–49.

Stern, Nicolas and Joseph E. Stiglitz. 1997. "A Framework for a Development Strategy in a Market Economy: Objectives, Scope, Institutions and Instruments." Working Paper No. 20. London: The European Bank for Reconstruction and Development.

Stiglitz, Joseph E. 2002. *Globalization and its Discontents.* New York: W. W. Norton.

Tertzakian, Peter. 2006. *A Thousand Barrels a Second: The Coming Oil Break Point and the Challenges Facing an Energy Dependent World.* New York: McGraw-Hill.

Tikhomirov, Vladimir. 2000. *The Political Economy of Post-Soviet Russia.* New York: St. Martin's Press; London, UK: Macmillan Press.

Transparency International. 2007. *Global Corruption Report 2007: Corruption in Judicial Systems.* Cambridge, UK: Cambridge University Press.

Tregubova, Elena. 2004. *Proshchanie kremlevskogo diggera.* Moscow: Ad Marginem.

UNCTAD. 2005. *World Investment Report 2005: Transnational Corporations and the Internationalization of R&D.* New York and Geneva: United Nations.

—. 2006. *World Investment Report 2006. FDI form Developing and Transition Economies: Implications for Development.* New York and Geneva: United Nations.

VTsIOM. 1993–2000. Monitoring obshchestvennogo mneniya, VTsIOM, Intertsentr, Akademia Narodnogo Khozyaistva, Moscow.

Volkov, Vadim. 2002. *Violent Entrepreneurs: The Use of Force in the Making of Russian Capitalism.* Ithaca, NY: Cornell University Press.

Wedel, Janine R. 1998. *Collision and Collusion: The Strange Case of Western Aid to Eastern Europe, 1989-1998.* New York: St. Martin Press.

Welfens, Paul J. J. 1999. *EU Eastern Enlargement and the Russian Transformation Crisis.* Berlin: Springer-Verlag.

Williamson, John. 1990, 2002. "What Washington Means by Policy Reforms." In *Latin America Adjustment: How Much Has Happened.* Edited by John Williamson. Washington, D.C.: Institute for International Economics. <http://www.iie.com/publications/papers/williamson1102-2.htm> (10 January 2003).

Winder, Jonathan M. and Phil Williams. 2003. "Russian Crime and Corruption in an Era of Globalization: Implications for the United States." In *Russia's Uncertain Economic Future.* Edited by John P. Hardt for the Joint Economic Committee, Congress of the United States. Armonk, NY: M.E Sharpe.

Wines, Michael. 2000. "Russia Unveils a Bold Economic Blueprint." *New York Times,* 29 June 2000.

Wolf, Charles Jr. and Thomas Lang. 2006. *Russia's Economy: Signs of Progress and Retreat on the Transitional Road.* Santa Monica, CA: RAND.

World Bank. 2005. "Dying Too Young: Addressing Premature Mortality and Ill Health Due to Non Communicable Diseases and Inquiries in the Russian Federation." <http://web.worldbank.org/WBSITE/EXTERNAL/COUNTRIES/ECAEXT/0,,contentMDK:20661159~pagePK:146736~piPK:146830~theSitePK:258599,00.html> (5 January 2006).

Statistical Appendix

Table 1 Macroeconomic Data

	1992	1993	1994	1995	1996	1997	1998	1999	2000	2001	2002	2003	2004	2005	2006
GDP, % growth		−14.5	-8.7	−12.7	−4.1	−3.6	1.4	−5.3	6.4	5.1	4.7	7.3	7.2	6.4	7.4
Industrial production, % growth*,	−18.2	−14.2	−20.9	−3.0	−4.5	2.0	−5.2	11.0	11.9	2.9	3.1	8.9	7.3	4.0	3.9
Unemployment, %	4.9	5.5	7.5	8.2	9.3	9.0	13.2	12.4	9.9	8.7	9.0	8.7	7.6	7.7	6.9
Inflation, CPI 12-month change, end of period	1528.7	875.0	307.0	197.5	22	11	84.4	36.5	20.2	18.6	15.1	12.0	11.7	10.9	9.0
Fixed investments	−40.0	−12.0	−24.0	−10.0	−18.0	−5.0	−12.0	5.3	17.4	10.0	2.8	12.5	13.7	10.9	16.7
External debt, $ billion								130.8	115.5	102.0	95.7	96.9	95.7	70.1	43.2
Forex reserves, $ billion including gold				17.2	15.3	17.8	12.2	12.5	27.9	36.6	47.8	76.9	124.5	168.4	303.0
Average gross wages						164	108	62	79	111	142	180	237	301	408

Note: * (1) New methodology from 2005, figures for 2001-2004 revised, not comparable with previous years.

Sources: Russian Federal State Statistics Service (http://www.gks.ru/wps/portal/english) and Central Bank of the Russian Federation (http://www.cbr.ru/eng).

Table 2 Distribution of Population by Per Capita Average Money Income

(percentage of the total, in rubles)

	2002	2003	2004	2005
Part of the population with average per capita monthly money income, rubles				
<1500.0	17.3	9.9	6.2	3.2
2500.1 – 3500.0	23.0	17.5	13.2	8.9
1500.1 – 2500.0	18.1	16.7	14.4	11.5
3500.1 – 4500.0	12.6	13.4	12.8	11.5
4500.1 – 6000.0	11.8	14.3	15.0	15.0
6000.1 – 8000.0	8.2	11.4	13.4	14.9
8000.1 – 12000.0	6.1	10.2	13.7	17.3
over 12000.0	2.9	6.6	11.3	17.7
Total	**100**	**100**	**100**	**100**

Source: Russian Federal State Statistics Service

Table 3 Russian Federal Budget

(2006 and 2007)

	2006, % of GDP	2007, % of GDP	2006 %	2007 %
Total revenues	**22.7**	**22.3**	**100**	**100**
Total, excl. social tax	21.5	21.1	95	94.7
VAT	5.4	6.6	23.8	29.7
Profit tax	1.8	1.9	7.9	8.3
Excise taxes	.3	.3	1.5	1.5
Natural resource fees	4	3.4	17.6	15.3
Export and import duties	8.2	7.7	36.3	34.4
Other revenues	2.9	2.4	13	10.7
Total expenditures	**16.3**	**17.5**	**100**	**100**
Total, excl. social tax	15.1	16.3	93	93.2
General administration	2.4	2.6	15.6	15.0
Defense	2.5	2.6	15.6	15.0
Security	2	2.1	12.4	12.1
Production, transport, etc	1.3	1.6	8.1	9.1
Housing	.2	.2	1.0	1.0
Education	.7	.9	4.6	5.1
Health care	.6	.7	3.4	3.8
Social policy	.8	.7	4.7	3.9
Transfers to regions	5.4	5.9	33.3	33.7
Other expenditures	.4	.3	2.3	1.4
Surplus	**6.4**	**4.8**		

Notes: Figures for the year 2006 include supplementary budget approved in November 2006 and based on economy ministry's GDP estimate of 27,220 billion rubles ($1,039 billion).

Figures for the 2007 are based on GDP estimate of 31,200 billion rubles ($1,177 billion using the approved average exchange rate assumption of 26.5 rubles to the dollar) included in the 2007 budget.

Source: Russian Finance Ministry (http://www1.minifin.ru/).

Table 4 Import and Export of Goods

(Billion of U.S. Dollars)

	1992	1993	1994	1995	1996	1997	1998	1999	2000	2001	2002	2003	2004	2005	2006
Exports					89.7	86.9	74.4	75.6	105.0	101.9	107.3	135.9	183.2	243.6	304.5
Imports					68.1	72.0	58.0	39.5	44.9	53.8	61.0	76.1	97.4	125.3	163.9
Current account					10.8	-.1	.2	24.6	46.8	33.9	29.1	35.4	59.5	84.4	96.1

Sources: Russian Federal State Statistics Service (http://www.gks.ru/wps/portal/english) and Central Bank of the Russian Federation (http://www.cbr.ru/eng).

Table 5 Transactions with the International Monetary Fund

(May 1984 – May 2006)

Year	General Resources Account			Poverty Reduction and Growth Facility/ Enhanced Structural Adjustment Facility Structural Adjustment Facility/Trust Fund			Total		
	Purchases		Charges	Loans		Interest	Purchases and Loans		Charges and
	Disbursements	Repurchases	paid	Disbursements	Repayments	paid	Disbursements	Repayments	Interest paid
1992	719,000,000	0	0	0	0	0	719,000,000	0	0
1993	1,078,275,000	0	56,082,833	0	0	0	1,078,275,000	0	56,082,833
1994	1,078,275,000	0	122,264,400	0	0	0	.1,078,275,000	0	122,264,400
1995	3,594,250,000	0	193,954,079	0	0	0	3,594,250,000	0	193,954,079
1996	2,587,861,200	359,500,000	323,567,770	0	0	0	2,587,861,200	359,500,000	323,567,770
1997	1,467,252,800	359,500,000	423,093,268	0	0	0	1,467,252,800	359,500,000	423,093,268
1998	4,600,000,000	673,921,875	528,876,040	0	0>	0	4,600,000,000	673,921,875	528,876,040
1999	471,429,000	3,101,138,750	528,469,919	0	0	0	471,429,000	3,101,138,750	528,469,919
2000	0	2,189,497,343	523,542,056	0	0	0	0	2,189,497,343	523,542,056
2001	0	2,997,937,522	398,106,279	0	0	0	0	2,997,937,522	398,106,279
2002	0	1,147,587,215	161,637,500	0	0	0	0	1,147,587,215	161,637,500
2003	0	1,356,065,590	100,706,947	0	0	0	0	1,356,065,590	100,706,947
2004	0	1,117,424,465	75,829,729	0	0	0	0	1,117,424,465	75,829,729
2005	0	2,293,770,240	18,064,962	0	0	0	0	2,293,770,240	18,064,962

Source: International Monetary Fund (http://www.imf.org).

Table 6 Public Revenues and Expenditures, and the Stabilization Fund

(as percentage of GDP)

	1993	1994	1995	1996	1997	1998	1999	2000	2001	2002	2003	2004	2005	2006
Revenues*	14.5	14.1	12.9	12.5	13.3	11.4	12.6	15.4	17.8	20.3	19.5	20.1	23.7	23.4
Expenditures*	15.9	18.1	18.6	20.9	20.9	17.4	16.8	14.6	14.8	19.0	17.8	15.8	16.3	16.0
Balance*	-6.5	-11.4	-5.7	-8.4	-7.7	-6.0	-4.2	.8	3.0	1.4	1.7	4.4	7.5	7.4
Stabilization fund, $ billion												18.9	43.0	89.1

[TBN}Note: * Fiscal indicators for federal government.

Sources: Russian Federal State Statistics Service (http://www.gks.ru/wps/portal/english); Central Bank of the Russian Federation (http://www.cbr.ru/eng).

Table 6 Oil and Gas Production and Consumption

(1991 – 2006)

	1991	1992	1993	1994	1995	1996	1997	1998	1999	2000	2001	2002	2003	2004	2005	2006
Oil production*	9326	8038	7173	6419	6288	6144	6227	6169	6178	6536	7056	7698	8544	9287	9552	9769
Oil consumption*	4999	4597	3875	3359	3025	2686	2689	2554	2625	2583	2566	2606	2622	2634	2628	2735
Natural gas production**	599.8	597.4	576.5	566.4	555.4	561.1	532.6	551.3	551.0	545.0	542.4	555.4	578.6	591.0	598.0	612.1
Natural gas consumption**	431.1	417.3	416.0	390.9	377.8	379.9	350.4	364.7	363.6	377.2	372.7	388.9	392.9	401.9	405.1	432.1

Notes: * (thousand barrels daily; ** billions of cubic meters).

Source: *BP Statistical Review of World Energy June 2007* (http://www.bp.com/statisticalreview).

Table 8, Foreign Direct Investment

(1985–2005, Millions of U.S. Dollars)

	1985-1995 (ANNUAL AVERAGE)	2001	2002	2003	2004	2005
Inflows	1,282	2,748	3,461	7,958	15,444	14,600
Outflows	869	2,533	3,533	9,727	13,782	13,126
Inward FDI, as a percentage of gross fixed capital formation	1.8	4.7	5.6	10.0	14.3	10.5
Outward FDI, as a percentage of gross fixed capital formation	1.2	4.4	5.7	12.3	12.8	9.5
Inward FDI, as a percentage of GDP			12.4*			17.3
Outward FDI, as a percentage of GDP		7.8*–				15.7

*Note: investment is the sum of equity, reinvested earnings, and intracompany loans. The percentage refers to the year 2000.0.

Sources: UNCTAD (2005). *World Investment Report 2005: Transnational Corporations and the Internationalization of R&D.*

UNCTAD (2006). *World Investment Report 2006. FDI form Developing and Transition Economies: Implications for Development.* New York and Geneva: United Nations.

Index